ROOTS OF THE STATE

A Series Sponsored by the East-West Center

CONTEMPORARY ISSUES IN ASIA AND THE PACIFIC

John T. Sidel and Geoffrey M. White, Series Co-Editors

A collaborative effort by Stanford University Press and the East-West Center, this series focuses on issues of contemporary significance in the Asia Pacific region, most notably political, social, cultural, and economic change. The series seeks books that focus on topics of regional importance, on problems that cross disciplinary boundaries, and that have the capacity to reach academic and other interested audiences.

The East-West Center promotes better relations and understanding among the people and nations of the United States, Asia, and the Pacific through cooperative study, research, and dialogue. Established by the US Congress in 1960, the Center serves as a resource for information and analysis on critical issues of common concern, bringing people together to exchange views, build expertise, and develop policy options. The Center is an independent, public, nonprofit organization with funding from the US government, and additional support provided by private agencies, individuals, foundations, corporations, and governments in the region.

BENJAMIN L. READ

Roots of the State

Neighborhood Organization and Social Networks in Beijing and Taipei

Stanford University Press · *Stanford, California*

Stanford University Press
Stanford, California

Printed in the United States of America on acid-free, archival-quality paper

Library of Congress Cataloging-in-Publication Data

Read, Benjamin Lelan, author.
    Roots of the state : neighborhood organization and social networks in
Beijing and Taipei / Benjamin L. Read.
        pages cm.—(Contemporary issues in Asia and the Pacific)
    Includes bibliographical references and index.
    ISBN 978-0-8047-7564-9 (cloth : alk. paper) —
    ISBN 978-0-8047-7565-6 (pbk. : alk. paper)
    1. Neighborhood government—China—Beijing.   2. Neighborhood
government—Taiwan—Taipei.   3. Citizens' associations—China—
Beijing.   4. Citizens' associations—Taiwan—Taipei.   5. Social
networks—China—Beijing.   6. Social networks—Taiwan—Taipei.
7. Beijing (China)—Politics and government.   8. Taipei (Taiwan)—Politics
and government.   I. Title.   II. Series: Contemporary issues in Asia and the
Pacific.
JS7365.B453R43 2012
320.8'5—dc23

                                                                2011039938

Typeset by Newgen in 9.75/13.5 Janson

Contents

Illustrations

Figures

Acknowledgments

It is my pleasure as well as my obligation to convey thanks to some of the many people and institutions that have contributed to my research.

My closest family members—my parents, Charles and Helen Read; my sister and brother-in-law, Emily and Rob Davies; my wife, Qi Yingwei; and my grandparents, the late Lelan and Elizabeth Read—have given me tremendous encouragement and love over all the years. I hope that Yingwei and I can give the same to our daughter Hazel. I dedicate this book to all of them.

Roderick MacFarquhar, Elizabeth J. Perry, and Robert D. Putnam of Harvard University's Government Department provided wise guidance and inspiration. I especially thank Liz for her counsel and untiring support over many years. I am also grateful to Vivienne Shue for teaching me and nudging me onto this path.

Among many outstanding academic colleagues in China, Taiwan, and South Korea who also provided extensive help and stimulation, I particularly thank Chen Chun-Ming, Chen Dung-sheng, Cho Soosung, Dai Jianzhong, Hsi Dai Lin, Li Lulu, Chan Wook Park, Shen Yuan, and Yu Yanyan. The generosity and hard work of Ethan Michelson made possible my participation in the Beijing Law and Community Survey; his companionship as friend and research collaborator has been wonderful. Working on the Taipei survey with Amanda Ho and the other careful and competent staff at Focus Survey Research was a pleasure as well. Robert Pekkanen collaborated with me on a conference and edited volume that enriched this book, and he kindly shared a draft of the English version of his coauthored book reporting results from a large survey of Japan's neighborhood associations.

At all stages in the project, fellow social scientists and others based at U.S. institutions provided what were often invaluable thoughts and comments, as well as general inspiration. Sincere thanks and much more are due to Fred Boehmke, Cheris Chan, Kent Eaton, Antje Ellermann, Ken Foster, Jonathan Fox, Mary Gallagher, George Gilboy, Steven Heydemann, Marc Howard, Alan Jacobs, Chris Jensen, Iain Johnston, Diana Kapiszewski, Ching Kwan Lee, Lauren MacLean, Mark Massoud, Dean Mathiowetz, Kevin O'Brien, Tracy Osborn, John Parrish, Eleonora Pasotti, Elliot Posner, Jeremy Press- man, Elizabeth Remick, Tom Rice, Roger Schoenman, Adam Segal, Naunihal Singh, David Siu, Jae-Jae Spoon, Eric Thun, Kellee Tsai, Lily Tsai, and Mike Urban.

During field research I enjoyed special assistance from Chang Po Chien, Fann Meei-yuan, Cheryl Lai, Lai Shien-Song, Lin Cheng-hsiou, Liu Jinglai, Sun Zhaojun, Tan Baogui, and Yao Manjiang. Among many other friends who have given support and companionship, Scott and Tiphaine Roberts, and Chris Thun, deserve special thanks, not least for sharing their homes in Bei- jing during times when it was not easy to come by accommodations that were affordable, comfortable, and legal all at once.

Chen Juan, Jeong Hoi Ok, Li Wanru, Liu Kankan, Shih Li-wen, Christo- pher Siegel, and Su Kuei-han provided, at various points, patient and skillful research assistance as well as advice.

My fieldwork received support from a Fulbright-Hays Fellowship, a grant from the Committee on Scholarly Communication with China of the Ameri- can Council of Learned Societies, and a grant from the Urban China Research Network of the Lewis Mumford Center for Comparative Urban and Regional Research at State University of New York–Albany. The Hauser Center for Nonprofit Organizations at Harvard University provided a year and a half of fellowship support as well as intellectual stimulation.

A Junior Scholar Grant from the Chiang Ching-Kuo Foundation for International Scholarly Exchange made much of the Taiwan research pos- sible. From what is now called the Center for Democracy and Civil Society at Georgetown University, I received a most helpful visiting faculty fellowship. Multiple offices at the University of Iowa made resources available to me: the Center for Asian and Pacific Studies (travel funding); the Obermann Center for Advanced Studies (an interdisciplinary research grant); and the Benjamin F. Shambaugh Memorial Fund (workshop funding). Finally, the University of California, Santa Cruz, has provided generous start-up funding as well as a stimulating community in which to complete this book. Heartfelt thanks to all of these institutions.

Librarians Annie Chang, formerly of University of California, Berkeley, and Nancy Hearst of Harvard helped me find valuable pieces of information. Ethan Michelson, Charles Read, and Shelley Rigger did me the large favor of reading the manuscript and helping me polish it. The two anonymous reviewers provided very perceptive and helpful comments. I also appreciate the work of Stacy Wagner, my editor at Stanford University Press; Katherine Faydash, who copyedited the book; and Jay Harward, who oversaw phases of the book's production. I owe thanks as well to the East-West Center, sponsor of the book series of which this publication is a part, and series co-editors John T. Sidel and Geoffrey M. White.

Finally, I am greatly indebted to the many, many people in China and Taiwan (and others in South Korea) who made this project possible by answering questions, making introductions, hosting me, and otherwise facilitating my work. Although they must go unnamed here, I am deeply grateful to the neighborhood leaders and staff in Beijing, Taipei, and other cities who tolerated and assisted me.

None of these individuals has any responsibility for errors and shortcomings in my work.

Some tables, figures, and passages in this manuscript have been adapted from "Mediating the Mediation Debate: Conflict Resolution and the Local State in China," *Journal of Conflict Resolution*, vol. 52, no. 5 (October 2008), and from "State-Linked Associational Life: Illuminating Blind Spots of Existing Paradigms" and "The Multiple Uses of Local Networks: State Cultivation of Neighborhood Social Capital in China and Taiwan," two chapters I contributed to *Local Organizations and Urban Governance in East and Southeast Asia: Straddling State and Society* (edited by Benjamin L. Read with Robert Pekkanen, published by Routledge in 2009).

Note on Names, Terms, and Romanization

This book uses the pinyin romanization system for Chinese words and names, with certain exceptions. In Taiwan, many people and places (cities, for instance, though not usually neighborhoods) have their own preferred or published romanization, which takes precedence here. For a few proper nouns, customary spellings like Chiang Kai-shek and Kuomintang are employed.

Personal names and place names cited from newspapers, official records, and other public sources are real. Pseudonyms (always in pinyin) are used for the names of neighborhood research sites and for individuals referenced in accounts drawn from interviews and site visits. The handful of exceptions, in which real names are used by permission, is flagged in the notes.

Administratively speaking, Beijing covers a sprawling territorial expanse, approaching the size of New Jersey in area, including sixteen districts and two counties. This book focuses on the eight districts that constitute its urban core. Except where noted, Taipei here refers entirely to the capital city (*Taibei shi*), not to the separate region that surrounds it, formerly known as Taipei County and now called New Taipei City (*Xinbei shi*).

There is no single, standard translation for *lizhang*, Taiwan's official neighborhood leaders. I refer to them as neighborhood wardens (NW), and sometimes with the untranslated term. In some English-language documents they are called borough chiefs or borough wardens. This seems inapt, however, because where the term "borough" is used in large cities such as London, Montreal, and New York, it denotes an area much larger than a typical *li*. For the sake of brevity I have left untranslated the term *liganshi*, referring to the civil servants sent by district offices to work with wardens, although "neighborhood officer" or "neighborhood liaison" would suffice. China's *jumin weiyuanhui* have long been straightforwardly translated as residents' commit-tees (RC). In Beijing and elsewhere, nomenclature has evolved over the past twelve years or so, as these bodies have gradually been relabeled as community residents' committees and made into one component of larger offices called communities (*shequ*). Chapter 2 discusses the terminological and institutional nuances. For the sake of simplicity, this book refers to them generically as residents' committees, except in places where the precise organizational details are relevant.

ROOTS OF THE STATE

Chapter One

Introduction

Administration at the Grass Roots in East and Southeast Asia

From the main avenue, the route to Chongxing community still runs through the alleys known as *hutong*—not the elegant kind often found in the old Manchu quarters, but the ramshackle warrens of southern Beijing, some barely wide enough for two pedestrians to pass. In the furious run-up to the 2008 Olympic Games, the city built a brick wall and a cosmetic ribbon of lawn and shrubs to hide this maze. Behind that facade, capillary-like lanes wend past doors that lead to small courtyards, around which cluster cramped homes, many of them single rooms. On the way, you pass the old office, where the women of the residents' committee once spent winters gathered around a coal-burning stove—now rented out to boisterous migrant workers. Characters chalked in cursive on a nearby blackboard exhort residents to mind the Eight Honors and the Eight Shames, one of the ideological refrains of the Hu Jintao era.[1] As placards, bulletin boards, and posters of all kinds have done for decades around China's cities, whether trumpeting such national campaigns or conveying more prosaic imperatives, they also signal the presence and authority of the neighborhood organization.

Set in its own courtyard where several alleys join, the new office of this body announces itself with bold sign plates emblazoned with the names of the district, street office, and community, paired with a red-lettered counterpart denoting the Communist Party committee. Inside lie several freshly painted meeting rooms and offices, among them the desk of the party secretary Liao

Jian, a middle-aged woman who moved into the nearby *hutong* in 1986, initially working as a manager in a state-owned store. She leads no fewer than sixteen other staff members, who busy themselves with a slew of responsibilities: from issuing health insurance cards to mediating quarrels, organizing charity drives, and counseling residents on birth control (a rack in the front reception room holds boxes of condoms, free to anyone willing to take them). Signs on the walls display organization charts and tabulate basic facts: 9,100 persons live in the neighborhood; there are five hundred courtyards, each with a designated liaison, and 76 residents' representatives. This is, in short, a kind of nerve center amid the dusty old homes. Through this nexus, dozens of state programs and tasks take root in the jumbled terrain of this corner of urban society.[2]

A thousand miles to the south, in the city of Taipei, the neighborhood of Wenchang similarly flanks a bustling arterial road. There, too, finding the office means plunging into the lanes off this main thoroughfare, through gently curving alleys wide enough for a car but intersecting at odd angles. Next to a steel security door with eight mail slots, a bright blue sign marks the neighborhood office, although the entrance is otherwise no different from those of the other apartment buildings nearby, most two to four stories high, with tile walls and narrow balconies. Pressing a button brings a routine greeting through the intercom from Bai Zhengmin, Wenchang's elected warden. Visitors exchange shoes for plastic slippers before stepping into the living room of the three-bedroom home that Bai and his wife share. Although it holds trappings of family life such as sofas, the Buddhist shrine, and the dinner table, this room is also a nerve center of its own.

Bolted to a wall are the components of a broadcasting system that Bai uses regularly for immediate communication with the neighborhood's 5,700 residents, his voice echoing through the alleys from a microphone on his desk. In a study off the living room, a set of monitors displays real-time pictures from twenty-nine video cameras scattered throughout Wenchang; police officers sometimes stop by to consult the stored images. Here, too, the neighborhood's full-time civil servant signs in for his daily visit and works on many kinds of government business requiring local outreach: support for the poor and disabled, the military draft, health insurance cards, and more. On the walls hang a detailed satellite photograph of Wenchang and a map showing its precise boundaries, contact information for Bai's twenty designated block captains, and a whiteboard calendar of meetings at the district office and the nearby activity center. Half private domicile, half public space, this focal point receives a steady trickle of inquiries and requests in the form of phone calls and personal visits from constituents, government staff, and all manner of others.[3]

Each of these two offices, described above as they existed in 2010, forms one cellular component of immense systems of urban governance. These systems, in the People's Republic of China and the Republic of China, respectively, are profoundly different from each other in some ways. Yet in other ways they are closely related. They also contrast with how neighborhoods are run in many other parts of the world. In a country like the United States, for example, the term "neighborhood organization" generally suggests a form of self-contained, small-scale activity: Saturday potlucks in the local park, efforts to protect and celebrate historical homes, the circulation of directories with children's names and ages. It indicates a loose form of self-governing voluntary association that may be entirely apolitical or may participate in urban politics episodically. With few exceptions, people in such historically liberal settings also take for granted that neighborhood groups are far removed from governance writ large. Military conscription, verification of welfare eligibility, household registration, and other parts of the machinery of the modern state would seem inappropriate for this kind of entity. As Whyte and Parish pointed out in a comparative comment in their landmark study of China's cities, "Americans tend to feel that it is illegitimate for city administrations to try to reach down into neighborhoods and formally organize them as part of the urban administrative system" (1984, 24).

In China and Taiwan, and in several other countries in East and Southeast Asia, neighborhood groups also imply social gatherings, recreational activities, community centers, and the like. But in these societies, such organizations—at least, in their official and universally mandated form—have substantially different structures and political roles.[4] They grow out of a more regimented vision of how society is to be ordered, which in most cases descends from origins far in the past. They constitute a dense network of standardized cells, with state-defined boundaries, covering all or virtually all of the urban geography. They are intended to help govern society, not merely to provide a focal point for conviviality.

The neighborhood institutions discussed in this book are examples of systems that I call administrative grassroots engagement (AGE), in which states create, sponsor, and manage networks of organizations at the most local of levels that facilitate governance and policing by building personal relationships with members of society. Their leaders serve as the state's designated liaisons in the neighborhood and as such work closely with officials and civil servants. The administrative programs to which they lend assistance run the gamut from welfare to conscription, from census taking to public health. To one degree or another, they help police to monitor their neighborhoods, and in some cases they help gather information on constituents for purposes of political surveillance. At the same time, these parastatal entities also provide a range of services to their constituents, listen to and act on their suggestions and complaints, and organize social and volunteer activities for them to take part in if they choose. To be sure, they are not the only roots of the state, which intersects with those it governs in countless ways, of which urban neighborhoods are but one. Yet the root metaphor captures something fundamental about the shape and ambitions of this institutional template. It points as well to a widespread social basis for an active, proximate, and responsive state, a basis that coexists with many forms of disagreement, contention, and resistance. The purpose of this book is to explore the vision of the state-society relationship embodied in these institutions as it plays out in practice.

James Scott memorably characterized modern states as yearning to take the impenetrable complexity of natural and social ecologies and render it "legible"—measurable, taxable, and regularized (1998, 2, 183–184). Indeed, anyone visiting the institutions examined in these pages will marvel at the many examples they provide of "seeing like a state," from the records they keep on women's use of birth control in Beijing to the micro-level neighborhood maps and video surveillance found in Taipei. It is tempting to apply a Foucauldian framework to such practices, as some have fruitfully done.[5] But it is not clear that such perspectives explain how these bodies can be deadening and alienating to certain constituents, yet vital and appealing to others. More generally, as this book shows, to focus merely on the baleful gaze of the state would lead to a partial and biased understanding of these systems. Doing so would leave us ill prepared to understand their extensive associative functions, how they serve as an important (sometimes the most central and vibrant) nexus of neighborhood life.

Varieties of AGE institutions have appeared in many parts of the world. State socialist systems such as that of the former Soviet Union featured official neighborhood-based organizations with wide-ranging responsibilities (Friedgut 1979; Roeder 1989). Cuba has them to this day in the form of Committees for the Defense of the Revolution (Fagen 1969; Kruger 2007), and Nicaraguan revolutionaries once sustained a similar network of Sandinista Defense Committees (LaRamée and Polakoff 1997). They also crop up in systems that are neither Leninist nor Asian. For instance, in the early 1970s, Peruvian authorities worried about political unrest among urban squatters created thousands of block-level neighborhood committees in the shantytowns of Lima and other cities.[6]

Although they are by no means unique to the countries of East and Southeast Asia, some of the most elaborate and persistent examples of this type of organization are found there (Table 1.1). As discussed in Chapter 2, most descend in one way or another from imperial or colonial periods. Early or premodern states in East Asia developed institutions of local control to collect revenue and to deracinate deviants and threats, and Japanese colonizers spread and refined these systems. Today, security and fiscal goals remain two of the powerful imperatives that drive public authorities to reach down into the warp and woof of local life. Yet today's states look to the grassroots level for a great variety of purposes. As it turns out, local organizations provide a highly convenient platform for projects of just about every stripe.

To the extent that they have attracted theoretical attention at all, they have generally been conceptualized along totalitarian lines. Yet—strikingly—such organizations exist in free societies and authoritarian polities alike. In Japan, Taiwan, South Korea, and Indonesia, they have endured long after the passing of the autocratic regimes that first spawned them. In China and Singapore, as well as in the region's democracies, they have also persisted through a process

TABLE 1.1

Cases of administrative grassroots engagement in cities of East and Southeast Asia

Country	Neighborhood level	Subneighborhood level
China	*Jumin weiyuanhui, shequ jumin weiyuanhui*	*Jumin xiaozu*
Indonesia	*Rukun warga* (RW)	*Rukun tetangga* (RT)
Japan	*Chōkai, chōnaikai, jichikai*	*Kumi*
Singapore	Residents' committees, neighborhood committees	
South Korea	*Tong, tongjang*	*Banchanghoe, banjang*
Taiwan	*Li, li bangongchu, lizhang*	*Lin, linzhang*
Vietnam	*Cụm dân cư*	*Tổ dân phố*

NOTE: Countries are listed in alphabetical order. Only currently existing institutions are included; historical predecessors are not.

of economic growth that has transformed the nature and meaning of residential neighborhoods for many urbanites. Why this is so forms a high-level puzzle that this book aims to solve.

Each of the AGE institutions has its own unique characteristics; they cannot be simplistically equated with one another. Important aspects of their organizational structures vary across cases. Residential areas in Taiwan are led by a single individual, a neighborhood warden (NW; *lizhang*) like Bai, who obtains the position by winning elections held every four years. This person works out of a government-supplied office, which may be set up in his or her home or elsewhere in the area. The network of wardens and their chosen block captains (*linzhang*) was once intended to mobilize and incorporate the local citizenry under the externally imposed rule of Chiang Kai-shek's Nationalist Party (the Kuomintang, or KMT). Yet in the past two decades it has transformed into a remarkably democratic institution, as Chapter 3 shows in detail. Indeed, in terms of the rigor of their elections, the neighborhood wardens may be the most democratically chosen leaders of their type in the world. Each comes to his or her position through formal processes of campaigning and balloting, in races that are often sharply competitive. Yet they are paid stipends by the state and work closely with a civil servant (*liganshi*) sent from the district administrative center.

In China, the comparable institution has, since 1954, been called a residents' committee (RC; *jumin weiyuanhui*), a team of neighborhood auxiliaries under the leadership of a director (*zhuren*). In recent years, this institution has been encased in an increasingly elaborate organizational architecture and packaged as a "community" (*shequ*). The RC elections take place every three years, although, as we will see, these carefully choreographed affairs offer little latitude for residents to contravene the arrangements of the street offices, the ward-level agencies that oversee the committees. The communities contain within them cells of the Chinese Communist Party, and their directors often double as party secretaries, although the posts may also be held by different people, as in Chongxing's case. Like their counterparts in Taiwan, the staff of the community receive monthly stipends for their service.

Just as the details of their composition vary, ultra-local administrative bodies across the region also range from those tightly linked to—indeed, almost part of—local government to those with a considerable degree of formal autonomy. For example, Japan's *chōnaikai* do not fall under the command of local government, researchers have argued; they cooperate extensively with city authorities, but on a voluntary and negotiated basis (see Chapter 8). Taiwan's wardens are legally obliged to obey higher levels of government, but as Chapter 4 shows, in practice they have considerable independent standing and clout. In China, neighborhood leaders are selected and installed by the party and the government, which can remove them from their positions whenever they please; the leaders are not in a position easily to refuse their requests. There and in other authoritarian settings, these local institutions perform a political surveillance function that is not found today in the democratic cases, by reporting to higher levels on people and activities that are deemed threatening by the ruling regime. Moreover, the systems of China, Vietnam, and Singapore strongly condition the local political environment, for instance by discouraging, precluding, or constraining organizations that might challenge the state's grassroots bodies. In Asia's democracies, in contrast, state-backed grassroots groups are subject to a higher degree of restraint by voters, the media, and other means of oversight. In these more open contexts, alternative forms of organization proliferate, thus constituting at least potential competitors for resources and popular participation.

Without losing sight of these important differences among countries and between regime types, this book makes the case that all these state-supported structures may nonetheless be analyzed within a shared conceptual category. At the highest level of abstraction, it asks why it is that these kinds of institutions have shown such staying power—not merely persisting under autocracies but also surviving and flourishing after democratic transitions in Japan, South Korea, Indonesia, and Taiwan. It thus purposefully compares one of the most authoritarian cases, the Chinese RCs, with the most internally democratic case, Taiwan's *li-lin* system, a comparison explained later in this chapter.

Researchers have published a scattering of English-language case studies on such organizations, some of them deftly executed, painting their subjects in vivid colors. Yet, as argued later in this chapter, the social sciences remain without a convincing understanding of them. This can in part be attributed to the tendency for Asia to remain marginal in theory building. More fundamentally, scholars steeped in the liberal tradition tend to fixate on wholly independent citizen initiatives, whether in the form of social movements or less contentious types of association. They often regard state-backed institutions, conversely, not only as deleterious but also as uninteresting, inherently stale.

At the same time, generations of observers have repeatedly been drawn to the subject of China's RCs, attracted by what they find repellent in them. Many such accounts come from Westerners, but by no means all; for example, Jung Chang's best-selling memoir, *Wild Swans*, gave special attention to the prying neighborhood committees of both Manchukuo and the postrevolutionary order (1991).[7] The organizations elicit such curiosity, I believe, because of the way they transgress what outsiders take to be boundaries between public and private, and between state and community.[8] Typically, the author expresses an appalled shock at the committee's surveillance of and intrusion into residents' lives.[9]

Among Beijingers, and in Taipei as well, the lowly neighborhood leaders are more likely to form the subject of humor. For years, whenever women of the residents' committees were mentioned, it was almost obligatory for people to poke fun at them as the "small-footed tracking squads" (*xiaojiao zhenji dui*), a trope spread even in comedy routines on state television.[10] In Taipei, the former vice president Lien Chan held, for four years during his term as chairman of the KMT and before his second presidential election defeat, a block captain position under the warden of Ren'ai *li*.[11] This drew wisecracks from some quarters: "Serving as neighborhood warden rather than president—that would be about right for him," one academic joked.

Responses of both discomfort and mockery help to frame the issues posed by administrative grassroots engagement and the questions that this book seeks to answer. These institutions constitute ornate extensions of officialdom fused into the structure and governance of the smallest of urban territorial units, which, depending on one's perspective, could appear unsettling, amusing, helpful, wasteful, or simply the normal condition of things. As Friedgut wrote about ultra-local institutions in the Soviet Union: "The point of the Soviet community organizational effort . . . is to make the regime your neighbor by having your neighbor represent the regime" (1979, 239). Put differently, in the approving term used both in China and in Taiwan, they act as a bridge (*qiaoliang*) connecting the people and the authorities.[12] The question is, What are the subjective attitudes and responses of people who actually live in such close proximity to these manifestations of state power? How do they perceive and understand this statist apparatus? How do they interact with it on an everyday or an occasional basis? Building on the answers to this fundamental set of questions, we go on to inquire further about the possibilities and problems of organizations designed to transgress any clear state-society boundary, to intermediate between the two at an intimate level. How should we understand the kinds of relationships that connect ordinary people with these ultra-local government intermediaries, and what effects do hierarchical authority patterns have on community networks? Finally, is it possible for what began as heavily top-down organizations to provide a basis for truly democratic participation and a channel for bottom-up political influence?

Those who are disconcerted by the kind of state structuring and oversight embodied in the RC and the *li-lin* will be surprised to learn that, as of the 2000s, at least, the systems both enjoyed substantial public support. Contrary to what one might expect, patterns in authoritarian Beijing and democratic Taipei display certain broad similarities. In both cities, one portion of the population took a dim view of them, seeing them as intrusive, grasping, or simply irrelevant and useless. Survey data and interviews show, however, that such perceptions are not the majority. More often than not, residents saw reasons to value their neighborhood organizations, as detailed in Chapters 5–7. Thus, both cities showed a divide in popular attitudes—and interviewees in the two capitals gave many of the same reasons for taking one position or the other.

Explaining these patterns—approval and disapproval alike—as this book aims to do, requires arguments at several levels. First, we observe in both Beijing and Taipei the enduring popular resonance of a collaborative (rather than arm's-length) vision of state-society relations. Many see as appropriate the presence of a permanent locus of authority in the neighborhood, a liaison to police and other authorities, and a source of help for themselves or for disadvantaged residents. At the same time, this orientation is by no means uniform or uncontested. It contends with other ideas: for instance, those insisting on a right to privacy and personal autonomy in the domestic sphere.

But such ideational constructs take us only so far. It is not merely abstract notions but rather the tangible milieu of the local social environment that forms the context in which residents interact with their RC or warden. This environment, and particularly the extent of leaders' ties to their communities, varies from place to place in both Beijing and Taipei, for instance between long-standing neighborhoods of older homes and newer high-rise apartments. Some RC staff and most *lizhang* draw on years or decades of familiarity with their neighborhoods, but they also build at least nodding acquaintance with broad circles of residents through the many functions they perform and services they provide. These range from giving free blood-pressure checks to responding to countless queries and complaints, and mediating local disputes, all of which can develop or reinforce connections with constituents. In many cases these are relatively thin relationships rather than thick, intimate ones—

but as Granovetter noted in his classic article, "weak ties" can have special strength and efficacy (1973). Examining the alley-level social terrain shows us that putting community ties toward state-mandated purposes, intermingling horizontal bonds with vertical lines of authority, is neither wholly contradictory nor entirely unproblematic, as discussed below.

Finally, for a portion of the urban population, state-fostered neighborhood structures provide a welcome and convenient venue for active participation—whether in purely social functions like festivals and exercise classes or in many forms of voluntary service. In both Beijing and Taipei, much of this participation fills government-defined roles that are intended to channel people's energies into pursuits that serve the state rather than make demands of it. Persistent scholarly debates have revolved around the nature of and motivations for such supportive activity. Programs like volunteer neighborhood patrols duplicate the kinds of missions that civil society organizations might pursue, and I argue that participants' motivations are much the same as those that underlie nonstate volunteering, although service in official auxiliaries also has its own distinct appeals.

All in all, the resemblance between patterns found in Beijing and in Taipei, and in the general reasons people feel as they do, is striking. Just as instructive, though, are the contrasts between the two capitals. Although residents of Taipei overwhelmingly feel that the *li-lin* system should continue to exist, compared to their Beijing counterparts they are less inclined to see it as an essential institution, something they would miss if it were gone. Even so, the social footprint of the neighborhood apparatus is in some ways larger there; a broader swath of Taipei residents join in activities sponsored by these organizations. Most significant, Taiwan's case illustrates the possibilities for vibrant democracy inherent in these entities. Through them, citizens cast votes in meaningful and competitive elections, choosing local leaders with strong standing from which to negotiate with the urban state. Taipei shows that AGE systems, born as tools of authoritarian control and cooptation, may evolve into highly democratic loci of bottom-up participation—even though bitterly fought elections at the neighborhood level and links to national political parties complicate community life in their own ways.

This study argues against foregrounding three factors that loom large in other aspects of politics for the purpose of understanding these neighborhood institutions. The RCs and the *li* operate as extensions of powerful states; in China's case, the state routinely employs repressive force against what it sees as threats. Yet even in Beijing, let alone in Taipei, most urbanites do not experience these organizations acting toward them in a coercive capacity. As well, partisan political allegiances—among Chinese Communist Party members in Beijing, and adherents of the two major parties in Taipei—have a place in this story, but residents are not strongly divided along these lines in terms of their basic attitudes toward these bodies. Finally, these intermediaries participate in an intricate fabric of ongoing negotiation, with their constituents and with higher officials, over various kinds of resources, opportunities, certifications, and more. In certain cases, specified in the chapters that follow, these exchanges can be thought of as following a patron-client pattern. Most, however, do not rise to the level of what should properly be called clientelism, a potentially vast category that requires sensible boundaries if it is to have meaning. All three of these factors have their place, but none deserves a unique spotlight.

So many states in East and Southeast Asia continue to retain and support grassroots institutions like these partly because they provide such a convenient platform for administrative interventions, but also because they root themselves so deeply in parts of urban society. Whether or not these institutions democratize, and even when they remain part of the surveillance apparatus of a repressive state like China, they nonetheless can win the acceptance or even support of a large portion of society. They do so in large part on the basis of interpersonal social networks, which take many forms and correspond only weakly and partially to a clientelism model.

The questions addressed in this book have special resonance in the world of East Asian studies and the China field. For example, these research communities have long grappled with issues surrounding the state-society relationship, including whether publics in the region are particularly receptive to a close partnership between the two of the kind that these grassroots organizations represent. Prominent scholars have provided arguments in the affirmative. The late Benjamin I. Schwartz, in an essay titled "The Primacy of the Political Order in East Asian Societies," argued that "the conception of the supreme jurisdiction of the political order in all domains of social and political life" has been "a more or less enduring dominant cultural orientation" in China through the ages and in countries influenced by Chinese civilization, such as Japan, Korea, and Vietnam. He clarified that this refers not to totalitarian control but to an assumption that the political order, or state, has special "centrality and weight," that it appropriately claims jurisdiction over and intermingles with the religious, economic, intellectual, and social spheres rather than remaining clearly delineated from them (Schwartz 1996, 114–115).[13] In a similar vein, the anthropologist Robert P. Weller wrote that, customarily in China and Taiwan, "state and society are not thought about as separate entities in tension with each other," although he noted that this is evolving as ideas from other parts of the world are borrowed and adapted (1999, 139).

Such perspectives, of course, are by no means unique to East Asia. Stepan, for instance, surveyed a closely related political vision he identified as organic statism, a set of normative principles that call for the elements of society to join together harmoniously in concert with public authority, and under its guidance (1978, 26–45). He showed that this strain of political philosophy extends back to thinkers such as Aristotle and Aquinas and influences doctrines as diverse as those of the Catholic Church, Lenin, and many other figures and forces in the modern world. One aim of this book is to assess the extent to which these kinds of ideational or cultural orientations influence popular attitudes as well as underpin institutional arrangements created by elites; it also weighs them against competing ideas and other factors. More broadly, as the above illustrates, the phenomena examined in this study take regionally specific forms and speak to themes in Asian studies but also inform our understanding of general concepts in the world of politics. Before continuing, then, it is necessary to consider a few other conceptual building blocks, as well as their tensions and limitations.

Organizations at the Local and Neighborhood Level

Urban neighborhoods generally seem to occupy a category lying between units of government and citizen associations—perhaps falling into the gap between them and constituting neither. In most cities of the world, neighborhoods are not a fundamental unit of governance. Often it is at much larger units that the real action begins. Each of London's thirty-two boroughs is the size of a city all by itself, with an average population around 230,000. Chicago's fifty wards hold more than fifty-five thousand people each and generally contain multiple neighborhoods within them. In global perspective, to situate layers of administration or representation below these is clearly the exception rather than the rule.

Matthew A. Crenson, in his study of Baltimore, addressed this as he noted the conceptual challenges of specifying the nature of politics in urban neighborhoods. "One is not likely to find anything that deserves to be called a government along the streets of most residential areas," he pointed out (1983, 9).[14] He found neighborhoods important for the social energy they might mobilize, their capacity to generate informal solutions to urgent problems—such as responding to store lootings when a snowstorm paralyzes the city's regular infrastructure. Other researchers look to neighborhoods for resources of different kinds. Sociologists and others have viewed them as cradles for transformative social movements or other forms of civic action (Fainstein and Fainstein 1974; Castells 1983; M. R. Warren 2001; Sampson, McAdam, MacIndoe, and Weffer-Elizondo 2005). They can be places where citizens engage in political discussion, trading information as they decide how to vote (Baker, Ames, and Renno 2006). Others have seen them as possible sites for participatory democracy, and as avenues that can bring residents into involvement in politics (Berry, Portney, and Thomson 1993; Smith 2000; Schmid 2001; Thomson 2001). Still others explore private local governance in homeowner associations, whether from an approving, critical, or simply analytical perspective (McKenzie 1994; Caldeira 2000; Meyer and Hyde 2004; Nelson 2005; Glasze, Webster, and Frantz 2006).

Whether or not they are explicitly organized around the concept of civil society, a concept for which I borrow Diamond's definition, for the most part they share its essential premises (1999).[15] The assumption is that government exists at higher levels, but moving outward, away from city hall and into the residential quarters, one crosses a boundary into the nonstate sphere. As sites of autonomous organization and incubators of political commitment, neighborhoods can empower citizens by encouraging political participation and providing experience in democratic self-governance, while at the same time making government more accountable by articulating interests and exerting pressure on public officials. In this way, this vein of analysis parallels widespread, though contested, arguments that civil society enhances politics both by enriching the practice of democracy and by supplementing electoral mechanisms with direct forms of action.[16]

In practice, neighborhood organizations can be a mixed blessing in their contribution to the civic life of a city. Putting more power in the hands of ultralocal units may not always serve desirable social ends. McKenzie, echoing others, expressed concern that the intensification of homeowner self-government might hollow out broader public institutions (1994, 21–23). Moreover, even at such a small scale, organizations do not necessarily take the same stance as their members on issues that matter most to them (Swindell 2000). Territorial associations of this kind sometimes pursue exclusionary goals, aiming to keep minority or low-income residents out of the locality. As well, high socio-economic status individuals and homeowners tend to be more politically active than others (Crenson 1983, 211; Rosenstone and Hansen 1993, 158; Verba, Schlozman, and Brady 1995, 453; Rossi and Weber 1996). Organizations in affluent parts of a city may lobby for public resources more effectively than their counterparts elsewhere, another way in which they might exacerbate inequality.

Even setting aside these concerns, the rather thin social and organizational lattices found in many residential areas lack the sturdiness to support the weighty aspirations of civil society theory. In liberal democratic contexts, such organizations stay more or less free from state intervention but also enjoy little state support. It is largely up to residents themselves to organize or not as they please. Thus, neighborhood organizations in the United States can be here today, gone tomorrow, waxing and waning with the vagaries of residents' concerns and cohesion. For example, Crenson found that some community organizations lapsed into inactivity in the time between his interview with their leaders and his completion of the study (1983, 294).

Governments not willing to leave neighborhoods in such an uneven and ephemeral condition embrace them more tightly. Even in liberal democracies, cities have experimented with efforts to nurture more active and persistent community involvement. Washington, D.C., for example, created thirty-eight Advisory Neighborhood Commissions, which meet monthly to discuss issues like traffic, parking, zoning, and policing.[17] Five American cities (Birmingham, Alabama; Dayton, Ohio; San Antonio, Texas; St. Paul, Minnesota; and Portland, Oregon) studied in one landmark project established special structures intended to "reach out to their neighborhoods and successfully incorporate the participation of average citizens into public policymaking" (Berry, Portney, and Thomson 1993, 1). Citizens' boards or councils, in some cases linked to neighborhood associations, gave residents new channels through which to control things like planning, zoning, and budgets. Yet the results were mixed. The investigators found, for example, that such institutions did seem to increase citizens' trust in government. But rates of community participation in the target cities were no higher than in comparison cities, a finding described as "sobering testimony to the difficulty of stimulating political participation" (Berry, Portney, and Thomson 1993, 97).

Cases like those represent only modest departures from the pure civil society model, remaining at the low end of a scale of state guidance. Moving across this continuum into greater degrees of administrative engagement entails leaving, at some point, the boundary of civil society and entering the realm of corporatism, which can be thought of in broadest terms as state structuring of associational activity and interest representation.[18] Schmitter distinguishes two variants: societal corporatism, in which interest groups form at their own initiative and acquire exclusivity and special treatment largely through their own power, and state corporatism, in which controls are imposed from above and groups exist in a highly dependent relationship to the state (1979, 20–22). Corporatism, of course, resonates closely with and seeks justification in ideas such as the organic statist vision discussed above (Stepan 1978, 46–48). Particularly in the rubric of state corporatism, East and Southeast Asian countries have provided many examples.[19] The neighborhood context explored in this book provides an opportunity to examine this concept more deeply outside of its most commonly studied manifestation, that is, government shaping of negotiations between business and labor (see Molina and Rhodes 2002). Cases like Taiwan's *li-lin* shed light on the underexplored territory between the extremes of societal and state corporatism—situations involving more than the state merely presiding over the table at which self-organizing groups sit, yet less than the bottling up of public constituencies in bodies that suppress their interests in the guise of speaking for them.

Past a certain point, state structuring of local associations can become all-out control, bringing us to the world of mass organizations. Accounts of communism, fascism, and totalitarianism all highlight such bodies as a means through which ruling parties extend their grasp to dominate specific sectors of society, with groups for youths, workers, women, neighborhoods, and so forth (Linz 1975; Linz and Stepan 1996). Through these institutions, regimes strive to accomplish such obvious goals as spreading official beliefs, values, and doctrines; exercising surveillance over political threats or opposition; and drawing the population out of passivity and into active displays of loyalty. In his survey of what he calls administered mass organizations (AMOs) in dozens of authoritarian states, Gregory Kasza also points out several other functions:

preempting autonomous groups, consuming members' time through sundry diversions, and projecting an illusion of mass democracy through "pseudopolitical activities." Force and coercion are integral to the AMO: membership is generally compulsory, and at a minimum, "alternative organizations are ordinarily prohibited" (Kasza 1995, 13, 27, 59). Some research on postcommunist systems further argues that such Leninist structures sour the population on all kinds of associational activity, leaving behind a persistent blight on the civic landscape even after the regimes that created them collapse (Howard 2002, 2003).[20]

Kasza and others have crafted compelling portraits of an institutional form that oppressive states around the world deployed in the twentieth century. There can be no question that true mass organizations are tools of control, transmission belts that powerfully extend an authoritarian ruling party's reach throughout society. Even so, a careful look at East Asia's post–third wave democracies suggests the need to supplement the AMO with a related but distinct theoretical category. We need a conceptual framework within which to understand what might be called AMO successors, like Taiwan's post-Chiang *lizhang* or Indonesia's post-Suharto *rukun tetangga*.[21] These structures were once imposed by the state, and they continue to be guided by it, yet they have become much more open to community-level input and steering than in the past, and they no longer exclude other groups within the same setting. They attract the willing and voluntary participation of extensive segments of the population. In China, the state's tight leash on the RCs and their basic conformity to the mass organization model have long been clear (Townsend 1967; Whyte and Parish 1984; Benewick 1991; White 1991, 1993). Yet even this case diverges from some elements of the transmission-belt concept. For example, as shown in later chapters, the RCs do not coerce or conscript residents into participation. Quite the contrary, they often must go to great lengths to coax constituents into taking part in their activities; in this regard, the shoe is on the other foot.

In short, the concepts through which we generally understand the world of organizations at the ultra-local level are not yet refined enough to explain, in an adequate way, the actual functioning of a large category of existing groups. Moreover, when we open up these organizations to examine the power dynamics and interpersonal networks within them, we confront a similar set of unresolved theoretical questions.

Competing Perspectives on the Intersection of Power and Local Networks

Administrative grassroots institutions graft part of the apparatus of government into the fibers of community networks. In doing so, they raise a particular set of questions, implicated in long-standing theoretical debates.

In studies of the role of social networks in politics, interpersonal links are commonly understood as falling into one of two distinct categories: horizontal and vertical. Horizontal ties are those that connect "agents of equivalent status and power," whereas vertical ties bind together "unequal agents in asymmetric relations of hierarchy and dependence," as Robert Putnam puts it (1993, 173). Many other scholars make the same distinction (Eisenstadt and Roniger 1984; Fox 1994; Rose, Mishler, and Haerpfer 1997). Horizontal ties emerge in many types of settings; the term is found everywhere, from the business world to ethnographic studies. Indeed, the word "horizontalism" has become a shorthand—even a rallying cry—for the practices of popular movements that "reject the hierarchical template bequeathed to them by established politics" and embrace "democratic communication on a level plane" (Sitrin 2006, 3). It is commonly held that the voluntary organizations of civil society provide an especially fertile source of horizontal bonds, and some, like Putnam, assert that these bonds constitute an essential mechanism giving civil society its power.[22] Although many have registered caveats and dissents to this simple notion, it remains widely accepted.[23]

The flip side of the valorizing of the horizontal is a suspicion of enduring ties linking ordinary citizens to authorities. Vertical relationships, involving power asymmetries, are held to be very different from, and antithetical to, the trusting, egalitarian bonds that are said to connect peers. Putnam strongly delineates this distinction in an argument that equates vertical ties specifically with patron-client relations. "A vertical network, no matter how dense and no matter how important to its participants, cannot sustain social trust and cooperation," he writes (Putnam 1993, 174). Other kinds of research, as well, have explored organizational contexts in which horizontal and vertical relationships work at cross-purposes. In Migdal's study of state capabilities in the developing world, for example, weblike societies with diffused sources of social control "capture" and subvert the efforts of government policy implementors (1988).[24]

In contrast to perspectives positing a sharp distinction between horizontal and vertical connections, others emphasize the possibility for the two to intermingle, and even to enhance one another. The concept of state-society synergy, championed by scholars in development studies such as Peter Evans, Elinor Ostrom, and others, exemplifies this. In the right conditions, it holds, collaboration between community and government can enhance rather than destroy internal networks of solidarity. Vertical links to the external political world can provide opportunities that the community cannot create on its own (Evans 1996a, 1119; see also Evans 1996b; Das Gupta, Grandvoinnet, and Romani 2000; World Bank 2004).[25] Specific examples depict community groups cooperating with public agencies to facilitate infrastructure and welfare programs, such as sanitation systems and water resource management.[26] Many other researchers have echoed these themes in studies of ways in which local groups and government can work together without subverting one another's basic purposes (Salamon 1995; Brown 1998; Woolcock 1998; Warner 1999; Grootaert and van Bastelaer 2002; Woolcock and Narayan 2006). Even some analyses of state socialist systems have employed this general framework. Roeder, for example, saw grassroots organizations in the former Soviet Union as encouraging citizens to facilitate the work of the government in a form of coproduction (1989). And as Chapter 8 explains, the idea of synergy also resonates with a strain of argument found in ethnographic accounts of cities in Japan and Indonesia, which sees public authority as blending harmoniously with urban communities.

By delving into the multifaceted reality of the state-society interface in a variety of contexts, this book shows the need for more conceptual nuance than is often found in treatments of these subjects. The rich literature on clientelism has, in fact, long noted the many different forms that vertical networks may assume, some of them involving considerable trust between superiors and subordinates. These social structures can be very enduring, and they run the gamut from coldly instrumental alliances to affect-laden ties.[27] Similar patterns of persistence and diversity have been identified in China-specific research on *guanxi*, with one review pointing out the seeming contradiction of the "combination of instrumentalism and sentiment" that this term connotes (Gold, Guthrie, and Wank 2002a, 8).[28]

Thus, the notion of clientelism suffers from a lack of definitional consensus, as scholars have noted (Stokes 2007, 604; Taylor-Robinson 2009). Some recent conceptualizations have responded to this problem by focusing on vote buying.[29] Yet this phenomenon has many nonelectoral manifestations, and for politicians to ply voters with offerings of cash can in fact suggest relatively low levels of dependency. In this study, I start with a broader definition of clientelism as "a relationship based on political subordination in exchange for material rewards," as Fox puts it, but I emphasize that there can be no black-and-white boundary distinguishing patron-client ties from all other interpersonal bonds (1994, 153). Instead, the extent to which a given relationship is clientelistic varies with certain conditions: the magnitude of material resources exchanged, the lack of alternatives available to subordinates, and the amount of personal discretion and arbitrary authority held by the superior.

It follows that hierarchy—inequalities of status and power—does not always entail clientelism, and it need not undercut horizontal solidarity. The capacity of vertical networks to atomize the subordinates, and to ensnare them in relationships of dependency, turns on specific circumstances and power dynamics. In the factories and schools of Mao-era China, as Chapter 7 notes, conditions were ripe for such factionalism and fragmentation. Influential studies have shown that cadres could arbitrarily dispense rewards or political penalties and demand displays of personal loyalty. Contexts like residential neighborhoods in the China of the past two decades, to say nothing of democratic Taiwan, present much milder, circumscribed forms of authority. Hierarchical relationships should be seen as a continuum running from the wispiest strands of power all the way to the kind of abject, atomizing dependency that constitutes the most pernicious forms of clientelism. Out-and-out dependency on local authorities is quite uncommon in the neighborhoods of Beijing and Taipei; rather, what we generally find is a range of much thinner forms of mutual obligation.

Even so, the synergy perspective and related visions of state-society harmony can hardly be applied uncritically to grassroots administrative institutions. They embody an optimistic perspective, in explicit contrast with theories that highlight the dysfunctional aspects of public institutions. Yet synergy is also an ideal or at least felicitous condition that is difficult to bring about. Evans and company seem, for the most part, to have sought out particularly unproblematic cases of state-community cooperation. In practice, many state agencies remain more prone to smother local initiatives than to engage them as partners, as they acknowledge.[30] The Chinese case displays elements of synergy within an institution that strives (with only partial success) to continue the stern grip that the party-state has long maintained on local organizational life. Even in relatively freewheeling Taiwan, the *li-lin* system shapes and channels community energies in ways that undercut nonstate alternatives even as it also can empower urban citizens.

Practical Reasons Why This Matters

The theoretical questions introduced above are what have primarily driven this study. Yet there are also compelling reasons for studying administrative grassroots engagement that have to do with its practical impact and its empirical effects on political systems.

The organizations in question have a sprawling presence throughout the region; their very pervasiveness suggests that they deserve far more attention than they have received. Japan boasts nearly three hundred thousand neighborhood and village groups working closely with local government. The vast Indonesian network of community organizations plays a central role in the lives of tens of millions of urban and rural poor people. In Taiwan, some 146,000 citizen-volunteers serve as block captains. Although nonstate groups (whether religious, clan based, recreational, charitable, or oriented toward social change) also flourish in many parts of Asia, to ignore this quasi-public sector is to miss an immense part of the picture of how associational life and governance interact.

But these institutions also deserve attention because of the practical uses to which many of them are put. They provide an important mechanism through which governments strive to accomplish their goals. Networks of deeply rooted local organizations are useful to the state in a number of different ways. They help it acquire information about people under its jurisdiction, which allow it more precisely and effectively to apply policy and interventions from police or other agencies. They convey information about laws, policies, campaigns, and initiatives to individual constituents. They embed state action within personal, face-to-face relationships, and thus endeavor to legitimize it. Finally, they encourage citizens to involve themselves in tasks that facilitate governance.

Some of these purposes—such as reporting information on dissidents to authoritarian regimes—many readers will find deeply troubling. In most cases, these institutions also work to further social policy goals, controversial though some of these may be in their own right. For example, in both China and Indonesia, local women's associations are enlisted by the state to popularize family planning programs (Shiffman 2002; White 2006). Grassroots bodies form an essential component of the social security infrastructure in many cases, helping connect disadvantaged populations with government agencies whose purpose is to provide assistance. Whatever their flaws and abuses, these networks of organizations constitute a potential resource for just about any developmental undertaking.

Comparison Across National Boundaries and Regime Types

Much of this book explores individual-level variation in how ordinary people perceive and interact with the organizations in question. It also compares different kinds of neighborhoods in the two primary cities and, to a lesser extent, discusses variation between these capitals and other, more peripheral municipalities. It also observes change over time, both in terms of recent developments in neighborhood structures as well as the historical trajectories that brought them to today. But perhaps most ambitiously, the book ventures a cross-national comparison. In a framework that considers analogous organizations in Japan, South Korea, Indonesia, and Cuba while also touching on other cases, it presents a focused study of Beijing and Taipei. We thus explore two institutions that are similar in many ways but different in others, notably their degree of democratic accountability, the potential intrusiveness of the state action that they facilitate, and the overall political milieu of which they form a part.

Despite the island's many historical connections to the mainland, China and Taiwan do not necessarily make an obvious pair for comparison. The former, of course, is a giant of a country, nearly sixty times as populous and three hundred times the land size of its neighbor off the Fujian coast. The latter is several times wealthier as measured by per capita gross domestic product, in contrast. Its experience with Japanese colonial rule from 1895 to 1945 was very different from the mainland's shorter but far more violent occupation by Japan, leaving divergent legacies. In terms of political economy, Taiwan has often been compared with other East Asian states that experienced post–World War II growth spurts (Vogel 1991; Wade 1992; World Bank 1993). Later-blooming China does not fit all the same economic patterns, for example in the role of foreign direct investment (Naughton 2007, 404).

Politically, the two states have come to be governed by significantly different political regimes. In the past three decades, many of China's people have enjoyed unprecedented levels of affluence and a surprising degree of personal autonomy and freedom of action. Yet for all of its reforms, the country remains dominated by the Chinese Communist Party, which represses autonomous political forces, places limits on public debate, and imprisons many dissidents. In Taiwan, the ruling Kuomintang accepted the formation of an opposition party, the Democratic Progressive Party (DPP), in 1986 and lifted martial law in 1987. This political opening proceeded through the extension of competitive elections to legislative and executive races, thus leading to the DPP's control of the presidency from 2000 to 2008 and to what is acknowledged as a consolidated democratic regime, including extensive freedom of press, speech, and association.

These systemic differences are reflected in the local institutions under study in this book. Although the RC and *li-lin* systems have many things in common, they also differ in important ways. To compare them is not to equate them in empirical or moral terms. The RCs play significant roles in a few programs that do not exist or are much less restrictive in Taiwan, such as the family-planning system. The coercive apparatus for which they gather information is capable of considerable repression, whereas the Republic of China respects basic civil liberties. The genuine electoral mechanism in Taiwan's neighborhoods puts teeth into what in the Chinese case are at best soft and intangible forms of accountability to constituents. Still, both institutions extend the reach of very strong states, which take micro-level governance seriously. In Taiwan's case, neighborhood officials even play a role in conscripting young men for mandatory military service, a program with no parallel in the cities of the mainland.

China stands as one of only five remaining Communist Party–led dictatorships, a club that once had as many as sixteen members and left behind many more successor states (Brown 2009, 3). Comparing systems within this category to other kinds of polities can be tricky and also controversial. Ken Jowitt, criticizing other Sovietologists like Jerry Hough, wrote about the dangers of assimilating Leninist phenomena to external concepts and warned of "the very different meanings formally similar behavior can have in institutionally distinct contexts" (1992, 126). From this perspective, Leninism constitutes a clearly demarcated gestalt. An unyielding application of such an approach would run contrary to the spirit of this book, which insists on the need to question the margins of accepted categories and explore liminal cases between them. Still, in undertaking comparison of state-sponsored organizations, it is indeed crucial not to lose sight of the significant differences in the political systems whose roots they partially constitute. This will involve, for example, carefully parsing citizens' political or quasi-political behavior (Shi 1997) while not straining to make more of such participation than is empirically supported, an error that has been justly criticized (LaPalombara 1975, 1978).

Only with multiple qualifications can China today be included in the category of Leninist regimes as they were once understood. It has embraced market mechanisms in far-reaching ways, accepted extensive globalization, forsaken class conflict, and turned away from charismatic leadership toward rule by technocrats.[31] Although Taiwan has diverged much farther from any standard template of Leninism, its former ruling party once tried to model itself on this pattern as well.[32] Indeed, this has been considered one of many parallels between the People's Republic and the Republic of China. As Bruce Dickson wrote in comparing the trajectories and capacity for adaptation of the CCP and the KMT, whose histories have intertwined repeatedly: "Both parties shared the same traditions of governance based on centuries of imperial rule, both were embedded in the same political culture, and both were initially organized as Leninist parties" (1997, 3). The two have also been compared in a recent study of dominant-party adaptation (Friedman and Wong 2008). The Taiwan-China duo has even been called "an experimentally ideal comparison" (Gilley 2008, 1).

Side-by-side study of local phenomena across the Taiwan Strait has shed at least as much light as macro-level research has. Teresa Wright identified parallels between student activism in Beijing and Taipei in 1989 and 1990, noting that "student protestors in both movements exhibited strikingly similar behaviors" despite the contrasting fates of the two struggles (Wright 2001, 8). Culture, and specifically political culture, in China and Taiwan has offered fertile ground for investigation (Brown 2004; Chu 2008). Most important from the perspective of this study, local governance and associations have provided especially thought-provoking bases for comparison (Weller 1999; Hao and Liao 2008; Madsen 2007, 2008; Solinger 2008; Weller 2008).

In this context, I must call attention to three points about the explicit cross-national comparison in this book, which is mainly China-Taiwan, and specifically Beijing-Taipei. First, there is obviously no assumption that these two primary cases stand for the cities of the PRC and ROC as a whole. As political nuclei and prosperous economic hubs, they are distinctive in certain ways, and in Appendix 2 I note some dimensions of variation. The book largely confines itself to the two primary cities, but data from various sources, including my exploratory research in other cities, support certain broader conclusions, and I assert that the findings from the capitals provide at least a solid starting point for addressing the analytical questions raised here. Second, I have not tried to give China and Taiwan equal treatment in every section of the book. The aim here is to compare the two cases in a way that is evenhanded and illuminating but not mechanical. Much more has been written about the Chinese case and China in general, thus necessitating extra weight in some places, whereas on certain topics there is simply more to say about one case or the other. Finally, the broader comparative framework incorporates several other cases in East and Southeast Asia. As Chapters 2 and 8 explain, despite these countries' obvious differences from each other, their local administrative institutions are linked by historical ties and show related patterns in their engagement with constituents. Ultimately, though, the basis for comparison does not rest on a shared lineage but rather on the common qualities of AGE institutions and the *problematique* of vertical and horizontal allegiances that they present.

Research in the Lanes and Alleys

This book takes inspiration in part from a long tradition of research on the interconnections between states and societies.[33] It aims to further this program through particularly up-close and fine-grained forms of comparative study. The questions posed here created the challenge of comprehending the myriad ways in which ordinary people of all kinds interact with and perceive ultra-local governance institutions. In my efforts to do so, I gathered several different kinds of sources and data. Here I discuss them in brief, saving a more detailed explanation for Appendix 1.

From the beginning it was clear that things like formal documents and official policies could play only a supporting role in this study. It was crucial to get at the actual encounters between residents and these extensions of the state, in as immediate and unvarnished a way as possible. This called for, among other things, adopting something like an ethnographic approach and observing these encounters in context and as they occurred. Accordingly, in these pages the reader will witness, as I did, the kinds of quotidian matters that make up the day-to-day life of these vast networks of grassroots administration. We listen to squabbles between occupants of adjacent units in Beijing housing blocks. In places like Chongxing we sit on uncomfortable stools, sipping hot water and inhaling fumes from coal stoves. We consider things like exercise classes, parking spots, stolen bicycles, welcome or unwanted smells from food stalls. In places like Wenchang, we probe into a realm of elections in which the margin of victory can be a few dozen votes or less. All this is well-nigh essential for understanding these organizations, and it reflects my strong belief that social science needs to stay attuned to the actual lives and concerns of men and women from many parts of the population. In taking this kind of approach, I have been inspired by other work that examines politics using a magnifying glass rather than a radio telescope—that demonstrates, as the title of Edward Schatz's recent compilation puts it, what immersion contributes to the study of power (2009).[34]

This project began with sixteen months of field research in Beijing (August 1999 to December 2001). I gradually established ten neighborhood research sites around the city. With two exceptions, the sites were not arranged through official channels; I contacted them through cold visits or through informal personal contacts. I chose the sites in such a way as to obtain geographic dispersal and a variety of housing types and populations. Four of them are old neighborhoods, lying inside what was once the city wall; two of these have been demolished and rebuilt as of this writing. The others consist of postrevolutionary apartment blocks and new housing developments. I made a total of 140 visits to the ten sites, with most visits lasting a morning or an afternoon, sometimes a full day. Most of the time was spent sitting in the RC office, observing what took place there, chatting with and asking questions of the staff. Elsewhere, I have explained what I see as the possibilities of such a site-intensive approach in greater detail (Read 2006, 2010). In the summers of 2003, 2004, 2007, and 2010 I conducted follow-up research in eight of the neighborhoods. Table 1.2 lists these Beijing field sites. In addition to my work in the capital city, I made short trips to six other cities in China (Benxi, Guangzhou, Hengyang, Qingdao, Shanghai, and Shijiazhuang) to visit neighborhoods and learn how the committees vary from place to place.

I undertook similar kinds of site visits in my research on Taiwan. As government and quasi-governmental structures in Taiwan are more open and less politically sensitive than their counterparts in China, I found that less time and trust building was required to be confident I was obtaining valid answers to the fundamental questions. Between 2003 and 2011 I spent a total of about five months there on five separate visits. Most of my research examined

TABLE I.2
Beijing neighborhood research sites

Site	Method of first contact	Total visits	Description
Anfeng	Introduced by an acquaintance[a]	6	High-rise homes belonging mainly to employees of a single work unit, built in 1980s on city's near north side; committee was a *jiashu weiyuanhui* (see Chapter 2)
Chongxing	Formal request	15	Old, single-story, courtyard-based homes in the alleys of south Beijing
Dengdao	Cold visit	16	Six- to eleven-story buildings, built in 1980s on east side
Duzhuang	Introduced by an acquaintance[b]	5	Mixed work unit and other apartment buildings, central Beijing
Shawan	Introduced by an acquaintance[a]	6	High-rise apartment towers, built in 1980s on west side
Shimen	Cold visit	29	Six-story 1970s-era apartment buildings on near west side
Shuangqiao	Cold visit	13	Old, single-story, courtyard-based homes in central Beijing. Demolished and re-built as of 2003
Wutai	Cold visit	13	New high-rise commercial housing on city's northern periphery
Xiyingjie	Formal request	8	Old, single-story, courtyard-based homes in the alleys of south Beijing. Demolition and rebuilding started in 2000.
Xianningjie	Cold visit	29	Six-story apartment buildings, built in 1970s on east side

NOTE: Neighborhood names are pseudonyms. The method of first contact with the RCs is reported because of the importance of avoiding model neighborhoods in China; see Appendix 1.

[a] I discontinued research at this site at the request of the RC.

[b] I did not visit the RC office but conducted five long, private interviews with a member of the committee staff.

Taipei, although an additional trip to the small city of Chiayi in the southern half of the island provided comparative perspective. During this fieldwork I interviewed and observed some twenty neighborhood wardens, as well as candidates for warden positions, neighborhood-based civil servants, and police officers. In six *li* I was able to make three or more visits over multiple years, and I observed the December 2006 neighborhood elections in Taipei. The neighborhoods that I visited in Taipei are listed and described in Table 1.3.

As a second component of the research, I conducted a series of forty-eight private interviews with Beijing residents concerning their interaction with the RCs. In addition, I drew on information gathered by others. I was generously given access to a set of twenty-five transcripts from interviews by two

TABLE I.3
Taipei neighborhood research sites

Site	Warden	Total visits	Description
Andong	Zhou Mintong, then Liu Xiutao	3	Southern periphery of city; a few families have extensive landholdings. Both NW were KMT.
Boren	Wang Shuiqing	1	Central area of city, apartment buildings interspersed with large businesses and markets. KMT NW has served ten terms since 1968.
Fushou	Yang Xueli	1	Far south of Taipei, including large section of mountainside. DPP NW
Guomin	Zhou Ruiqi	2	South Taipei. KMT NW
Haisheng	Kang Mingyi	2	South Taipei. KMT NW
Luzhou	Zhang Junhua	1	Mountainside neighborhood in north Taipei. Former *li ganshi*, running as a nonpartisan, defeated a longtime incumbent in 2006.
Pingshan	Huang Maosen, then Wu Jiaqian	7	Mixed area including large section of mountainside in northeastern Taipei. Both NW were KMT.
Puzhao	Zeng Yalang	4	Central area of city, affluent neighborhood. DPP NW
Qianqiu	Qiu Jinyue	1	South Taipei. KMT NW
Shengfeng	Chen Boyu	10	Affluent neighborhood in northern part of city. KMT NW
Wenchang	Bai Zhengmin	16	South Taipei, near two universities. Nonpartisan but DPP-leaning NW
Yanping	Gao Kunshan, then Xu Peilan	3	South Taipei, includes part of a hillside. Both NW were KMT.
Yicheng	Xie Jinyuan	2	South Taipei. Five-term KMT NW whose family has extensive roots and a large temple in the neighborhood

NOTE: *Li* and warden names are pseudonyms. In neighborhoods for which more than one *lizhang* is named, the first is an incumbent defeated in the December 2006 elections. In a few cases, the number of visits includes interviews conducted outside of the neighborhood in question.

Chinese researchers, Dai Jianzhong and Li Guoqing, who were studying related matters. I also hired Dai and his wife, Tan Baogui, to carry out a further set of twenty-five interviews on my behalf from 2003 to 2005. Interviews for a separate project on homeowner organizations (*yezhu weiyuanhui*) provided further material on newly built neighborhoods. Between 2000 and 2007 I studied twenty-three such cases, all but one of them in Beijing, Shanghai, and Guangzhou. In Taiwan, together with three research assistants, I conducted in-depth interviews with about thirty residents of Taipei to gain perspective on their attitudes toward and interaction with the *li-lin* system.

I found it essential to bring the findings from ethnographic and interview research into dialogue with quantitative data that could capture citizens' attitudes and experiences in broad perspective. Thus, I augmented the qualitative work with data from two original surveys. One was the Beijing Law and Community Survey (BLC), parts of which I helped design in collaboration with the principal investigators Ethan Michelson and Li Lulu. Interviews for the survey were carried out in the summer of 2001 and produced a data set containing responses from 1,018 individuals in twenty-five neighborhoods, scattered throughout seven of the city's eight core districts. In late March and early April 2006 I commissioned and supervised the Taipei Neighborhoods Survey, a telephone survey of the city's residents that replicated important aspects of the BLC while also adding questions specific to the Taiwan context. As in Beijing, the survey assessed respondents' perceptions of, interaction with, and participation in the *li-lin* system. This resulted in 1,140 completed interviews with residents living in 372 of Taipei's officially defined neighborhoods, which at the time numbered 449 in total.

In both China and Taiwan, I also conducted many interviews with officials of various kinds at levels above the neighborhood. In Beijing, these included national-level bureaucrats at the Ministry of Civil Affairs and city officials in the Civil Affairs Bureaus, district governments, and street offices. In Taipei, these included city officials at every level below the mayor (city civil affairs and society bureau officials, district chiefs and staff), as well as officials of the national Ministry of the Interior. Yearbooks and especially the detailed records compiled by the election commissions after every round of voting provided crucial information on Taipei's neighborhoods as well. Around China and in Taiwan, I also benefited from many fruitful discussions with local academic researchers. Various published sources such as newspaper reports, policy documents, handbooks for neighborhood staff, and the like have supplemented the other sources of data. Finally, ten days of field research in Seoul provided the basis for a comparative sketch of its neighborhood administrative system.

Outline of the Book

This study proceeds as follows. Chapter 2 discusses the history behind administrative grassroots organizations, which in East Asia can be traced back to the *bao-jia* of imperial China, a premodern system intended to regiment and control society under the Qing and earlier dynasties. It explains the evolution of the neighborhood governance institutions of contemporary China and Taiwan from the postwar period to the present day. Parsing the extensive duties of today's organizations in Beijing and Taipei shows the substantial functional similarities between them, as well as key points of divergence.

The question of leadership selection in these two core cases forms the focus of Chapter 3, which scrutinizes the procedures through which neighborhood leaders are selected. It lays bare the elaborate state manipulation of the elections in Beijing, which produces RC staff that have essentially been handpicked by city government. In sharp contrast, Taiwan's balloting procedures, which became immensely more competitive over time, have changed the dynamics of local governance. Free and open elections make the *lizhang* accountable to their electorates and give them a much stronger position from which to make demands on city government.

Chapters 4 and 5 explore the ways in which constituents of various types look upon and interact with these organizations. First, participant observation and other sources are brought to bear in an effort to understand neighborhood power dynamics—exactly what kinds of actual authority local leaders have and how this is experienced by residents, ranging from high-status households to potentially more dependent welfare recipients and (in Beijing) migrants. This section also examines these leaders' relationship with nongovernmental organizations and social movements. Next, survey evidence is analyzed to provide a large-N perspective on citizens' perceptions of and encounters with these institutions.

The book then turns to an examination of the complex social networks that surround the RCs and the *lizhang*. The neighborhood institutions typically attract a tightly knit core of committed participants. The question of what motivates people to serve as block captains (small-group leaders and the like in Beijing, *linzhang* in Taipei), and how nonparticipants see them, is assessed in Chapter 6 against a backdrop of theoretical accounts of state-mobilized activism. In Taiwan, the competitive nature of neighborhood politics, including the ability of *lizhang* candidates and other nonincumbent groups to organize freely and to receive public resources, means that even government-supported organizations can contribute to bottom-up social action. In both cities, substantial numbers of residents have at least thin forms of interaction with their ultra-local representatives: light acquaintance, occasional meetings, or phone calls. Chapter 7 identifies the various bases for these widespread networks, and explains their significance.

Chapter 8 widens the focus of the argument, moving from the paired China-Taiwan comparison to a broader consideration of administrative grass-roots engagement in other East and Southeast Asian countries, specifically Japan, Indonesia, and South Korea. It identifies the complex historical inter-connections among these cases and considers the related, though geographi-cally distant, case of Cuba. While noting the many distinct features of each of these cases, it highlights general patterns that accord with findings from Beijing and Taipei.

Finally, Chapter 9 brings together the strands of evidence and argument for summary. In their own ways, organizations like the RCs and the *li-lin* challenge us to rethink dichotomies like vertical and horizontal, state and non-state. We find in them neither pure synergistic harmony nor arid coercion. The social networks surrounding them blend elements of hierarchy, camara-derie, exchange, public power, and neighborly cooperation. Understanding them requires embracing a world of enduring, hybrid categories, to whose ancestry we now turn.

Chapter Two

The Little Platoon
Structuring the Neighborhood

The Nature of Administrative Organizations at the Grass Roots

Chapter 1 introduced the basic concept of administrative grassroots engagement (AGE): networks of state-sponsored organizations at the ultra-local level that facilitate governance and policing by building personal relationships with members of society. Here I explain this concept further and sketch out some of the historical processes that brought this kind of institution to such widespread presence in East and Southeast Asia today. From there, the chapter proceeds to a careful look at the Beijing and Taipei cases.

As we will see, these institutions are sticky: once created, they tend to persist and evolve, developing new purposes even as they shed others. In part, this stems from their tremendous utility to government. From a state's perspective, cooperative links with local organizations are useful in several basic ways, all of which spring from the human presence and interpersonal networks that they embody. Rather than trample on local knowledge à la Scott's high modernism, they instead afford access to it, thus making it possible to gather information that would otherwise be impossible or costly for distant bureaucrats to obtain (1998, 4, 88). They help bring trouble, threats, and deviants—however defined—to the attention of the authorities. They also allow for information flows in the other direction, which provides a way for the state to disseminate announcements, policies, and other messages efficiently. This propagating of information can be used merely to inform—for instance, telling parents where to take their children for vaccinations. The same function also can be used to persuade: to blunt local resistance to redevelopment plans or to convince people to adopt new forms of trash disposal and recycling. Organizations at the grassroots level can address conflict locally, thereby relieving burdens from higher levels of the state. To a greater or lesser extent they are intended to fill a space that could stand empty or be occupied by less cooperative forms of association.

As systematically as a tractor-towed seed drill, states implant such organizations in uniform patterns, which ensures their near-ubiquitous presence. They thus may compete, quietly or overtly, with uncultivated, spontaneously formed groups at the grassroots level—although at times the two may cooperate with each other.[1] Governments often disburse stipends to their core personnel and also grant them offices, equipment, and operating funds. Furthermore, they bestow on them the stamp of authority through symbols and placards as well as policies and laws. In a curious form of doublethink, states also play down the official status of these bodies, putting them forward within thick clouds of community talk, as an embodiment of societal organization. Notionally, they express a form of solidarity both rooted in the community and integrated with the nation as a whole. At the same time, they provide a channel through which ordinary people can articulate demands, address local issues, and sometimes vote for representatives.

Figure 2.1 lays out seven cases of administrative grassroots engagement along two dimensions. The vertical dimension portrays the extent of each institution's administrative role: the degree to which it has duties of policy implementation; information gathering; and in some cases, political surveillance. The horizontal dimension shows how internally democratic each organization is: the degree to which its leaders are elected through open, fair, and participatory procedures.[2] The first thing one might note is the existence of considerable variation along both dimensions, as discussed below. Also evident is that the organizations' administrative role and internal democracy are only weakly correlated. The Chinese case exhibits a high degree of administrative responsibility together with a very low level of democracy, but some organizations that are much more democratic, such as those in the Indonesia and Taiwan cases, still carry out a significant set of administrative tasks. Finally, the internal democracy of these local institutions and the democratic or authoritarian nature of the country's national-level political regime (a third

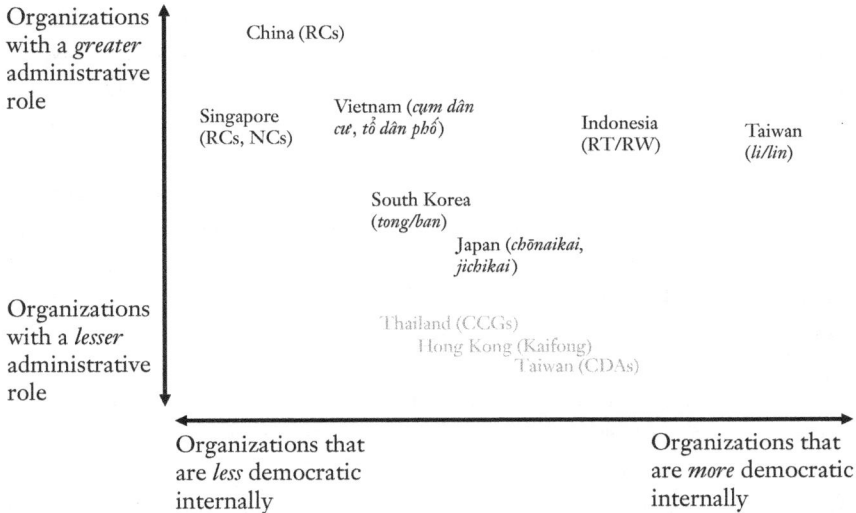

Organizations with a *greater* administrative role

Organizations with a *lesser* administrative role

China (RCs)

Singapore (RCs, NCs)

Vietnam (*cụm dân cư, tổ dân phố*)

Indonesia (RT/RW)

Taiwan (*li/lin*)

South Korea (*tong/ban*)

Japan (*chōnaikai, jichikai*)

Thailand (CCGs)

Hong Kong (Kaifong)

Taiwan (CDAs)

Organizations that are *less* democratic internally

Organizations that are *more* democratic internally

Figure 2.1.   Cases of administrative grassroots engagement in East and Southeast Asia, by role and internal democracy.

Estimates are from the author's research on China, Taiwan, and South Korea, and from various secondary sources on Vietnam, Singapore, Japan, Thailand, and Indonesia. The names in gray are not full-fledged cases of AGE: they have fewer administrative functions and a less widespread presence than the other cases.

dimension, not pictured in Figure 2.1) are imperfectly correlated as well. Although authoritarian countries like China and Singapore predictably run their neighborhood organizations in undemocratic ways, the four democratic states vary greatly in the procedures used to constitute theirs. South Korea, for example, is a thriving democracy at the national level, but its part-time neighborhood liaisons (*tongjang*) are not voted into their positions; rather, they are appointed by ward offices, though sometimes at the recommendation of residents. Only some members of its tightly woven network of household cluster leaders (*banjang*) are elected, and then only informally so.

The neighborhood organizations in urban China, Vietnam, and Singapore cluster together on these continua, although they are hardly copies of one another. (Whether by coincidence or not, in both China and Singapore the relevant body is called a residents' committee in English.) In Singapore, the government's omnibus consociational ringleader, the People's Association, runs an elaborate network of grassroots groups, the most widely dispersed of which are the residents' committees (Seah 1987; Ooi 2009).[3] In Vietnam, cities like Hanoi have resident groups composed of twenty-five to thirty households. Each of these has a head and assistant heads, and the groups in turn are assembled into resident clusters (Koh 2006, 44–50). These three cases are the most government-dominated of the institutions considered here. Their members are guided or directly managed by higher levels of city administration. In all three cases, they also are subject to control through parallel systems running all the way up to the monistic parties that dominate political life: the Chinese Communist Party (CCP), the Vietnamese Communist Party, and the People's Action Party, respectively.

In each of these three cases, the grassroots body in question centers on a group, essentially a team of staff, although in none is the team formally employed by the government. In China, as Chapter 3 shows, these individuals are "elected" to their positions in what for the most part are heavily constrained vetting and balloting procedures, designed to ensure that committee members are acceptable to the authorities and can be relied on for support. They work close to full-time and must answer to the state in something close to an employee relationship. In Singapore, members of the city-state's 551 residents' committees are also appointed from above, but they do not spend long hours on duty in the same way; rather, they come together for monthly meetings with police officers and staff from the Community Development Secretariat (Ooi 2009, 179–184). Hanoi's resident group leaders also work informally but hold multiple meetings each month with ward officials, who rely on them heavily for tasks ranging from mediation to selling government bonds to reporting on neighbors, according to Koh. He writes that these leaders are elected and that nominations are subject to "practically zero" party control but also that candidates cannot have "committed offenses or crimes against the law or the [Vietnamese Communist Party]" (Koh 2006, 48).

Four other cases—in Japan, Taiwan, Indonesia, and South Korea—once were carefully controlled from above, much like their counterparts in Singapore and China, and likewise served as buttresses for authoritarian systems. Since the democratization of each of these countries, however, they have evolved in ways that set them apart. Japan's neighborhood associations possess considerable autonomy; they are not subject to any formal levers of control by city governments. Their degree of independence is such that some scholars discuss them as a form of civil society, indeed as a characteristic and central form of civil society organization in Japan (Pekkanen 2006). Yet one might easily see them as occupying a gray area. With few exceptions, they work hand in hand with local authorities, mainly in ways that oblige local government rather than resist or make demands on it. For example, many regularly collect fees, publicize announcements, and perform other tasks for the city bureaucracy.

In Indonesia, the micro-level organization of society takes the form of the *rukun tetangga* (RT), whose roots can be traced back to Japan's occupation in World War II, as discussed in Chapter 8. In cities like Jakarta, each RT corresponds to a segment of a neighborhood that contains just a few hundred residents. Several of these entities, in turn, are clustered together to form larger units called *rukun warga* (RW). Once dominated by the Suharto regime, the leadership of these bodies has become politically pluralized since the beginning of Indonesia's democratic transition in the late 1990s. They remain, however, closely tied to the wards, the next-higher rung on the urban administrative ladder.

The RT and RW are one example of a governance structure that manifests itself in the countryside as well as in cities (Sullivan 1992, 134–135). Similarly, Taiwan's Local Government Act invokes villages and neighborhoods together in the same passages and treats them all but identically; official texts and academic analyses often conceptualize them as two facets of a single system (*cun-li zhidu*). Although the rural versions of these institutions also constitute important sites at which state designs and administrative programs mesh with local society, this book confines itself to the urban cases. It does so in part as an arbitrary way of imposing boundaries on the comparative framework. Also, though, the rural counterparts of urban organizations can be very different. In China, for example, villages have much more extensive responsibilities than their neighborhood cousins, with the management of land rights, control over major productive assets, provision of roads and schools, and other duties lying partly or entirely within their remit.[4]

Figure 2.1 also includes three other organizations, with their names rendered in gray because they are not full-fledged cases of AGE: they have fewer administrative functions and a less widespread presence than the other cases. The purposes of such associations constitute a subset of those found in the others. Thailand's cooperative community groups (*chumchon yoi naikaet tesaban*) and Taiwan's community development associations (CDAs; *shequ fazhan xiehui*) are urban bodies encompassing some but not all neighborhoods, initiated in government programs, receiving public funds. They aim to promote neighborhood cohesiveness and self-governance, and they serve as channels through which to distribute largess from public coffers to particular constituencies and community projects (Mahakanjana 2009).⁵ Hong Kong's *kaifong* associations emerged after World War II to address welfare, relief, mediation, and education needs. They also served as channels through which authorities of the colonial government kept in touch with Chinese society. But the rather patchwork set of *kaifong* received little, if any, government funding, and the associations were judged to be in decline by the late 1970s (Lau 1983, 130–136; see also Wong 1972). Other such bodies could be included in Figure 2.1 as well. They remind us that the phenomenon identified here as administrative grassroots engagement shades into other forms of local organization.

In divergent regime types, the political tasks of these organizations vary widely, even as they draw on the same basic mechanisms and engage in many overlapping practices. Unsurprisingly, in authoritarian contexts, such as China, Indonesia (pre-1998), Vietnam, and Singapore, a primary purpose of state-fostered organizations is to help maintain the grip of a ruling party. They can do this by keeping a lookout for political dissent and reporting illicit behavior, just as in another region Cuba's Committees for the Defense of the Revolution have done by exercising "revolutionary vigilance" (Dominguez 1978; Colomer 2000). Or regime support can take subtler forms, such as inculcating loyalty to Suharto's so-called New Order, building national unity, or identifying and recruiting leadership talent. The cases of Japan, Taiwan, South Korea, and Indonesia (post-1998) teach us that these organizations can shed their more intrusive, control-oriented functions. In these countries, democratic governments still find countless uses for them. States of both regime types use these organizational platforms for delivering services; gathering popular input; stimulating voluntary activity; and otherwise performing liaison work that is congruent, rather than at odds, with residents' interests and needs. Simultaneously, community associational networks often build themselves around the nucleus that is established by government structuring. It is characteristic of administrative grassroots engagement to meld together all these conceptually distinct functions so that the boundaries among them blur.

Do such institutions truly constitute a distinct category? To be sure, even in liberal democracies like the United States, governments strive to maintain certain kinds of personal links with constituents. Bureaucracies employ specialists to act as intermediaries with those who receive special state support or supervision. For instance, social workers establish relationships with welfare recipients; parole officers keep tabs on the parolees in their charge. Community policing efforts bring police officers into closer contact with the localities they serve, and initiatives like the Neighborhood Watch program encourage ordinary citizens to report suspicious activity to the state. The organizations considered in this book, however, are substantially more institutionalized than Neighborhood Watch groups, more deeply embedded in local society than most community policing initiatives, and more functionally diffuse than welfare caseworkers.

Why is this kind of institution so prominent in East and Southeast Asia? No simple answer suffices. After all, state-sponsored organizations are hardly unique to this region. Corporatism as a concept was first theorized in Europe, and Latin America has provided many cases as well. China's and Vietnam's neighborhood bodies have counterparts in current and former state socialist regimes elsewhere, from Cuba to the former Soviet Union. And as noted above, the general questions of government's relationship to associational life are even relevant in strongly liberal systems. Precisely because there are so many ways in which local organizations can be valuable for state programs, these institutions are found in many places.

Still, their distribution in the world is far from random. Despite their political diversity today, the countries that develop these institutions have a set of general properties in common. First, establishing this form of grassroots presence requires considerable bureaucratic coherence and organizational capacity: a strong state. The East Asian model is usually invoked to discuss patterns of industrialization and economic development, or sometimes labor or human rights (Amsden 1989; Öniş 1991; Wade 1992; Kohli 1994; Evans 1995; Peerenboom 2007). Yet many of the qualities that underpinned the region's approach to economic development and civil liberties also influenced the evolution of local associations.

Most of these states shared internal or external security concerns in the second half of the twentieth century. Whether in socialist systems like China or Vietnam, fearing threats to the revolution, or under conservative regimes like Park's Republic of Korea, Chiang's Republic of China, and Suharto's Republic of Indonesia, wary of communist expansion, officials were driven to construct organizational networks capable of monitoring the populace and co-opting dissent. Although security is only one of many purposes to which such institutions are put today, such concerns were central motivations for the effort to monitor and influence society at the neighborhood or household level. Finally, the doctrines of liberalism found little resonance in the corridors of power here. These systems lacked principled prohibitions on government organization of the populace; to the contrary, this was considered the norm. Just as bureaucrats largely shunned the idea of a laissez-faire approach to building the economy, they also did not believe that societal organization should be left alone to grow haphazardly from the grass roots up. Instead, corporatist intervention, the active shaping of organizations, made just as much sense to them in overseeing urban and village governance as it did in guiding firms or labor groups.

These preconditions do not constitute a full explanation of the emergence of administrative grassroots engagement, but they help show how some states are more likely to develop such institutions, whereas others are unable or unwilling to do so. Cases are thus absent, rare, or attenuated in the poorest and weakest of developing-world states, as well as in countries with a long-standing liberal tradition. Certainly this set of prerequisites—strong states, security concerns, and collectivist rather than liberal traditions—figured prominently in both China and Taiwan (as well as in other cases like South Korea, Singapore, and Indonesia) for formative portions of the post–World War II era. But another factor cannot be ignored, and indeed deserves an extended discussion. Rulers in each case also had particularly robust historical templates to look to in constructing the machinery of ultra-local governance. Before launching on an excursion centuries back into East Asian history, we must remind ourselves that the premodern or colonial histories of individual countries can take us only so far; the state-sponsored organizations of Singapore, for example, do not seem to have sprouted from British seeds. Although templates from the past are not a necessary condition for administrative grassroots engagement, they give it a substantial boost.

Intertwined Roots in East Asian History

The parallels between the residents' committees (RCs) and prior organizational forms lie in the use of individuals possessing local knowledge and situated outside the formal governing hierarchy to extend the power of the state. A recurring and critically important theme of local Qing administration was the state's effort to leverage a relatively small bureaucracy into a relatively large amount of revenue collection and control by delegating, selling, or ceding powers to intermediaries (Ch'ü 1962, 9–13; Moore 1966, 162–174; Kuhn 1975, 258). The state proper extended downward only to the level of the county magistrate himself. The magistrate, as Duara writes, "was able to administer a jurisdiction of roughly 300,000 people only by 'contracting' out many administrative functions to local individuals and groups with the experience to run the business of government" (1988, 46). This contracting or delegation took many forms. Notoriously, the clerks and runners of the magistrate's headquarters, or *yamen*, took responsibility for day-to-day processes such as collecting taxes and wielded their authority to great personal advantage (Ch'ü 1962, 36–73; Kuhn 1979, 108; Shue 1988, 98). The state also maintained extensive relationships with the educated local elite, referred to as gentry. The gentry played a role in such activities as maintaining public works, collecting taxes and corvée labor, managing efforts for famine relief and mutual aid, organizing local militia, delivering moral lectures to the local population, and mediating disputes (Ch'ü 1962, 168–192; Shue 1988, 85). In addition to enlisting the gentry's participation, the state also sometimes drew on the leaders of lineage communities or other local organizations such as the sluice-gate associations (Freedman 1966; Duara 1988, 26–38). In commercial centers, merchants and their guilds were tapped as well, for the purpose of self-regulation and taxation (Rowe 1984, 252–321; Wakeman 1993).

A further manner in which the state recruited local people to serve its ends was the establishment of what are sometimes called decimal hierarchies for policing and tax collection, particularly the *bao-jia* and *li-jia* systems. What makes these distinct from the other governing mechanisms is that they were intended to penetrate to the most local level, that of the individual household; they were rooted in the place of residence; and by design they elicited the participation of ordinary commoners and were kept separate from gentry involvement. In the *bao-jia* system, as it was formulated in the early Qing period, each group of ten households was to form a *pai*; each group of one hundred households, a *jia*; and every thousand households, a *bao*.[6] The designated heads at each level (*paitou, jiatou,* and *baozhang,* respectively) shouldered specific responsibilities, mainly revolving around security. Households posted door placards listing the names of all their adult males; individuals had the duty of reporting any crimes, or the presence of criminals, to the heads, who in turn reported to the authorities. *Bao-jia* leaders themselves, as well as their constituent households, were to be held responsible for crimes committed in their jurisdiction, thus giving all an incentive to discourage or report wrong-doing. The *bao-jia* also gradually acquired tax-prompting responsibilities that were initially channeled through the parallel *li-jia* (Hsiao 1960, 3–143; Ch'ü 1962, 150–154).

The regimentation of this system displayed a clear martial logic (Kuhn 1970, 24–28). One might say, with apologies to Edmund Burke, that it sought to create a literal arrangement of society into a cellular pattern around the "little platoon" (2007, 44). Quite contrary to what Burke envisioned in this metaphor, historian Hsiao Kung-ch'üan did not see much in the *bao-jia* that could cultivate the germ of public affections or proceed toward a love of one's country and mankind. Military-style organization employed in this way deliberately sowed "fear and distrust," he believed: "By enlisting the help of the local inhabitants, the government extended its control to the remotest hamlets without multiplying the number of government officials; by putting the *pao-chia* under the supervision of local officials, it prevented the *pao-chia* heads from acquiring undue power or influence. Under this system the people became potential informers against wrongdoers or lawbreakers among their own neighbors—in other words they were made to spy upon themselves. Such mutual fear and suspicion were instilled in their minds that few of them dared to venture into seditious schemes with their fellow villagers" (Hsiao 1960, 46).

Despite periodic attempts at revival, the *bao-jia* system had inherent flaws. Illiterate locals lacked the skills to maintain household registries properly; unit heads sometimes possessed little real authority over the gentry and faced reprisals for reporting on actual criminals; it was often difficult to recruit people for *bao-jia* duties because of the risks and responsibilities involved; and those who did serve tended to abuse their powers. Hsiao concludes that the *bao-jia* nevertheless helped deter crime and maintain order in generally peaceful areas and periods, although Ch'ü is more skeptical (Hsiao 1960, 72–83; Ch'ü 1962, 151). By the mid-nineteenth century the system had begun to lapse into disrepair, and it decayed further along with the general decline in Qing authority that was to culminate in the dynasty's 1911 collapse. Yet it would be revived again and again by modern states that sought to remedy the above-mentioned shortcomings.

The Qing had extended the *bao-jia* system to Taiwan starting in 1733, though Ching-Chih Chen judges that it "fell far short in its actual performance" (1975, 393). Not long after Japan's 1895 acquisition of the island, Gotō Shimpei and other colonial administrators adapted the Qing's local control organizations, known as *hokō* in the tongue of the metropole. By 1903, there were 4,080 *bao* and 41,660 *jia* on the island, figures that had increased by about 50 percent as of 1942 (Chen 1975, 399). The heads of these units were freighted with duties relating to public health, road construction, taxation, and more, in addition to surveillance and registration functions. Caroline Hui-Yu Ts'ai concurs with Chen that the Japanese implemented this system far more effectively than had the Qing. Rather than merely borrowing it, they "synthesized, internalized, and improved on it" (Ts'ai 1990, 54). For the first time, the *bao-jia* were backed up by a tightly integrated network of modern police stations. The *bao* leaders, who set up offices in their own homes, were elected by the heads of households, although police commonly manipulated the voting and allowed only preauthorized candidates (Ts'ai 1990, 214–216). Despite its colonial nature, which at times elicited protests by intellectuals, the system sank deep roots into Taiwanese society, Ts'ai writes: "a *hosei* [*baozheng*, or *bao* leader] was one type of the traditional local elites, often being honorifically addressed as '*hosei san*,' who had considerable influence in the local and police administration and possessed a real hold over social education and economic development in his locality. In contrast to *pao-chia* headmen of imperial China, therefore, *hokō* headmen in colonial Taiwan were highly regarded by local residents" (1990, 523). Yao Jen-to makes similar points in his Foucauldian interpretation of this institution.[7] By co-opting such leaders and putting them in the service of Japan's modernization projects, the system "served as a catalyst for creating an islandwide identity for the Taiwanese, despite the political and social distress that the *hokō* system inflicted upon them" (Ts'ai 1990, 579–580).

As Japan occupied and colonized other parts of Asia in the twentieth century, it established either *bao-jia*, as in mainland China, or differently named but substantively similar bodies (Chen 1984; Kasza 1995, 18–19). Korea, whose dynastic heritage also included state-imposed systems of household registration and collective responsibility, was organized into small groups called *ban* in 1917.[8] In 1940, these were redubbed "patriotic *ban*" (*aegukban*; Seo 2002, 2). As one historian explains, "each association consisted of ten households, and this became the basic unit for a variety of government programs for collection of contributions, imposition of labor service, maintenance of local security, and for rationing" (Eckert 1990, 321). Japan introduced similar units, named *tonarigumi*, after an institution from the home islands, to Java during its wartime occupation (Kurasawa 2009; Sullivan 1992, 136).

In the early 1930s, the Kuomintang (KMT) reintroduced the *bao-jia* in rural areas of China as part of its attempt to establish local dominance and wipe out the communist movement (Kuhn 1975, 297). Demonstrating again the portability of this institutional template, the Nanjing government drew in large part on rules adapted from Japan's colonial administration on Taiwan while restoring the organizations, in an ambitious though poorly implemented effort stretching to sixteen provinces (Ts'ai 1990, 552, 558). Beginning in 1940, the Japanese occupiers brought *bao-jia* back to cities they had taken during their invasion of China. When the KMT regained control of major cities after Japan's surrender in 1945, it kept the *bao-jia* system in place and attempted to use it to facilitate police work, population registry, tax collection, and draft conscription (Schurmann 1966, 369–371).

One might imagine that anything associated with previous rulers (and the Japanese conquerors in particular) would have been rejected by the postwar governments of South Korea, Indonesia, Taiwan, and mainland China. But to the contrary, each reestablished systems of ultra-local administration in both countryside and city. In Korea, the Syngman Rhee government kept the *ban* in place with another change in nomenclature; this time it was renamed "citizen's *ban*" (*kungminban*; Seo 2002, 2). Although its heyday of mass mobilization came in the 1970s under Park Chung Hee's "revitalization," the basic structure remains intact even now. Meanwhile, in Indonesia, anticolonial leaders quickly reconstituted successors to the *tonarigumi* (and their companion bodies, the *aza*) under the new labels RT and RK (*rukun kampung*) in 1947, during the independence struggle against the Dutch. Mayors and military commanders, in particular, fostered them during the Sukarno years. When Suharto came to power he further solidified this system, purging it of communist infiltration and integrating it into a far-reaching corporatist reworking of society (Kurasawa 2009, 61–67). Although the Korean and Indonesian neighborhood bodies remain shadow cases in this book, we return to them at points in the chapters to come, and especially in Chapter 8.

Post–World War II Trajectories

As the communist forces took control of China's major cities one by one at the end of the 1940s, they faced the challenge of maintaining order while also removing from power hostile or unreliable individuals who had worked for the Nationalists. Their solution was to keep parts of the old security forces in place, but only as long as necessary. After a brief period of accommodating the *bao* heads in what was then called Beiping, for instance, CCP leaders called for mass struggle against them and abolished the system entirely. Naturally, the communists had no quarrel with the basic principle of mobilizing local residents for policing and other purposes; indeed, they had employed similar "mutual guarantee units" in some of the territories they captured during World War II (Chen 1986, 102–106).

The establishment of CCP power in China's cities brought profound upheavals in the social and political structure of urban life. Some of these changes were immediate, such as the rooting out of the Kuomintang power apparatus; others unfolded gradually, such as the reallocation of housing stocks. But by no means did the new order constitute a complete break from the past. The new regime's grassroots institutions in fact bore a distinct resemblance to the precursors discussed above. This is not to say that organizations like the RCs were mere copies of earlier patterns. Rather, they appear to have emerged from a mix of traditional precedent, the lessons learned during the CCP's own administrative experiments en route to its seizure of national power, and the situational imperatives faced by a young government trying to entrench itself in unfamiliar urban terrain after decades of rural struggle.

In the aftermath of the urban takeover, the communists busily created several kinds of mass-based organizations. They were particularly keen to acquire control of key industrial firms and to mobilize the working class into new unions. In addition to such functional or workplace-centered associations, however, the new regime also found it necessary to establish residence-based organizations. This was in part an effort to integrate the many urbanites who did not belong to schools, factories, or administrative institutions. The effort was driven, too, by the regime's eagerness to mobilize the citizenry against real or perceived domestic enemies of the revolution at a time of war in Korea and threats from Taiwan and the United States. After initially relying on individual activists and ad hoc committees in neighborhoods, the regime organized formal residents' committees on an experimental basis starting in Tianjin in 1951 (Schurmann 1966, 374). By mid-1953, Beijing's mayor Peng Zhen was advocating that they be standardized and adopted nationwide; this was done over the months and years that followed (Peng 1991, 240–241).

The RCs were by no means merely the old *bao-jia* dressed up in new clothing.[9] If the main purposes of the *bao-jia* were to facilitate household registration and to make residents themselves responsible for helping detect and deter criminals, the RCs' functions were substantially broader. They had the job of promoting the common welfare by organizing things like sanitation and relief efforts. With their special focus on city dwellers who had no other connection to the new regime's governing institutions—particularly unemployed housewives, and those who had received little or no schooling—the committees carried out programs designed to reach out to these constituencies, educate them, and integrate them into what was conceived of as a new and progressive society.[10] Literacy classes and newspaper-reading groups, both revolving around the publications and discourse of the Communist Party, were among the ways the RCs tried to build ties to these once wholly disenfranchised individuals; they also organized activities and sometimes reading rooms for children. They attempted to contribute to a new social order in other ways as well, for instance by educating women about their right to free themselves from coerced marriages under the 1950 Marriage Law.[11] They also strived to mediate disputes among neighbors, a function that has received particular attention over the years (Lubman 1967, 1997; Clark 1989; Wall and Blum 1991; Diamant 2000a; Guo and Klein 2005; Read and Michelson 2008).

Like their pre-1949 predecessors, however, they had important security functions, came to acquire household registration duties, relieved government of the burden of dealing with many day-to-day affairs, and involved recruiting and empowering selected ordinary citizens to bear those responsibilities. The ways in which they served the state also went considerably beyond the scope of their predecessor organizations. They were intended to communicate government policies and announcements to the neighborhood (and at least nominally to communicate residents' opinions to city authorities), and to mobilize residents to respond to government campaigns. Their post-1949 reemergence owes to a confluence of factors: the imperatives facing the young regime as it consolidated its control over the cities, techniques of mass mobilization that the CCP developed on its own and borrowed from the Soviet Union, and patterns of delegation that party elites and urbanites alike drew from both the distant past and recent experience.

In Taiwan, colonial administrators abolished the *bao-jia* on the eve of Japan's surrender in August of 1945 (Ts'ai 1990, 513). But with Chiang Kai-shek's government assuming control of the island soon thereafter, it is hardly surprising that a successor to this institution was quickly put into place, given both its legacy in Taiwan and the Kuomintang's recent deployment of it on the mainland. Like the Japanese in the late nineteenth century, the KMT arrived as an external force keen to harness and guide the energies of local leadership and, especially after the uprising of late February 1947, to ferret out resistance.[12] The total number of *li* and *cun* in 1946 was very close to the number of *bao* four years earlier—6,301, up from 6,168—which attests to the continuity between the two institutions (Chen 1975, 399; Schafferer 2003, 86). Indeed, the view that the village-neighborhood (*cun-li*) system emerged from the *bao-jia* seems to command a firm consensus among researchers and officials alike. Po Ching-Chiu, a longtime scholar of local government in Taiwan, explains that because the Japanese had used the name *bao-jia* for their "hated" system of control, the new rulers switched to *cun-li* terminology "to avoid misunderstanding on the part of the compatriots of Taiwan province" (Po 1971, 209). Ts'ai attests that "in the neighborhood (*lin-li*) organizations in today's Taiwan remains a diluted form of the *hokō* system from the period of colonial Taiwan" (1990, 544). Then-mayor Ma Ying-jeou, in a March 24, 2003, address to the Taipei City Council, linked the current system to the dynastic *bao-jia* and stated that, "although the position of *lizhang* only has 58 years of history, its predecessors go back more than three hundred years in time" (City of Taipei City Council 2003). A research report on village and neighborhood governance circulated by the Ministry of the Interior dedicated three full pages to tracing the roots of today's institutions back not merely to the Qing but to the Qin dynasty, founded in 221 B.C. (Tseng 2004, 17–19).

As with their precursor organizations, Taiwan's early *li* (and rural *cun*) were meant to bring locals of some stature into semiformal work on behalf of the government. They combined elements of co-optation, information gathering, and administrative responsibility with a host of public service functions. As of July 1969, the *lizhang* received modest stipends of NT$150 per month (up from $100 previously), plus a newspaper subscription and a few other small benefits (Po 1971, 214). Each warden was paired with a government civil servant (*liganshi*), both because the puny compensation meant that the *lizhang* could work no more than part-time and no doubt to ensure that he did not neglect key administrative tasks. Early national-level guidelines regarding villages and neighborhoods affirmed that these positions should exist but said little about specific duties assigned to them; rather, responsibilities were spelled out in local codes, a situation that still holds today. Drawing on examples of such codes, Po shows that the warden and the civil servant were given long lists of responsibilities, generally overlapping in content. They were to handle

various jobs pertaining to core state functions like distributing tax bills, prod-
ding residents to pay these levies, announcing and explaining new government
policies, and issuing various certificates and affidavits. Particularly prominent
were tasks related to military conscription and service: handling draft notices,
exemptions, benefits for soldiers' families, and the like. Other items on their
agendas aimed more at citizens' well-being, such as helping implement land
reform and rent reduction, providing relief for disaster victims and the poor,
and even checking on truant children. Po argues that the *liganshi* was intended
to be the "center of gravity" of neighborhood work, with the warden in a secondary role, but that in practice the wardens were at least as important (1971,
216–220).

Like other levels of the ROC's governing structure, the *li* also encouraged
structured forms of popular participation. Under the Japanese, *bao* leaders
had been elected by household heads, although candidates were subject to a
number of eligibility requirements and the results subject to the authorities'
veto. Starting in 1946, wardens too were chosen by constituents, first through
indirect balloting by local assemblies and, from 1950, in direct elections
(Schafferer 2003, 85–91). As the island's national political regime gradually
democratized, the role of the *lizhang* slowly but unmistakably changed, as later
chapters detail. Non-KMT and even Democratic Progressive Party (DPP)
candidates began to win warden positions that had come to be dominated
by the ruling party. Over time, the network of wardens became pluralized in
terms of political affiliations, more closely reflecting the mixed preferences of
the electorate—even in Taipei, where the Kuomintang organization remains
particularly strong. The *lizhang* also developed more independence from
political parties and city governments alike. Today, party headquarters and
state *liganshi* both treat the wardens not as subordinates but as autonomous
actors who deserve respect.

Just as significant, other kinds of political groups and action not only
emerged in the neighborhood setting but also became accepted and routine.
Notions of community development were discussed in Taiwan as early as
the 1960s, when they became popularized through agencies of the United
Nations. In the 1990s, President Lee Teng-hui promoted the spread of community development associations (discussed further in Chapter 6). Although
they often received state support, these groups were meant to be self-initiated
citizens' organizations, arising to fill needs not met by the neighborhood
administrative network and cutting across its boundaries (Lin 1996, 16–24).

Cities saw the rise of local political movements over issues like parks, redevelopment, and quality of life.

Meanwhile, extensive debates arose within government and among
researchers as to what the relationship should be between the official community structures and other organizations. Studies proliferated, with some
proposing to abolish the *li-lin* system, or at least reform it. In Taipei, these
ideas came to a head in the neighborhood-governance reform program introduced in 2002 by a young Civil Affairs Bureau director who had come into
politics by way of popular activism. As explained in Chapter 4, the resistance
against even these modest reforms, which would have chipped away a few of
the wardens' prerogatives and benefits, reflected the deeply entrenched position of this institution in the island's sociopolitical system. All in all, the *li-lin*
system has evolved in cumulatively momentous ways, but this came through
a slow and quiet process. Many of the responsibilities that cities give to the
wardens today are similar to those of four decades ago. Democracy came to
Taiwan gradually, and its effects trickled down bit by bit to the neighborhood
level, without sudden upheavals.

In certain key respects the institution of the residents' committee, too, has
stayed constant over the years; it has remained a parastatal, neighborhood-
based organization, carrying out a mixture of tasks on behalf of the government as well as providing services to constituents. But the committee has gone
through a process of evolution in which historical turning points as well as
socioeconomic trends have figured prominently. The Great Leap Forward
was the occasion for one important development. Though better known for
the crash program to transform the rural economy through industrialization
and communization, the late 1950s also saw a somewhat parallel attempt to
build urban communes. Beginning in mid-1958, this campaign had several
overlapping goals. Salaff writes: "Like the rural communes, the urban would
create a totality of urban living—bringing together industry, agriculture,
commerce, culture, education and defence" (1967, 94). They were intended
to rid the cities of their noisome residue of prerevolutionary culture, to rouse
the population to active political engagement, and to mobilize the productive
efforts of those adult urbanites who remained outside the labor force. The
street offices and RCs tried to carry out the latter by organizing residents
to work in small-scale factories, workshops, and even their homes, turning
out handicraft goods, sewing clothing, or performing finishing tasks on the
products of state enterprises. Although the urban communes were short lived,

these local collective enterprises lived on. Many proved economically unviable in the long term, but successful ones were often taken over by higher administrative levels. Still, as of the 2000s, some of Beijing's longest-serving RC veterans dated their involvement back to this campaign.

Launched by Mao Zedong in 1966, the Cultural Revolution was a second major watershed for the residents' committees, as it was for the entire urban governing structure. This movement, even more calamitous for China's cities than the Great Leap had been, was Mao's final attempt to restore the purity of the revolution by encouraging youth, workers, and other groups to attack the very system that he and his confederates had themselves created. In its initial phases, the primary arenas of mobilization and struggle were schools and factories. Then, starting with the municipality of Shanghai in January 1967, the leadership signaled its approval for the takeover of government institutions themselves by "rebel" factions. First city governments, then districts, street offices, and even residents' committees themselves were upended, contributing to a general breakdown in order.

During this period, the extant committees often came under criticism from their constituents for the more unpopular policies of the time that they had been charged with carrying out (Salaff 1971, 295–298). As order was restored around 1968, the street offices eventually cashiered many RC incumbents and replaced them with so-called revolutionary residents' committees—the same basic institution under more radical leadership. These continued to conduct well-established political activities, like study groups, with all the more vigor, and moreover led rallies and struggle sessions against residents who had been designated class enemies. In cities like Beijing, they also helped the housing authorities determine whose homes should be shared with other households, as the once-wealthy occupants were finally parted from what property they had managed to retain. In the late 1960s and 1970s, millions of youths were sent to the countryside to learn from the peasants, and RCs had to report any who sneaked back to their parents' homes.

Officials and government documents often state that RCs languished in paralysis during the aftermath of the Cultural Revolution. This appears somewhat misleading, because in fact the RCs persisted as an institution and continued to carry out many of the same administrative, political, and economic tasks that they had for years. Regardless, rebuilding the RCs became part of the broad effort to repair the damage done to the state apparatus during the turbulent final chapter of Mao's rule. It also formed part of the response to a set of administrative challenges to China's cities that grew more and more acute through the 1980s and 1990s. The long-term decline in the fortunes of state enterprises posed a double problem. First, layoffs and factory clos-ings left millions of urbanites without employment, fueling unrest. Second, workplaces (*danwei*) that had once incorporated a large fraction of the urban population became less effective as administrative tools. Consequently, cit-ies increasingly turned to the government structure itself, as opposed to the workplaces, to carry out both oversight and social security functions. More-over, cities faced a rising tide of rural migrants, whose mobility made them particularly difficult to monitor. Upheavals like the 1989 protest movement also convinced the party-state of the need to consolidate its organizational infrastructure. The difficulties caused by these developments led urban gov-ernments to devote increasing attention and resources to the RCs (Choate 1998; Read 2000).

The Continuing Evolution of Neighborhood Institutions in China and Taiwan

As everyone who has set foot there knows, China's cities have undergone breathtaking development and expansion in the past two decades (Logan 2002, 2007; Wu 2007). In Beijing, like in other cities, many prerevolutionary neighborhoods and early socialist housing blocks have come under the wreck-ing ball, reemerging as modern condominium towers but scattering existing communities and stirring conflict in the process (Cai 2007). Apartments once owned by work units and allocated to employees were sold to their occupants at low prices in the 1990s, and new private developments have risen, many on the urban periphery, as the city sprawls outward onto former village land.[13] In the 2000s, and particularly under the administration of Mayor Hau Lung-Bin, Taipei began to pursue urban renewal projects as well, though more slowly and on a smaller scale than in Beijing.[14] New organizations (*yezhu weiyuan-hui*) received the blessing of China's State Council in the 1990s as a means of giving homeowners more control over the property management companies that run such new private developments—although in Beijing and elsewhere, establishing and maintaining such groups has proved difficult and has led to ongoing struggles (see, e.g., Read 2003, 2008a). In Taipei, parallel organiza-tions, called management committees (*guanli weiyuanhui*), became a normal feature of life in the large, modern condominium blocks that housed roughly a quarter of the population by the mid-2000s.[15]

A small number of academic studies have examined Taiwan's neighborhood wardens in the postdemocratization era (e.g., Chuang 2005). Little scholarly research on them has been published in English. The attention they have received has focused on their role as local party operatives (*tiau-a-ka* in Taiwanese, or *zhuangjiao*, "cornerstones"), particularly in the KMT's mobilization apparatus (Rigger 1999; Wang and Kurzman 2007). This role is indeed worth attention, but the discussion here highlights their position in the urban state structure, later turning to consider their partisan political dimension. The basic framework of neighborhood (and village) governance today is defined in articles 3 and 59 of the Local Government Act (*difang zhidu fa*) of the Republic of China (ROC), implemented in 1999 and amended multiple times since.[16] In recent years, the ROC government and city authorities have commissioned a modest amount of research on the *li-lin* system while considering options for its future development (Hsi and Fan 2003; Chen 2004; Tseng 2004). In Taiwan, unlike China, the government does not feel at liberty to modify the neighborhood system however it pleases, as it has a life of its own; wardens, their communities, and the politicians who draw on their support do not necessarily welcome change.

In broadest perspective, Taiwan's *li* system has maintained a notable stability over the years in terms of its core structure: the warden-*liganshi* dyad. Transformation has come not so much in the form of organizational shakeups but rather in shifts of power and accountability in the context of gradual democratization and political pluralization, as explained in later chapters. In China, change in the RC system has also brought an evolution of power dynamics, though not one that has led to greater electoral democracy. The organizational structure of China's neighborhoods, however, has been in flux, even as the government has, if anything, tightened rather than loosened its control over this structure.

The changes in China's neighborhood governance apparatus have proved challenging to interpret. Sometimes, outsiders confidently pronounce them moribund, a lifeless vestige of the totalitarian past.[17] At other times, they appear to leap back to life in dramatic and frightening ways. As a Shanghai-based Western journalist wrote of her neighborhood committee in June 2003: "Until two months ago, Mrs. Li and her comrades seemed anachronisms, but China's SARS outbreak, coverup and ensuing public panic have revealed deep fissures in the Communist infrastructure, and have prompted the government to revitalize some of the repressive elements of the Cultural Revolution."[18] Either way, such accounts often perceive dramatic transformations—the neighborhood organizations are dead, or they have been "reactivated," or they have democratized—when in fact change has unfolded gradually over decades, and accords with none of these terms.

The long-term effort to reinvigorate the residents' committee system has proceeded under the banner of community building (*shequ jianshe*), extolled at the highest levels of the Chinese Communist Party and coordinated by the national Ministry of Civil Affairs (Kokubun and Kojima 2002; White and Shang 2003; Benewick, Tong, and Howell 2004; Derleth and Koldyk 2004; Wong and Poon 2005; Bray 2006; Dutton, Lo, and Wu 2008). It has also been the subject of a substantial amount of Chinese-language research (e.g., Lei 2001; Yu 2006; He 2007). Despite the ministry's appropriation of the discourse of community, the animating force behind *shequ jianshe* has been a highly statist conception of this malleable term. Rhetoric to the contrary, what the Ministry of Civil Affairs has in mind is not the fostering of self-organizing communities as collectivities empowered to act as a group toward independently determined goals. As we will see, the project has, at best, an ambiguous relationship to the building of the kind of interpersonal networks and solidarity among citizens that might normally be termed "urban community." Rather, its primary aim is to bolster and reequip the state's organizational mechanisms within residential neighborhoods while devising new ways to make this organization useful to residents and viewed favorably by them. As Heberer and Göbel argue in their thoughtful study of communities in Shenyang, Chongqing, and Shenzhen, "the reorganization of China's *shequ* has greatly increased the infrastructural power of the Party-state, as it has deepened the CCP's penetration of the urban grassroots" (2011, 5).

This initiative bears a resemblance to projects undertaken by China's leaders to build links to societal groups in other spheres, such as through business and entrepreneurs' associations (Unger 1996; Kennedy 2005; K. Tsai 2007; Unger 2008). It fits with Jiang Zemin's and Hu Jintao's push to keep the CCP in touch with the population as a whole as opposed to merely its historical core constituencies. This process also mirrors the more widely studied effort to rebuild rural authority through the villagers' committees.[19] In both cases, the government has sought to recruit new leaders possessing basic managerial skills and credibility with constituents.

Discussions of the *shequ* often emphasize ways in which they depart from the long-standing RC system, or see the former as summarily replacing the latter (Bray 2006, 537–543; 2008, 398; Chen and Lu 2007, 423–425; Chen, Lu, and Yang 2007, 506; Hurst 2010, 253, 258). Although the communities do represent change in some ways, the perspective taken here sets what is indeed new about them in the context of fundamental continuities with past structures. As of the summer of 2011, neither the constitution nor the 1989 organizational law under which they operate had been modified to say anything of *shequ* as an organizational structure—despite what is said to be years of internal debate within the National People's Congress and the Ministry of Civil Affairs. Although eventual change surely should be expected, and although it is now widely prefaced with the term "community," the residents' committee still has a special legal centrality in neighborhood affairs, as reflected in official documents and statistics.

The Ministry of Civil Affairs encouraged a nationwide process of experimentation and, by the early 2000s, had designated more than two dozen urban districts as trial zones in which organizational innovations were encouraged. Ambitious leaders at the city or district level vied to promote their own small variations and embellishments on the *shequ* theme. They prepared model communities for showing off to streams of domestic and international visitors.[20] But each rearrangement of the institutional furniture has carefully stayed in the same basic architecture: firm party and state control, incorporating some degree of popular participation in selective and structured ways. In Beijing, the experimentation process has played out in a series of steps and missteps spanning many years. In the 1990s, RCs around China were encouraged to raise their own funds by developing economic points (*jingji dian*) and tertiary industry (*sanchan*), which for them meant renting out spare rooms, sheds, and sundry spaces to serve as tiny stores, lunch stands, fruit carts, barbershops, and the like. Beijing's street offices largely reined this in over time, asserting control over these scraps of real estate and renting them out on their own behalf, though still in the name of community services. In 2000, a large batch of RC personnel were hired with special status as community cadres through a competitive testing process, an effort to bring in staff with stronger training and office skills.[21] Results were mixed, not least because of envy on the part of existing staff, and many quit, but the city continued to apply the same kind of basic training and testing procedures to later waves of recruits. Meanwhile, facilities emblazoned with the word "community" cropped up everywhere, from public exercise equipment painted in bold primary colors to networks of small medical clinics. An experiment in one district divided the neighborhood teams into a deliberation level of advisers and an implementation level who put in the long hours in the office. The path forward was formed in part through trial and error.

Table 2.1 displays the basic organizational structure of large cities in China and Taiwan as of the late 2000s, showing how administrative grassroots engagement continues to form a vast extension below the formal levels of municipal government. In Taiwan, large cities are divided into districts and further divided into *li*, which are sometimes translated as "boroughs" but are referred to simply as neighborhoods here. Just as in the earlier years of the ROC's administration of Taiwan, each *li* is overseen by a warden. The cities of the Republic of China had nearly 5,000 such *lizhang* in total in 2009; there were 1,735 in just the seven major cities. As of the 2000s, Taipei's wardens received a monthly stipend of NT$45,000 (about US$1,500) from the state, ostensibly to cover expenses but also serving as a de facto salary. They also controlled annual neighborhood-improvement budgets of NT$200,000 (about US$6,500), to be spent with the city's approval. Just as in the 1960s, each works hand in hand with an unelected civil servant (*liganshi*) in carrying out his or her responsibilities to the state and to constituents.

Neighborhood-level governance in China has long been less centered on individual leaders; rather, it has revolved around a team, the residents' committee. The contrast with Taiwan is somewhat less sharp than it first appears, however, as the committees, too, have leaders: the director (*zhuren*), who in most cases is a party member and often is the same person as the party secretary.[22] In the past decade, with the widespread adoption of *shequ* vocabulary, the RCs have been renamed community residents' committees in many parts of the country, including Beijing, although this book generally uses the original term for the sake of simplicity. Like the *li-lin* system, the RCs form an immense network covering almost all neighborhoods of China's cities, with the exception of some newly built housing developments and recently urbanized areas. Their members receive stipends that vary by the individual's education, experience, and pension status, as well as by the wealth of the locality, ranging from a few hundred to 2,000 yuan (about US$50–$300). In Beijing, some of the best-compensated committee members were receiving 1,600–1,800 yuan monthly as of 2010, two to four times the levels of a decade prior. In Beijing, the neighborhood staff work what can generally be thought of as

TABLE 2.1

Levels of urban administration and grassroots engagement in China and Taiwan

	CHINA (PRC)			TAIWAN (ROC)	
Level	Chinese term	Total nationwide	Level	Chinese term	Total nationwide
City government	Shi zhengfu	655	City government	Shi zhengfu	7 (39)
District government	Qu zhengfu	856	District office	Qugongsuo	49
Street office	Jiedao banshichu	6,524	(No corresponding level exists)		
RC or community residents' committee	Jumin weiyuanhui or Shequ jumin weiyuanhui	83,413	Neighborhood warden, neighborhood office	Lizhang, li bangongchu	1,735 (4,835)
Block captain (residents' small group)	Jumin xiaozu	1,287,000	Block captain	Linzhang	35,528[a]

SOURCE: Data for China are for 2008 and come from *Ministry of Civil Affairs* 2009 (number of cities and districts, p. 55; number of RCs and residents' small groups, p. 83). Data for Taiwan are for 2009 and come from the Administrative System (*xiang zhen shi qu can li lin shu*) table of the *Statistical Yearbook of the Ministry of the Interior* (http://sowf.moi.gov.tw/stat/year/list.htm, accessed March 30, 2011).

NOTE: Nonshaded sections refer to what this book considers levels of formal government administration; shaded sections refer to levels of administrative grassroots engagement. For Taiwan, the figures predate the changes of December 25, 2010, which fused the counties of Taichung, Tainan, and Kaohsiung into the cities of the same names, respectively, and promoted Taipei County to New Taipei City. The numbers outside parentheses refer only to Taiwan's seven larger cities, that is, municipalities and provincial cities, excluding those administratively subordinate to counties (*xian*). Numbers in parentheses include such smaller cities (*xian xia shi*), which have no district offices but do have *li* and *lin*.

[a] National-level figures do not distinguish between *lin* in villages (*cun*) and *lin* in urban *li* for regions outside of the seven major cities. The total number of *lin*, including village *lin*, was 147,863.

full-time or close to full-time, usually six to eight fixed hours daily. Many of Taipei's wardens put in similar hours, although some have other jobs as well. In both places, work can easily spill into nights and weekends as they handle trouble, special events, and requests from constituents. Indeed, for many wardens, being available at all hours is a source of pride and a campaign talking point.

Large Chinese cities have long had, in effect, three levels of state administration rather than the two levels found in Taiwan. In addition to the city government and district governments, there are also street offices (sometimes called subdistricts or wards in English). Chinese bureaucratic discourse technically has identified the street offices not as a level of government (*yi ji zhengquan*) but as a delegated organ (*paichu jiguan*) of the district government. Regardless of this nuance, from an analytical perspective they stand as part of the formal apparatus of the party-state. For decades, the street offices have directly organized and managed the residents' committees, which serve as their local contacts. The offices have maintained a specialized staff to supervise the RCs and frequently call the committee members in to attend meetings and receive instructions. The process of merging and consolidating RCs in cities around the country, and of building a more bureaucratized *shequ* structure around them, has both streamlined the system and introduced further complexity. As of 2009 there were approximately 83,000 RCs around the country; despite China's rapid urbanization, the total number of these organizations has fallen from well more than 110,000, as committees have been amalgamated with one another.[23]

In both China and Taiwan the basic neighborhood organizations receive help from a final layer of organizational structure that lies below them, made up of what I loosely translate as "block captains" and discuss further in Chapter 6. The *lizhang* chooses a set of *linzhang* (about twenty on average, in large cities), who receive small monthly stipends and assist the warden in his or her duties. Similarly, China's RCs select dozens of people living around the neighborhood as their designated liaisons to the households in their immediate proximity. Although national figures include only the formal category of residents' small group leaders, on the ground the set of assistants includes other categories that are not found in official statistics, going under a variety of terms like "floor leader," "courtyard leader," and such.

Neighborhood work, in both cases, centers on physical offices. In Taipei, as the vignette presented in Chapter 1 showed, the city sets up the equipment and furnishings for the neighborhood office (*li bangongchu*) in the residence of the elected warden if he or she requests it, or otherwise finds office space nearby. These spaces—a room or two—are basic, functional, and often homey. In the early era of China's RCs, committee members worked out of their homes as well. As of the late 1990s, many of Beijing's RCs operated out of primitive quarters like the old Chongxing office, a small, run-down room just like any other in the *hutong*; trips to the bathroom required walking down the alley to the putrid public toilet. Better-equipped ones, like Xianningjie, had four women working out of a converted apartment in one of the state-built housing blocks. The offices were gradually expanded and upgraded so that by 2010 they constituted the most immediately recognizable aspect of the *shequ* program. By that point, neighborhoods had extensive suites of offices, forming the headquarters of the new communities, often in newly constructed or renovated buildings. Inside stood contemporary work desks, computers, and filing cabinets; neighborhood staff increasingly used e-mail in their work, and sometimes even text messages. These increasingly resembled the modern offices of formal state agencies, whereas those in Taipei (even ones not implanted in wardens' homes) maintained a more casual look. This reflected both the increasing bureaucratization of the *shequ* and the fact that warden offices generally are taken down and moved when the position changes hands.

Table 2.2 provides a sense of how closely intertwined these organizations are with the residential fabric of the two capital cities. For the past four decades, the city of Taipei has tinkered with the configuration of its districts, which went from sixteen in 1968 to twelve since 1990. It has also rearranged its *li*, which once numbered 608, peaked at 780, and have since been reduced to 456.[24] On average, a *lizhang* in Taipei oversees an area containing approximately 5,800 people, including children. The comparable figure for Beijing's core districts is now almost the same, with almost six thousand people, on average, in each *shequ*. Here the consolidation of the RCs has made a conspicuous impact; as recently as 2000, the same eight districts had more than twice as many neighborhoods (3,885), with an average of only 1,700 residents in each.[25] Even as the total amount of housing has rapidly expanded, with many new condominium estates springing up (particularly in districts like Chaoyang), the number of RCs has decreased as they have been merged with one another and folded into the *shequ* architecture. In many places, this has meant that what were once separately administered, relatively homogeneous pieces of the population, sharing, for instance, a common type of housing or institutional affiliation, are now lumped together. In the city's newly built

TABLE 2.2

Scope of administrative institutions in Beijing and Taipei

| | BEIJING | | | TAIPEI | |
Level	Number of units	Average population per unit	Level	Number of units	Average population per unit
District governments	8[a]	1,350,000	District offices	12	218,733
Street offices	102	105,882	(No corresponding level exists)		
Community residents' committees	1,810	5,967	Wardens	456	5,756
Block captains (residents' small groups)	40,324	268	Block captains (linzhang)	9,534	275

SOURCE: For Beijing, figures for population, street offices, and community residents' committees come from Tables 1.1 and 3.3 of the *Beijing Statistical Yearbook 2010* (2009 data), http://www.bjstats.gov.cn/nj/main/2010-tjnj/index.htm, accessed March 30, 2011. Figures for residents' small groups come from unpublished data from the Beijing city government, 2006, on file with the author. For Taipei, figures are derived from February 2011 data posted in the statistical section of the Taipei city government Department of Civil Affairs Web page, http://www.ca.taipei.gov.tw, accessed March 21, 2011.

NOTE: For Beijing, the total population figure of 10.8 million people is the long-term resident population (*changzhu renkou*), which includes individuals from other parts of the country (*waidai renkou*) who have lived in Beijing for at least half a year. Only data from the eight districts constituting the urban core of Beijing are reported here: Dongcheng, Xicheng, Chongwen, Xuanwu, Chaoyang, Haidian, Fengtai, and Shijingshan. The outlying, substantially rural suburbs that are part of the massive Beijing administrative region, including eight other districts and two counties, are not included.

[a] The outlying, substantially rural suburbs that are part of the massive Beijing administrative region, including eight other districts and two counties, are not included.

areas, the creation of the organizational architecture of the RCs lags somewhat behind the pouring of concrete and selling of homes, but it eventually
catches up.[26]

If the piece of the city supervised by each of these organizations comprises
several thousand people, just how intimate can the connection between leaders and the population be? As later chapters show, this depends on characteristics of the neighborhood such as type of housing, stability of residency,
and who the leaders are. Beijing's RCs have a certain advantage in this regard
in that they are composed of multiple members—six people on average.[27]
Among them, they generally know many, though far from all, residents. Even
in Taipei, with but a single warden and one (usually nonresident) *liganshi* per
neighborhood, the scale is still small enough to make it possible for neighborhood leaders to have personal acquaintance with a substantial fraction of
their constituents, and vice versa. The lowest level of organization—the *lin* in
Taipei and the small group in Beijing—brings these institutions into even
greater proximity to constituents. In the former case, 275 people reside in
each such unit, on average; in the latter, 268.

These figures, however, do not account for other affiliates and groups that
play a role in ultra-local governance. In Taipei, neighborhoods often have
volunteer security patrols, community development associations, and other
entities that can form part of the warden's network, although as we will see
they can also be entirely separate from and even hostile to the incumbent
lizhang. In Beijing, peripheral bodies have an even wider presence, including security patrols and the aforementioned floor heads, courtyard heads, and
entryway heads. To take one example from my research sites, the particularly
large Xianningjie *shequ*, created through the merger of six old RCs, had 228
such volunteers in its 2010 population of more than four thousand households. Moreover, one thrust of the *shequ* program since the late 1990s has
been to push Communist Party members who are retired or otherwise no
longer active in a work unit to affiliate with the community-level party structures. Although this initially met with reluctance (neighborhoods were seen
as organizational backwaters relative to the *danwei*), by 2006 there were just
more than a quarter million community party members in Beijing's eight core
districts, an average of 146 per *shequ*.[28] Xianningjie boasted more than six hundred, grouped into eight party branches.[29] These related networks add to the
reach and salience of the primary neighborhood organizations.

In the case of Beijing, finally, the community-building process has bulked up the numbers of people working in the revamped neighborhood offices, such that the staff roster now extends well beyond the RC proper. By 2010, communities commonly had a total of twelve to twenty people working in the new offices. The party committee had previously been, for the most part, a subset of the residents' committee members, who would meet periodically. It had come to be set apart as a more distinct, standing leadership entity, containing some members who worked full-time at desks in the office but did not belong to the RC. Xianningjie, for example, had been led in the late 1990s by a female party secretary whose education was cut short in the Cultural Revolution at the age of fifteen; a decade later, the secretary and vice secretary of the party committee were two seasoned bureaucrats, both men, with long experience in formal state-sector institutions. Moreover, much of the ordinary business of the community was handled by eight new facilitators (*xieguanyuan*), who also were not part of the residents' committee itself. Mostly young graduates of technical colleges and the like, many from other provinces, they handled particular functional areas like social welfare, the registration of non-Beijing residents, and disability benefits. Created in part as a way to boost employment, in other parts of the city such service-stand (*fuwu zhan*) positions were held by unemployed locals.[30]

Setting aside these additional personnel, Table 2.3 presents a profile of the people who serve as core staff members in the neighborhoods of Beijing and Taipei. A detailed discussion of the selection processes in the two capitals is reserved for Chapter 3. Although, as we will see, little or no electoral democracy is involved in the choosing of RC staff, the state-led revitalization of the committees has made stipends considerably larger than in previous decades, and therefore the hiring process has grown more competitive. Once staffed largely by people from favored class and political backgrounds (particularly those from working classes or those whose families had supported the revolution) with scant education who were paid little or nothing, Beijing's committees now generally employ vocational high school, high school, or technical college graduates who often have substantial organizational experience from previous jobs. Significant numbers of four-year college degree holders serve as well. Now as in the past, many more women than men occupy these positions, but far from the stereotypical bound-footed old lady of yesteryear, the average staff member now is in her midforties. Nearly 50 percent are members of the

TABLE 2.3
Descriptive data on RC directors, RC members, and neighborhood wardens

	Beijing: RC directors	Beijing: All RC members	Taipei: Wardens
Average age	45	46	54
Men	30%	22%	86%
Women	70%	78%	14%
Party membership or	84% CCP	49% CCP	53% KMT
affiliation	16% non-CCP	51% non-CCP	8% DPP
			39% no party
Education			
Postgraduate	1%	0%	2%
College	20%	9%	27%⎫
Technical college	48%	34%	⎭
High school or	27%	47%	47%
technical high school			
Middle school or less	4%	9%	25%
n	1,622	11,074	449

SOURCE: For Beijing, unpublished figures from the Beijing city government, on file with the author, reflecting the results of the 2006 RC elections. For Taipei, the figures for average warden age and sex ratios, as well as education, are from the official record of the December 2006 elections: *Taibeishi di shi jie lizhang xuanju shilu* (City of Taipei Election Commission, 2007), Table V-10. Party affiliations, reflecting nominations at the time that warden candidates registered for the election, are from "Taibeishi di 10 jie lizhang xuanju dangxuanren zhengdang zhanyou bili tongji biao," City of Taipei Election Commission Web site, http://mect.cec.gov.tw, accessed January 1, 2007.

NOTE: For Beijing, only data from the eight districts constituting the urban core of Beijing are reported here: Dongcheng, Xicheng, Chongwen, Xuanwu, Chaoyang, Haidian, Fengtai, and Shijingshan. The "Beijing: All members" column includes data on directors in addition to the nondirector members. The proportion of CCP members includes probationary party members. In the Taipei source data, those with college and technical college degrees are combined. The lowest category, containing 25 percent, is labeled "other" in the source; this is presumed to mean middle school or less.

Communist Party—up from just less than 40 percent in 2000—which reflects diligent efforts by the authorities to shape the composition of the committees and to ensure their political reliability.

Turning back to Taipei, the ranks of the *lizhang* are even more overwhelmingly male than the RCs are female—although the 2010 elections brought more women than ever to these posts.[31] With an average age of fifty-four, they are almost a decade older as a group than the RC staff. The Kuomintang's nominees have the majority of warden posts in the Nationalist-leaning capital, but only barely, as many win without a party label and a smaller contingent has come to office under the DPP banner. Contrary to what one might expect, given Taipei's generally higher degree of socioeconomic development, the wardens' education level is somewhat lower in general than that of their

TABLE 2.4
Occupational backgrounds of RC directors, RC members, and neighborhood wardens

Beijing categories	Beijing: RC directors	Beijing: All RC members	Taipei categories	Taipei: Wardens
Certificate holder	57%	22%	Public sector	47.2%
Retired	25%	45%	Commerce	27.6%
Still employed	10%	9%	Service sector	11.3%
Laid off	6%	20%	Freelance	5.9%
Other	2%	3%	Industry or worker	1.4%
			Medical	1.2%
			Agriculture or farmer	1.2%
			Education	1.2%
			Homemaker	0.7%
			Other or missing	2.4%
n	1,647	10,313		424

SOURCE: For Beijing, unpublished figures from the Beijing city government, on file with the author, reflecting the results of the 2006 RC elections. Data for Taipei are compiled by the author from records of the 2006 elections, downloaded from the Web site of the Taipei Election Commission, http://mect.cec.gov.tw, accessed January 1, 2007.

NOTE: Columns may not sum precisely to 100 percent as a result of rounding. For Beijing, only data from the eight districts constituting the urban core of Beijing are reported here: Dongcheng, Xicheng, Chongwen, Xuanwu, Chaoyang, Haidian, Fengtai, and Shijingshan. "Laid off" includes a small number of individuals said to "have maintained employment relations with their original *danwei*." The "still employed" are mainly concentrated in Haidian and are likely associated with large state *danwei* there, a vestige of the *jiaweihui* (see Chapter 4). For Taipei, most data from the district of Datong were missing in the original source, so only figures from the other eleven districts are used here.

counterparts in Beijing. Thus, there is a smaller fraction of college-educated *lizhang* in Taipei than there are college-educated RC directors and RC members in Beijing, and a much larger proportion with less than a high school education in the former group compared to the latter. As virtually anyone may run for these positions and win election in Taiwan, those with little schooling are not excluded, as they are through the hiring procedures in Beijing.

Information on the occupational backgrounds of RC staff is available only in relatively crude categories and is not broken down by industry. The data do show, however, that one-fifth of Beijing's committee members came to their positions after having been laid off from previous employment, and 45 percent are retirees. Field research indicates that, as one would expect, many of the people in the latter category took forms of early retirement (sometimes in their forties) during the downsizing of the state-owned and collective enterprises. The figures also show many committee members, and a majority of RC directors, to be holders of special certificates for neighborhood work, issued by the city government after its training and testing process. Although this does not reveal the nature of their previous employment, it further illustrates the city's commitment to promoting individuals who meet formal standards qualifying them for quasi-bureaucratic work. In Taipei, the (self-reported and sometimes less-than-clear-cut) prior occupations of the wardens are coded by sector, and the data show two clear pools from which most emerge. Just less than half have a background in the public sector, whether as civil servants, employees of state firms, or political organizations. About 40 percent worked in businesses of various kinds, in many cases having run shops in their neighborhoods.

All this starts to bring into focus a picture of the social background and status of neighborhood leadership in the two capitals. The RC members and wardens are not considered part of the municipal bureaucracy, yet they also do not have the type of professional identity associated with trained social workers. In neither city do these positions carry particularly lofty prestige; in each case, although residents often treat the leaders with dignity out of respect for their titles, they also may well privately chuckle at the relative pettiness of these positions—or they might do both depending on circumstances. Comparatively speaking, the RCs have stood a few notches lower in perceived status than the *lizhang*. Service in the committees is viewed as women's work; as the figures show, relatively few men seek such positions, whether because of their image or because the pay is lower than what they might earn elsewhere. People who otherwise would be hard pressed to find any desk job may prize these posts, but those with professional accomplishments or upward mobility often see them as a sidetrack at best. This may evolve, however, with the formalization of the community structure. Top *shequ* leaders (particularly in the party committees, as opposed to the RC proper) have deeper managerial or administrative experience than those of the past. In Taipei, the position of *lizhang* is relatively more remunerative, and winning one can be seen as a respectable achievement even for a person with success in other lines of work. As discussed in Chapter 5, wardens sometimes hold prominent places in locally influential clans or other associations and thus have stature in their own right. Their work, too, is widely understood in gendered terms; the respectful term "uncle warden" (*lizhang bo*) is common, whereas the female equivalent is not.

With this as backdrop, we may take a close look at what these organizations do. The functions of the RC and *li-lin* system are similar in many respects, despite the obvious differences between the two, starting with the contrast in their specifically political purposes. As extensions of a hegemonic party-state, China's RCs embody the principle that the CCP's unique leading role reaches all the way to the grass roots. Taiwan's *li*, by contrast, lie open to wardens of all political persuasions, whose party activities, if any, are supposed to be incidental to their work on behalf of constituents and an ostensibly nonpartisan city bureaucracy. This granted, staff of both institutions facilitate a wide range of state programs. Their duties are set out in formal laws and policies, but in practice their work often diverges from what is written in official documents. Rather than reproduce these texts, I summarize some of the most salient elements below. The most prominent aspects of their government work include the following:

- *Conveying information from the state.* Whether in the form of government publications (books, pamphlets, bulletins) or briefings conducted by officials, the RCs and *lizhang* regularly receive updated information about state laws, campaigns, programs, and policies. Part of their function is to help convey this material to residents and educate them on it. This is done through visual displays situated in public places throughout the neighborhood (whether simple bulletin boards, colorful chalkboard presentations, or illuminated panels) or through interpersonal contact with constituents. In China, the RCs sometimes conduct classes in their offices. Taiwan's wardens distribute announcements of upcoming elections.
- *Facilitating welfare programs.* In both Taiwan and China, the staff of the organizations keep in touch with disadvantaged individuals such as those in certain categories of unemployment, those with disabilities, and elderly persons with no independent means of support. On the basis of what can be very detailed knowledge of residents' circumstances, they help the state determine eligibility for public assistance.
- *Participating in public health programs.* Grassroots engagement institutions regularly take part in things like cleanup drives and hygiene campaigns, and in Beijing they are linked to a network of local health clinics. During the 2003 outbreak of severe acute respiratory syndrome (SARS), both the *lizhang* and the RCs helped with emergency measures, notably by keeping in touch with and assisting residents who had been placed under quarantine.
- *Assisting the police.* In Taipei, the *lizhang* maintain close contact with police about neighborhood security matters. In Beijing, this cooperation is even

tighter, more routine, and has an important political dimension. Officers from the local public security substation (*paichusuo*) are assigned to cover one or two RCs on an ongoing basis. They visit the committee office regularly to find out about or respond to problems or crimes in the neighborhood. The RC staff not only gather information on behalf of the police but also accompany officers should they need to visit a resident's home. In the Chinese case, in addition to everyday problems like burglary, the committees also keep an eye out for political offenses and work with police to deal with dissent. For example, during the government's campaign against the *falun gong* sect, which was officially deemed an "evil cult" after it staged a large protest in 1999, RCs were tapped to identify followers and attempt to dissuade them from public activities.

• *Maintaining the system of household registry (hukou).* Here again the two cases differ somewhat. In Taiwan, the *lizhang* are not centrally involved in updating the official records on each household, although their close partners the *liganshi* are, and *lizhang* sometimes help them. In China, assisting the police stations' efforts to increase the accuracy of these lists is an important part of the RC's work. Controls on population mobility are not nearly as rigid as they were in the prereform era. City government and police nonetheless continue to maintain household registry rolls, which identify the residents at particular addresses, their ID numbers, and demographic characteristics. An important part of this comprises efforts to register and keep track of the large population of rural migrants.

Wardens and *liganshi* communicate with families of young men who are due for their mandatory military duty, a program not found on the mainland. Conversely, some functions are found only in China. Most significant, there the RCs constitute one portion of the system through which the government implements its family-planning policy. The committees maintain records on women of childbearing age in the neighborhood. In principle these are supposed to specify such details as the method of birth control each woman uses, although in practice the staff only occasionally pester women for such information. They carry out family-planning educational programs but also report unauthorized pregnancies to officials at higher levels. As previously noted, in recent years, communities in Beijing, Shanghai, and elsewhere have also come to play a role in the cities' medical insurance programs. Residents can now take care of paperwork related to their insurance cards in the *shequ* offices.

It is important to note that the actual character of these state-assigned functions varies, and most of them are ambiguous in their relationship to residents' interests. They could involve doing things that intrude, inconvenience, or otherwise strike people as noxious. Yet perceptions range widely, and in many cases, as discussed later in the book, residents perceive these functions as beneficial. For example, RCs' policing-related tasks certainly help the authorities sniff out political dissent—a form of surveillance that some, though not necessarily most, residents object to. Yet the bulk of their work with the police revolves around trying to prevent break-ins, talking to former offenders in the neighborhood, and mediating disputes—all of which are quite likely to be seen in a favorable light.

Duties related to administration and policy implementation constitute only one facet of the work of these organizations. Another important aspect is arranging social and volunteer activities, in the following major forms:

- *Voluntary service activities.* The RCs and *lizhang* help organize willing residents into various types of service roles, of which the *linzhang* and small-group heads are prime examples. Beijing's volunteers help the residents' committee with many aspects of its work, from disseminating announcements to keeping in contact with welfare cases. They may also make themselves useful to neighbors by doing small chores like going door-to-door to collect fees for sanitation, gas, or electricity; helping deliver mail or newspapers; or cleaning up public areas. The *linzhang*, too, assist in various ways and communicate information, although they are rarely enlisted in administrative work. Neighborhood security patrols are another type of voluntary service that is found in both Beijing and Taipei.
- *Group recreational activities.* These take many forms. In China, some residents' committees lead singing groups, and others dance and exercise classes. Taipei's community centers, funded by the city and supervised by wardens, sponsor similar activities. Like the *lizhang*, RCs also lead outings to parks and other attractions, and some maintain activity centers. In Taipei, the neighborhood wardens often organize festivals around major holidays.
- *Charity.* In China, the RCs lead charity collection drives. In response to what are usually government-organized campaigns, the committees encourage residents to contribute to causes like relief for victims of floods and earthquakes. They sometimes go door-to-door to solicit funds or post notices requesting that people come to the committee office to donate.

At the same time, these organizations carry out a number of other functions that are intended to be useful to constituents:

- *Listening to input from residents, and conveying certain kinds of requests upward.* The staff serve as sounding boards for all manner of complaints and suggestions from their constituents, usually over local matters: noise, waste disposal, and crime prevention are just some of the most frequent topics at issue. In both cases, the neighborhood institutions often attract (among others) the discontented, the lonely, and the troubled in considerable numbers, who simply come in search of someone to talk to.
- *Mediating disputes between neighbors and within families.* Usually at the request of one of the parties to the conflict, RCs intervene in squabbles between households over such matters as noise, shared utility bills, and the use of common facilities like kitchens and courtyards. The *lizhang* have similar responsibilities, although in Taipei disputes can also be sent to more formal mediation centers in district offices.
- *Providing a range of small goods and services, often free of charge.* For instance, neighborhood offices in both cities sometimes have blood-pressure meters that can be used to give free tests to anyone who wants one. In Beijing, the RCs sometimes purchase commodities like dish detergent and sell them to residents at bulk rate. The committees also were used in recent years to distribute free water-saving spigots to their constituents as part of a city resource conservation program.

These three broad areas of activity are closely interrelated. Most of these organizations' administrative duties depend on the gathering of local knowledge to which bureaucrats in state offices far removed from the neighborhood would have no access. Maintaining household registry records, for instance, requires finding out who has moved into and out of the area, who is renting or subletting local homes, and so forth. Helping with police work calls for detailed information on neighborhood matters to watch for unusual activity and keep an eye on known offenders and problem spots. The welfare-related duties require being well informed regarding the needs of potential recipients of state aid, as well as the resources those families possess, such as assets, employment, or relatives, to assess their eligibility. The organizational and service functions of the RCs and the *li-lin* system help them try to mobilize active support, to build a positive image in the neighborhood, and to create interpersonal ties with constituents, all of which may facilitate their government work to the extent they are successful.

Conclusion

This chapter began by considering the general nature of administrative grassroots engagement, then reached far back into the past to consider early precursors of urban governance institutions in China and Taiwan. These antecedents are only part of the reason why the RC and *li-lin* systems exist today—as shown, security imperatives and other factors can drive modern states to develop such systems even in the absence of predecessors. Yet historical templates clearly helped encourage their persistence through the twentieth century and beyond, despite momentous changes of regime. At the same time, these systems have evolved over time, diverging from one another and deviating from their own pasts in important respects. In Taiwan, even in the 1950s and 1960s the dichotomy between the *lizhang* and the *liganshi* made clear that the former was more of a community representative, albeit a co-opted and cooperative one, and the latter more of a state emissary and supervisor. Over time, in the context of Taiwan's democratization, this division of roles became even clearer: the warden developed greater independence, even as the two continue to work together and assist each other. Broad though their responsibilities are, residents need not go through them for many routine items of business; for example, specialized offices (*huzheng shiwusuo*) can handle most household registry matters.

In China, the RC system was always meant as a neighborhood-based complement to the work unit as a locus for both service programs and administrative control. In the rubric of the *shequ*, the state has pumped further investment into this system. It has consolidated this network from a larger number of relatively informal neighborhood outposts into a smaller number of more modernized centers with functionally differentiated staff. This process has pushed the community-RC nexus in Beijing toward looking more like a formal bureaucratic agency—indeed, with facilitators sitting behind a counter receiving most guests, some of the new offices even feel a bit like the lobby of a bank branch. Effectively, part of the street office apparatus that managed the RC from a distance of twenty minutes' stroll has been internalized inside the neighborhood structure. Indeed, the logical next step of abolishing the street offices has been put forward by national civil affairs officials as a goal.[32] Inside, though, its beefed-up staff continues to perform the roles of earlier RCs, along with certain newer duties and speaking partly in a new vocabulary.

With the next chapter, we turn from a conceptual and historical overview of these structures to an up-close look at their workings in practice, starting with the procedures through which neighborhood leadership is constituted.

Chapter Three

Elections, Bogus and Bona Fide

The previous chapter gave an empirical introduction to the dense networks of institutions that certain states cultivate at the ultra-local level. For a first cut at understanding how they work, our attention naturally turns to the question of who controls these organizations and, in particular, the mechanisms by which leadership is constituted in them. How exactly do specific individuals come into their positions as intermediaries between state and community? To what extent are constituents free to pick leaders of their choice? To what extent do government officials choose them or have influence or veto power over the selection? How competitive and how participatory is the process? The answers to these questions form an essential basis for inquiry into accountability relationships in everyday practice.

Cities in both mainland China and Taiwan regularly hold elections for neighborhood leaders. Elections at this level can be viewed as something of an anomaly, even an oddity, in democratic theory and practice. Local elections in general are typically deemphasized in the study of comparative politics; researchers tend to focus on democracy as a national-level regime type. A consideration of voting in the neighborhood context takes us at least one or two steps below even what is normally studied within the rubric of local politics.

Neighborhood-level elections present challenges on both practical and less tangible levels. In logistical terms they can be labor intensive to organize. In addition, winner-takes-all elections produce decisive results, with one side clearly achieving victory and attaining office, but the consequent shutting out of those on the other side can seem to fly in the face of norms of harmony and consensus. Small wonder, then, that in many cities around the world, politics at the neighborhood level does not revolve around formal electoral contests for leadership positions but rather involves more casual decision-making and consensus-building procedures.

The injection of partisan politics into neighborhood affairs, as in the Taiwan case, presents a further twist. Political parties in many countries develop networks of local supporters, of course, who may take titles in the party such as precinct captain and the like. But elected, state-recognized offices are often nonpartisan below a certain level. For candidates to run in neighborhood-level elections under the banners of large political parties introduces several complications. Resources may flow downward as parties sow a crop of loyalists, on whom they later lean for support in other electoral campaigns. And the emotions that inflame national political contests are kindled in neighborhood-level campaigns, sometimes producing lines of division that otherwise would remain latent.

Comparative Glances at Other Asian Countries

East and Southeast Asian cases of administrative grassroots engagement display many different forms of leadership selection: in some cases, the choice is made by government officials; in others, by community elites; and in others, by a formal or informal election process. Patterns at the local level do not necessarily match those of the national political regime. South Korea and Taiwan initiated their processes of democratization at roughly the same time, in the mid- to late 1980s. The two countries are considered East Asian exemplars of third-wave democratization (Huntington 1991). Yet urban governance in South Korea has evolved differently from its counterpart in Taiwan. The cities of both countries elect their own mayors. Indeed, in 2008 Lee Myung-bak and Ma Ying-jeou assumed the presidencies of the Republic of Korea and the Republic of China, respectively, after each had bolstered his political résumé through a stint as mayor of the capital. In Seoul, the twenty-five districts (*gu*) have executives and councils that are both popularly elected.[1] Elections go no lower than the district level, however. The city's 522 ward offices (*dong samuso*) are led and staffed exclusively by civil servants.[2] The districts and ward offices in turn select the part-time *tongjang* that serve as city governments' links to neighborhoods, although residents may nominate people for these positions. An official in Seoul's Dongjak district argued that elections cost money and generate administrative hassle, and also might inconvenience residents; the system serves its purposes just fine without them, he said.[3] The neighborhood group leaders (*banjang*), the nominal heads of tiny clusters of households, generally are selected in a consultative process rather than through formal balloting. Thus, the democratization of higher levels of the state does not necessarily bring electoral institutions to its local roots.

Theodore C. Bestor carefully described the organizational structure and leadership selection process of the Tokyo *chōkai* that he called Miyamoto-chō. Of the several dozen formal and informal officers, three of the most important were elected to their positions: the neighborhood association's president and two auditors. The election process was entirely self-managed by the association itself and free from influence by the city government. It was also shaped by the decisions of local elites made in closed-door conclaves. At a general meeting, Bestor wrote, a nominating committee privately agreed on a slate of candidates from among those that neighborhood leaders deemed acceptable; these candidates were then presented to the meeting attendees, to be approved by acclamation. He observed that although "the selection process may seem authoritarian, arbitrary, and totally under the control of a self-perpetuating oligarchy," still "supporters maintain that the lengthy rounds of discussion among leaders and other residents preceding these and most other decisions automatically provide checks and balances in the decision-making process" (Bestor 1989, 176, 188).

A survey of many thousands of Japanese neighborhood associations in 2006 and 2007 by Pekkanen, Tsujinaka, and Yamamoto found that in cities nearly half of association presidents are picked by the board of directors, and about two-fifths are elected by the membership. Less commonly, the leadership rotates among households. As for the directors, the presidents themselves often choose them; in other cases the board selects its own members, or board positions rotate. In only about one-sixth of the cases do urban residents elect their association directors (Pekkanen, Tsujinaka, and Yamamoto n.d., chap. 3). Thus, Bestor's depiction of leadership selection in Miyamoto-chō, though dated, hardly seems atypical even today. Neighborhood groups in Japan choose their leaders independently of government, but the choice process ranges from one in which many residents vote to one in which a small core of elders and activists anoints the locality's top steward (Pekkanen 2006, 100).[4]

Indonesia demonstrates a different pattern: one in which local branches of the city government organize elections neighborhood by neighborhood. During the long period of Suharto's rule, residents voted on the leadership of community-level units (the *rukun tetangga*, or RT, and the larger *rukun kampung*, or RK) but hardly in a free and fair way, as candidates were subject to stringent screening on political criteria and required the approval of state authorities (Sullivan 1992, 143). Since the *reformasi*, Kurasawa reports, elections have become much more open and leaders at the RT and higher levels from any political background are eligible. In the neighborhood in the South Jakarta ward of Lenteng Agung where she conducted years of field research, successive rounds of voting gradually passed local leadership from supporters of the government-backed Golkar Party in the 1980s and 1990s to backers of Megawati Sukarnoputri's party after 2001. The RT elections are presided over by a small committee including officials from the ward, and one person—usually a man—from each household was allowed to cast a ballot. Kurasawa notes that although residents voted freely, "local government was still heavily involved in organizing and possibly influencing the election" (Kurasawa 2009, 70).[5]

Thus, a quick glance at countries around East and Southeast Asia, ranging at the national level from fully consolidated to recently established democracies, shows three general patterns. In one, neighborhood leaders are more or less appointed by local government. In a second, local chiefs are selected informally through consensus building and consultation, a format that tends toward choice by a small coterie of community elites. A final pattern is one of formal elections managed by branches of the city government, which may find ways to put its finger on the scales. These are not mutually exclusive; other cases show a mix of practices, with elections in some localities and not in others.[6]

Mechanisms of leadership selection in these other cases of urban neighborhood organization elsewhere in the region are perhaps the most instructive points of comparative reference for the purposes of this book. But it is also worth bearing in mind the rural cousins of the wardens and RCs. Taiwan's villages have long elected their leaders, under the provisions of the same law that covers city neighborhoods. In China's case, villagers' committee elections have attracted extensive study since the 1988 promulgation and 1998 strengthening of the law authorizing them. Strictly in terms of the procedural quality of elections in China's more than six hundred thousand villages, specialists have found that openness and fairness have improved over time, yet remain highly mixed (O'Brien and Han 2009). Implementation of the election law has been uneven from locality to locality. In her four-province survey, Lily Tsai, for example, found that only 41 percent of the villages in her sample were free from interference by township and other authorities in preelection procedures such as nominating candidates and determining the makeup of the election oversight committee. Although almost all villages held contested elections, only 77 percent had secret ballot booths and only 54 percent permitted campaign speeches (L. Tsai 2007, 206). A further set of questions, raised by these and other observers, concerns the ability of elected village leaders to effectively exercise power in democratic ways; after all, elected village heads are still subordinate to the local Communist Party chiefs, and indeed these posts are often held by the same person. Even so, the distance that China's villages have traveled in the past two decades puts into sharp relief the way that cities lag behind them in terms of grassroots electoral reform (Li and O'Brien 1999; Benewick, Tong, and Howell 2004; Kennedy 2007; Alpermann 2009; Manion 2009; Schubert 2009; Landry, Davis, and Wang 2010). In the problems that remain, we also see echoes of the tight controls that still keep a grip on their urban counterparts.

Beijing's Elections

The Organizational Law stipulates that RC elections are to be held every three years. The Chinese media regularly report on successive rounds of these elections with accolades for the high level of citizen empowerment that they embody. Sometimes, even newspapers outside of mainland China have blithely conveyed official claims that one or another electoral exercise represents a "significant development in grassroots democracy" (see, e.g., Li 2002). At other times, independent journalists have remained appropriately skeptical.[7]

Every triennial cycle, Beijing's RC elections are loudly heralded in newspapers and on neighborhood chalkboards alike, the latter calling on residents to actively participate. An example from Shimen, on the near-western side of the city, gives a sense of what this process actually entailed. As early as the previous September, the four RC staff members there had been anticipating the elections of the summer of 2000, the city's fourth round. They all expected to step down from committee service with the change of term (*huanjie*). We're too old, they said, with typical self-deprecation. We're poorly educated; we have to make way for others. But they also seemed downcast at the thought of losing their positions, which for years had supplemented their small pensions and given them a sense of purpose. They had worked together daily for the better part of a decade, although an earlier colleague had been lost to cancer in 1997. The coming transition weighed on their conversations throughout the year.

The first meeting in preparation for the elections was held in March 2000, as the street office began to make arrangements concerning whom it would replace and whom it would keep. By June 23, two days before the election, almost all the details had been worked out.[8] The balloting coincided with a merging of neighborhoods, part of the ongoing process of consolidating the RC system into a smaller number of larger organizations. Shimen would absorb four smaller committees, all *jiaweihui* belonging to nearby work units.[9] Almost all the staff from those committees would be dismissed, and in Shimen as well there would be a thorough, though not total, changing of the guard.

Contrary to the women's previous expectations that all four of them would be relieved of duty, it had been determined that Director Ding Xiaoli would retain her position as neighborhood party secretary while dropping from director to vice director. The street office had already selected the incoming director: Lian Xiaohong, thirty-eight years of age, one of the city's newly trained and certificated community affairs cadres. Lian's inauguration speech had been prepared; gifts of towels and bars of soap for the voters were ready. Although the leadership positions were a foregone conclusion, the election was not entirely sewn up in advance. Apart from the director and vice director positions, the new committee would have three other members, for which four candidates would compete. Kong Shuying, a former day-care attendant with little schooling who handled cleanliness and hygiene, and Jiang Xiayun, a round-faced party member who dealt with family planning and other work requiring clerical skills, were not in the running and would step down, Ding explained. Their all-female team, which had worked together cheerfully since the early 1990s, would thus break up. But she expected that veteran mediator Tai Jin would win reelection to one of the three seats.

Lian and two others, including a woman from the propaganda (*xuanchuan*) section of the street office, were going over the election meeting agenda with Lao Sun, the seventy-year-old director of one of the *jiaweihui* to be merged. Possessing only basic literacy skills, Sun was nervous and unsure of herself. Under Lian's tutelage, they planned everything that Sun would say, including offhand remarks like "It's really hot out." The voters would be forty-two carefully chosen residents' representatives, twenty-four of whom lived within the existing boundaries of Shimen, and eighteen in the newly merged neighborhoods. Ding explained that the representatives were "mainly activists and entranceway leaders"—residents on good terms with the RC who could more or less be counted on to play their limited role in the proceedings uncomplainingly.

The meticulously planned vote went off without a hitch, but with one surprise. Tai Jin was not, in the event, chosen by the residents' representatives; rather, they turned her out by a margin of three votes. The humiliation and loss of face caused by this rejection was so overwhelming that Tai broke down in tears. Ding later explained that some of the activists felt that she was "lazy" and "liked to take it easy and put her feet up," thus her failure to win back her seat. A Shanxi native in her fifties, who had once worked for a street office on the other side of town, then held a factory job, had been tapped in her place.

As the Shimen example illustrates, RC members are still all but handpicked by city officials. This is so despite law and official rhetoric that would suggest a more open process of election by their neighborhood constituents and despite evidence that residents would prefer democratic procedures (Chen and Lu 2006). The government and party manage the staff selection through various mechanisms. For each neighborhood, an election committee is formed before the balloting, a committee dominated by the street office and including participants (typically party members) from entities like the local police station and nearby work units, as well as nominal representation of ordinary residents. Data from the Beijing city government presented in Table 3.1, combined with findings from fieldwork, document this in considerable detail.[10]

The nomination process is the first means through which the elections are kept under control. In principle, groups of residents, or at least groups of chosen household representatives, may nominate candidates. But as the 2006 figures show, in all but a handful of cases the selection of candidates is done by resident small groups, which are designated by the RC itself. Even this misrepresents the process in suggesting that nominations generally bubble up from below. In fact, fieldwork strongly indicated that street offices shaped or entirely determined the list of candidates in advance, sometimes in consultation with the RC incumbents. The neighborhood's election committee vets the list of candidates, which provides an opportunity to weed out any names not to the authorities' liking.

TABLE 3.1

RC elections in Beijing, 2000–2006

	2000	2003	2006
Total number of RC elections held	3,552	1,684	1,622
NOMINATION METHOD			
Nominations by 10 or more electors	NR	NR	0.6%
Nominations by 5 or more household representatives	NR	NR	2.8%
Nominations by resident small groups	NR	NR	96.5%
COMPETITIVENESS			
Cha'e (at least one seat was contested)	5.0%	NR	42.8%
Deng'e (no competition at all)	95.0%	NR	57.2%
SCOPE OF PARTICIPATION			
All residents	0.2%	0.7%	0.4%
Household representatives only	0.5%	8.7%	6.6%
Residents' small-group representatives	99.3%	90.7%	93.0%
RESULTS			
Candidates who lost	1.5%	9.5%	6.9%
Incumbents who were reelected	43.9%	47.1%	56.2%

SOURCE: Unpublished figures from the Beijing city government, on file with the author.

NOTE: NR = not reported. Only data from the eight districts constituting the urban core of Beijing are reported here: Dongcheng, Xicheng, Chongwen, Xuanwu, Chaoyang, Haidian, Fengtai, and Shijingshan.

Residents' committee elections feature only a modest degree of contestation, as seen in the Shimen case, although they have grown somewhat more competitive over the years. In 2000, 95 percent of the elections in Beijing had no competition at all; in these equal-to-the-quota (*deng'e*) elections, there were no more candidates running than there were positions to be filled. By 2006, only 57 percent of all elections held were of this variety, and the rest involved competition for at least one seat on the committee (*cha'e*). In some cases, two or three candidates compete for one or two of the RC positions. To the best of my knowledge, the RC director's position has never been open to competition. Arranging elections in which, for instance, eight candidates run for seven slots is a way to create a vague impression of democracy, and sometimes to get rid of a troublesome or unpopular incumbent. Indeed, this happens commonly, and provides one mechanism through which the neighborhood's preferences are registered. In Duzhuang, for example, one incumbent committee member withdrew her candidacy in advance of the election upon realizing that the activists would select her as the one to be eliminated out of seven candidates for a six-person team.[11]

The scope of participation in RC elections is, in the large majority of cases, also sharply limited. In a small number of Beijing elections between 2000 and 2006, all eligible residents of the neighborhood (or one from each household) were permitted to vote. In 2003, for instance, 11 neighborhoods permitted all residents to vote, and 146 allowed one member of each household to do so— although no data are available as to how many actually voted in these cases. But in each of those three rounds, more than 90 percent of elections featured participation only by residents' small-group representatives. As in Shimen, what this meant was a group of some thirty to fifty constituents chosen for electoral duty by the street office and the residents' committee themselves on the basis of factors like their cooperativeness as well as prestige they may lend to the proceedings. In my field research sites, these occasions were choreographed and rehearsed to ensure at least a large majority in favor of the official slate of candidates, if not a display of total unanimity.[12]

The final two rows in Table 3.1, presenting partial statistics on the results of the elections, show that very few candidates lose in RC elections, as a result of their limited competition and high predictability. Thus in 2006, only 7 percent of those running failed to be elected. The numbers also show, however, that the elections serve to ratify staffing decisions made by the street offices that keep the committee membership in a dynamic state of frequent change. After each of the three rounds, only about 45 percent to 55 percent of the incoming RC members were incumbents held over from the previous term.

Like other election and organization data, information on the Communist Party's presence in the residents' committee structure is generally not reported to the public. But Table 3.2 presents some fragmentary aggregate figures. The Chinese Communist Party (CCP) can, of course, quite effectively manage the RCs through its control over the three levels of formal administration

TABLE 3.2
The Communist Party at the neighborhood level in Beijing, 2000–2006

	2000	2003	2006
Proportion of RC directors who are CCP members	NR	NR	84.3%
Proportion of RC directors who are also community party committee directors	NR	NR	66.8%
Proportion of CCP members among all RC members	39.8%	47.6%	49.2%
Community party members, total number	NR	214,153	263,217

SOURCE: Unpublished figures from the Beijing city government, on file with the author.

NOTE: NR = not reported. Only data from the eight districts constituting the urban core of Beijing are reported here: Dongcheng, Xicheng, Chongwen, Xuanwu, Chaoyang, Haidian, Fengtai, and Shijingshan.

from the city through the districts and down to the street offices. But these data illustrate that the party has also, through the selection and election process, ensured that it dominates the membership and leadership of the committees themselves. The fraction of RC members who are also party members is the only relevant figure reported for all three election years from 2000 to 2006, reflecting the priority that has been placed not merely on maintaining but also on increasing this proportion. It grew by almost ten percentage points over this period, standing at just under 50 percent by 2006. As the top two rows of Table 3.2 show, the authorities go to special lengths to reserve top committee posts, in particular, for CCP loyalists. And the growth in the number of community party members (*shequ dangyuan*) follows from efforts to develop the neighborhood as a site of party activity, particularly for followers who no longer take part in party life at their workplaces.[13]

In short, party and state authorities in Beijing use elections as occasions to clean out and refresh the ranks of the RCs, but these exercises have very little to do with democracy.[14] Beijing is not out of line with other cities in this regard. As some researchers have conscientiously documented, China's urban community-building efforts have included a number of local experiments with elections, which seem to promise advances in democratic governance.[15] But as yet, no fundamental change has occurred in how leaders are chosen in the great majority of communities. In the six cities outside of Beijing where I conducted supplementary research, modest variations on the RC institutional theme could be found, as discussed in Appendix 2. For the purposes of this chapter, findings can be summarized quite simply. A number of cities have experimented with electoral procedures by relaxing one or more of the above constraints, although not so far as to render the elections free and fair by any standards. In none of these cases had RC elections departed from the basic pattern of careful management and near-complete control of outcomes by the local party-state. Investigation by other researchers has thus far further confirmed this basic picture (Gui, Cheng, and Ma 2006; Keng and Chen, 2007; Heberer 2009; Heberer and Göbel 2011, 36–38, 71–78).

Taipei's Elections

Most of the remainder of this chapter focuses on Taiwan's neighborhood elections, which, as free and open contests, have the most to teach us about the possibilities and problems of ultra-local democracy. Once dominated by Kuomintang (KMT) hegemony not unlike that of the CCP in the mainland's neighborhoods, warden elections became increasingly fluid as Taiwan moved toward multiparty competition. As is the island in general, Taipei is well accustomed to the rituals of democracy. The hard-fought quadrennial presidential elections, and to a lesser extent mayoral and legislative contests, occasion large rallies and parades. Intrinsically small scale as they are, the warden campaigns do not bring out mass displays of political fervor; armies of partisans do not gather in front of the Presidential Office Building, as they do at times of national-level contestation. Nonetheless, they elicit remarkably voluble, sometimes heated, competition.

This competition is encouraged by the design of neighborhood-level institutions and in many ways actively stoked by city government. The city election commission, for example, formally registers all *lizhang* candidates about four weeks before the vote, randomly assigns them ballot numbers, and collects statements from the candidates that are then distributed to all households in the city in an election announcement. Candidates are encouraged to establish a campaign headquarters (*jingxuan banshichu*)—indeed, sometimes *lizhang* hopefuls set up two such headquarters. Further, after the election, the city reimburses candidates the equivalent of hundreds of U.S. dollars, thus defraying expenses incurred in their races.[16] For many neighborhoods, the district offices also set up campaign activity sites (*jingxuan huodong changsuo*) in the days before the balloting, where competitors can make their appeals. In short, the warden system contains multiple provisions ensuring that in most neighborhoods the votes are hotly contested—though also others that tamp competition down.

Table 3.3 shows that neighborhood warden elections in Taipei have indeed featured a considerable degree of competition among multiple contenders. In the January 2003 round, for example, 1,377 hopefuls vied for 449 positions. To be sure, not every neighborhood is contested in every round; in that year, forty-three of the *li* had but a single candidate running unopposed (City of Taipei Election Commission 2003, 217). But records show that the 2003 races pitted an average of slightly more than three candidates against one another. In one neighborhood, Shuanglian of Datong district, no fewer than ten individuals ran, as eight men and one woman tried (but failed) to unseat KMT incumbent Xu Chengjiao (City of Taipei Election Commission 2003, 437). Indeed, city officials felt overburdened by the number of

TABLE 3.3
Neighborhood warden elections in Taipei, 1998–2010

	1998	2003	2006	2010
COMPETITIVENESS				
Number of candidates	1,231	1,377	930	953
Number of neighborhoods	435	449	449	456
Average number of candidates per *li*	2.8	3.1	2.1	2.1
RESULTS				
Newly elected	31.3%	35.0%	30.3%	25.4%
Incumbents reelected	68.7%	65.0%	69.7%	74.6%
TURNOUT				
Ballots submitted	705,762	726,845	616,416	1,429,088
Eligible voters	1,804,949	1,926,401	1,984,221	2,020,906
Voter turnout	39.1%	37.7%	31.1%	70.7%

SOURCE: 1998 and 2003: City of Taipei Election Commission 1998 and 2003. For 2006: "Taibeishi di 10 jie lizhang xuanju ge xingzheng qu xuanju gaikuang," computer file retrieved from the City of Taipei Election Commission Web site, http://mect.cec.gov.tw, accessed January 1, 2007; *Taibeishi di shi jie lizhang xuanju shilu* (Taipei: City of Taipei Election Commission, 2007). For 2010: "Taibeishi di 5 jie shizhang, di 11 jie yiyuan ji di 11 jie lizhang xuanju houxuanren ge qu, ge li depiao ji dangxuan qingxing," from the commission's Web site, accessed February 15, 2011.

candidates. Thereafter, a procedure of collecting monetary deposits, previously employed only in races for higher-level elected offices, was applied at the warden level. Each contender put down a deposit of NT$50,000, equivalent to roughly US$1,500. A losing candidate received the deposit back only if he or she won the support of at least 10 percent of all eligible voters—not just of those who actually turned out—in the neighborhood (City of Taipei Election Commission 2006). Although lightening the workload of election officials and discouraging those who would throw their hat in the ring frivolously (*fulan canxuan*), this also no doubt detracted from the elections as a focus of popular political engagement.[17] Consequently, the races of late 2006 and 2010 saw only 2.1 candidates per *li* on average. The city imposes other controls on the elections as well, for better or for worse. For each neighborhood, on the basis of the number of eligible voters, the city sets a maximum for candidates' campaign expenses; in 2003 this ranged from NT$86,000 (about US$2,700) to NT$151,000 (about US$4,700; City of Taipei Election Commission 2003, 17–25).

Voter eligibility in Taiwan is established through the household registration system. A resident may cast votes in the neighborhood warden election (just as in other elections) as long as he or she has lived in the neighborhood and been registered there for at least four months. This has two notable implications: there is no need for a separate system of voter registration, and figures for turnout are relatively precise. As a consequence, we know that almost 38 percent of the electorate voted in the January 2003 round of *lizhang* elections in Taipei, by most countries' standards a respectable turnout for local contests. In the December 2006 round, with the overall number of candidates reduced by the deposit system, turnout shrank to about 31 percent. Taipei's turnout figures then jumped to a remarkable 71 percent on November 27, 2010. The reason: for the first time, neighborhood elections in Taipei and four other cities took place together with voting for mayors and city councils. This constituted an abrupt break from a tradition of holding neighborhood votes separately, a long-standing system that many believe was meant to encourage wardens to devote more time to getting out the vote for their party in higher-level elections, undistracted by the task of defending their own seats.

Even before this turnout-boosting reform, the elections had succeeded in replenishing the ranks of *lizhang* with ample numbers of fresh faces. In each of the three elections from 1998 through 2006, almost a third (32 percent) of Taipei neighborhoods replaced incumbents with new leaders, on average.[18] The higher turnout of 2010 coincided with lower turnover. Possibly it brought to the polls voters less informed about the warden races, who tended to give their support to familiar names.

As Shelley Rigger, Christian Schafferer, and others have observed, Taiwan has a long history of voting, dating back even to the period of Japanese colonization. Elections were also held throughout the four-decades-long authoritarian period. Nationalist domination came to discourage all but ruling-party contenders, but the scope of competition gradually increased to encompass non-KMT (*dangwai*) candidates and, after 1986, contenders from opposition parties, notably the Democratic Progressive Party (DPP; Rigger 1999, 2011; Schafferer 2003). This basic pattern of gradual pluralization has played itself out in neighborhood elections just as at higher levels.

From 1968, when it became a special municipality (*zhi xia shi*), through 2010, the City of Taipei held eleven rounds of neighborhood warden elections. The early elections were wholly dominated by the Nationalists. Indeed, as Figure 3.1 shows, as late as 1985, on the eve of the lifting of martial law, the city had scarcely any wardens who were not affiliated with the KMT. In the years of Lee Teng-hui's presidency, as democratization broadened through the 1990s, the party continued to hold a large majority of Taipei's

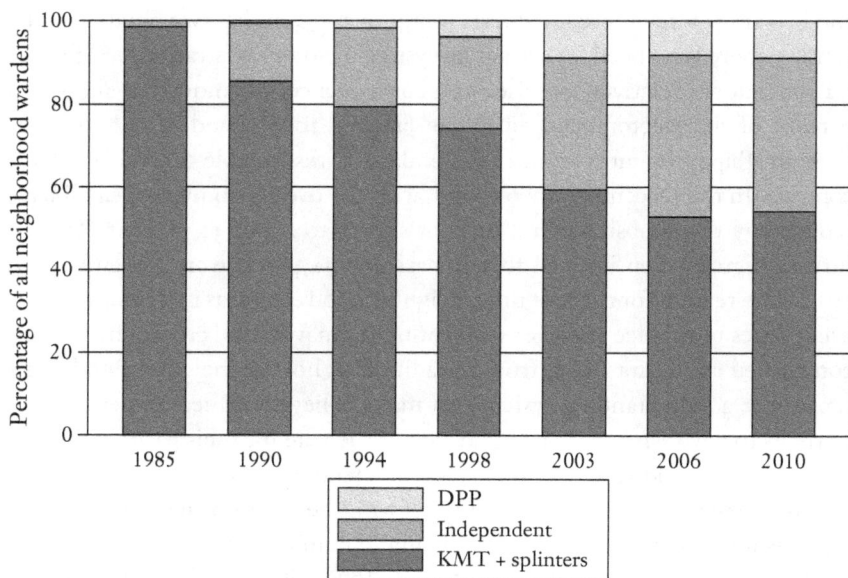

Figure 3.1.   Party affiliation of Taipei neighborhood wardens, 1985–2010.
As of 2011, after the eleventh round of neighborhood elections, the city of Taipei had 456
neighborhood wardens in total, but this number has fluctuated. In 1985, they totaled 630; in
1994, only 435. Data are from City of Taipei Election Commission 1985, 1990, 1994, 1998,
and 2003. For 2006, the source is "Taibeishi di 10 jie lizhang xuanju dangxuanren zhengdang
bili tongji biao"; for 2010, "Taibeishi di 5 jie shizhang, di 11 jie yiyuan ji di 11 jie lizhang xuanju houxuanren ge qu, ge li depiao ji dangxuan qingxing," from the commission's Web site,
http://mect.cec.gov.tw, accessed January 1, 2007, and February 15, 2011, respectively.

neighborhood positions. The party of Chiang Kai-shek's family and Lee
Teng-hui continued to hold a large majority of Taipei's neighborhood positions throughout the 1990s. But just as candidates from the Democratic Progressive Party made inroads in the national legislature during that period,
they also acquired warden posts in parts of the city holding concentrations
of supporters, notably the Wanhua, Datong, and Zhongshan districts. In the
2006 Taipei phone survey, almost 19 percent of all respondents identified
themselves as having an orientation toward the DPP or other parties in the
pan-Green camp.[19] In the three elections from 2003 through 2010, the DPP
has maintained a steady 8 percent or 9 percent fraction of the city's *lizhang*,
neither losing much ground during the party's overall slump in President

Chen Shui-bian's final years in office nor making appreciable gains along with Su Tseng-chang's strong mayoral challenge.[20] Most striking, the fraction of winning candidates who run without the imprimatur of any party grew every year for more than two decades.[21] By 2010, only 54 percent of the wardens had KMT nominations, and 168 out of 456, or about 37 percent, were independents. Some of these nonpartisan neighborhood wardens lean toward the Green camp, others lean Blue, and still others are truly neutral.

The KMT, of course, has a long history of using its material resources to boost its candidates. For many years, it would even invest funds in candidates for neighborhood positions; these cornerstone wardens would then pitch in to mobilize voters in support of candidates for city council, the Legislative Yuan, and other offices. But with the KMT's grip on national-level power broken in the 2000s, under pressure to divest assets seen as ill-gotten holdovers from the authoritarian period, the party's resources available for its loyal wardens shrank. This no doubt helps explain why the capital city, which leans Nationalist in elections for the mayoralty, legislature, and presidency, has undergone such dramatic pluralization in neighborhood-level politics over the past twenty-five years.

It would be natural to assume that the DPP might hold much larger proportions of neighborhood warden positions in cities outside of Taipei, particularly in the south, where much of its base lies. But election records from other cities show this not to be the case. Even in Kaohsiung, a city governed exclusively by DPP mayors from the election of Frank Hsieh in 1998 through the reelection of Chen Chu in 2010, relatively few neighborhoods have Green leaders. In that city's 2010 round of *lizhang* balloting, the KMT took 27 percent of the warden slots to a mere 11 percent for the DPP. Yet in Kaohsiung and the other three newly amalgamated municipalities, the Nationalists lacked the strength they displayed in the capital; nonparty candidates won a large majority of neighborhoods.[22]

The workings of Taipei's neighborhood elections can be illustrated by an extended look at the campaigns of Bai Zhengmin, the warden whose home-based *li* office was described at the beginning of Chapter 1.[23] A DPP supporter proud of his Taiwanese identity, Bai retired from his job in the Forestry Bureau in 1989, the year he turned fifty-two. He first attempted to win the wardenship of Wenchang Li in 1994, when he took on the fifty-six-year-old incumbent, Shao Jiancheng. Shao had served two terms already and enjoyed the backing of the KMT, the party whose authoritarian rule and domineering ways had given Bai a large stock of accumulated antipathy over the decades. The 504 votes he won that year were 124 fewer than Shao's; the presence of another DPP-leaning candidate in the race diluted Bai's support, though in this and later races Bai ran as an independent.

At the next opportunity, in 1998, Bai took on Shao once again. Turnout in Wenchang Li was almost identical that year, but without a second challenger in the race, Bai defeated Shao by 1,006 to 612. A grudge match shaped up in 2003, when Shao sought to reclaim the seat. This time, Bai won reelection by an even larger margin, 1,202 to Shao's 464, permanently laying this rivalry to rest—although, like other incumbents, he sometimes thought he detected the hand of his old opponent behind later challengers.

By late 2006, Bai had accumulated more than eight years of continuous experience as warden of Wenchang. This had given him a detailed knowledge of his constituency. Preparing for his fourth race, he said, he or his wife personally visited about 1,000 of the neighborhood's 2,200 households. Knowing well who favored him and, of those, who was likely to turn out on Election Day, he targeted these contacts selectively and amassed a solid base of support. Nonetheless, two other men threw their hats into the ring. One, Li Muchun, was the fifty-one-year-old proprietor of an automobile repair shop along the thoroughfare that makes up one of Wenchang's boundaries. The other, Liang Yilong, listed no occupation on his application but had worked as a cement layer and a cook. His candidacy carried a whiff of rebellion. Liang served as one of Bai's twenty block captains, a holdover from Shao whom Bai had kept.

Li had deep roots in the locality, and Bai considered him the greater threat of the two. Both Li's uncle and grandfather had previously served as Wenchang's warden. Still, the family's local clout had diminished over time as the neighborhood's population grew to what was then 5,404 people, most of whom were not born locally. Bai estimated that 15 percent of Wenchang's residents were part of the Li clan.

Ran Wenling, the *liganshi* assigned to Wenchang, was obliged by civil service rules to maintain neutrality in the warden race. But she confided that she would be greatly dismayed if Bai were to lose, as that would mean she might have to work with one of the challengers, whose tactics she deplored. Liang, she said, had viciously slandered Bai behind his back. Liang did not make the attacks in his printed campaign literature but spread rumors by word of mouth: that Bai's wife was buying votes, that Bai had padded the voter rolls with people who did not actually live in the neighborhood (*youling hukou*), that Bai had promised he would not run again but would turn the position over to Liang, and that Bai refused to answer his doorbell.

By December 29, the day before the election, Wenchang was thoroughly festooned with campaign paraphernalia. Bai, who prided himself on relatively modest promotional expenditures, had nonetheless bought one hundred pennants and twenty large banners with his name, picture, and the number 2, his assigned position on the ballot. His opponents had hung up similar materials, taped to streetlights or stretched across fences. That evening, the three candidates each held a get-out-the-vote activity (*zao shi huodong*). In Li's case, this centered on a small truck carrying one man beating a drum and two crashing cymbals. Some thirty other supporters wore vests with Li's ballot number and slogans: "#1—innovation—development." They loudly chanted slogans, following behind as the truck toured the neighborhood.

Bai's rally started half an hour later, at 7 P.M., in the city-funded community activity center that he had helped win for the neighborhood. The woman who ran the center was among Bai's allies, and a large display on the wall unabashedly promoted his reelection. Soon the room was packed with supporters of all ages. Six campaign banners were held aloft, and glowing light sticks were distributed to children. The group set out to make the rounds of the fifteen blocks that constituted Wenchang, with Bai in the lead hailing the apartment buildings through an amplifier. "Dear fellow neighbors," he called out, identifying himself and his ballot number. "Please cast a vote for me." Bai's entourage proceeded along the edge of the neighborhood, going by motor-scooter stores and betel-nut stands. It filed past Li's garage and campaign headquarters, from which stony faces looked out. At one point, the rival groups passed each other in an alley; cordial waves were exchanged. About eighty people had joined Bai's procession by the halfway point. His rally concluded next to a park, where it won the attention of residents taking out their household trash at the designated hour.

Like all elections in Taiwan, Taipei's tenth round of *lizhang* elections was held on a Saturday. The balloting follows procedures that voters and election workers alike are familiar with from long experience in elections at many levels. Neighborhood politics, in this way, draws on skills and practices cultivated in other parts of the democratic system. Starting at 8 A.M., Wenchang's voters went to one of two polling stations, each a classroom in the local elementary school, depending on which of the neighborhood's twenty *lin* they lived in. Several official election workers, wearing green identification cards, carefully oversaw the issuing and collection of ballots and controlled entry into the classrooms. They were assisted by observers representing the candidates or political parties, each with a yellow-colored card. A handful of police officers kept watch in the hallways. The ballots were printed with the candidates' names and pictures. An elaborate poster explained twenty-seven different valid ways in which a ballot could be marked by a voter and twenty kinds of markings that would invalidate it.

At 4 P.M., the polling stations closed. A row of students' desks was set up in the classroom where the votes for *lin* 1–9 had been collected, dividing the room in half and creating a protected space for the count. Two dozen spectators stood in the back or squatted on tiny grade school chairs, accompanied by the police officers. At the front of the room, a team of volunteers and officials, ten people in total, carried out the tallying ritual. Two people removed ballots from the box, one at a time. One person, back to the audience, facing the classroom's chalkboard, read the full name of the indicated candidate out loud and held the ballot up over his or her head, for the audience to verify. Another person, standing at the chalkboard, repeated the name and, with a crayon, scored a mark on a big piece of paper, forming five-stroke *zheng* characters that each stood for five votes. Still another person confirmed the mark and handed the ballot to a final individual, who stacked them in a pile. One doubly marked ballot was shown to the room and discarded as invalid. At the end, the election workers held up the emptied ballot box and showed it to the audience.

Bai sauntered in while the count proceeded. Election officials in the other polling station, quicker to finish, had already issued him a stamped and signed carbon copy of the tally from *lin* 10–20. The combined figures produced the official result: Bai Zhengmin, 962; Li Muchun, 197; Liang Yilong, 388. Much to Bai's private satisfaction, neither of his challengers met the minimum threshold of 428 votes necessary for a refund of their deposits, and Li failed to qualify for government reimbursement of election expenses, to boot. As Bai and his wife walked the two blocks back to their home, a group of supporters lit off strings of ear-splitting firecrackers.

Back in his living room-cum-warden office, Bai reflected on the election in his patient, methodical way between congratulatory calls from well-wishers. He would have to dismiss challenger Liang Yilong from his block-captain post—not out of spite, he insisted, but because Bai's other, loyal *linzhang* would not tolerate the turncoat in their midst. Bai did not begrudge the fact that Liang had, as early as two years prior, sprinkled promises of *linzhang* positions around the neighborhood as a way of wooing backers. "I would have done that myself the first time around if I had been smarter," he said. At 8:30 P.M., two officials came to the door to deliver framed congratulatory scrolls from the head of the district office; Huang Lu Ching-Ju, commissioner of the city's Department of Civil Affairs; and Hau Lung-Bin, the mayor. After they had left, Bai—never enamored of the city's KMT-dominated official-dom—declared that he would throw those tokens away.

Although Bai's convincing victory gave him the luxury of feigning nonchalance, other incumbents were in dismal moods. Elsewhere in the same district, eleven out of thirty-nine wardens suffered outright defeats, and two others had chosen not to defend their seats. On the other side of Taipei, the high-minded and usually jovial Huang Maosen had lost by eighty-one votes to a brash challenger. A phone call found Huang so despondent that I waited a week to visit and learn what had happened—circumstances that are discussed in Chapter 6. For present purposes, it is enough to observe that participants take the neighborhood races very seriously. Just as at the national or municipal level, the ballot box provides a brutally decisive way of resolving the question of leadership. The *li* are big enough in scale for the contests to be earnestly fought, small enough for affirmation or rejection by one's neighbors to be intimately felt.

This account from one neighborhood in 2006 shows important features of the elections, such as the rigor of the vote counting and the ways races pit against one another not just individual candidates but also teams of their supporters. More broadly, what should we conclude about these events as exercises in ultra-local democracy? On what basis do candidates make their appeals and on what criteria do voters assess them? As one would expect in any small-scale environment, the contests are highly personalized. Voters choose among neighbors who at least are likely to have met them in person, asked for their vote, and perhaps offered them hospitality in their election headquarters—or who may even be a relative. In many but not all neighborhoods, the campaigns have a pronounced partisan dimension, and voters who strongly identify with either the KMT or the DPP camp typically back like-minded candidates. As we have seen, the elections can feature negative campaigning, whether in the form of whispers or attack flyers stuffed into residents' mailboxes, which can contain wild allegations. Still, there are also legitimate, substantive issues at stake, such as priorities for spending government funds, plans for using public space, and controversial development projects.[24] Incumbents generally run on

their record of specific accomplishments, like improvements to the neighborhood's infrastructure, security arrangements, and landscaping. In the end,
those who turn out in such elections care about who runs the neighborhood.
One resident, for instance, cited Bai's honesty and openness with *li* finances
among reasons for his avid support.

In the Wenchang election described above, more than 36 percent of eligible voters turned up at the polling stations, five percentage points more than
the city average that year, perhaps driven in part by the three-way contest.
Data from the 2006 Taipei survey shed further light on the nature of popular
participation in neighborhood politics, which is also explored in Chapter 6.
Just more than half of the city residents in the sample told interviewers that
they voted in the 2003 *lizhang* elections.[25] As Figure 3.2 shows, participation
in neighborhood contests has a strong class correlation; the less education
respondents had, the more likely they were to vote. This is unusual in the
context of general studies of political behavior, which have found a strongly

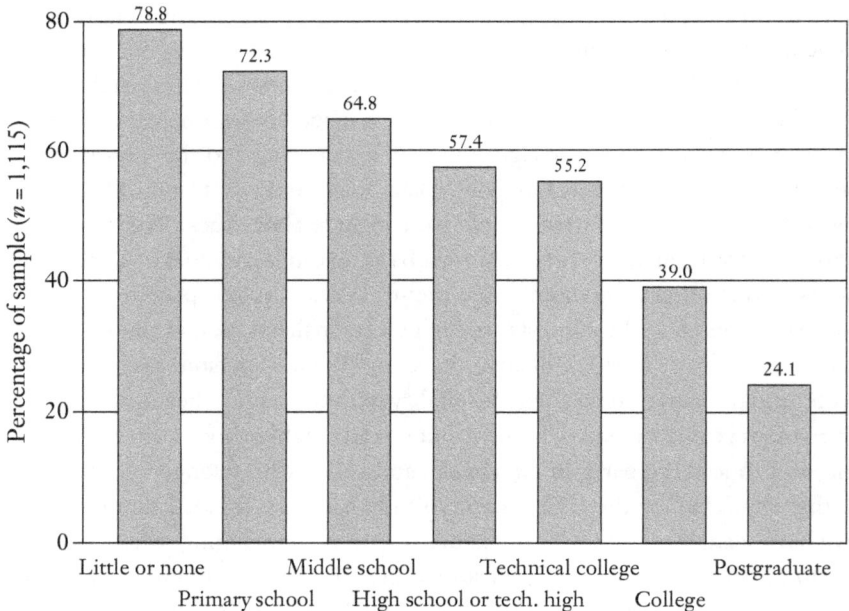

Figure 3.2.   Voting in neighborhood warden elections, by education.
Data from the 2006 Taipei Neighborhoods Survey.

positive correlation between education and voting (Rosenstone and Hansen 1993, 3; Miller and Shanks 1996, 56). But it reflects the distinctive nature of neighborhood politics in Taipei, resonating with details that we glimpsed in the above account from the late 2006 elections. It is people like the neighborhood shop owners, clan elders, and friends of mechanic Li Muchun who are most engaged with the warden system.

The survey also indicates that citizens want to keep the right to vote for their community leaders. Almost three-quarters of respondents (73 percent) expressed support for the current system of popular balloting for neighborhood warden. Only 18 percent favored a change to government-appointed neighborhood leaders, an improbable notion but one that Ministry of the Interior officials have contemplated. A nationwide survey conducted in 2004 by Professor Chen Chun-Ming of Shih Hsin University on behalf of the ministry obtained very similar findings; election was favored over appointment by a margin of 77 percent to 15 percent among urbanites.[26]

Vote buying has long left an odor of corruption around Taiwan's elections (Wang 2004; Wang and Kurzman 2007). Even in Taipei, middle-aged or older citizens have memories of the warden handing out cash before elections. In the capital city, this illegal practice has greatly diminished in prevalence, however. A question in the 2006 telephone survey of Taipei residents asked, "In the past five years, have you heard anything about your *lizhang* buying votes?" More than 80 percent of residents answered no, and fewer than 6 percent answered yes, with others saying that they did not know. This of course does not mean that such abuses actually took place even in this small fraction of cases, but it provides one form of benchmark.[27] Of the sixty-seven respondents who answered in the affirmative, only four lived in neighborhoods run by a DPP leader, which suggests that, to the extent it still exists, this practice remains largely associated with the Kuomintang. Still, the paucity of reports of it in the survey data corroborates the finding of in-depth interviews that vote buying by wardens has become a rare occurrence in Taipei.[28]

It must be noted that on this important point, other parts of Taiwan differ from the capital. In the city of Chiayi, for example, money is still regularly offered to voters at election time. There, several neighborhood leaders and others confided that while vote buying was not a part of every campaign, it remained fairly common. In elections for higher offices like the national legislature, the large district size made payoffs to individual voters impractical. Candidates for Chiayi's city council, by contrast, often resort to such payments. Neighborhood leaders made natural channels through which to influence elections in this way; their community ties gave them a keen sense of who might be swayed by this form of persuasion. (No warden acknowledged buying votes him- or herself.) All informants who discussed the practice agreed that NT$1000 (roughly US$34) was the going price for a voter's favor.

One seasoned member of the KMT elite in Chiayi initially declined to talk about vote buying: "That's not something that can be brought out on the table for open discussion." Later, though, this person warmed to the subject and explained:

> Usually a candidate for city council needs three thousand votes in order to be sure of winning. And in general vote buying goes through the *lizhang*. But if a candidate pays NT$10,000 for ten votes, for example, that might only translate into two votes in the final results. Some voters take the money, then don't vote for you. People over fifty will vote as bought, not younger folks. Sometimes the *lizhang* themselves pocket half the money. So if you ended up actually winning five votes out of the ten you bought, you would be saying a prayer of gratitude [*ni jiu a mi tuo fu*]. To get three thousand votes for sure, you'd need to buy fifteen thousand.[29]

A full understanding of why vote buying has attenuated in Taipei while it flourishes elsewhere must await further research. Possibly, enforcement is stronger in Taipei, and thus the risks to parties have come to outweigh potential gains. It may be that voters' need and taste for such inducements diminishes with higher living standards or that the price becomes unaffordable. Perhaps stronger civic norms lead voters to reject the idea of putting their electoral allegiance up for sale. Regardless of which is the most important cause, the result is that, at least in the capital, one of the most glaring ways in which candidates and parties manipulate the democratic system is no longer widespread.

Conclusion

All in all, Taiwan sets the highest standard for democratic elections in urban AGE institutions, certainly relative to mainland China but also in comparison to parallel bodies around the region. By design, Taiwan's neighborhood structures conjure up a boisterous form of political contention. The island's rigorous ultra-local contests draw on the resources of the city electoral commissions, with their long experience registering candidates, setting up polls, reporting the count, and everything else required to make a fair vote happen. They also rely on the practiced democratic competence of the population. In providing a focus for participation and civic engagement, the warden elections present one plausible incarnation of the kind of active neighborhood politics that, as Chapter 1 noted, theorists have deemed desirable, if elusive. China's RC elections show us a different picture, essentially a simulacrum of democratic procedure with very little of its actual content, quite consistent with the pseudopolitics that Kasza's model of the administered mass organization would suggest (1995).

This chapter has explained a basic contrast in the procedures through which neighborhood leaders are chosen in Beijing and Taipei. Both RCs and neighborhood wardens are subject to oversight from state administrators, which sets significant constraints on them. But as later chapters argue further, the competitive electoral structure of the *lizhang* system makes a difference. It creates a sturdy basis for a warden's authority, something he or she can invoke as a source of leverage in dealings with constituents and the state. It also means that wardens live under the shadow of competition. They obtained their seats, typically, by beating out rivals, uprooting not just the previous *lizhang* but also his or her network of supporters and designated *linzhang*, sometimes slighting or even embittering significant fractions of local society. They know they need not please every voter, and indeed they sometimes ignore those whose support they can do without. But they face the prospect, and in some cases the certainty, of future challenges; neighbors who covet their positions are watching and waiting. This shapes local civic engagement in Taiwan and gives it a distinctive cast.

To the eyes of Western political researchers, at least, the contrast between the remarkably democratic electoral procedures of Taipei and the tightly controlled pseudoelections of Beijing could hardly be starker. Given this, we might well expect an equally sharp contrast in the way that citizens of the two cities perceive these institutions. But in fact, no such night-and-day difference is to be found in the data, qualitative or quantitative. Rather, as mentioned in Chapter 1, residents of Beijing and Taipei express many similar patterns of perception, as well as some notable contrasts. Figure 3.3 shows an example. In both cities, survey respondents were asked to assess their RC or neighborhood

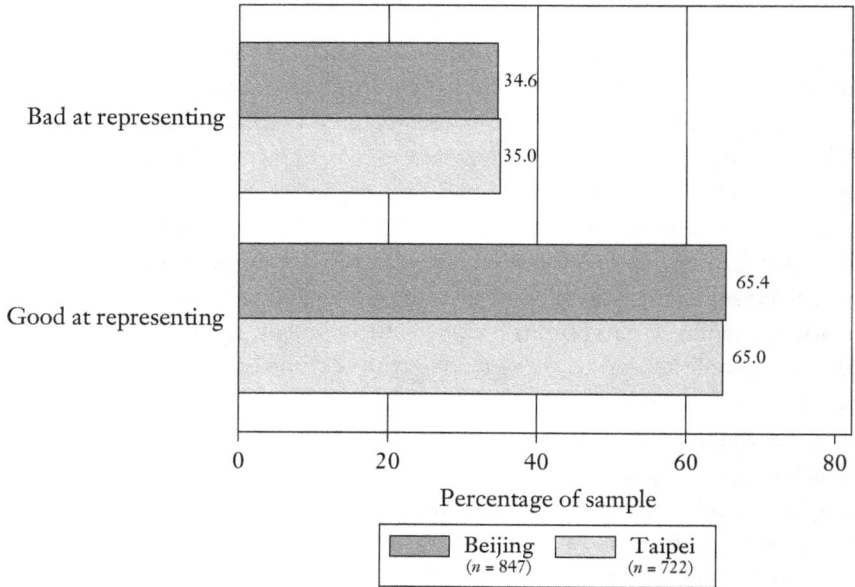

Figure 3.3. Neighborhood organization's perceived effectiveness at representation.
Respondents who said that they did not know how effective their neighborhood organization was at representing them (158 individuals in Beijing, 418 in Taipei), as well as a small
number of refusals and missing responses are omitted here. Data are from the 2001 Beijing
Law and Community Survey and the 2006 Taipei Neighborhoods Survey.

warden in terms of how effective the organization or leader was at representing them to the city government. What is striking is the similarity of the
distributions of responses.[30] In both cities, a clear majority gave an affirmative
nod to the neighborhood representatives in terms of representational ability, whereas a substantial minority disagreed. This puzzling dimension of the
comparison between the capitals is explored in the coming chapters.

Chapter Four

Power Relations at the Alley Level

What is the nature of constituents' relations with their *lizhang* and residents' committees (RCs)? Do residents shun or embrace these organizations, which work so closely with the state, and in many respects extend its reach into the intimate residential environment of the neighborhood? To what extent must they fear the power of these intermediaries or develop clientlike dependency on them? At this point, we turn from looking at the neighborhood organizations as institutions to analyzing the ways in which they interact with constituents on an everyday basis. The previous chapter established one major element of the relationship between constituents and local leaders: the extent to which the former have direct electoral control over the selection of the latter. But these elections, be they fair or stage-managed, happen only once every few years. A complete answer to the above questions must strive for a full-spectrum understanding of local power dynamics. We begin by exploring the neighborhoods' connection to higher levels of city governance, then ask exactly what kinds of carrots and sticks the RCs and *lizhang* have at their disposal to apply or withhold in dealings with residents.

Beijing: Under the Eye of the Street Office

The RC's general freedom from democratic electoral constraints does not mean that there exist no other mechanisms by which residents can try to hold it to account, as we will see. Nonetheless, the committees are primarily accountable not to their constituents but to the street offices that oversee them. It is impossible to understand these neighborhood institutions without grasping the nature of their interaction with these state organs to which they report. The committees are subject to an endless stream of orders and instructions from their minders in the street offices and the police substations, and they are expected to translate these into real action.

Although they are even more obscure than the RCs themselves, the street offices constitute a crucial element of city government in China. As explained in Chapter 2, they come directly under district governments in the urban administrative hierarchy, that is, in cities large enough to have multiple districts. Managing the residents' committees is one of their most important functions, and without the RCs the street offices would be hard pressed to accomplish the ambitious administrative tasks that they are given.

Beijing's street offices govern areas containing from several tens of thousands to well more than 100,000 residents, with around 106,000 on average. The number of residents' committees that each supervises varies, but the average declined from thirty-seven in 2000 to eighteen in 2009 with the consolidation of the neighborhood governance system into larger communities.[1] Personnel rosters range in size from merely a few dozen staff members per street office in smaller cities to well more than one hundred in larger ones. They are led by a director (*zhuren*) and one or more vice directors; as in all state organs in mainland China, this leadership group overlaps with a party committee. A street office typically occupies an entire building of its own, which often works in tandem with a police substation (*paichusuo*) that has jurisdiction over the same area.

Inside a street office the director oversees a more or less standardized set of functional bureaus.[2] The party structure, for instance, encompasses branches of the Chinese Communist Party's (CCP) organizational, propaganda, and disciplinary departments, as well as mass organizations like the labor union, women's federation, and youth league. The government structure includes offices for city planning, security, labor, education, statistics, economic management, and other portfolios. Each of these may call on the residents'

committees to carry out tasks that require local knowledge or personal contact with constituents. As of the early 2000s, it was the Residents' Bureau
(*jumin ke*) that took primary responsibility for managing the residents' committees. Inside this bureau, a number of staff served as liaison cadres (*waiqin
ganbu*), handling a few RCs each and visiting them on a regular basis. The
liaison cadre was a highly important figure to the committee members; this
overseer assessed their work and enforced discipline while also providing useful information about upcoming policy changes. The staff were given a constant stream of instructions from the street office, whether over the telephone,
through in-person visits by *waiqin ganbu* or other officials, or in general meetings held regularly at street office headquarters. These minders also demanded
a sheaf of detailed quarterly and year-end reports from the RC, covering each
of its areas of administrative responsibility (*kou*). As of 2010, the enhancement
of the neighborhood-level bureaucratic structure had internalized part of this
supervision in the community itself, and staff in one part of the city told me
they no longer reported to liaison cadres—although the specialized offices
within the street office continued to keep close tabs on them.

The RC member's relationship to the street office is in many respects one
of employee to employer. Work in the RC is, first and foremost, a kind of
job. Staff in Beijing were expected to spend roughly thirty hours per week on
duty, showing up at the office for one three-hour shift in the morning and one
in the afternoon, five days a week. In practice, the staff are given a degree of
flexibility with their hours, and sometimes they arrive for their shifts late and
leave early. They also are expected to carry out special after-hours assign-
ments when necessary, however. Moreover, residents often feel free to contact
them at home, even at odd hours, if urgent needs arise.

The nature of neighborhood institutions and the work that they do varies
somewhat in different parts of Beijing. Later chapters explore the significant
contrasts between older city quarters and new high-rise housing, but other
features deserve mention as well. Each of the four central districts occupies a
quadrant in the heart of Beijing, together covering the area that the old city
wall once contained as well as swatches of territory beyond it. (In 2010 plans
were announced to consolidate these districts, collapsing Xuanwu and Chongwen into Xicheng and Dongcheng, respectively.)[3] This kernel is surrounded
by four much larger districts, which have been called near suburbs (*jinjiao*)
and are designated "expansion districts," as indeed, much of the recent expansion of the city's population has taken place in them.[4] In Chaoyang, the aver-

age number of residents per RC ballooned to more than nine thousand by 2009, about twice the figure for those in the central districts, which themselves had grown much larger with the merging together of small neighborhoods into larger ones. Until recently the four peripheral districts, with their high concentrations of postrevolutionary factories, schools, and other *danwei* compounds, had large numbers of *jiaweihui*, in other words, RCs run by work units. In Haidian, as many as 64 percent of RCs had this status in 2000. Compared to regular committees, my field research indicated, the duties of the *jiaweihui* tended to be somewhat quieter and more predictable, as residents shared a common identification with the *danwei* and were subject to administration from work unit institutions that overlapped with neighborhood functions. The committees have since been brought under more uniform administration by the city government, and the *jiaweihui* was phased out as a separate category.[5]

The microculture of RC work is an amalgam that has elements stemming from the demands and incentives emanating from the street offices, as well as a workaday employee subculture of getting by and cutting corners. The extent to which an RC keeps focused on its many appointed tasks depends heavily on constant oversight and vigilance by the street office. Even in committees that were quite diligent and committed to their work, conflicts of interest with state purposes and criticism or correction by superiors inevitably occurred. The Shimen RC was dressed down by its liaison cadre for having organized a day trip to Tianjin for party members and activists, paid for out of the committee's funds, without having asked in advance for permission from the street office. Chastened, the staff laboriously wrote out an application for retroactive approval, lying about where they had gone.[6] Some RCs clearly take bribes and engage in other forms of abuse, although their corruption cannot exceed the modest scope of their local authority. My RC informants rarely told me about any serious wrongdoing of their own, but they did complain about nearby committees that had taken kickbacks from entrepreneurs or failed to report to the street office minor fees that they levied. Like employees anywhere, RC staff quite often grumble among themselves about the onerous chores they are assigned; they feel, with considerable justification, that they are saddled with innumerable tasks from what seems like every nook and cranny of the city government.

At the same time, RC staff are often proud of their work and of their positions. As petty as it is in the country's organizational hierarchy, the status of being even the most minor of state-designated deputies and being politely addressed as director (*zhuren*) or other such titles by the more deferential of visitors are the source of no small satisfaction. Although some are cynical about their work or view it as just a job and nothing more, many others consider themselves honorable foot soldiers, tirelessly assisting the government in providing for constituents' needs. Even though their actual powers are limited, the symbols thereof—things like red sleeve badges, the committee's official seal, and the offices in which they work—affirm their self-worth. This has particular value to those whose previous employment offered no particular sense of status or ended abruptly in layoffs or early retirement. In contrast, recently recruited staff who once held more prestigious or remunerative jobs, for instance in schools or businesses, sometimes confided to me that they felt downright embarrassed to be working in such a lowly position and handling such petty matters.[7]

Personal dynamics among committee members varied greatly from neighborhood to neighborhood. Relations among the staff were amicable in some cases, but others were strained, with tension along several fault lines. Members tended to be acutely conscious of status differences, such as between old-timers with little education and rookies with high school diplomas or more. The community cadres hired in Beijing aroused considerable jealousy and complaints from their peers who earned half their salaries or less. With hiring and firing decisions determined in secret by the street office, committee members clearly showed their tension and unease around the time of staffing changes or RC mergers that foreshadowed downsizing.

Some aspects of the world of the residents' committees have an almost camplike quality in that they involve elaborate sets of contrived activities that are undertaken with an earnestness seemingly out of proportion with their prima facie significance. The street offices regularly hold contests among the RCs for excellence in certain areas of work or for the best-designed propaganda display of a certain type, which generate a sense of friendly competition among teams. The RCs also vie for district- and city-level awards. Committees may deliberate at great length over minute decisions about which residents will serve as the head of an entranceway or a residents' small group. Staff members put great care into the drawing and redrawing of organizational charts and the artful chalking of blackboard slogans, employing their skills in crafts, drafting, and calligraphy. All this can make for an atmosphere of structured group fun. The atmosphere of levity that at moments infuses the RC office, and the frivolous nature of some of the office activities, belies and veils the entirely serious role that these institutions play in many areas of urban governance.

Taipei: Independent Political Standing in the State Rubric

On paper, the organizational structure of the lower reaches of Taipei's government is not so different from its counterpart in Beijing. Article 59 of the Local Government Act states that neighborhood and village leaders serve under the command and supervision (*zhihui jiandu*) of the heads of cities, districts, and townships as applicable. The first paragraph of Taipei's instruction manual for wardens further states: "Although *lizhang* are elected by the people, and the District Chief does not have the power to appoint and dismiss them, nonetheless with regard to operational matters in the administrative system, the *lizhang* is in a directly subordinate relationship to the District Office. The *lizhang* comes under the command and supervision of the District Chief, and in turn commands and supervises his or her subordinate *linzhang*" (City of Taipei Civil Affairs Bureau 2003b, 1).

In practice, the relationships among Taiwan's *lizhang*, *liganshi*, and the district offices are considerably more complicated than these official texts would suggest. Indeed, there are differences in perspective among people who are themselves part of this system.

The *liganshi* form an important part of the link between state and citizenry—both in their own right and by working with the neighborhood warden. In some ways, they are analogous to the *waiqin ganbu* of mainland cities, in that they are full-time civil servants sent from the lowest level of the formal bureaucracy to liaise with neighborhood leaders. Typically, they punch in at the district offices in the mornings, then proceed to the neighborhood in the afternoons, working in the neighborhood office or making house calls. Their names and photographs are publicly posted, and they make themselves available for residents to reach on government-issued cell phones until 10 P.M. There is no limit on the amount of time a *liganshi* may serve in a particular jurisdiction, but after a new warden is elected, he or she is often reassigned.

Although *waiqin ganbu* and other representatives of the street office clearly come as overseers and taskmasters to the RCs, the *liganshi*'s relationship to the warden is considerably different. The former do exercise some degree of restraint over the latter; for example, major expenses must be approved by the civil servant, who is supposed to put a stop to any illicit use of power or public money. Yet this supervisory role is muted. According to a man who had served in both capacities: "The warden is like the top executive [*shouzhang*], and the *liganshi* is like his chief of staff. The warden has to do more outreach and interaction with the residents, and the *liganshi* does more paperwork, preparing material for meetings, that kind of thing."[8] Indeed, some *liganshi* do act like assistants to the elected neighborhood leader, at least in certain capacities. One eighty-five-year-old warden, who had been elected to ten consecutive terms since 1968, had worked with the same middle-aged civil servant for twelve years. At his office in central Taipei, he sat drinking tea with visitors while she answered the phone and fielded requests. In a nearby neighborhood, another *liganshi* complained that the warden for whom she worked, driven by ambitions to vault into the heights of the city council, harangued her to respond immediately to all complaints by residents rather than within the stipulated three-day period. She protested: "Some people say that the *liganshi* is the *lizhang*'s secretary. But we are formally appointed civil servants. We help the warden to be a bridge between the residents and the district office. If the government has requests, we help to take them to the community to carry out."[9]

Veteran neighborhood leader Bai Zhengmin observed that in the authoritarian period of Kuomintang (KMT) rule, these district personnel acted more like bosses of the neighborhood leaders and checked whether they harbored any forbidden political ideas. Although this is no longer the case, Bai also rejected the idea that authority relations between the two should be seen as the reverse of this earlier pattern.

> A lot of wardens have a mistaken idea. They think: "I'm really big as a *lizhang*; the *liganshi* is there to work for me." But this is wrong. In fact, both of them are given orders and overseen by the district chief. So they ought to be equal, even though the *lizhang* was elected whereas the *liganshi* passed a test and was appointed. Because the wardens are older, and because they're elected, the district chiefs are usually very polite to them, and the *liganshi* says that he or she is "helping" them. But this cultivates an incorrect idea.[10]

As he suggested, even Taipei's twelve district chiefs, figures of towering stature in the city government, hardly act as bosses to the wardens. One described her relationship with the several dozen neighborhood leaders beneath her as subtle (*weimiao*):

> I'm supposed to be their superior. But the wardens are elected, and the mayor is elected, while the district chief is an appointee. Because of this structure, they can go above me and talk directly to the mayor. They think: "I don't have to take you seriously." I know that one district chief lost his position because he was pushed out by the wardens. This gives them a lot of airs. They say things like, "Do you want to keep your job?" So to say I'm afraid of them would be putting it too strongly, but there's some truth to that.[11]

The ambiguity and variation in these relationships underscores the point that the *lizhang* have considerable independent standing and are by no means mere lackeys at the bottom rung of the urban hierarchy. Still, the state channels many kinds of work through the neighborhoods, and one way or another, this curious team of one elected local and one civil servant carry it out. One *liganshi* discussed the extensive work she does on behalf of the district office's military service bureau. She estimated that she personally delivered one hundred draft letters (*bingdan*) to families with teenage boys over the course of a year. After this came home visits, physical exams, and various forms of follow-up, especially with families claiming deferrals. She explained why all this could not be done by mail, without human intervention: "We have to determine the family's actual situation. If they were only reached by mail, they could refuse the letter. Some people keep moving from place to place. So we have to go and find them ourselves. We try to find someone with a relationship to the family [*guanxi ren*], that way it's easier for us to find them and follow up. We can tell if the young man is likely to shirk his military service. We have the *guanxi ren* sign for these letters; that way, they can't deny that they received it."[12] The warden, for his part, helped take the notices around as well, and he assisted with many other state-assigned tasks. In abstract terms, neighborhood elections ensure the seating of wardens with deep roots in the area; the *liganshi*, in turn, draw on those networks in the course of carrying out their work for the district.

The *lizhang*, unlike neighborhood staff in China, have a mandate from the voters and cannot be summarily dismissed for insubordination. A close examination of wardens who left their positions during the 2003–2007 term illustrates this. By April 2006, city authorities had removed 2 of the 449 elected in 2003, both because of serious offenses.[13] One, You Qingfa of Shilin district, was convicted of corruption (and subsequently stabbed a fruit peddler in an argument).[14] Even more remarkably, Chen Chao-chin of Beitou district was stripped of his position and later sentenced to prison for paying and encouraging the man who shot to death city council member Chen Chin-chi in 2002.[15] These cases remind us that the ranks of the wardens, even in the capital city, are not free of rough characters and crooks. But more important, the extraordinary circumstances involved make clear that it is only in the event of criminal wrongdoing that the Taipei government dismisses a *lizhang*. It issues evaluations of neighborhoods and *liganshi* alike, designating some as being of excellent accomplishment (*jiyou*), but these have little consequence for the wardens. ("When we get reelected, that's how you really know we're excellent," said one.)[16]

Indeed, many wardens pride themselves on standing up to government officials, even berating them. In Chen Boyu's neighborhood, a piece of land belonging to the National Property Administration of the Ministry of Finance had become an unkempt eyesore. Chen arranged a meeting with a bureaucrat from that agency, along with representatives from the Taipei government. The national official, he said, behaved disrespectfully. Chen rebuked the man, calling him a "dog official" (*gou guan*), a breathtaking insult. He continued: "I'm the *lizhang*, I was elected here. Even if President Chen Shui-bian came he would have to be polite to me." He followed this up on the spot with a phone call to the bureaucrat's superior. Afterward, Chen reported, the man became much more polite. "That was the most satisfying scolding I've ever given." Similarly, Bai Zhengmin proudly related, on more than one occasion, the story of how he had told off a district official for assigning lazy personnel to his neighborhood.

In China, committee staff can provide suggestions and feedback to their higher-ups and may be able to obtain action on certain local problems by drawing their superiors' attention to them. Beyond that, they have a very limited capacity to make requests, and many committee members told me they felt that the street offices discouraged serious initiatives on their part. In comparison, Taiwan's wardens, in certain circumstances, have a much greater ability to reach upward, pressing demands on the municipal bureaucracy.

One source of clout for the wardens stems from their ties with city councilors (*shi yiyuan*) and even mayors. City councils employ a single nontransferrable vote system with multimember districts, much like the national legislature before its 2005 reforms. As of 2011, Taipei had sixty-two councilors spread across just six electoral zones, each of which comprised two of the city's administrative districts.[17] Correspondingly, each zone held large numbers of constituents: 341,558 people in the smallest and 569,343 in the largest (City of Taipei Department of Budget, Accounting, and Statistics 2011, 888). The neighborhood system is thus an important means through which city council candidates bring themselves into contact with voters on a scale that is small enough to involve human interaction but larger than one-on-one. Shelley Rigger explained the basic pattern and identified it as a form of clientelism:

> A city council member might act as a patron for several neighborhood leaders, while simultaneously acting as a client to the mayor. In this case, the neighborhood leaders would rely on the council member to ensure that community complaints were resolved quickly. In exchange, they would mobilize the neighborhood to vote for that council member. The council member, in turn, would encourage those neighborhood leaders to turn out their supporters to vote for the mayor, while the mayor pressured the city bureaucracy to take special care of the council member's neighborhoods. (1999, 42)

This kind of mutual back scratching indeed remains part of the fabric of urban political life. Wardens often build connections with one or two go-to council members; the latter develop a stable of congenial wardens. Yet Taipei's *lizhang* can, by and large, only gently steer voters toward their favored council members; excessive pressure could backfire. As the wife of warden Chen Boyu put it: "If you went up to people's homes, knocked on their doors and simply told them whom to vote for, they would think you were insane. It would give them a bad impression of you. They would assume you had been paid off."[18] Thus, although the relationships that Rigger discussed certainly exist, they typically take a wispier and less binding form than might be imagined.

The KMT, in particular, is known for its prowess in vote allocation (*peipiao*) techniques. These attempt to allocate supporters in a multimember district to specific candidates, so that each receives enough to be elected but not so many that votes are wasted (Rigger 1999, 41). Chen, however, supported the council member with whom he had developed a long-standing, mutually beneficial relationship rather than the one his party suggested he encourage residents to favor. He would not go so far as to host a dinner for the special purpose of introducing constituents to a politician: "I don't do that. It's awkward later if they don't get votes."[19] But in early 2007 he did invite two city council candidates to the *weiya* banquet he held at a tony seafood restaurant, a customary piece of hospitality at the end of the lunar year and a celebration of his reelection. Six tables of supporters were present, some politely sipping the wine that was offered in large pitchers and others knocking it back with abandon. The politicians made short speeches, apologizing for the fact that the several other *weiya* on their evening's schedule prevented them from joining the guests in imbibing more than lightly.[20] This kind of encounter characterized the kind of support that a Taipei warden might give to a higher-level political ally: hardly delivering votes but providing opportunities to win them. Day trips organized by neighborhood leaders offered a similar kind of platform: councilors might arrange to meet the sightseers where they stopped along the way, having previously stocked their busses with cases of bottled water.

Bai Zhengmin, a diehard DPP supporter at heart but outwardly independent to his Blue-leaning neighborhood, distributed a flyer to his constituents in advance of the 2006 city council and *lizhang* elections. The text read, in part:

> In my eight years as *lizhang*, a number of city council members have supported me irrespective of party or faction, helping me win many improvement projects for the community. In particular, widening Wennan Street, expanding the sidewalk on Jinhua Road . . . , repaving the sidewalk on both sides of Lane 170, and accelerating by 20 years the renovation of the neighborhood's drain-water pipes—all these things could only have been completed in a smooth and timely way through close cooperation and joint efforts between your warden and city council members. . . .
>
> If you like the Nationalist Party, please concentrate your family's votes on one of the following: (15) Chiang Nai-hsin (5) Ken Li Kuei-fong (10) Wang Hsin-i.
>
> If you like the Democratic Progressive Party [DPP], please concentrate your family's votes on one of the following: (14) Po-ya Chou (2) Chia-ching Hsu (19) Lin Hsin-chien.[21]

This appeal thus deftly emphasized Bai's nonpartisan image, gave a hint of his educated polish, and reminded voters of his own accomplishments. Its suggestions did not accord with any partisan vote-allocation scheme, nor did they more than gently nudge voters toward his favored council members.

The clout that *lizhang* exercise through such ties is normally modest and behind the scenes, but a series of events in 2002–2003 illustrated the collective power they can wield. In the last year of his first term as Taipei's mayor, Ma

Ying-jeou developed a set of adjustments to the city's grassroots governance system, called the neighborhood administration reforms (*lizheng gaige*). These came on the heels of the city's half-year postponement of the ninth round of warden elections to January 4, 2003, a move that stirred controversy in its own right.[22] The reforms were the brainchild of Lin Cheng-hsiou, a former student activist who had been appointed director of the city's Civil Affairs Bureau at the tender age of thirty-one. The city had readjusted neighborhood boundaries and trimmed more than seven hundred block captains from the rolls. It further proposed subjecting the expenses of the wardens to discussion and approval at public meetings, diminishing the latitude of the wardens in choosing *linzhang* by encouraging the appointment of members of condominium boards in certain areas, diverting half of the US$60 monthly subsidy each *linzhang* received to other public purposes, and discontinuing the wardens' own holiday bonuses (City of Taipei City Council 2003). All this was to be done in the name of increasing accountability and fairness in the use of public resources, but the planned changes were unveiled without extensive consultation with those they would affect.

Though relatively modest in scope, the reforms still entailed "cutting a piece of flesh" out of the neighborhood leaders and their teams of block captains, as Yang Xueli put it.[23] They made their displeasure known. Yang was himself an uncharacteristically young part of the Civil Affairs apparatus; he won the leadership of Fushou Li in the 2003 elections as a thirty-two-year-old. At the warden inauguration ceremony on January 16, in front of television cameras, he tore up his appointment certificate promptly after receiving it from the deputy mayor.[24] This act of defiance was only part of the occasion's drama: dozens of other wardens boycotted the ceremony, some raised a protest banner, and Lin's speech was cut short. Mayor Ma persisted in his effort to push through the reforms but met with a storm of criticism from city council members of both the Blue and the Green camps. Ma apologized, the reform plan was postponed and partially gutted, and five months later Lin was transferred to a lower-profile city office.[25]

This episode vividly illustrated how the neighborhood leaders can mobilize and, on the basis of their reciprocal ties with politicians at higher levels, have their voices heard. To be sure, collective action of the kind that took place in 2003 is rare. Although wardens have their own associations (*lianyi hui*) at the city and district levels—something that also distinguishes them from their counterparts in China, who have no such corporate bodies—these are not typically tools through which political force is exerted. Rather, wardens more commonly work their relationships with city council members, and skills they may have in navigating the urban bureaucracy, to finagle a grant here, expedited projects there. There is no guarantee of success, but savvy and well-connected *lizhang* can obtain special treatment in matters like the repaving of roads, the sprucing up of parks, and the repair of other infrastructure. Some do everything possible to claim credit for such morsels of pork. In Yanping Li, for example, Gao Kunshan's name remained stenciled on many sidewalk benches even after this four-term warden lost his seat in 2006.

In short, on paper, the RC staff and *lizhang* occupy analogous positions in their cities' organizational charts. In both cases, their offices carry trappings and insignia designating their work as authoritative. Both carry out duties on behalf of the state, and in both cases, oversight mechanisms exist in the bureaucracy to keep them on task. Yet within this framework of broad similarity, their status and power vis-à-vis superiors are very different. When push comes to shove, RC members serve at the pleasure of the street offices and are kept closely under their watch. The intensified bureaucratization of China's neighborhoods in recent years brings this oversight even closer than before, internalizing it within the community structures. The elected wardens, by contrast, are not nearly so subject to the beck and call of the district. Though lodged within the rubric of the state, they occupy a more self-confident position there, with much firmer standing to make demands of superiors and to choose what degree of cooperation to offer them. The *lizhang* are rather like the state's partners, people it must work with regardless of attitude or temperament; the RCs are more like its informal employees.

The Inquisitive and Coercive State

Having secured a general grasp on the contours of the relationship between the state and its grassroots-level intermediaries, we can turn to an examination of the complex power dynamics between the latter and their constituents.

During Taiwan's authoritarian period under Chiang Kai-shek and Chiang Ching-kuo, the island's neighborhood leaders formed one component of the police state. It is widely agreed that they never constituted a primary pillar of the KMT's security apparatus; their more important purpose was to co-opt the island's population and mobilize support. But for four decades they unquestionably helped the ruling party keep watch over the cities. As noted by Bai Zhengmin, who lived through the entirety of this period: "For instance, the police would ask the wardens to investigate whether someone had thought problems. They would use the wardens as informants. It was pretty fright-ful. Now there's none of that."[26] Indeed, with the democratization of the *li* system, and of the political regime as a whole, neighborhood leaders feel that much of the power they once wielded over their domains is a thing of the past. The danger of alienating voters makes wardens reluctant to impose anything unwelcome on their constituents.

Still, the wardens and the *liganshi* are involved in various forms of monitor-ing and certification on behalf of the government. They often consult closely with police about crime and security in the neighborhood, and along with the block captains, they are formally tasked with reporting an extensive list of ille-gal or suspicious behaviors (City of Taipei Civil Affairs Bureau 2003b, 75–76). They sometimes may be asked for information by officials of other agencies, such as those handling land administration and taxation. One kind of affidavit from the warden, attesting that a child lives in the area, can be required to obtain admission to a local school, and another can validate low-income stu-dents' eligibility for special support. The *liganshi* have a broad set of oversight duties, extending even to providing guidance to the local temples and making sure they are free of strange powers and improper spirits (*guaili luanshen*).

The Republic of China state implements a number of ambitious programs, such as a military draft and a household registration system, which require information-gathering and personal contact, as previously noted. The process of updating the household registers, however, is primarily handled by a special-ized set of administrative offices (*huzheng shiwusuo*) and their staff. Compared with the mainland's RCs, which expend tremendous effort helping the police with the endless task of figuring out who lives where, neighborhood personnel in Taipei are less centrally involved with this process. The civil servants paired with the neighborhood warden, *liganshi*, take the lead on other administrative matters, such as welfare casework. Moreover, the *lizhang* are spared from hav-ing to undertake anything like the mainland's family-planning enforcement, as Taiwan has nothing comparable to this program. In short, neighborhood leaders there rarely come to their constituents in an information-gathering or coercive capacity.

In China, though, the kind of informant role that Bai described is not just something of the past; the RCs have acted as collectors of information throughout their history and continue to do so. Not only are they a key component of the surveillance network maintained by the security apparatus; they also help the state to act on that information and to intervene, at times as part of political campaigns. Because of the special importance of understanding the position of grassroots institutions in a repressive setting, it is appropriate to take a particularly careful look at this aspect of the Beijing case here.

To understand neighborhood power dynamics in this setting, it is necessary to appreciate, in a clear-eyed way, the processes of information gathering and state coercion in which RCs play a part. It is also necessary to contextualize this and appreciate its limits and constraints. Although in certain respects these entities are backed by the formidable resources of the state, including the police, what this means to individual constituents varies. The system operates in such a way as to minimize the use of overt coercion, reserving it for exceptional circumstances. Most important, the RC itself in fact has relatively few sanctions that it can apply in dealings with constituents. For example, unlike the work unit, the RC has no control over people's salaries or their access to housing. Residents can opt not to cooperate with it. Indeed, most of the time they can ignore it entirely if they choose.

The Chinese government does not hesitate to intervene in cases of serious criminal activity, perceived threat to state security, or violation of key policies. The RC plays two important roles in such intervention. The first is that of antenna. It finds out about the violations in the first place and brings them to the attention of the authorities. Through its command of detailed information about micro-level circumstances, it can also make intervention easier and more effective.

A striking example of this appeared one day in the Chongxing neighborhood with the arrival at the RC office of Huang Jun, a member of the district court's enforcement staff, along with his assistant.[27] A local man had been judged by the court to be in default on a debt of 50,000 yuan. He had contracted for and received 100,000 yuan worth of remodeling on a music hall that he owned but had paid only half that sum. Huang's task was to carry out a forcible implementation (*qiang zhixing*) of the court's ruling, one of several such jobs on his day's schedule. This, he said, would entail confiscation of all the man's substantial possessions, as well as those of his wife and mother, who lived with him. Their initial visit to the home, however, revealed few assets other than a refrigerator.

Before returning to the debtor's home, Huang interviewed the committee staff to acquire information that would help him go about his task, with his associate taking notes: In the committee's judgment, does the music hall indeed belong to the debtor, or did he transfer ownership to someone else? Was it true that he had been involved in other business activities, such as reselling steel products? Does he come back home often? Does it look like he has money because of what he wears and what his mother wears? The committee staff—drawing on the kind of knowledge that neighbors have of one another in the cramped alleys and courtyards—supplied such details as which of his family members slept in which rooms and the fact that the women in the family wore necklaces and rings.

There was nothing distinctively authoritarian about the enforcement action itself; similar pieces of unpleasant business like repossessions or evictions happen under all kinds of governments. What is distinctive is the way neighborhood personnel facilitated this action, drawing on the kind of micro-level detail that only someone deeply embedded in the local milieu would possess. The incident provides an indication of the informational leverage that the state's enforcement arms can receive from its local operatives and how this might help them carry out their duties. It is also important to note that the enforcement was in no way initiated by the RC; the committee assisted but did not cause it to happen. Its role was quiet and behind the scenes, as is often the case.

In addition to acquiring information, the RCs also may take part in the intervention itself. Committees I observed or learned about did so in cases such as enforcing household registry, persuading expectant mothers of unapproved children to leave town or even to have abortions, and talking to residents engaged in things considered criminal or deviant by the state. This participation by the RC staff has two purposes. It is intended to make the intervention more effective. Committee members generally go to the resident's home as a team, which emphasizes their numbers and their determination. Their presence conveys the idea that the local representatives of the state will be watching to ensure future compliance. It is also aimed to make the intervention less jarring and gentler. The RC members play up their personal sympathy toward the resident and the long-term common goals that everyone is expected to agree to. They may even distance themselves from the policy or rule that is being enforced but ask for compliance as a personal favor.

Yet eliciting cooperation from residents even on minor matters can be remarkably difficult. One RC staff member, Jiang Xiayun of Shimen, echoed the frustration of countless others in declaring in exasperation: "Residents' work is hard to do. You have every kind of person out there [*Bu hao zuo, zhe jumin gongzuo. Shenme yang de ren dou you*]."[28] Beijing citizens displayed a formidable repertoire of resistance to the entreaties of the RC, and this illuminates an important aspect of neighborhood power dynamics.

The trouble that upset Jiang that day was one of the most common headaches faced by the committees: nonpayment of fees owed to it. Deadbeats simply ignored the handwritten reminder slips left on their doors by the staff and dodged when they happened to see them around the building. Residents also stymied the RC by depriving it of other minor forms of cooperation. In Wutai, a new high-rise development, dog owners helped themselves to the use of the dog-free elevator on the way to their pet's daily stroll.[29] In other neighborhoods, residents flatly declined RC requests to clean up the areas around their apartments that they had strewn with disused furniture and other castoffs.[30]

People regularly turned down even simple requests made to them in person by the RC director. In the Shimen neighborhood, as in many other parts of the city, a new cheat-proof electricity system had been installed that required each household to purchase and plug in prepaid cards to obtain current rather than paying after the fact on the basis of readings from a meter. Shared fixtures like hallway lights also required their own cards. A woman from building 18, entryway 4, came in to complain to the RC that the hall lights were not working, even though her card still had eleven kilowatt-hours of power left.[31] Director Ding called two phone numbers at the housing office and demanded help in her polite-but-insistent manner, but she was told that the new cards were designed to stop working even with a certain amount of credit remaining. Ding explained this to the resident, hinting that she should go purchase a card herself and then collect from the other people in the entryway. But the resident insisted that the RC should, instead, buy cards on the residents' behalf, and she left in a huff when this request was turned down. Ding then called another resident who lived in the same entryway to ask her to go buy an electricity card. She cajoled her, sympathetically: "I know it's a bother, but won't you . . ." The resident declined. Ding and her colleagues were again left to gripe about the thankless and intractable tasks that fall on their shoulders.[32]

All the above incidents tell us something about the power wielded by the RC—or rather, the limitations thereof—precisely because of its thoroughly quotidian nature. Even in the pettiest of requests, for things that would benefit the residents themselves, it is often difficult for the RC to get constituents to accept its suggestions.

Another type of snub to the RC, and a far more significant one, was refusal to provide information, which happened quite frequently. One family refused to give a committee member their telephone number even when she showed up in person to ask for it.[33] Sometimes residents even articulated a principled defense of their right to keep information away from the RC, as in the following case. In the year 2000, rent on publicly owned housing was scheduled for an increase of several hundred percent from its once-nominal level. Low-income families could apply for an exemption, but it was up to the RC to verify their eligibility. The committees did so in part by drawing on their existing knowledge of applicants' circumstances but also by putting up posters around the neighborhood stating applicants' names and their self-reported incomes along with a request that "the masses please exercise surveillance" (*qing qunzhong yu yi jiandu*) and report any apparent discrepancies.

In Dengdao, one resident, a poised and confident stage actor around the age of forty who worked in a drama troupe, came in to pay his cable television bill and asked about the names on the poster outside the office. The greenhorn RC staffer, Wang Xin, explained the need to confirm applicants' suitability for the exemption. The man objected to the term "surveillance by the masses," saying it sounded like something out of the Cultural Revolution. Wang explained that it was the law. The visitor continued with thick sarcasm: "What are we supposed to do, knock on their door and check and see if they're wearing tattered clothing and riding old bicycles?" This was not the masses' job, he said. Wang and her colleague beat a retreat to a fallback position: This is just something we're required to do, they explained. It's just a formality.[34]

Two particularly forthcoming RC members in Wutai explained that this type of sentiment was becoming prevalent in the affluent high-rise neighborhood where they worked. One put it this way: "The residents now want a human right: privacy [*baomi*]. It isn't just one or two residents that want it. They don't think we should do things like they were done in the past." Her colleague Ke Chunrong continued:

> There's a conflict between the policy and the reality. People buy homes here and want privacy. For instance, those in business especially don't want us to know about how many homes they own. The government is still experimenting with the right way to go on policy. In the United States, it's OK to have secrets. But here the state requires us to know the situation of each resident, for instance to do household registry and the census. At the age of fifteen, everyone is

supposed to get an identification card and be registered. But some residents don't want to answer our questions.[35]

This growing notion that a right to privacy trumps the obligation to divulge information is one basis for citizens feeling a sense of power against the RC. Another type of empowerment is residents' taking complaints over the RC's head, to its superiors in the street offices and elsewhere. One vivid example of this occurred in Xianningjie. In the fall of 1999, a pudgy young farmer from the rural suburbs south of Beijing began selling vegetables from a cart he rolled into the neighborhood every morning. After an extended debate among themselves, the committee members decided to take him under their informal sponsorship in the name of providing community service. They would also collect from him a monthly fee of 45 yuan, without consulting or obtaining permission from the street office.[36] This arrangement worked smoothly all winter long, but nine months later the committee found itself in hot water when a resident complained to the street office's letters and visits (*xinfang*) office as well as its city management (*chengguan*) office. The tipster had alleged not only that the produce vendor bribed the RC but also that he overcharged customers by injecting the vegetables with water. This resulted in a furor that the RC defused only after making long and defensive explanations to the street office on the telephone and to a city management officer who showed up in person to investigate.[37]

Not every street office is necessarily so quick to follow up on complaints of RC misbehavior by residents. Moreover, allegations of corruption seemed to be particularly effective at getting the attention of higher authorities, whereas other complaints might elicit a less forceful reaction. Nonetheless, it is notable that in two other sites, RC staff members were fired during the time of my field research as a result of allegations of corruption by constituents.[38] These cases give a sense of the ways in which Beijing residents at least sometimes can avail themselves of mechanisms to check the RCs rather than put up with actions they consider abusive.

Finally, in a number of cases of outright exasperation, residents defied the committees through covert acts of sabotage and even overt action by individuals or groups. Construction activity was often the occasion for vigorous resistance. In two instances, locals ganged up to physically obstruct unwanted or excessively noisy construction projects, in one case blocking the building company from pouring cement.[39] In an older neighborhood where most homes lacked their own bathrooms, controversy erupted over an attempt to rebuild a public bathroom. Here a local entrepreneur who ran a convenience store out of his dwelling had prevailed on the authorities to modify the bathroom next door so that there would be more space separating it from his residence. When other residents realized that the reconfigured facility would have the men's and women's sides facing each other with little privacy, a group of more than ten gathered to stop the workers from completing the job.[40]

Sometimes residents went so far as to issue demands of their own to the neighborhood staff. Fed up with a street-office-sponsored restaurant located near her home because of its noise and dumping of greasy wastewater, a resident mobilized her neighbors to sign a petition calling on the restaurateur to cooperate, and she criticized the RC staff to their faces for failing to do more to support her.[41] A welfare recipient who was angered by being asked to reapply for minimum-income aid threatened to impregnate his wife with a second child, an act that would jeopardize the salary bonuses of not just the residents' committee but the entire staff of the street office.[42] When a housing office closed up a much-used bicycle shed to put it toward commercial purposes, residents threatened the RC that they would knock the building down brick by brick.[43] When the police and RC, seeking to put a stop to a rash of car theft and burglary, put padlocks on one of the gates of a fenced-in neighborhood, inconvenienced residents promptly broke them off.[44]

The behavior recounted here varies from mere foot-dragging at one extreme to serious challenges to authority on the other. Not all of it was directed at the RC itself, as in the case of the bicycle shed and the public bathroom, but such incidents nonetheless represent direct opposition to arrangements that the committee was charged with explaining and defending. Some of these actions were merely situational responses to an inconvenience or a disliked local policy decision that did not necessarily imply opposition to the committees per se. Others were attempts to redress real or perceived abuses committed by the neighborhood organization. Still others represented a fundamental rejection of the premises of some aspects of RC work—for instance, in the case of the actor, the idea that residents have an obligation to report information about their neighbors. Although the meanings of these disparate acts varied, they give an indication of the considerable constraints under which RCs operate. Far from being able to impose their wishes on residents as they please, they must deal with constituencies that are often willful and assertive.

The RC does have the power to nag and harangue. Its members can post insistent notices on residents' doors; accost them in the alley upon running into them; or visit their homes in the evening, repeatedly if necessary. This can be one way of obtaining compliance on minor matters such as the payment of fees or minor quarrels between neighbors. But even in deploying such soft enforcement techniques, the RCs are often constrained by reluctance to offend local sensibilities.

The problem of carrying out the city's dog policies in one neighborhood, Xianningjie, provides a good example. Beijing's dog rules, printed on large, imposing posters that the RCs pasted up in prominent locations, required owners to obtain licenses costing thousands of yuan each—a prohibitive expense for many—and outlawed dogs more than thirty-five centimeters in height. But in many places, Xianningjie included, dog lovers flouted the rules, particularly by neglecting to get licenses. One resident groused to the committee that dog droppings were everywhere and that leashless beasts running around made her child afraid to go outdoors. The RC director admitted that it was embarrassing having regulations so clearly displayed, yet so obviously not upheld, but said that the RC did not wish to offend dog owners in the absence of a strenuous enforcement campaign by the police.[45]

Important as it is to understand the limits of the committees' power and the willingness of many Beijingers to stand up to them, it is also vital to underscore the considerable degree of cooperation they elicit. Everyday compliance, you might say, is as pervasive as everyday resistance.

Anyone stepping into the RC office is potentially subject to questions about themselves or their neighbors—often with equal parts politeness and persistence. One warm morning in March a woman arrived at the Chongxing office on an errand; not recognizing her, the staff began its gentle inquisition. What is your name? Where do you live? The woman answered and informed them that she had just moved into house 4 in courtyard 19. The staff proceeded to ask her more questions and to inquire about the woman who lived on the other side of the courtyard from her; the visitor obligingly answered.[46]

Entirely mundane, this type of interaction is played out again and again on a daily basis. Unlike those who dodge the RC rather than face its questions, or the actor who vocally challenged his committee on even the idea that he should report information about his neighbor, in this case the subject displayed no objection, however she might have felt about the encounter herself. The Chongxing RC not only was able to update the household records but also was able to acquire basic information about the visitor's neighbor without even having to ask the neighbor for it; indeed, probably without the third party ever knowing.

Indeed, for many purposes, we must discard a simple state-versus-society perspective on the micro-level interactions between citizens and their neighborhood committee. Often the office is perceived not as an intruder but as a potential resource. Later chapters elaborate on this as well, but a few examples illustrate this point. In instances in which one resident has aggrieved or irritated another, the latter commonly seeks to enlist the RC as an ally. In one of the high-rise apartment buildings of Anfeng, a controversy broke out in early November 2000 over renovations that a middle-aged male resident undertook on a unit he owned in the building. In violation of explicit rules, his workers tried to dispose of used plaster, boards, and sticky wallpaper by jamming it down the building's trash chute from the fifteenth floor, thus clogging it up. Another resident reported this deed to the RC and identified the man as responsible for the clog. Piqued by this violation, and by having to pay a worker 20 yuan to pick out the obstruction, committee member Hu called the man's home and summoned him to the office. He initially denied responsibility and demanded (unsuccessfully) that Hu identify the witness who had turned him in. After a long argument, Hu's further threat to convene a meeting of all residents from the fourteenth to the sixteenth floors to determine responsibility for the incident led him to stop denying the accusations, although he never paid restitution.[47]

Even the state's forceful suppression of *falun gong* provides vivid examples of the complexity of power dynamics at the ultra-local level. Commencing in July 1999 and continuing for years, this was the most aggressive political campaign in a decade. As James W. Tong makes clear, the assault on the sect comprised multiple coordinated elements. The media sounded a shrill and sustained Klaxon of condemnation. Security forces and the judiciary applied coercive muscle, with thousands of practitioners detained, many sentenced to "reeducation through labor," and uncertain numbers physically abused in custody, in some cases to death. At the same time, an immense but quieter effort, in work units and residential areas, sought to change the minds of Li Hongzhi's followers (Tong 2009).[48] All over Beijing, RCs were mobilized to disseminate official denunciations of the group and to report, monitor, and cajole its adherents.

In the midst of all this—some swayed by the government's education campaign, others reaching their own conclusions—Beijingers had widely varying assessments of the sect. Many viewed it as pernicious, even though the government's heavy-handed crackdown also drew quiet criticism. In two cases that came up in my visits and interviews, families of *falun gong* followers came to RC staff in efforts to shake their loved ones free from this unorthodox and all-consuming faith. In Duzhuang, the committee was instructed by police to look into the circumstances of the several local *falun gong* followers. Committee staff, including my informant, went to visit the home of a woman in her seventies suspected of having joined the sect. She denied it, but later her husband, hoping to turn her away from the group, came to the RC and provided them with evidence of her participation in it: a *falun gong* book, about twelve audio tapes, and a video.[49]

A similar incident unfolded late one Monday afternoon in an RC office across town in Shawan. A middle-aged man came in at his own initiative to talk with the committee staff. He was in despair because his wife had, over the course of three years, become so absorbed in the *falun gong* sect that she was neglecting him, their two sons, her job, and everything else in their lives. She had been arrested at least once recently and apparently had been beaten. Despite this experience, several other believers continued to call her and come by her home, and she continued to go out with them to attend sect activities. Their sons, the husband continued, had begged her with folded hands to give it up, but she refused. She believed that she was impervious to pain; that going to jail for the *falun gong* cause was glorious; and that if she died for her beliefs, she would become a Buddha.

The purpose of the man's visit was to request that the RC take his wife to the police station and scare sense into her by telling her how long she could be put in prison for. He asked that they arrange a time when she and her fellow sect members could be rounded up together. According to his plan, the RC and the police would confront them as a group and ask them whether they would acknowledge that their activities were criminal. This, he felt, might solve the problem once and for all, and it was preferable to simply talking to her in the setting of their home. Their conversation about how to put pressure on his wife continued for the better part of an hour, and eventually the man spoke to the beat cop on the phone about how they would proceed.[50] These episodes are extraordinary in that they involved a particularly intensive political campaign and individuals cooperating with the RC against the wishes of a spouse. But they are also broadly revealing in that they show just how complex power can be at the neighborhood level, whether in such unusual circumstances or in ordinary ones.

Taking into account all of the above examples, we are reminded that RCs form part of a vast and powerful policing apparatus. They help the state acquire fine-grained information about urban society. Fearsome as the state's might can be, residents' individual experiences with its neighborhood extensions are highly varied and usually mundane. Most law-abiding permanent residents of cities like Beijing do not personally encounter the RC intervening in their lives in a political capacity. The RC itself has no direct coercive role; it falls to other state agencies such as the police to provide the actual muscle, should it be called for. This means that its own independent latitude for determining when coercion is applied is limited. The committees themselves have but modest ways of applying pressure to constituents, and often they hesitate even to bring those to bear. Coercion turns out to play surprisingly little role in how the RC handles its everyday duties.

From a regime-based macroscopic perspective, then, there is a sharp contrast between the neighborhood warden and the RCs; the latter's political surveillance and facilitation of policies like the family planning program have no parallel in today's Taiwan. Yet from the alley-level point of view, the contrast in actual power relationships between residents and these state intermediaries is not as stark as one might think.

Special Subpopulations and Requests

What about the organizations' ability to bestow positive favors on cooperative residents? To what extent do people develop clientelist ties with the RCs or wardens, depending on them for significant benefits, rewards, or protections? In both cities, the answer to this question varies among different types of constituents. Most residents are never or only rarely in a position to require special favors or treatment from their neighborhood staff. Yet there are partial exceptions to this.

MIGRANTS

Migrants from rural areas do not constitute a salient category of the *li* system's business in Taipei, as Taiwan's household registration system is designed merely to track where people live, not to deter migration or to deny benefits that are accorded to a protected urban population. In China's major cities, of course, such sojourners from the countryside form an immense and under-privileged group, and helping to monitor them is one task of the residents' committees. Lacking the permanent right to live in the metropolis represented by a local household registry, migrants' position in the metropolis is inherently insecure (Solinger 1999; Zhang 2001). To live and work in Beijing, such people were required to carry at least the forms of documentation known as the three permits: an identity card (*shenfen zheng*), a work permit (*laowu zheng*), and a temporary residence permit (*zanzhu zheng*). Women and girls older than the age of fourteen also needed a certificate indicating compliance with the family-planning policy.[51] Without all required permits, such outsiders could be detained by police and sent back to their home provinces. Though sporadic, enforcement of this was at times quite stringent, especially around certain holidays and sensitive events when the police came under pressure to show the city at its most orderly.

The RCs came into this picture in two important ways. First, although temporary residence permits are issued by the police station, getting one required approval by the residents' committee. The RC often took migrants' applications and delivered them to the police station on their behalf. The criteria for receiving such a permit appeared fairly loose. The main purposes were to compel migrants to show evidence of legitimate employment and housing in the city; to give the administrative apparatus a sense of who the many migrants were and where they lived; and to relieve them periodically of the application fee of 10 yuan. The committees thus channeled the paperwork and also held the potential to influence the approval or denial of applications.[52]

Second, RCs often played landlords, in effect, to migrants who set up shop in one of the handful of rooms or shacks in the neighborhood that the committees might control. Such outsiders typically worked as tailors, barbers, small restaurateurs, or peddlers of fruit and vegetables, providing what could be labeled as community services; generally, they lived as well as worked in their rented space. Street offices kept an eye on this practice and periodically examined the RC's portfolio of migrant businesses and its accounting books to confirm that it was receiving its proper share of the rent. Migrants under the sponsorship of the RC in this way naturally had a vested interest in keeping on the committee's good side. Often they developed long-term relationships in which the RC served as their protector; they, in turn, refrained from making trouble for the committee; acquiesced to its administrative impositions; and provided it with a flow of goods, services, and favors.[53]

One afternoon spent at the Shuangqiao office with Bian Ruiying, a forty-four-year RC veteran, displayed several manifestations of this type of relationship. First she sent a younger staff member over to the street office to deliver a pair of pants that had been repaired free of charge by a migrant tailor who operated under their aegis. Later she held an extended conversation with a cook from Henan who had worked at the restaurant next to the RC office since 1992 and with whom she was well acquainted. The cook, a man in his late twenties with a wife and child, was considering leaving his 2,000-yuan-per-month job to open a clothes stall like many others in the markets lining nearby streets. Bian, savvy to the vicissitudes of the local economy, counseled against it: "None of them are making money, you silly youngster" (*Dou bu zhuan qian, sha xiaozi*). She nonetheless obliged him by giving him a rundown on people at the police substation who might set him up with stall space, and she eventually paged one of them on his behalf using the office phone. Later, Bian spoke with the Preventive Care Department of a nearby hospital regarding a vaccination that a third migrant, like other such temporary visitors, was required to receive. She agreed to find the man who was due for his shots and assured the hospital employee that he would be "well behaved" (*laoshi*), as she had helped him find housing in the past. Bian also promised that police would chase the man away if he or she did not cooperate.[54]

These three minor interactions typify the ways RCs treat the floating population with a mixture of paternalistic solicitude and administrative sternness, and receive gifts and cooperation from them in return. Committees often coached their favorite migrants on when to expect a late-night document-checking raid by the police or what hoops to jump through to get their permits in order.[55] Although permanent residents tended to have their own home phone lines, migrants sometimes relied for telecommunications on the RC's office phone, which often doubled as a pay phone, especially before cellular devices became widespread. The committees, in turn, requested things like having their wives submit to required birth-control checkups. In one case, migrants helped the RC by donating blood that went toward the quota the neighborhood was expected by the health bureaucracy to meet; in exchange, the committee gave them eggs to help them recuperate.[56]

Migrants are by no means abjectly dependent on Beijing's RCs. Mobile by nature, they often pick up roots and travel around to find better combinations of business opportunity, accommodation, and sponsorship. Ming, a young tailor from Zhangjiagang, made an unexpected return to the Shuangqiao office one afternoon in April 2000. Once based in the neighborhood, he had been kicked out by the beat cop because his wife talked back to the officer, and he had also refused to pony up the fee for the temporary residence permit. Despite this past run-in, Ming received the warmest of welcomes from the staff, particularly from Director Fang, who praised his talents to the skies and complained that clothes she had paid others to make since he left fit her poorly. Fang and the others teased him about how he must have lost money while trying to work in other cities, and they began energetically recommending venues available in Shuangqiao where he might set up shop again. They assured him over the course of a long chat that many of his old customers, themselves included, were eager to see him return. Noncommittal, Ming left a phone number where he could be reached at his current operation in Dongsi, a few kilometers away.[57]

The number of migrants living in a Beijing neighborhood may range from a handful to hundreds, depending on rental costs and accessibility to outsiders. But of those, the number who relied directly on the RC for provision of accommodations, the sponsorship of their business, or other kinds of employment was relatively few. Moreover, the utility of the support and cooperation they can provide to the committee is limited. Migrants are useful to the RC as a source of revenue, small gifts like tailoring services, and help with odd jobs. But they are not a group the RC turns to for help in carrying out most of its core responsibilities. Migrants, for instance, were not asked to provide information on permanent residents, who in any event tend to disdain and shun them. In fact, as we will see in Chapter 7, sponsorship of outsiders often turned out to be a political liability for the RC, irritating some of its other constituents and sapping their goodwill.

WELFARE RECIPIENTS

A second category of individuals who might be in a position of dependence with respect to the neighborhood organizations is welfare applicants or recipients. In both Beijing and Taipei, grassroots personnel form part of the system that verifies their eligibility for benefits.

In Taipei, low-income residents, elderly residents with middle to low incomes, and individuals with physical disabilities are among those potentially eligible for monthly subsidies and other forms of state assistance. The role of the neighborhood office is to help the city's Society Bureau determine these people's sources of income and assess whether children or other family members can provide for them. In one case, an elderly woman came to Bai Zhengmin's home office to confer about her welfare benefits. Her husband had divorced her, moved to China, then died; subsequently, she began receiving low-income subsidies. The government, however, discovered through bank records that she had a son and two daughters living in the United States and, presuming that they were sending her funds, moved to cut off her aid. The woman claimed that her children had no ability to support her. After talking to her at length, Bai said that he believed her and would go to the district office to talk to the welfare officials on her behalf.[58]

Thus, a neighborhood leader, whose stamp is required on welfare certifications, might intervene for or against a resident in such circumstances. The warden is hardly in a position to determine the outcome single-handedly, however. The application and verification process also involves the *liganshi*, the civil servant who is responsible for helping to maintain the integrity of the process. Ultimately, Society Bureau staff review the documentation and make the final determination of eligibility.

As part of the Civil Affairs system, China's RCs have always been involved in welfare work. The cases they handle fall into a number of standard categories, including relatives of individuals currently on active military duty (*junshu*), family members of martyrs (*lieshi jiashu*), the disabled (*canji ren*), elderly individuals with no family members or other resources to depend on (*gu lao hu*), and specially disadvantaged households (*te kun hu*). Poor households in Beijing in the year 2000 could be eligible for two main types of state aid: the minimum income guarantee, in which cash assistance was granted to ensure a base monthly income of 273 yuan per household member, and the assistance card, which could be used to acquire around 40 yuan worth per month of oil and cereals at state grain stores.

The residents' committees are responsible for keeping an eye on these special-status households, visiting them periodically and helping them as necessary, and serving as their liaison to the street office. Together with the street office, they organized receptions for all aid recipients at least once per year. Like their counterparts in Taiwan, the RCs also play a role in determining people's eligibility for benefits. Current welfare recipients have their cases reviewed by the street office twice per year, and the RC is responsible for verifying that these individuals do not, for instance, have other sources of income that would render them undeserving of state aid. As the case of the actor mentioned earlier in this chapter indicates, the RC are sometimes called on to assess eligibility for other kinds of benefit programs outside the standard categories managed by the Civil Affairs bureaucracy.

This at least potentially puts the RCs in a position to exercise power over certain types of disadvantaged residents. The committees collect information on such individuals both through home visits and anonymously from neighbors. New and ongoing welfare applicants come to the RC office and make their case for eligibility. They are asked detailed questions about employers and sources of income, dependents and other family members, and all other factors that might be taken into consideration. An RC welfare officer might, for instance, probe into whether a male visitor observed at the home of a single mother was a new spouse who could have income sufficient to support the family.[59]

Sometimes the circumstances of welfare applicants are complicated enough that the RC has to undertake a considerable inquiry. In March 2000, Shao Lihua came to the Shimen office seeking both state aid under the minimum-income guarantee and an exemption from the upcoming rent increase on public housing. Confident and highly articulate, a Christian with a child in middle school, Shao said her former husband refused to make his court-ordered child support payments. After their divorce, the three-room apartment they shared was split between the two of them, with her former husband's brother taking the other half. Finding this situation unpleasant, Shao rented her rooms to a tenant while she and her daughter sought accommodation elsewhere. She earned a mere 462 yuan per month. After an hour-long conversation that delved into various conflicts between Shao and her neighbors, Director Ding asked her to get formal certification of her employment and income situation from her work unit, and to obtain documentation concerning her tenancy from the housing office.[60] Notably, Shao was anything but obsequious or deferential toward the committee; indeed, she regaled them with biblical quotations and references to God's judgment that made them visibly uncomfortable (three of the four members were atheists; the fourth confided to me once that she was a secret believer in Buddhism.) She also did not hesitate to make a grossly politically incorrect reference to former CCP Chairman Mao Zedong in the course of talking about her tiff with the neighbor.[61] Other cases proved that applicants for special benefits could in fact be entirely disrespectful.[62]

Thus in both Beijing and Taipei, neighborhood leaders are not at liberty to make an up-or-down decision about welfare benefits on their own authority. Rather, they serve as preliminary fact finders and advise the relevant higher-level agencies: street offices and (in Shao's case) the housing office in Beijing, and districts in Taipei. Neighborhood leaders have influence, but ultimately these authorities make the final decisions and issue the assistance in question. Further, welfare applicants, far from being at the mercy of neighborhood staff, can appeal to these offices directly if they wish.

HIGH-STAKES DECISIONS

Once in a while, neighborhood organizations became involved—directly or tangentially—in other matters of high value or importance to constituents, such as major assets or special approvals. On two occasions in Chongxing, for example, I observed individuals request help in asserting their right to a contested home. In this older neighborhood, with single-story housing units lying helter-skelter in a maze of alleys, property rights had a special degree of ambiguity to them. Parts of the surrounding area were scheduled to be demolished and rebuilt—although specific plans and timetables were still under debate in the city government and remained obscure to everyone in the neighborhood, including the RC. As bona-fide residents and homeowners stood to receive compensation in the form of cash or replacement housing once the demolition plans went through, the otherwise dilapidated and unappealing courtyards of the neighborhood took on potential value again, bringing old disputes to new life.

A man named Geng, around forty years old with a mustache and a limp, approached the committee, holding in his hand a summons from the district court; he was being sued by a neighbor over the tiny one-room shack he lived in. Thirteen years prior he had rented a room in one of the Chongxing courtyards, although his official place of residence was his mother's home in a nearby neighborhood. While residing in his rented accommodations, he cleaned up a corner of the courtyard where garbage had been piled and built the shack on it, which he used as a kitchen. The neighborhood committee, then under a different director, gave this little project their blessing and considered him to have done a good deed by improving the courtyard's sanitary condition. Later the landlord evicted him from the rented room and he and his wife, a non-Beijinger, moved into what had been his kitchen; now the landlord was suing him to get the shack as well. Because the summons asked him to bring relevant documents to court, Geng explained, he hoped the RC would write him up an affidavit supporting his claim.[63]

A similar incident had unfolded during a previous visit. A seventy-three-year-old man who had never himself lived in the neighborhood spent considerable energy discussing the former home of his aunt. His audience consisted of Liao Limei, a middle-aged committee member distinguished by her rather prickly personality, frumpy perm, and especially her penchant for jean jackets and faux-leather pants. The visitor spared no effort to try to impress Liao with his credentials and connections—he was a Qinghua University graduate, he said; he had friends working in the district government; and he had close connections with none other than Jia Qinglin, he intimated more than once.[64] His aunt, it turned out, had passed away back in the 1960s. In her old age she had entered into a *yanglao songzhong* arrangement, in which another woman would take care of her up until her death, at which point her home would become available for use by her caregiver. This agreement was carried out and the caregiver's relatives continued to live there. Now, decades later, the elderly nephew of the original owner was contesting it on the grounds that there was no written documentation of the deal. The nephew did not make any explicit requests of the RC during this encounter, but it became clear that his purpose was to try to head off an effort by the home's current occupants—who showed up with a lawyer during one of my later visits—to get the RC to verify formally that the *yanglao songzhong* transfer had been real and legitimate. (The man's name-dropping succeeded only in making Liao disgusted with the visitor, as she vocally expressed after his departure.)[65]

These two encounters illustrate that in exceptional circumstances, the RC can indeed find itself called on for support regarding a matter of real importance to the interested parties. But they also show that its actual power to weigh in decisively on one side or the other can be fairly limited. In neither of these two incidents did the RC issue any statements or certifications of its own approval; in fact, its standard practice as dictated by the street office was to turn away all such requests concerning housing matters. The street office and the housing authority prefer to retain for themselves the power to issue documentation, consulting the RC when necessary.[66] In assessing the RC's power vis-à-vis residents, we must take into account that it occasionally may have some input on matters concerning major assets or opportunities but also that even on those rare occasions, its independent authority to influence outcomes is modest.

Years after the above encounters in Chongxing, as of 2010, the neighborhood's seemingly inevitable demolition had yet to take place. Nearby *hutong* areas with similarly decrepit housing such as Xiyingjie, though, had been razed and rebuilt into apartment buildings and stores. The process leading up to the demolition plainly revealed the subservience of the RC relative to the higher powers of the city. The Xiyingjie committee staff, who had no say whatsoever in the fate of the neighborhood, merely went about the emptying alleys, encouraging residents to accept the buyout offers, nagging the few holdouts who sought better deals, trying to answer questions, and helping with paperwork. As in other such cases, the committee itself was essentially disbanded, and its members moved away along with everyone else, although at least one would later return to a new home in the area.[67]

As mentioned in Chapter 2, urban renewal (*dushi gengxin*) projects have picked up pace in Taipei in recent years, although on a scale much smaller than that of Beijing. There, the demolition of a residential building requires a supermajority vote of those who own homes in it. In a neighborhood near one of Taipei's new subway stations, the *lizhang* actively advocated (and implausibly claimed sole credit for) a renewal project that would garner special city subsidies.[68] In other places I visited, wardens played a more passive role, facilitating discussions among developers and groups of residents and providing advice to constituents who sought it. Thus, the neighborhood leaders play a part in the planning and negotiations related to renewal efforts, although decisions are up to the homeowners themselves. Even if they exercise only limited power on such matters as the wrecking and raising of whole buildings, the wardens do wield influence in their localities in many kinds of ways.

Four days after his Taipei neighborhood, Shengfeng, voted him back for a second term, Chen Boyu sat at a table in a small meat-porridge shop with two of his block captains and another resident. In the course of this casual dinner, the store's proprietor, one of the block captains, passed on a message from Fang Jiaqing, the manager of a nearby parking ramp: she wanted to "smooth things over" now that the 2006 elections were complete. "There's nothing to smooth over," Chen said, but he also chuckled: "She really backed the wrong horse [*ya cuo bao*], didn't she?"

Chen's main opponent, Mo Deming, had garnered fewer than six hundred votes against more than one thousand for Chen. Failing to anticipate this lopsided defeat, Fang and a local business group had supported Mo after having repeatedly been denied approval to hold fairs on a public square in the neighborhood. Mo had favored these events, which, though ostensibly charitable in nature, would have brought in as many as forty fee-paying vendors selling food and setting up carnival-style games. Chen calculated that a five-day fair would have generated NT$400,000 (about US$12,000) in revenue for the sponsor, and they could be held as often as once a month. He felt that most of his constituents preferred to be spared the noise and mess of an activity that would have resembled the night markets found in other parts of Taipei. Even a sympathetic *lizhang* would not have the power to authorize the use of public space in this fashion, he explained, but the notary office would send him or her a copy of the application before forwarding it to the parks department, which might be swayed one way or the other. By 2010, an arrangement had been worked out between Chen and Fang's group and approved by the city commerce bureau: occasional weekend-long fairs were held in the square, but vendors paid much lower fees and sold only crafts and secondhand goods, with no food or games. Chen, who said he received no money from these events, judged them to be "healthier" and more suited to Shengfeng Li. By bringing in hungry patrons, they also presented a boon rather than a challenge to local eateries like the porridge shop.[69]

An affluent newspaper editor confided that his warden knowingly signed off on a false statement attesting to his adoption of nonexistent children, affording a tidy tax write-off.[70] One knowledgeable interviewee mentioned that a resident had once asked the *lizhang* for help getting her child into a different school district, and then had become angry when the neighborhood leader refused even to try to wrest this favor from the bureaucracy.[71] As these examples make clear, Taipei's neighborhood leaders vary in their willingness to collude in efforts to bend the rules in such serious ways. In areas like welfare benefits, they are often constrained by oversight mechanisms. Still, on occasion they have more latitude than do Beijing's RCs to offer or deny favors carrying significant monetary or other consequences.

Neighborhood Governance and Independent Initiatives

The final questions to be addressed in this chapter are the following: Can state-backed organizations launch or form partnerships with independent initiatives? Or does government support smother any possibility of independent political action? As noted in Chapter 1, versions of these questions have been addressed by many scholars studying citizens' groups, nonprofit organizations, and related topics.[72] They arise in any assessment of the role of the state in connection with associational activity; the stifling of creative or contentious forms of action is a potentially damning consequence of government sponsorship. In theories of civil society, independence from such suffocating control is at least part of what allows organizations to exercise a beneficial influence. Yet answers may vary. For example, studies of Japan's neighborhood associations have generally highlighted their seemingly ingrained reluctance to step out of line or branch out into activities seeking to influence rather than lend a hand to local government (Broadbent 1998; Pekkanen 2006). An ethnographic study of Indonesia's post-Suharto *rukun tetangga* and *rukun warga*, in contrast, showed them avidly forming partnerships with nongovernmental organization (NGO) activists and submitting joint proposals to donor agencies to support local projects (Kurasawa 2009, 75).

In China's cities, where civil society remains weak and politically suspect, relationships between the RCs and nonstate civic organizations are few and tentative. No such cooperation with NGOs was to be found in any of my Beijing sites throughout the 2000s. The position of RCs in homeowner struggles that have emerged in new housing developments on the city's periphery illustrates the way the system discourages committees from forming alliances with any independent force. Since the mid- to late 1990s, owners in many private neighborhoods have mobilized against property developers and management companies in clashes over issues like construction quality, fees, amenities, and maintenance funds.[73] Like many other localities, the city of Beijing and its district governments have generally taken a negative stance toward homeowner organizations (*yezhu weiyuanhui*, or YWH), particularly those of a feisty nature, even though national policy provides for them. As of late 2000, the city's 860 new neighborhoods had about 180 officially approved YWH. By 2010, according to one well-informed activist, the then roughly four thousand housing developments had some one thousand approved groups, of which only a small minority were democratically elected.[74] Specific circumstances vary, and in some new neighborhoods the homeowner movement emerged before the establishment of an RC. The city instructs the community party committees to assert leadership in matters such as conflicts with management companies and decisions over maintenance. Thus, in these struggles, the committees have stood on the sidelines at best and more generally have acted to impede the formation of independent homeowner groups.

What about in a context far more hospitable to civil society? In Taipei, not only are independent citizen groups better established, but also neighborhood leaders potentially have more latitude to pursue ties with them if they please. Taiwan's capital presents a mixed situation showing patterns that are instructive. Site visits and interviews in Taipei turned up no special conflicts between condominium management committees and the *li* offices, apparently because, under normal circumstances, the two kinds of organizations have every reason to cooperate with each other, if they interact at all. But leaders in other kinds of nongovernmental groups and those in the neighborhood administrative system each understand the other as heading a substantially different form of organization. The two often find themselves in adversarial positions, although they also may cooperate, and sometimes wardens themselves take stands on important local conflicts.

It is not uncommon for the NGOs working on urban issues in Taipei—concerning the environment, the preservation of historical sites, social equality, and other topics—to take a dim view of the wardens who lead the neighborhoods in which they work. For example, activists who had, for many years, led efforts to stop a major housing development on mountain slopes just outside Yangmingshan National Park criticized the several neighborhood wardens involved. Some of the wardens had, at times and to varying degrees, raised concerns about this project, but these tended to be practical and conditional; rather than opposing it outright, they asked how much more traffic would be imposed on the mountain roads, whether water and sewer provisions would be adequate, and so forth. Accordingly, activists saw the wardens as fitting in too snugly with a city government that cut corners on environmental impact assessments and public accountability in its haste to satisfy investors and construction companies.

A member of an organization pushing reforms and improvements to the urban environment said: "From what I've seen, usually the wardens have an attitude of opposition toward social movements. Often that's because what the social movement is trying to accomplish is directly contrary to something he would count as one of his governing achievements [*zhengji*]. He thinks the project is good for his track record."[75] As an example, she cited the case of a set of homes in central Taipei built during the period of Japanese colonization. Activists sought to preserve the buildings, which featured fine yards and trees. The local warden, however, backed plans to take them down and replace them with new housing. For their part, neighborhood leaders sometimes look askance at the NGOs, as seen in these remarks by Chen Boyu concerning one activist organization: "They have some good ideas. But when they do social movements they use some methods I don't like. They encourage people to go demonstrate. It isn't the ordinary people [*laobaixing*] who want such demonstrations, it's the organization there egging them on. And then you have students from the Urban-Rural Institute pushing these projects so they can write about them for their master's theses. They are being used. Why don't they run for election if they want to do these things?"[76]

Ping-Yi Lu, a longtime NGO activist and executive director of Tsuei Ma Ma Foundation for Housing and Community Services, argued that although older, traditional wardens were unlikely to cooperate with civil society organizations on issues involving any controversy, competitive elections were bringing in a new generation of leaders whose attitudes could be different: "Younger *lizhang*, or those who have challenged incumbents, they won because they were better able to attract younger or middle-class people with knowledge or commitment. So they are more open to the kinds of metropolitan issues that we advocate. These kinds of leaders have a different base of support, and so they might have reform agendas for making community life better, and may even cooperate with us. So there's a difference between old and new."[77] His organization and others have, in fact, undertaken a "professional *lizhang*" project intended to train neighborhood leaders who are open to the NGOs' style of civic activism—although they have found that the trainees often lost elections to their more traditional counterparts.

Incumbent or candidate wardens sometimes do take sides and become involved with movements on issues that command a strong consensus in the neighborhood. For example, in the southern reaches of Taipei a large hillside temple planned a tall memorial tower (*lingguta*) in which families would purchase space to store the ashes of their deceased relatives. Backed by KMT politicians, this project was granted a construction permit in 1996. At the time, Yang Xueli was running a noodle shop in the neighborhood, together with his wife. He threw himself into a local effort to oppose the memorial tower, including two marches at which paper funeral money was thrown in protest. Residents were wary of the project for several reasons: a few worried about the impact of the new building on the steep and fragile hillside, whereas others were concerned about the traffic and noise that would result from selling tens of thousands of spaces in a tower rising ten or more stories high. Many felt that the funereal landmark would bring bad fortune. The resistance effort that grew out of these various objections provided a shot in the arm for Yang's career in local politics. Buoyed by months of this campaign, he ran for warden in 1998, losing by only thirty-two votes. He went on to win the office as a DPP candidate in 2003, at which point he joined the previously mentioned resistance to the city government's neighborhood reforms. Meanwhile, the tower project was put on hold, even though the temple continued to advocate for it (Liu 2008).[78]

This example shows that *lizhang* can at least put up not-in-my-backyard-style resistance to outside encroachments—for better or for worse. One led an (unsuccessful) effort to prevent a home for AIDS patients being situated in his neighborhood. Another joined opposition to a development project that would have degraded the mountainside ecology. Yet even this kind of reactive protest is more the exception than the rule. Around the same time as the memorial-tower controversy, an even larger construction project was under way in the vicinity of Yang Xueli's neighborhood: the Maokong Gondola, a cable car connecting the city zoo with an area of the nearby mountainside popular for its teahouses. Yang personally opposed it on environmental grounds but took no action in his official capacity, explaining that he feared being "labeled as undercutting local development": "With a project like the cable car, the ordinary people think it's a positive thing, so it's hard to stop. Some environmental NGOs, like Green Citizens Action Alliance and a community college group, wanted me to ally with them to oppose it. If it just meant taking a bullet, politically speaking, that would have been all right. But I knew I would be slaughtered by heavy artillery if I took that stance. I didn't want to lose my position; I didn't want to be Don Quixote."[79] The four-kilometer-long system went into operation in 2007, reopening in 2010 after an eighteen-month closure caused by typhoon damage.[80]

Just like official neighborhood leaders elsewhere in East and Southeast Asia, *lizhang* are not generally found spearheading social movements. They can be perceived by activists as stodgy or even suspected of taking bribes from moneyed interests like property developers. But Taipei wardens' reluctance to become caught up in single-issue causes also reflects their more extensive democratic accountability relative to that of NGOs. These local leaders have to explain themselves to their entire electorate, or at least a majority of it, rather than just to those individuals who happen to care about a particular topic or grievance. Therefore, they generally weigh in on contentious issues only in ways that do not put them at odds with the wishes of their constituents. There are, however, occasions for them to cooperate with social movement forces on a case-by-case basis, on matters that offer both sides something to gain.

Conclusion

The power dynamics at play at the ultra-local level are subtle, and they vary extensively from individual to individual and from neighborhood to neighborhood, as later chapters explain further. This discussion has shown that Taipei's wardens have considerably greater freedom of action with respect to city government than their Beijing counterparts—they can talk back to officialdom in ways unheard of in China, and they can even pursue efforts to affect significant city-level decisions, at their own initiative or in concert with nongovernmental groups. This distinction is not to be minimized, particularly when assessing the capacities of these systems for civic action. Moreover, the fact that politicians in Taiwan continually seek their favor gives the wardens extra latitude for bending the rules here and there. In comparison, Beijing's RCs are kept on a shorter leash.

At the same time, the actual power relationships into which this translates in everyday dealings with urbanites present less of a clear contrast than might be imagined. The street offices and liaison officers, and the districts and *liganshi*, act as checks on the RCs and wardens. In authoritarian Beijing, some among the permanent, local population certainly encounter the neighborhood organization in ways that feel oppressive to them, but many do not. From residents' perspective, the experience of state power in connection with both of these institutions is occasional, situational, and quite complex. In neither case are neighborhood staff at liberty to defy the wishes of their constituents— certainly not in Taipei, where the shadow of elections always looms, but also not in Beijing, where many residents feel remarkably free to talk back to the committees and blow the whistle on perceived wrongdoing.

In both cities, there is some scope for favors and assistance to certain constituents and not to others. In Beijing, both migrants and welfare applicants are regularly subject to intervention by the RC that could potentially favor or harm them. Migrants in particular, with their status in the city so tenuous and with less chance of circumventing the committee and obtaining support from other government offices, may come to rely on its good graces. In Taipei, welfare applicants may be affected by the position taken on their case by the *lizhang*. Neighborhood leaders in both places, particularly Taipei, sometimes have the power to grant or withhold special treatment on high-payoff matters. It is clear that, in some cases, people in these two groups develop ties with the neighborhood organization that fit within the category of patron-client relationships discussed in Chapter 1. These relationships, in other words, may involve the exchange of loyalty and possibly material support from the subordinate in return for favored treatment on significant matters by the holders of power, in ways that are voluntary, particularistic, and fairly enduring.

Yet this type of patronage is limited both in scope (the fraction of the local population that it encompasses) and in depth (the degree of dependence or interdependence.) Generally speaking, only small subsets of the population might become enmeshed in such patronage relationships in an ongoing way. In neither system do neighborhood organizations themselves have the power to make final decisions on matters such as who will receive state welfare aid and who will not. In both cases, oversight by the civil service constrains these bodies from developing too much arbitrary power. All this is essential background for understanding residents' perceptions of the neighborhood organizations, to which we now turn.

Chapter Five

Perceptions and Interaction

As the previous two chapters have begun to show, the power dynamics between the official neighborhood organizations and their constituents assume many forms in both Beijing and Taipei. A grasp of these basic power relationships makes it possible to pursue answers to one of the fundamental questions posed at the outset: How do individuals perceive, interact with, and respond to these multifaceted organizations? We aim to make sense of their subjective understanding of these ultra-local extensions of state authority.

Many of the things that administrative grassroots engagement (AGE) institutions do on a day-to-day basis are unquestionably beneficial to residents, such as selling bulk-rate household goods, helping to handle certain types of paperwork, or offering advice on how best to approach the state bureaucracy. Others are more ambiguous in their relation to residents' interests. Things like upholding the rules on improvised, sub-code kitchens and sheds or intervening in hallway disputes are welcomed by some and not by others. The residents' committees (RCs) and the wardens make decisions that cannot help but displease parts of their constituencies—for instance, choosing whether to pave over a patch of flat land to turn it into parking spaces or to leave it as green landscaping. Still other aspects of their work inherently run the risk of alienating people, such as requesting sensitive, personal information or blowing the whistle on residents who violate important policies or laws. This is particularly true in the case of China's residents' committees, which engage in a pervasive form of political surveillance—albeit generally in a passive fashion—on behalf of the Communist Party–led government. But as we will see, the highly democratic *lizhang* of Taipei also are sometimes viewed as objectionable.

This chapter begins to examine what local residents think about these bodies, whether and in what ways they interact with their neighborhood leaders, and the micro-level considerations that shape those interactions. The chapter starts by laying out some general findings from a study of China's cities conducted on the eve of the reform era, which form an imperfect but nonetheless important baseline for inquiry today. It presents several quantitative measures of Beijing and Taipei residents' perceptions of and attitudes toward the RCs and neighborhood wardens. Statistical analysis of those measures helps to establish a basic grasp of what factors predict positive or negative assessments. We then turn back to interviews and ethnography first to examine community settings, then for an up-close understanding of those who turn up their noses on, look askance at, or simply disregard these extensions of officialdom. These unfavorable views are dissected to determine what their basis is and what they tell us about citizens' perspectives. With that in mind, we turn in the following two chapters to those who approve of and even embrace the city government's local liaisons.

Urban Life in Contemporary China was the first piece of research attempting to evaluate systematically the ways in which city people looked upon neighborhood-level institutions like the RCs (Whyte and Parish 1984). Serious up-close investigation in Chinese cities was impossible at the time, so the authors instead drew on interviews conducted in Hong Kong with 133 émigrés from the mainland. These interviews took place in 1977–1978; most of the informants had left China in the early to mid-1970s, and thus their impressions reflected experiences during the Cultural Revolution. The sample of interviewees was of necessity subject to potential biases arising from place of origin and selection mechanisms.[1] Nonetheless, this research produced a landmark analysis, one that successfully identified many sociopolitical features of residential neighborhoods that remain recognizable to this day. Although a great deal has also changed since the publication of the book, it provides a conceptual starting point.

In its discussion of the residents' committees, *Urban Life* advanced three basic points relevant to the concerns of this book. First was the finding that RCs, or at least their directors, were fairly unpopular. "In our interviews, about a quarter of our informants saw their residents' committee chiefs as helpful and friendly, another quarter saw them neutrally, and about half saw them as nasty and meddling" (Whyte and Parish 1984, 285). The reason for this mixed but largely dark assessment lay in the second finding: RCs wielded considerable power over their constituents and sometimes used it in oppressive ways, even though they lacked the comprehensive clout of the work unit, which compiled political dossiers and organized criticism sessions during campaigns. "In the 1970s, some residents came to have very strong feelings against their local leaders, especially against leaders who were sticklers for going by the book and constantly reporting suspicious activity to the police" (Whyte and Parish 1984, 284). Third, residents had little ability to check and restrain this power. The authors concluded:

> Neighborhoods, then [in contrast to villages], have not acted as buffers between the individual and the larger political system. . . . [N]eighborhoods also posed a danger if your household register at the ward police station was checked for negative class label and past political problems or if local neighborhood leaders turned against you. There was no way that neighborhood residents could control this aspect of their environment. . . . Even when the neighborhood was essentially neutral, or when neighborhood leaders were helpful individuals, neighborhoods did not represent one's interests or play a buffer role in the larger political arena. Neighborhoods were at best transparent entities between the individual and the state above, and it is perhaps not too surprising as a result that neighborhood structures seemed to generate little enthusiasm, interest, or loyalty among the people in our interviews. (Whyte and Parish 1984, 289–290)

Investigation of China's RCs a generation after Whyte and Parish's work shows that structurally speaking, certain things still accord with the picture they painted. For instance, their metaphor of the state using the committees to seek transparency, if we understand that word to mean unobscured access to important facts about its citizens and their activities, remains apt. It also remains true that thinking of the neighborhood organizations as interest groups would distort their actual nature. Yet on each of the three points identified above, things today look considerably different. As Chapter 4 indicated, for the most part, RCs no longer possess much arbitrary power to bring political oppression down onto the heads of urbanites. Residents have little formal power to check and restrain the committees, yet in practical terms they can and do speak up if they feel they are not being treated fairly. And at least in

Beijing, popular opinion about the organizations is not skewed toward the negative; instead, negative perceptions are in the minority.

Whyte and Parish's schema highlights political threat, and its opposite, buffering or protection from such menaces, as driving popular perceptions. This is plausible for Mao-era China, and it dovetails with the mass-organization models. But it leaves us less prepared to understand opinion in contexts in which such threats are rare or entirely absent. In today's China, where political repression takes (relatively speaking) narrowly targeted and predictable forms, the category of people for whom neighborhoods' complicity in repression looms as a large concern is correspondingly smaller. Still more in settings like Taiwan, or other postauthoritarian countries in which political dangers are largely a thing of the past, do different sets of considerations hold sway.

Evidence from the Surveys

Several sets of figures from the 2001 Beijing Law and Community Survey and the 2006 Taipei Neighborhoods Survey allow us to sketch the overall contours in public perceptions of the two cities' official neighborhood organizations. They show the range of attitudes that people hold toward these local leaders, from highly positive to highly negative, and illustrate in a rough way how the population is distributed among these various opinions.

Figure 5.1 presents the results from a simple question assessing approval or disapproval of the respondent's RC or neighborhood warden. In both Beijing and Taipei, just more than 60 percent in each capital answered that they were fairly or very satisfied. A little more than one-quarter of respondents, about 26 percent, gave a negative or neutral response. In both cities, responses overwhelmingly clustered toward the middle of the scale rather than the extremes; only a handful of people expressed particularly strong opinions about their neighborhood leaders, whether in a positive or in a negative direction. In Beijing, more than 15 percent volunteered a neutral response.[2] The pattern is similar to that seen in Figure 3.3, with roughly the same distribution—a majority of favorable responses and a minority of unfavorable ones—found in both cities.

A further question sought to measure how useful the neighborhood organizations are thought to be—or, put the other way, their perceived dispensability. Beijingers might, for example, feel a grudging acceptance of the RCs,

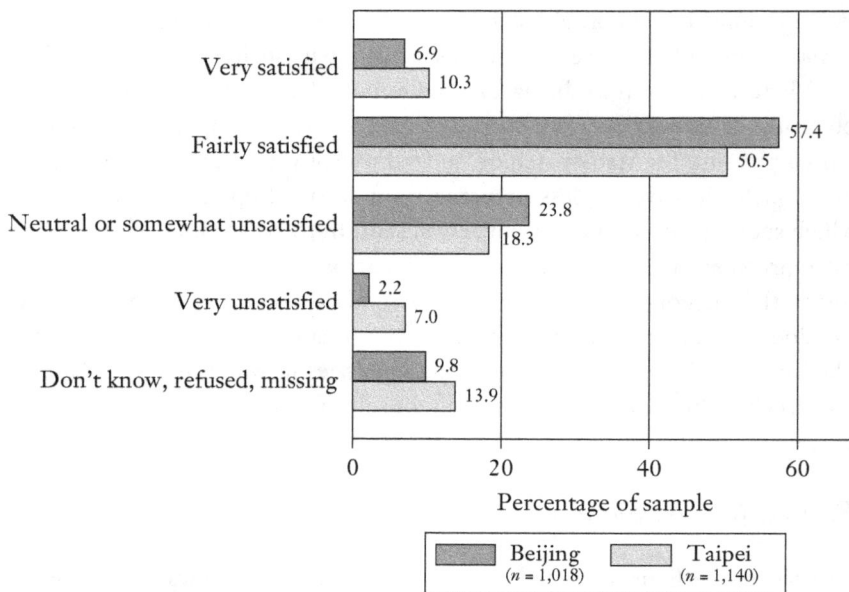

Figure 5.1.   Satisfaction with specific neighborhood organization.
Data are from the 2001 Beijing Law and Community Survey and the 2006 Taipei Neighborhoods Survey.

but only because they are a constitutionally mandated feature of the urban world that individual citizens could hardly do away with even if they wished to. The wording of this question posited the existence of a neighborhood without a residents' committee or a neighborhood warden and asked whether the absence of this institution would cause "trouble" (Figure 5.2). Here the responses show a meaningful difference between the two locales. In Beijing, almost 70 percent chose one of the two answers on the side of the scale corresponding to a perception of usefulness, that "some problems" or "big problems" would result from not having an RC. Only 6 percent opined that such a situation would not cause any problems. In Taipei, though, respondents were almost evenly split, only slightly favoring the two more useful (49 percent combined) over the two less useful (45 percent) responses. More than a quarter there felt that the absence of a warden would pose no problem at all. The Beijing average was an entire half point higher on a scale from 0 to 3. The survey results in Beijing accord with findings of other researchers who

What if there were no RC or NW?

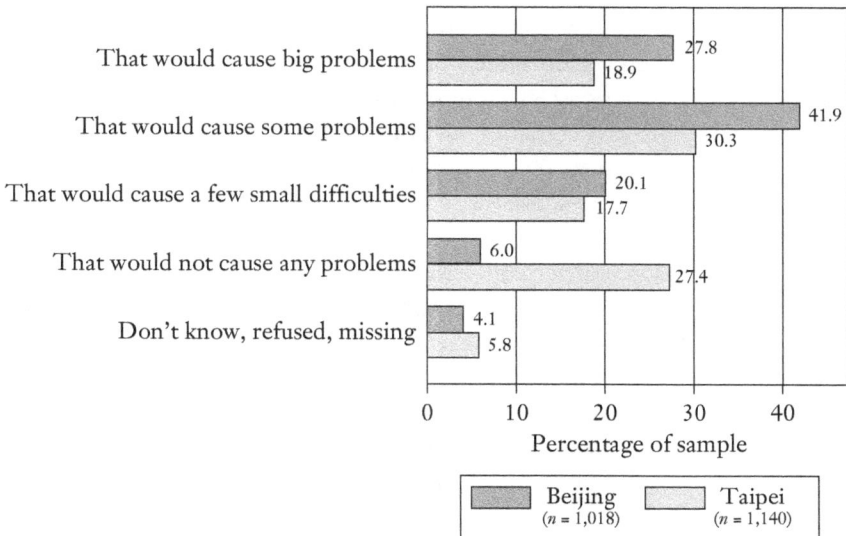

Figure 5.2.   Perceived usefulness of neighborhood system.
Data are from the 2001 Beijing Law and Community Survey and the 2006 Taipei Neighborhoods Survey.

have identified substantial support for these neighborhood institutions (Chen, Lu, and Yang 2007).

In Taipei, interviewees were also asked directly whether they felt that the warden system should be maintained or done away with. Fully two-thirds of respondents favored keeping the system when asked that question outright.[3] Twenty-four percent said that the system should be abolished. This basic distribution of opinion about the neighborhood warden is not idiosyncratic to Taipei alone. The 2004 national survey sponsored by the Ministry of the Interior, first mentioned in Chapter 3, found an overwhelming preponderance of support for both the *lizhang* system and its rural counterpart, the *cunzhang* system. Among 877 city dwellers around the island, 19 percent stated that they would like to see the warden system abolished, and 74 percent wanted it maintained.

As previous chapters have shown, Beijing's RCs undertake a number of administrative and security functions that Taipei's wardens do not. At times, they even request help from residents in pursuing some of these activities, and they may ask residents for information about their neighbors. Therefore, in the Beijing survey, a special set of four questions was asked to ascertain residents' willingness to cooperate with their residents' committee in various ways. All four questions asked about things that fall in the scope of the committees' real day-to-day activities, and they followed a pattern of increasing sensitivity. The first question was designed to be something wholly innocuous: helping the RC with a task that could be of benefit only to the neighborhood's residents. It involves not the disclosure of information to the RC, but rather providing general assistance to it. The remaining questions inquired about willingness to provide information. Telling the RC about a dispute between neighbors, as posited in the second question, could well be interpreted as doing the disputing parties something of a favor, perhaps leading to intervention that might resolve the conflict. The third question asks about willingness to disclose to the RC information about the identity or household registry status of a neighbor. Finally, the fourth question poses the possibility of providing information that could be truly damaging to one's neighbor, who might lose his or her welfare benefits as a result. For each of the questions, interviewees were asked about their willingness to "cooperate with the work of the Residents' Committee," with four answer categories ranging from "certainly willing" to "certainly unwilling," as well as a neutral category that was accepted but not offered.[4]

The results of the questions on cooperation are presented in Figure 5.3. Again, one should bear in mind that these are hypothetical scenarios rather than real-life occurrences, and they cannot be taken as reports on actual dealings with the RC. Still, they are useful as one more indicator of people's general orientations toward the neighborhood groups. For the most benign of the questions, the one concerning vaccinations, more than 73 percent of the respondents declared themselves somewhat or certainly willing to help the RC. As the questions moved farther toward matters that potentially or certainly encroached on neighbors' privacy, the expressed willingness to cooperate dropped off. About 33 percent suggested that they would turn in a welfare cheat to the RC, the most demanding measure of the four. This gives us another glimpse of the multiple perspectives in the Beijing populace concerning where the line falls between an obligation to help the committees and an obligation to respect others' privacy. No comparable questions were asked in Taipei, partly because gathering information for the state is a less central part

Willingness to assist RC in four hypothetical scenarios

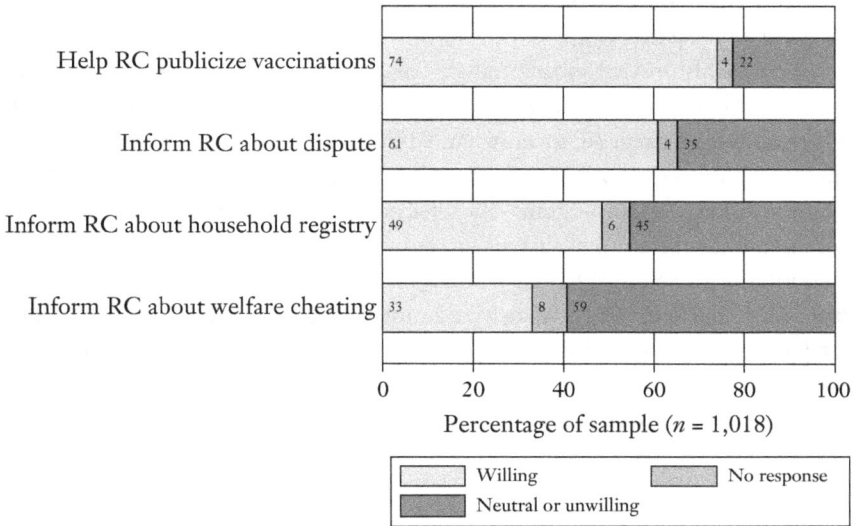

Figure 5.3.   Willingness to cooperate with RC.
"Certainly willing" and "perhaps willing" answers were collapsed together, as were
"neutral," "perhaps unwilling," and "certainly unwilling" answers. Data are from the 2001
Beijing Law and Community Survey.

of the duties of the neighborhood wardens, but data presented in the following
two chapters offer insight into related issues of public versus private interests.

In summary, the survey data presented here paint a broad-brush picture of
what residents of the two cities think about these institutions of administrative
grassroots engagement. This picture helps define the explanatory task of the
remainder of this book. The first key point is that opinion varies significantly
from person to person—there are those who embrace the RCs and neighborhood wardens and those who are thoroughly put off by them. This was also
the case in Whyte and Parish's findings from their 1970s research, although
their study, a wide-spectrum overview of the urban environment, focused on
the modal perceptions rather than on explaining variation. Yet in both Beijing
and Taipei, residents are far from unanimous in their views on these organizations; we must examine and explain this variety of opinion rather than setting
it aside. The diversity of perspectives that respondents express challenges, or

at least complicates, any notion of overwhelming community harmony, or cultural consensus—ideas that, as Chapter 1 noted, sometimes figure centrally in accounts of local life.

The data also reveal substantial similarities in the distribution of attitudes on the part of residents of Beijing and Taipei toward these organizations. This comes as a surprise, given what, to institutionally oriented political scientists, would seem to be fundamental differences between the RC and the neighborhood warden systems. As Chapters 3 and 4 have made clear, Taipei's neighborhood organizations are subject to a high degree of democratic accountability. Beijing's fall far short of that, and they play a role in political repression and seemingly intrusive administrative programs. In spite of this, the basic contours of opinion in the two capitals share a striking resemblance, with a majority supportive of the neighborhood system and a minority cool toward it. This, too, requires explanation.

Explaining Individual-Level Variation: A First Cut

Basic statistical analysis on some of the variables presented in the previous section offers a way to begin addressing this puzzle. Regression models estimated on respondents' attitudes toward neighborhood organizations shed light on what kinds of people tend to feel closer to these institutions and what kinds more remote from them. Two separate analyses are reported here. In Table 5.1, the dependent variable combines a respondent's assessment of his or her specific RC or warden in terms of general satisfaction and perceived representative efficacy (see Figures 3.3 and 5.1). In Table 5.2, the dependent variable is respondents' assessment of the usefulness of the system overall (see Figure 5.2). The coefficients on the two sides of the table—those for Beijing and those for Taipei—are not strictly comparable with each other, as there are differences in the models and in some of the survey question wordings. Still, it is possible to compare which factors prove significant, their signs, and their magnitudes relative to others in the same model. As it turns out, broad similarities emerge between the models for the two cities.

Among demographic characteristics, socioeconomic class emerges as an important predictor of individuals' attitudes toward the RCs and the wardens. In both cities, the neighborhood organizations tend to have somewhat more salience among lower-class rather than upper-class respondents, if income is

TABLE 5.1

Predicting evaluation of respondent's specific RC or NW: OLS regressions

BEIJING			TAIPEI		
Variable	*Coef.*	*SE*	*Variable*	*Coef.*	*SE*
DEMOGRAPHIC			DEMOGRAPHIC		
Female	0.046	(0.045)	Female	−0.026	(0.056)
Age	0.003	(0.003)	Age	0.002	(0.003)
Education, years	0.000	(0.008)	Education, years	−0.021*	(0.010)
Income, 2006 USD (1000s)	−0.384**	(0.147)	Income, 2006 USD (1000s)	−0.035	(0.018)
Retired	−0.126	(0.068)	Retired	0.290**	(0.111)
Homeowner	0.071	(0.048)	Homeowner	0.010	(0.075)
White-collar job	−0.028	(0.050)	White-collar job	0.063	(0.061)
Size of household	0.050	(0.031)	Subethnicity: Mainlander	−0.001	(0.111)
Life satisfaction	0.052*	(0.025)	Subethnicity: Minnan	0.029	(0.095)
Single rather than married	0.152*	(0.075)			
POLITICAL AND ADMINISTRATIVE			POLITICAL AND ADMINISTRATIVE		
Approval: Police and courts	0.194***	(0.027)	Trust in city government	0.189***	(0.043)
CCP or CYL member	0.034	(0.053)	Party ID: Pan-Blue	0.079	(0.071)
Correct household registry	0.066	(0.061)	Party ID: Pan-Green	0.058	(0.082)

(continued)

TABLE 5.1 (*continued*)

BEIJING			TAIPEI		
Variable	*Coef.*	*SE*	*Variable*	*Coef.*	*SE*
SOCIAL			SOCIAL		
Years in neighborhood (log)	−0.023	(0.033)	Years in neighborhood (log)	−0.005	(0.042)
Neighbors known (log)	0.023	(0.023)	Neighbors known (log)	−0.053	(0.032)
Sociability: Associations	0.032	(0.026)	Sociability: Associations	0.103***	(0.027)
			Generalized trust	0.116***	(0.034)
NEIGHBORHOOD			NEIGHBORHOOD		
High-rise building	−0.128	(0.087)	High-rise building	−0.191**	(0.072)
1- or 2-story building	0.246***	(0.051)	1- or 2-story building	−0.027	(0.097)
Neigh. avg. income, 1000s yuan	0.137**	(0.053)	Low-income pop. in li	−0.001**	(0.000)
			Area of li, km^2	0.000	(0.001)
			Age of warden	−0.007*	(0.003)
Constant	0.691**	(0.255)	Constant	1.425***	(0.306)
Observations	738		Observations	665	
R^2	0.157		R^2	0.144	

NOTE: The outcome variable is an index combining the respondent's satisfaction with his or her neighborhood organization together with his or her assessment of its ability to represent constituents. Separate models were estimated for Beijing and Taipei, and not all predictor variables were the same for both cities. Robust standard errors were used in Beijing because of clustering by neighborhood.

*$p < 0.05$. **$p < 0.01$. ***$p < 0.001$.

TABLE 5.2

Predicting usefulness of RC and NW system: Ordered probit regressions

BEIJING

Variable	Coef.	SE
DEMOGRAPHIC		
Female	-0.036	(0.085)
Age	0.009	(0.006)
Education, years	0.023	(0.016)
Income, 2006 USD (1000s)	-0.654*	(0.258)
Retired	-0.025	(0.124)
Homeowner	0.235**	(0.091)
White-collar job	-0.018	(0.098)
Size of household	0.157**	(0.052)
Life satisfaction	0.144**	(0.046)
Single rather than married	0.182	(0.152)
POLITICAL AND ADMINISTRATIVE		
Approval: Police and courts	0.492***	(0.053)
CCP or CYL member	-0.019	(0.102)
Correct household registry	0.130	(0.119)
SOCIAL		
Years in neighborhood (log)	-0.159*	(0.063)
Neighbors known (log)	0.023	(0.040)
Sociability: Associations	0.125*	(0.051)

TAIPEI

Variable	Coef.	SE
DEMOGRAPHIC		
Female	0.057	(0.086)
Age	-0.010*	(0.004)
Education, years	-0.007	(0.015)
Income, 2006 USD (1000s)	-0.079**	(0.027)
Retired	-0.016	(0.176)
Homeowner	0.080	(0.113)
White-collar job	0.160	(0.095)
Subethnicity: Mainlander	-0.196	(0.173)
Subethnicity: Minnan	-0.107	(0.151)
POLITICAL AND ADMINISTRATIVE		
Trust in city government	0.200**	(0.066)
Party ID: Pan-Blue	0.274*	(0.108)
Party ID: Pan-Green	0.122	(0.127)
SOCIAL		
Years in neighborhood (log)	-0.003	(0.065)
Neighbors known (log)	0.039	(0.049)
Sociability: Associations	0.130**	(0.042)
Generalized trust	-0.058	(0.052)

(continued)

TABLE 5.2 (continued)

	BEIJING				TAIPEI	
Variable	Coef.	SE	Variable		Coef.	SE
NEIGHBORHOOD			NEIGHBORHOOD			
High-rise building	0.203	(0.152)	High-rise building		-0.199	(0.108)
1- or 2-story building	0.128	(0.094)	1- or 2-story building		0.202	(0.150)
Neigh. avg. income, 1000s yuan	-0.123	(0.098)	Low-income pop. in li		-0.001*	(0.000)
			Area of li, km^2		0.001	(0.001)
			Age of warden		0.007	(0.005)
Cut point 1	-0.275	(0.482)	Cut point 1		-0.079	(0.474)
Cut point 2	0.811	(0.479)	Cut point 2		0.499	(0.474)
Cut point 3	2.125***	(0.483)	Cut point 3		1.478**	(0.476)
Observations	770		Observations		697	
Pseudo-R^2	0.092		Pseudo-R^2		0.030	

NOTE: The four-way outcome variable derives from a question assessing the respondent's perception of the usefulness of the neighborhood administrative system, as described in the text. Separate models were estimated for Beijing and Taipei, and not all predictor variables were the same for both cities. Robust standard errors were used in Beijing because of clustering by neighborhood.

*$p < 0.05$. **$p < 0.01$. ***$p < 0.001$.

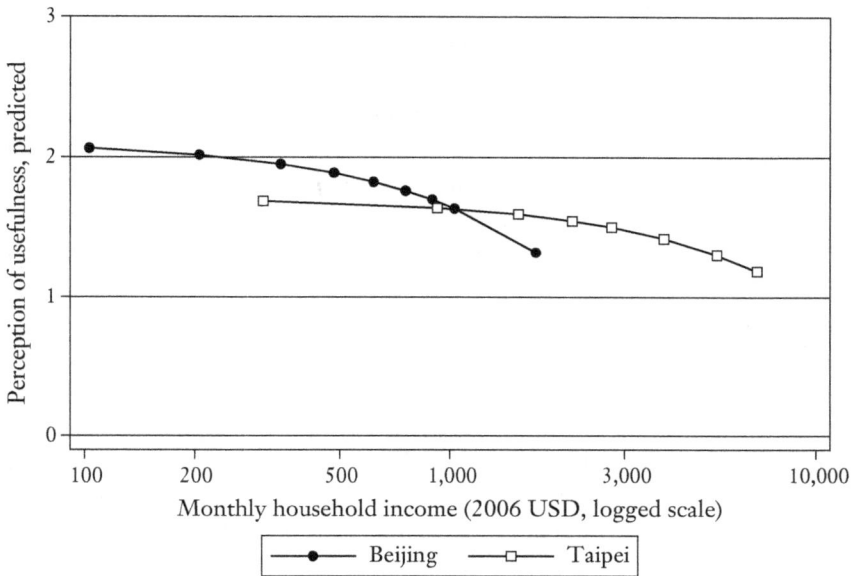

Figure 5.4. Perceived usefulness of RC or NW system, by income.
Data are from the 2001 Beijing Law and Community Survey and the 2006 Taipei Neighborhoods Survey.

taken as a proxy for class. This is shown in more detail in Figure 5.4, which displays this result in graphical form. On the basis of the regression models, predicted values of perceived usefulness of the RC or neighborhood warden for respondents of different income levels were separately calculated for the Beijing and Taipei data sets and plotted together.[5] As we observed in the previous section of this chapter, residents of China's capital see a substantially higher degree of usefulness in the system overall; most of the circles lie above all the squares. In Beijing, the perception of usefulness declines more sharply at the higher income levels. Chapter 7, in particular, illustrates why this is so. This finding resonates with other Asian cases, as well. Studies of Indonesia, for example, make clear that Indonesia's *rukun tetangga* system of ultra-local administration is much more prominent and deeply embedded in lower-class *kampung* while playing a quieter role in wealthier areas (Kurasawa 2009, 60, 68; Guinness 2009, 33).

To abstract from the data a bit further: poorer Beijing residents tend to strongly favor the kind of state paternalism that the RC system embodies; affluent Beijingers do, too, but their support is somewhat softer. In Taipei, by contrast, attitudes are much more constant across poorer and wealthier groups. There, in the context of a society that is relatively well-off overall, an individual's perception of the neighborhood governance system has less to do with where he or she lies on the income scale.

One would expect older respondents to have more favorable assessments of these institutions than younger ones, given the greater importance of the neighborhood environment to many elderly people, as well as the fact that neighborhood organizations in both cities have programs and activities targeted to them. Yet the data show otherwise; in three of the models age has no linear relationship to these attitudes, and in one case it has a slight negative correlation.[6] In Beijing, those with larger households tended to find the RC system more useful, perhaps because they have more occasions to seek its assistance. Other demographic variables had little predictive value. In Taipei, mainlanders' orientations toward the *li-lin* system did not differ, statistically, from those identifying as Minnan or Hakka.[7] As we saw in Chapter 2, the neighborhood institutions have a strongly gendered character, both historically and currently, beginning with the fact that it is mostly men in Taiwan, and mostly women in China, who lead them. But this does not mean that male and female respondents had different attitudes toward incumbents or toward the institution as a whole; gender was not statistically significant in any of these models.

Political factors are the next important category of predictor variables. In Beijing, perhaps surprisingly, Communist Party or Youth League members were no more likely than others to have a positive perception of the RCs. Although there could be more than one explanation for this, it must partly reflect the fact that—notwithstanding community party building as discussed in Chapter 2—the committees are not generally viewed as a crucial element of the Communist Party per se. In Taipei, in contrast, individuals' party identification does make some difference. As Table 5.2 and Figure 5.5 show, loyalists of the pan-Blue parties see somewhat more utility in the *lizhang* system than do others. The figure's bottom bar shows the distribution of the full sample on the question of whether the warden system should be abolished or kept, whereas the three bars above represent subsamples broken down by respondents' stated party preference. As noted earlier in the book, *li*-level gover-

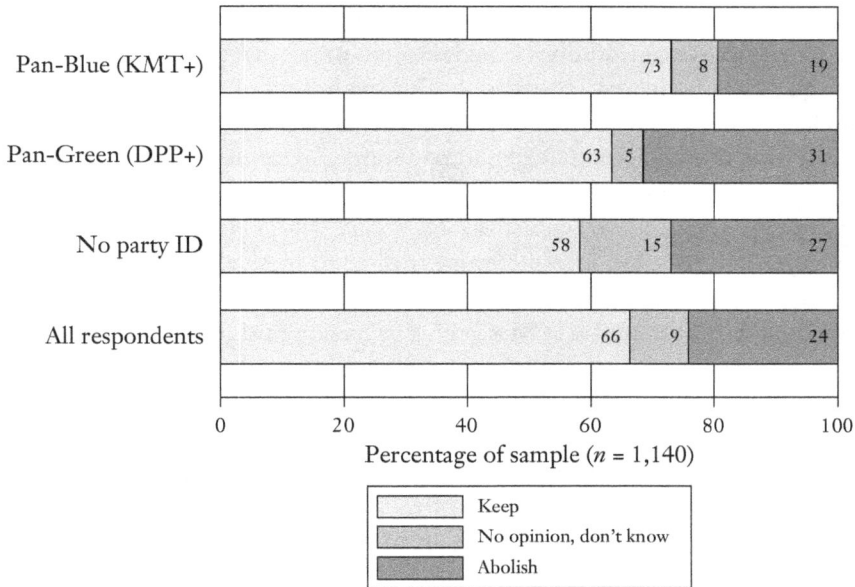

Figure 5.5.   Keep or abolish neighborhood warden system, by party ID.
Data are from the 2006 Taipei Neighborhoods Survey. Percentages on bars do not all sum precisely to 100 percent as a result of rounding.

nance has historically been a mainstay of Kuomintang (KMT) mobilization, and the Nationalists continue to enjoy disproportionate success in cultivating supporters in these grassroots positions, even if that edge has eroded considerably. One might expect, therefore, a sharp partisan divide in residents' attitudes toward the neighborhood warden system as a whole. These data indeed show a gap; a greater fraction of pan-Blue citizens (73 percent) than pan-Greens (63 percent) favored maintaining the network of *lizhang*. Still, the system enjoys broad support from citizens on both ends of the political spectrum, and even majority support among nonpartisans, the subgroup that expressed the most indifference to it.

Among political variables, more significant than party affiliation are attitudes toward government in general. This factor was operationalized through an index of attitudes toward police and courts in the Beijing case and a question measuring trust in city government in the Taipei case. In both cities, these factors have a strong and positive relation to each dependent variable.

Of course, on one level, it is to be expected that an individual's general attitudes toward state institutions would color his or her perceptions of a particular quasi-governmental organization. But the impact of this factor deserves underscoring. Taken with the other political findings, it indicates that orientations toward the RCs and neighborhood wardens are strongly bound up in a broader set of attitudes concerning state more than party.

Variables related to individual sociability and neighborhood context emerge as perhaps the most noteworthy of all in these analyses. Those who are joiners, frequently taking part in associations (*shetuan*) outside the neighborhood setting, tend also to be warmly disposed toward their RC or warden.[8] In both cities, those living in low-rise rather than more anonymous high-rise housing also had more favorable assessments of their neighborhood organizations.[9] Such general patterns suggest that these institutions operate in ways that dovetail with other networks of association.[10] They signal the need to understand state-organized systems of administrative grassroots engagement in a social framework, precisely as Chapters 6 and 7 do, given that human ties figure so centrally in their workings.

Statistical analysis, then, points to three basic factors shaping individuals' attitudes toward these organizations: class, politics, and sociability. Although the results from Beijing and Taipei vary in some details, broadly speaking, these factors apply in parallel ways in both cities. In other words, there are strong general similarities between the kinds of people who approve of the RCs and the kinds of people who approve of the neighborhood wardens. Quantitative correlational analysis can take us only so far. Individuals vary in their attitudes, and these models explain less than 20 percent of this variation. The statistical models have given us a start, a valuable sense of what patterns hold up to rigorous evaluation and where we should look for answers. For deeper understanding, we turn back to qualitative data, after first grounding the perceptions reported here in a more concrete picture of the contexts that give rise to them.

Profile of Interaction with Constituents

The RCs and the wardens succeed or fail in creating a positive image and relationship with residents largely on a person-by-person basis, hence the focus in much of this book on individual-level analysis. In the same neighborhood, different people often have highly divergent views of the committee or the warden. The RCs' customary style of operation, in which, for the most part, they deal with ordinary constituents one by one rather than collectively, works to reinforce the individualistic nature of people's responses. As we will see, Taipei's wardens engage with their communities in group settings—at social gatherings, during elections, at public hearings—somewhat more often, yet even so, residents' personal perceptions of the same leader vary greatly. Even more fundamentally, individual residents differ widely in the degree to which the neighborhood in which they live figures in their social landscape and daily life. This commonplace fact has profound consequences for the RCs and the *li* offices, which stay in far closer touch with some constituents (e.g., those who spend their work or leisure hours in the locality, those who have deep family or associational ties to it) than others. Data from the Beijing and Taipei surveys illustrate this, providing a detailed profile of residents' contact with and knowledge of their neighborhood organizations.

A rough measure of the degree of interaction that Beijing respondents have with the RCs is the number of neighborhood staffers with whom they have a personal acquaintance. Table 5.3 shows the number of committee members that the respondents in the sample report knowing, with knowing defined in the questionnaire as having spoken to them before. About three-quarters of everyone who was asked reported having the acquaintance of at least one member of his or her local residents' committee. Sixty percent knew at least two people on the committee, whereas at the other end of the distribution, one-fifth of the sample had met none at all. Overall, the large proportion of those who do know RC members provides a striking measure of the institution's continued salience.

In Taiwan, with but a single leader in each *li*, the same measure would not provide a useful comparison. Instead, familiarity was measured as follows. Early in the interview, residents were asked which *li* they lived in; more than nine out of ten were able to state the name of the official neighborhood in which they resided. In a later question, the interviewers asked for the name of the warden and assessed the match between the stated answer and the actual name of the elected leader of the respondent's neighborhood. This question was a demanding test of people's local political knowledge, as they had no practical way of feigning to know this if they in fact did not. As Table 5.3 shows, more than two-fifths of respondents knew the full name of the warden, and a full 58 percent could correctly state either the family or the given name.

TABLE 5.3
Familiarity with neighborhood leaders

(Beijing) How many of the staff members of this neighborhood's residents' committee do you know?	Respondents (%)
Zero	16.1
One	14.5
Two	20.8
Three	14.6
Four	8.2
Five	9.3
Six	4.0
Seven or more	6.0
Refused or didn't know	6.4
n	1,018

(Taipei) May we ask if you know the name of the warden in [respondent's neighborhood]? Could you tell us his or her name?	Respondents (%)
Correctly stated warden's full name	42.6
Knew only warden's given name or surname	15.3
Could not state warden's name	41.5
Refused or missing	0.6
n	1,140

SOURCE: 2001 Beijing Law and Community Survey, 2006 Taipei Neighborhoods Survey.

NOTE: The survey question defined knowing an RC staff member as having spoken to him or her before.

These results make clear that for a majority of Taipei residents, the identity of their state-defined community and its leader is not an obscure triviality but something of which they are well aware. This contrasts with at least one study from the United States, which found frequent discrepancies between neighborhood names used by the government and those used by the people living in them (Crenson 1983, 28–29).

We saw in Chapter 3 that people with lower levels of education were considerably more likely to vote in warden elections than were those with more schooling. Figure 5.6 shows that—in both Beijing and Taipei—the same kind of class-based skew applies to people's general degree of acquaintance with the official system of neighborhood organization. Among even college-educated residents of Taipei, roughly half were able to come up with some part of the *lizhang*'s name, and in Beijing, no sample subgroup knew, on average, fewer than two RC members. Still, it is clear that those with less schooling know relatively more about their neighborhood leaders. Once again, we see that

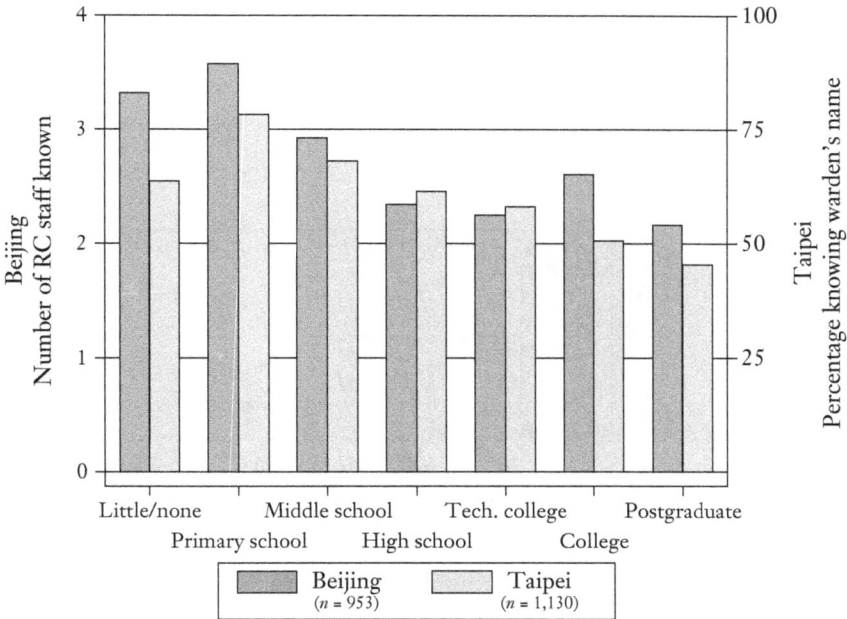

Figure 5.6.   Familiarity with neighborhood leaders, by education.
Data are from the 2001 Beijing Law and Community Survey and the 2006 Taipei Neighborhoods Survey.

AGE systems in China and Taiwan, as in other countries, appear to be grounded most firmly in lower social strata. Those with higher levels of education are less in touch with neighborhood-level administration.

So far, we have seen that majorities have at least a passing acquaintance with these local leaders. But we also want to know how frequently residents come into actual contact with their neighborhood organizations. The survey data show that, all told, a substantial amount of interaction takes place between RCs or *lizhang* and those they administer—but also that great variation exists from person to person. For a two-year period, the median number of contacts with RC members that Beijing residents reported was six, whereas the corresponding figure for Taipei was two (the mean number of contacts was much higher, forty-four in both of the cities, reflecting the weight of those at the high end of the distribution). Figure 5.7 presents a visual breakdown of the distribution. Perhaps the most immediately striking thing about

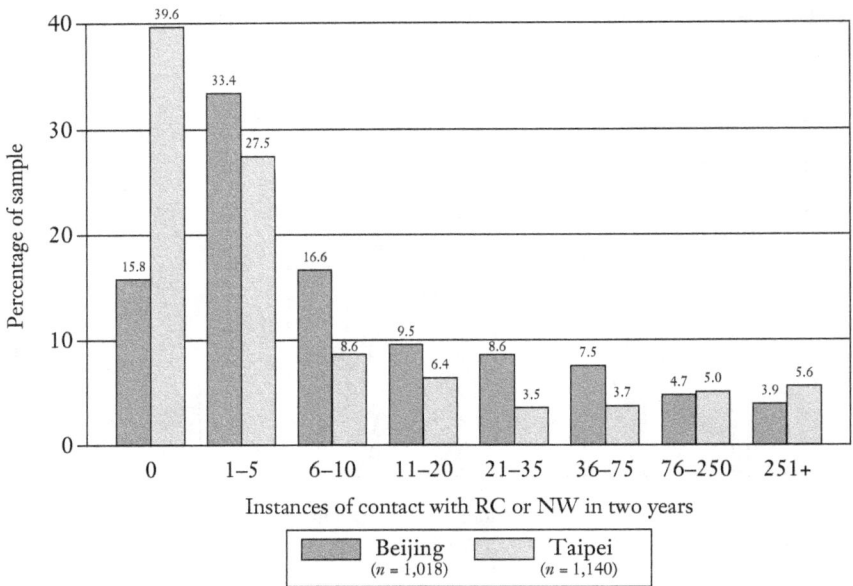

Figure 5.7. Frequency of contact with neighborhood leaders.
Data are from the 2001 Beijing Law and Community Survey and the 2006 Taipei Neighborhoods Survey.

this figure is the difference between the two cities in the proportion of the sample that had no contact at all with the neighborhood leadership. In Beijing, fewer than 16 percent had no contact in two years, whereas in Taipei, nearly 40 percent belonged to that category, a gap that discussion later in this book aims to explain.

Conversely, Figure 5.7 shows that more than 80 percent of the Beijing sample (59 percent in Taipei) reported some degree of contact with the neighborhood organization in the previous two years. For many residents this is sporadic and infrequent. But in Beijing around 30 percent reported contact with an RC staff member at least every other month or so, and in Taipei about 24 percent said the same regarding their *lizhang*. The thick tails in the distributions illustrate that a considerable fraction of citizens has quite frequent interaction with these organizations—yet there are also significant numbers who remain wholly distant from them, even more so in Taipei than in Beijing. The data show the vast presence of grassroots engagement as an inter-

In your relationship with the RC or NW . . .

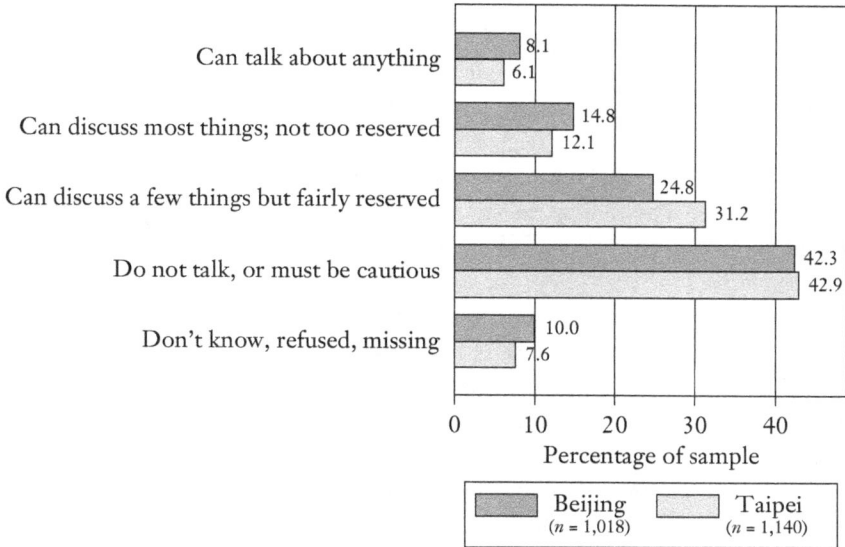

| | Beijing (*n* = 1,018) | Taipei (*n* = 1,140) |

Figure 5.8.   Openness with neighborhood leaders.
Data are from the 2001 Beijing Law and Community Survey and the 2006 Taipei Neighborhoods Survey.

face between state and society: though uneven and far from universal in their reach, these institutions are at least loosely in touch with large numbers of constituents.

Figure 5.8 reports results from a question, asked in both cities, aimed to determine how open or trusting respondents were toward their neighborhood leaders. This was, by design, a question containing an ambiguity on one end of the answer scale: a negative answer could either mean a lack of contact with the neighborhood organization or a lack of openness toward it.[11] Given the question wording—the most open answer category stipulated, "I can talk about *anything*" with my RC or neighborhood warden—it can be thought of as a stringent test of residents' relationships with their neighborhood representatives. The answer distributions for the two cities in Figure 5.8 display a striking similarity, despite the fact that their political and administrative functions contain such major contrasts. In both cities, a minority of between 18 percent and 23 percent provided one of the two open responses, whereas roughly

42 percent chose the most distant of the response categories. This observed pattern offers an important general truth about AGE institutions and how they fit into the sociopolitical milieu of these cities. Belying the lavish use of the language of community in both Beijing and Taipei, only a modest portion of the denizens of urban neighborhoods actually have a sense of strong, personal closeness with, or deep trust in, the leadership chosen to speak on the community's behalf. On a methodological point, we can also infer from the responses to the Beijing question that even in that generally authoritarian system, interviewees did not feel undue pressure to give only positive answers in the survey.

In both cities, then, a majority of residents has at least some degree of acquaintance with these local state intermediaries and interacts at least occasionally with them. Some 15 percent to 30 percent of the population is in quite regular touch with them, knows them relatively well, and has more than a merely businesslike level of association with them. At the opposite end of the spectrum, significant minorities in Beijing and Taipei have nothing to do with their RC or *lizhang* whatsoever. Urban society is thus deeply divided in its relationship to the neighborhood structures.

The Varying Density of Community Networks

To consider the ways in which administrative grassroots institutions embed themselves in urban society requires a moment of reflection on the neighborhood as a social space. Cities have been interpreted by some as fertile ground for associational ties and by others as barren terrain. Classic sociological studies have declared cities to be marked by alienation and an absence of the kind of community ties that village life is said to sustain (Wirth 1938). An analysis of mortality during Chicago's heat wave of 1995 observes that, for some urban residents, particularly among the elderly, social isolation can be near complete, and even deadly (Klinenberg 2002). Peter Evans reminds us, as well, that city dwellers often lack the solidarity required to exercise power in a sustained way: "The romantic vision that 'community' automatically entails homogeneity and unity of purpose is misleading even in traditional rural settings; urban communities contain an even more daunting spectrum of interests, identities, and political positions" (Evans 2002a, 14–15). Yet he and other sociologists have also emphasized the possibilities for community and solidarity that do exist in cities while noting that residents' social networks are only partially, and often weakly, centered on the place where they live (Fischer 1982; Wellman 1988; Forrest and Kearns 2001; Sampson 2004).

In line with these general observations, neighborhoods in different parts of Beijing and Taipei vary in terms of the nature and density of residents' interactions with one another and with local leaders. Some of this simply stems from the personality and competence of specific leaders. Ding Xiaoli, the director of the Shimen organization, brought a high level of commitment and empathy to her job; others can be dilatory and indifferent or worse. Observers at the local level or in city governments tend to emphasize the importance of the character and abilities of the people in the organization in explaining cross-neighborhood variation. One street office official said that, from her point of view, the key to a successful committee is cohesion among the members and having the right mix. It should include younger members who are relatively better educated as well as older members who have knowledge of the neighborhood and the respect of the residents.[12] A member of a committee elsewhere concurred: "Those RC staff who are hired from outside the neighborhood have a hard time doing the work. Why? First, they don't know the people, and second, residents don't approve of them; they won't give you face [mianzi] if they don't know you. . . . [If] young people don't know the RC member, they'll say: 'Why should I do that for you? I don't know you.'"[13] Comparing the experienced, local staff to newly hired young adults, one committee director said: "The old ladies may not have much education, but think how many years they've lived here and how familiar they are with the place. When they handle things, the residents tend to oblige them out of respect. Also, they don't care about keeping regular work hours, and if residents need something they're happy to go to their homes at night."[14]

As these observations suggest, the familiarity and local networks possessed by neighborhood leaders are of great importance to their work; these "weak ties," to again borrow Granovetter's term, give them credibility and entrée (1973). Two members of the Chongxing RC exemplified this. Cheng Guilan began working in that committee in 1959, at the age of just twenty-two, with only two years of formal education in her home village in Hebei Province. She served continuously for more than four decades. Gu Xiuhua moved to the neighborhood in 1975 from a different part of Beijing. With only five or six years of schooling, she had operated a lathe at a tractor plant on the other side of the city, taking early retirement at the age of fifty. In her mind, as she often stated privately, her thirty years of formal factory work put her in a category superior to that of Cheng, who had spent just two years in a collectively run workshop during the Great Leap Forward before beginning RC work. Yet the younger staff, with high school educations, saw the two as belonging as a common type.

Indeed, Cheng and Gu brought similar resources to their work in the committee—in particular, a far-reaching acquaintance with most of the 485 households who lived in the neighborhood's ninety-seven subdivided court-yards as of the year 2000. Apart from transients, they essentially knew every-one in Chongxing, and residents would nod their heads or greet them when they walked through the neighborhood's narrow, twisting alleys. Local children affectionately called them grandmother (*nainai*) when they came through the office; the other staff members were called auntie (*ayi*). One February morning, a nearby neighbor's coal stove had gone out, and Cheng skillfully used tongs to take over a red-hot coal honeycomb and reignite it for them. She also delivered gas canisters to welfare recipients on a three-wheeled pedal-powered cart.

It would be wrong to imagine that these women were universally loved by their constituents. Anyone living or working in such places develops a rich mixture of loyalties, favors, slights, and grievances over the years. Still, they unquestionably held the same values and outlook as many of their neighbors; in afternoon chats in the office, visitors, committee staff, and even police officers would roundly vent their disaffection at things like high-level corruption, the upending of the economic system in which they came of age, and bewildering changes in social mores. The deep embeddedness of these two longtime residents, or in more specific terms, their networks and local knowledge, infused all aspects of the committee's work, as the account of the court enforcer showed. Their time was running out, however. By 2003, the street office had arranged for both Gu and Cheng to step down from their positions. Gu continued to live in her stuffy, 12.3-square-meter room off a courtyard a few steps from the former committee office, living on the mod-est pension from her previous factory job and taking care of her disabled husband. By that time, the RC had been merged with others, and the area it governed had grown to more than seven times its previous size. Of Gu and Cheng's younger colleagues from the old Chongxing office, two had been retained in the merger. They were more recent arrivals to the neighborhood. In theory, their superior literacy skills and familiarity with the conventions of paperwork and record keeping would make up for their sparser and shallower local ties.

As deeply rooted as Cheng and Gu were in Chongxing, they were not born in the neighborhood. Indeed, Gu's home remained the property of the court-yard's prerevolutionary owner, albeit under heavy rent control. By Taipei standards they would not be considered true locals. Taiwan, of course, under-went plenty of wrenching change during the twentieth century, including col-onization by Japan and the post–World War II takeover by the Nationalists.[15] The population of the capital city increased by a factor of ten over the past six and a half decades. But the absence of a class-based revolution preserved many locally rooted social configurations, and these show up as marked con-trasts with the mainland in neighborhood governance. In Taipei and in other cities on the island, for example, it remains common for wardens to emerge from families and extended clans that trace their presence in the locality back for many generations. Fifty-one percent of the Taipei neighborhood wardens elected or reelected in 2010 were born in the capital city, which suggests a roughly half-and-half split between those with multigenerational local ties and those who built their own base in the community from scratch.[16] Some wardens are closely linked to temples in the neighborhood, which in many cases are dedicated to clan ancestors. Some win their offices on the coattails of deceased parents or spouses who previously held the same position. Others are entrenched in their communities by having run successful businesses there, such as one four-term warden in the city of Chiayi whose turkey-and-rice lunch restaurant had customers lining up out the door during my 2006 visit. In terms of its socioeconomic foundations, neighborhood leadership in Taiwan may more closely resemble the mainland's villages than its cities.

Zhou Mingtong was born in 1939 in a village near the area that would eventually be incorporated into Taipei as Andong Li. At the age of sixteen, with just a few years of education, he came to work on the Liu family's farm-land and two years later had married one of its daughters. Zhou's father-in-law, the owner of a local store, set him up to run for warden on the family's behalf. He won election in 1968, beginning what would be almost four de-cades in office. As of one evening in late 2003, he presided over a neigh-borhood of 2,800 households, and several members of his hundred-person volunteer patrol team were chatting in his ground-floor office. Zhou had been a beneficiary of rising land prices over the years; the amount he claimed to pay in property taxes implied holdings worth more than US$3 million. He had handily beaten four assorted challengers in the January 2003 election for his ninth consecutive term.

In the December 2006 election, however, Zhou was unseated by one of his wife's cousins, a fifty-six-year-old woman. Having grown up under the same roof with Zhou, Liu Xiutao began assisting Zhou with constituent service and reelection campaigns in her teenage years. In turn, his political connections helped get her started in jobs at KMT-linked trade associations and in campaign work for legislative candidates. Explaining the intrafamily rivalry, Liu claimed that Zhou had agreed to step down and given her his blessing to run in his place, but then had been convinced by supporters to run again. The campaign was bitterly fought, including attacks on her distributed via flyers in residents' mailboxes. In the end, she denied him a tenth term of office with an overwhelming win: 1,084 votes to 491.

In part, she won by reclaiming control of the Liu family's influence in the area, which is based on five generations of presence since their immigration from Quanzhou. The story of Andong thus illustrates, in part, the ongoing potency of kinship networks in some of Taipei's *li*, but also that contemporary wardens must forge other ties with voters to keep their seats. As Liu explained, votes from kinfolk no longer sufficed. First-generation arrivals to the city made up fully two-thirds of her constituents. The boundaries of the neighborhood had come to encompass several large families other than the nearly two hundred descendants of her own, which had its clan temple (*zongci*) elsewhere in the district. Liu's strong majority came to her not as an inherited patrimony but mainly through hard campaigning, steady confidence, and loyal volunteers.

If we step back for a more abstract perspective, we see that the network endowments of neighborhood leaders are closely linked to urban geography. In Beijing, the sharpest contrasts are between RCs in the older, city-center neighborhoods, on the one hand, and in newly erected high-rise developments containing privately owned condominiums, on the other hand. The former areas are typically composed of cramped housing built around narrow lanes, often run-down and dating back to prerevolutionary years. Between these extremes lie widespread tracts of four- to six-story apartment buildings, many of which were built in the 1970s or 1980s, with individual units sold to occupants during housing reform in the 1990s. In Taipei, the remaining stock of older, one- or two-story homes is relatively small. Sixty-nine percent of the telephone survey respondents lived in walk-up apartments, referred to in this book as low-rises, and 23 percent occupied high-rise towers known locally as

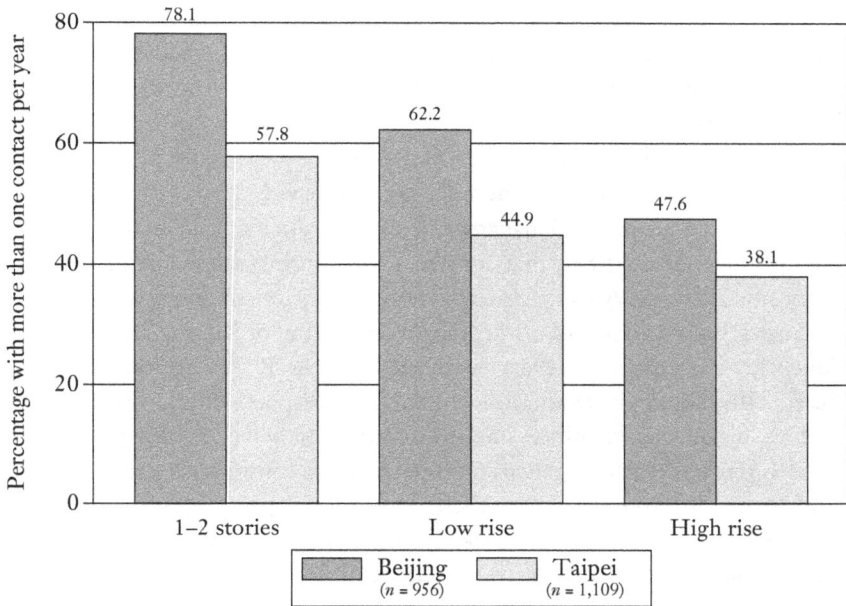

Figure 5.9.   Contact with neighborhood leaders, by housing type.
Data are from the 2001 Beijing Law and Community Survey and the 2006 Taipei Neighborhoods Survey.

da xia. These various forms of housing are more uniformly scattered throughout the city than in Beijing.

Figure 5.9 gives a visual depiction of the way residents' interaction with RCs and neighborhood wardens changes by characteristics of the locality. In both cities, people living in single- or two-story homes had relatively large amounts of contact with neighborhood representatives. Those in high-rise apartment buildings, by contrast, had this kind of interaction less frequently.[17]

The material and social conditions that brought about these patterns were plain to see on the ground, especially in old Beijing neighborhoods like Chongxing, Xiyingjie, and Shuangqiao. There the underdeveloped and trouble-prone condition of housing infrastructure enhanced the RC's role. Problems with sewers and sanitation were chronic. As of the early 2000s, not all homes and businesses had phones, and the RC office sometimes served as a convenient place to leave messages or make calls. Bathhouses, a local fixture because homes in such places often lacked hot-water heaters, sold packs of tickets through the committees. Property rights over things like shared space in courtyards were especially blurry, causing disputes to crop up more often than in other places.

In recently built neighborhoods like Wutai, by contrast, whole categories of issues that would elsewhere be taken to the RC are instead handled by professional property management companies (*wuye guanli gongsi*). Typically offshoots of the firms that construct the housing, these companies take responsibility for everything from collecting utility fees to hiring private security guards and contracting workers for redecoration or heating repairs. Consequently, there are fewer everyday matters for the RC to handle. Residents occasionally asked the committee to mediate disputes that arose between mothers-in-law and daughters-in-law, or from the behavior of pet dogs, but not as often or concerning as wide a spectrum of controversies as in the old neighborhoods. Homeowners in these developments often possess a sense of self-sufficiency that is rarely possible in older parts of the city. As one staff member put it: "Most people own their homes in Wutai. They are in their thirties or forties, and are fairly successful. They don't need help. So the RCs don't have a very large role [*zuoyong*] to play. RCs are good at 'taking care of the house and minding the courtyard' [*kan jia hu yuan*], and here people don't need that. People hire their own nannies. Also, for so long the government administered things so tightly. Now with reform, people like to have some privacy, to close themselves off from the rest of the world. And they do so in places like this."[18]

Much the same feeling of self-sufficiency can often be found in Taipei's modern apartment towers, where management committees (*guanli weiyuanhui*) handle many issues of everyday importance to occupants, from security to plumbing. Yet, as we will see, even in such settings, where many constituents live in contented insulation from street-level concerns, neighborhood leaders in both cities find ways to keep in touch, building networks anew where none existed before.

The Distant and the Critical: Interpreting Negative Perceptions

The social setting of the neighborhood, shaped by its particular history and the built environment in which people live, thus constitutes one overarching factor influencing the way people in Beijing and Taipei experience their institutions of ultra-local governance. Probing deeper into these experiences, much of the rest of this book endeavors to make clear why so many residents of Beijing and Taipei have at least a mildly favorable disposition toward their RCs and wardens. But the views of those who have neutral or negative perceptions, though not the majority, are important in their own right. Taking a look at these perspectives sheds light on the portion of the survey respondents who found the RCs not to be very useful or who believed that the *lizhang* system should be done away with. What is the basis for their skepticism? Do critics in the two cities find the same kinds of faults or different ones? We bear in mind the hostile attitudes toward RCs that Whyte and Parish found to be prevalent among émigrés in the 1970s and ask to what extent the same kinds of concerns are raised today—and more generally, whether these concerns match those we would expect people to raise about state-imposed mass organizations.

Certain grounds for complaint are specific to the context of either Taiwan or China. The political allegiances of the *lizhang*, and the role they play in electoral politics, provide one example. Even though overt vote buying in Taipei has largely died out, many people have vivid memories of the practice from the not-so-distant past, and they remain keenly aware of the fact that neighborhood leaders still carry water for political machines. One sixty-year-old widow, a former KMT member who had long since repudiated that party, felt no warmth toward her warden whatsoever: "I have no interaction with her; the only reason I know her is because she comes around asking for votes. Of course she is nice to you around elections, but after the election is over, there's no more of that."[19]

The more politicized of Taipei residents often see their *lizhang* through a lens colored by party loyalties. Supporters of the Democratic Progressive Party (DPP) sometimes chafed under KMT wardens. In Taipei's Zhongshan district, one retired business executive, a strong DPP partisan, claimed he had never met his previous *lizhang*, an affiliate of the Nationalist Party: "He never came out, never talked to us, no one ever saw him." But when a member of his own party was elected in 2003, espousing strong "Taiwan consciousness," this interviewee became an enthusiastic participant in community life. Drawing on his childhood in the period of colonial occupation, he volunteered as a Japanese-language teacher in the neighborhood office.[20] In some cases, Blue-leaning interviewees were similarly displeased by Green *lizhang* who had won control of their neighborhoods. Taiwan's national-level political polarization

often finds expression at the *li* level, with community development associations and factions surrounding warden candidates commonly taking on a partisan hue.

In short, political objections in Taipei had to do with local leaders using
their positions for the benefit of specific electoral parties. Objections of precisely this kind are not to be found in Beijing, of course, where the nature of
party mobilization is entirely different. China differs, as well, in the potentially more intrusive kinds of monitoring that the committees engage in. Three
political dissidents of my acquaintance spoke of the oppressive sense of having their comings and goings observed by the neighborhood organization,
which kept watch over them in concert with the police and other security
agencies. (On occasion, dissidents said that the RC members, as individuals,
expressed understanding and sympathy toward them.) Although their circumstances were exceptional, some ordinary people I spoke with also objected to
the way the RCs poked into what they felt was people's private business. As
a thirty-year-old man from a Beijing suburb said: "My residents' committee
likes to ask visitors questions, like who they are looking for, things like that.
So I personally don't like them very much, and a lot of young people feel the
same way."[21]

A number of interviewees who were critical of the neighborhood groups
cited the way that the committees are so closely tethered to the government.
One young person flatly described them as a "tool of control." A sixty-year-
old woman said: "None of the residents' committee staff live in this building,
and so no one takes care of things in this building, and there's no organization.
RC elections aren't done all that conscientiously; if you wanted to vote the bad
ones out, you wouldn't be able to. No one realizes that this is [supposed to be]
an autonomous organization of the masses."[22]

Even state officials—at least those of a reflective bent—sometimes
expressed reservations about the residents' committees' lack of real autonomy:
"From the government's point of view, it needs something below the street
office. Technically the residents' committee is supposed to be about 'self-
administration, self-service, and self-education.' But now our attitude toward
the RCs is ambiguous [*aimei*]. Should they be part of the government? Should
they be the tip [*moshao*] of the government? If it's going to be a residents'
autonomous organization, there should be elections. So we're now in a state
of drift. It's very interesting."[23]

These kinds of criticisms—concerning the committees' nosiness and the government's tight grip on them—accord with the factors cited by Whyte and Parish, and indeed with what we might expect to hear. Having noted the existence of such skepticism, it is important to add that this is by no means the most common line of critique among interviewees who take a negative view of their RC. Indeed, in many cases the problems cited by Beijing residents echoed those raised by people in Taipei.

As noted in Chapter 2, the RCs were originally meant to administer and tend to only those residents who had no work unit. Although their mandate is far broader now, it is still the case that people who are occupied with their careers outside of the neighborhood have less interaction with them. "The RCs' duties are mainly taking fees for sweeping the streets and for cable television. They have little contact with people like us who go to work," said a fifty-two-year-old low-ranking cadre in a state enterprise.[24] But those who are unemployed do not necessarily think more highly of the committees. One laid-off worker pointed out that the RC could not do anything to get him a job.[25] Other interviewees felt that the committees did little of value for anyone,[26] and others expressed complete indifference toward an institution they found dull and irrelevant.[27]

Many residents fault their RC for having limited ability or willingness to solve people's most pressing problems. Such people either did not feel that the committee's service functions added up to anything particularly impressive or did not believe that their committees even made an effort to be of use. "Mine doesn't do much. It's just an empty shell," said a thirty-eight-year-old woman working for a foreign company in Beijing. All that she knew for certain her committee did, she continued, was rent out a room or two to make money. Earlier in the year her sleep had been disturbed by the crowing of a rooster that someone in her building was raising. "I went to the RC, but they didn't want to do anything about it; they didn't want to hurt their relations with the person."[28]

In Taipei as well, some people are wholly unimpressed by the neighborhood leaders. One middle-aged woman complained: "It doesn't seem like the *lizhang* really do anything. It seems like they're just a waste of the country's money."[29] A small-business owner in Da'an district said: "I've always felt that the wardens aren't of much use. They probably just come out to distribute a few flyers and put up some notices. The city government could outsource that and it would cost a lot less."[30] A sixty-six-year-old woman living in a ten-story apartment building found her warden, living on the other side of the large *li*, inattentive to the concerns of those living in her area. "The *lizhang*'s own community is big, with lots of people in it, so as long as he takes care of the people over there he doesn't have to worry about reelection," she explained. When the national power utility made plans to install a transformer station in an empty lot near her home, it was an uphill struggle to get the warden even to talk to the company, and in the end the transformer went in anyway. Clearly, the electoral accountability of the *lizhang* does not necessarily make them responsive to all their constituents.[31]

In some cases, residents harbor grudges against their neighborhood leaders because of instances when they made a decision or enforced a rule that left them feeling burned. One woman, for instance, was resentful because, on the very day of the interview, the RC had told her to rip out the patch of melons that she had been growing in the small garden outside her first-floor housing unit.[32] In Taipei's narrow lanes, parking privileges alone generate an ongoing behind-the-scenes struggle, teeming with opportunities for malfeasance and offence. One woman reported: "The curb is painted red near the intersection because it's dangerous there where cars are turning. But the block captain who lives below us covered the red with gray paint, making it the same color as the road, so he could park there. I called the warden and complained about this. The warden, who of course is close with his block captain, replied in a delicate way: 'This is part of Taiwan's culture.' How can you call his breaking the rules and defying the law Taiwan's culture? I've never trusted the warden ever since."[33]

A broad category of criticism, in both cities, revolves around allegations that the neighborhood organizations look the other way when they are supposed to act as watchdogs—with the resulting suspicion that they have been paid off. It is also common to hear complaints having to do with the RC's or warden's relationship with nearby businesses, or other matters concerning money. Some in Beijing charged that the committees aimed too much at earning revenue by sponsoring commercial activity, thus bringing migrants into the neighborhood as proprietors or employees.[34] One Taipei resident was convinced her *lizhang* had been bought off by vendors operating food stalls, which she said produced offensive smells and oily waste that clogged drainpipes.[35] Another said that his former warden tried to collect money from residents in the name of the patrol team and seemed to spend it on banquets for supporters.[36] Another, an enthusiastic DPP backer, complained that she was unable to join government-subsidized neighborhood outings because her KMT warden had reserved all the slots for his cronies. She also had heard rumors that travel agencies gave him kickbacks.[37]

So far, much of what we have seen driving residents' opinions corresponds to practical concerns in the here and now. But other negative opinions do not fit this pattern. Perhaps most remarkably, some in Beijing felt that today's RCs fared poorly in comparison with those of the prereform era, like this man in his forties:

> The residents' committees aren't as effective as they once were. In the past, they would mediate disputes, and keep an eye on things. They knew everything about everyone in the area: where they worked, how they behaved [*biaoxian*]. Now they don't care as much. [I asked about mediation.] In the past, they would not only break up the dispute and tell the people not to argue, they would also get involved and arbitrate who was right and who was wrong. Nowadays, if you actually killed someone the police would come after you. Short of that, the RCs don't get involved much.

I asked this man, "Isn't it better not to have the committees bothering you?" No, he insisted, he liked them better the way they were before. "It's better to have them involved in neighborhood matters."[38]

A sixty-seven-year-old woman commented: "In the past, the RC cadres were all small-footed old women. Whether or not they were given money, they all dared to speak up and even were able to uphold justice. The mother-in-law of the committee director next door did RC work for eighteen years and never got a penny. Now they're on a salary system, and they're afraid to take things on. They're paid, but they end up not daring to speak. Going to the RC won't solve any problems, anyway."[39] Similar sentiments—the idea that neighborhood leaders today have departed from the purer ways of the past—could also be heard in Taipei, as in this interview with a sixty-year-old woman: "Nowadays the wardens and block captains have degenerated into election tools; the wardens are just 'cornerstones.' I'm not sure if they were elected in the past, because I've never voted for them, but I feel that in the past they had a sense of honor. Back then I know they didn't have salaries, but you could tell that they cared about the locality. Now they're elected and they're paid, but it would be better if they didn't receive salaries."[40]

Conclusion

This chapter has, first and foremost, provided an overview of the range of variation that one finds in exploring citizens' perceptions of and interactions with the RC and warden systems. Patterns in the survey data from the two capitals run curiously parallel in certain regards—yet they also diverge in others, such as the usefulness gap, which calls for explanation. In each city, some neighborhoods have close-knit and enduring community ties, whereas in others, such as those with immense new condominium buildings, residents are far less closely bound to one another. Most important, individuals vary—for one woman, the RC's or warden's office may be a prominent feature of everyday life, but her next-door neighbor might never give it a second thought. Analysis of the quantitative data has drawn attention to patterns like the special salience these institutions have among poorer, less educated, working-class folk. It also noted the role of political beliefs and affiliations, as well as sociability, in explaining some of the person-by-person variation.

The following two chapters explore the perspectives of those residents who accept or even embrace their state-backed neighborhood organizations. But as we saw in the quantitative data, a considerable portion of the survey respondents in both cities had negative perceptions of them as well. The detailed exploration here of the kinds of causes that underlie such critical responses reminds us of several things. Plenty of wardens and RC members are not particularly diligent or adept at delivering the forms of service and assistance that their constituents expect of them. Even when they do apply themselves to these duties, they do not always win plaudits from residents. More basically, there exist widely divergent opinions among citizens and even government officials about the appropriateness of the particular way in which these organizations balance the competing demands that they face.

Whyte and Parish concluded that the large amount of hostility toward China's RCs they found in the late 1970s among émigrés stemmed from, essentially, the oppressiveness of those institutions in the prereform environment. To be sure, we would only expect circumstances and perspectives to have changed significantly since the Cultural Revolution era. Yet at least from a liberal, Western perspective—and certainly from the mass organization models—we would also anticipate that many of the interviewees today would bridle at these state-managed institutions, particularly in their authoritarian form in Beijing. And in these interviews, we indeed find examples of this kind of critique: in those who accused the RCs of invading their privacy or those who ripped them for lacking the independent standing that they are supposed to possess. In Taipei as well, some citizens question whether the *lizhang* truly earn their taxpayer-provided support. These residents, we might infer, want to see the organizations act more like civil society groups, autonomous bodies with unimpeded freedom to advocate on the community's behalf. At least they want them to be more responsive and accountable.

Still, much of the negative opinion that exists does not necessarily accord with the principles behind these kinds of objections. The nostalgia some express for the organizations as they existed in the past is particularly anomalous in this regard. As one would expect, the democratically responsive *lizhang* escape some of the criticism that is trained on their authoritarian counterparts, for instance on grounds of political snooping. But many of the problems that interviewees in the two cities decry are largely the same. In both cases, negative perceptions are often formed in practical and situational ways, by unsatisfactory encounters that individuals happen to have experienced. In both cities, ties to business activity or favored associates bring suspicion, rightly or wrongly, on local leaders. Moreover, it appears safe to assume that most of those busy Beijing residents for whom neighborhood matters are simply irrelevant would feel no greater affinity to their nonauthoritarian counterparts in Taipei. In short, we find that regime-level differences do matter, but person-by-person perceptions are largely driven by other factors, in ways that show many parallels between the two capitals. One set of commonalities lies in the kinds of opportunities for participation, service, and recreation that the two systems use to solidify their ties to certain constituents, as explored in Chapter 6.

Chapter Six

Thick Networks and State-Mobilized Volunteers

All institutions of administrative grassroots engagement develop and rely on networks of volunteers, auxiliaries of an auxiliary. Whether the work done by these irregulars is entirely uncompensated or rewarded with small gifts or stipends, it occupies a different category from that of the neighborhood staff themselves, who take on far more extensive duties and are paid something close to a wage. The volunteers greatly expand the ranks of those who contribute to the work of these bodies, and they help to compose a core of individuals closely linked to local leaders and avidly taking part in the organization's activities. This chapter takes a detailed look at those who join these dense networks and aims to explain the nature of their participation.

In China, neighborhood volunteers are sometimes known as activists (*jiji fenzi*), a term that has a special meaning in comparative communism studies, one that has evolved over decades of scholarship. This chapter reviews and critiques this concept. Activists in China and other state-socialist settings have previously been understood as responding to coercion, acting out of ideological commitment, or chasing material incentives. I argue that such interpretations have only limited utility for understanding the role of volunteers in this setting today. Activists in the neighborhoods of Beijing choose to participate in this form of service for reasons that are not at all specific to the context of a Communist Party–led system and are similar to those motivating their counterparts in Taipei. Indeed, these have much in common with the motivations of volunteers everywhere: the rewards of working toward what they view as the public benefit and the camaraderie generated by spending time with like-minded peers. A theme of this chapter is the way in which, for a subset of city residents, several aspects of connectedness and participation overlap closely and reinforce one another. Close connections to one's neighbors, participation in community affairs, and voluntary participation in institutions of grassroots administration all tend to go together.

Thus, instead of an explanation specific to one regime type, we need a more general account of the effects of state encouragement and cultivation on different forms of local participation. At the same time, the differences between authoritarian and democratic forms of volunteer service and civic participation cannot be elided, as some other studies tend to do.[1] Beijing's neighborhood activists, just like the residents' committees (RCs) that organize them, still form an extension of the Communist Party's system of political surveillance. In Taipei, the *linzhang* and other volunteers help the state in various ways but not for the purpose of sniffing out dissent or reporting on neighbors. Moreover, although these forms of service were originally intended to provide extra reach and assistance to the government, in the democratic setting of Taiwan they also exert substantial bottom-up influence through competition, leadership succession, and other mechanisms. We must appreciate both the overlap and the distinctions between China's form of neighborhood volunteering and other kinds of state-mobilized participation in less intrusive contexts. Only by grasping both these things will we be able to make sense of the mixed and ambivalent ways in which neighbors perceive these volunteers.

Perspectives on Activists and State-Mobilized Volunteers

In the United States, voluntary service is customarily viewed as deriving from and closely linked with the nongovernmental organizations of civil society (Verba, Schlozman, and Brady 1995; Putnam 2000, 119–122; Smith 2000). In other parts of the world, the same assumptions do not necessarily hold. As Mary Alice Haddad has argued: "In a community where citizens think that the government should deal with social problems, organizations with close, embedded relationships with the government will be viewed as engaging in a legitimate activity and will garner volunteer support" (2007, 30). In her account of Japan, she points out that a community-based organization like a neighborhood association, parent-teacher association, or volunteer fire department, which "has frequent, habitual interactions with the bureaucracy and engages in the policy-making process with bureaucrats," can constitute an important site where citizens' voluntary energies are engaged (Haddad 2007, 36). Research on European countries such as Germany and Sweden has also pointed out a close link between the state and volunteering (Offe and Fuchs 2002, 231; Rothstein 2002, 296–299).

Volunteer service in state-socialist settings has long been interpreted as something wholly different from what would seem to be its counterparts elsewhere. The concept of activism has special resonance in the China-studies field, although equivalents for the term are found in other Communist Party–led systems as well. Numerous works have examined the Soviet equivalent, the *activ* (Meyer 1965; Bendix 1974, 403, 417–433; Little 1976, 446; Friedgut 1979). With its Maoist emphasis on mobilizing the masses and overcoming difficulties through the application of politically conscious will, the Chinese Communist Party (CCP) encouraged supporters to contribute their energies to the revolution in numerous settings, from villages to factories to schools.[2] Influential works of research over several decades have identified the distinction between activists and nonactivists as a major fault line in China's sociopolitical landscape; scholars have debated the extent to which this divide eclipses other relevant social categories along lines such as class, group interests, and so forth.

Activists, in the sense of local recruits who did not hold formal leadership positions, played a large part in the communist revolution, and their contributions as well as the party's use of the concept have been chronicled in many studies. For example, William Hinton describes in *Fanshen* how a struggle meeting conducted by *jiji fenzi* radicalized the villagers of Long Bow "like the waves on the surface of a pond when a stone is thrown in" (1966, 115). Activists have long been identified as a crucial part of the Maoist approach to revolution and administration, seen as heroic or sinister depending on the author's perspective. Focusing on CCP mobilization in the Shaan-Gan-Ning area based in Yan'an, Mark Selden highlights the local emergence of "peasant activist leadership" as an important part of the "mass line." Local activists not only served to overcome the gap between leaders and masses in keeping with mass line doctrine but also exemplified "a new conception of the communist ideal man" who spread progressive values, created community ties, and helped transform rural life (Selden 1971, 210, 274–276). Townsend's study of political participation also engages the concept of the mass line as "a particular instance of the CCP's desire for a generally high degree of activism and political consciousness among the people" (1967, 75).[3]

Townsend also finds an important differentiation (rather than solidarity) between activists and ordinary people, asserting that "the primary distinction to make in analyzing popular electoral participation, or mass participation in any political movement in Communist China, is that between activists and ordinary citizens" (1967, 132).[4] Others writing on the post-1949 period elaborated on the possibility that activism could create social ruptures rather than build solidarity. They began to portray activists as self-serving and calculating, seeking advancement by currying favor with superiors. A 1965 essay by sociologist Ezra F. Vogel argued that CCP rule had attenuated personal friendships on the mainland because people feared their friends would betray them to the authorities; those he labeled "activist-opportunists" were especially dangerous: "An activist who is anxious to join the Young Communist League or the League member anxious to join the Communist Party in order to advance his own career has to prove that he is very loyal to the régime. One of the best ways to prove it is by showing that friendships do not stand in the way of his loyalty to the régime, that when necessary he will report on a friend" (Vogel 1965, 48).[5]

An equally dark perspective is found in Richard H. Solomon's 1969 article on activists, which like Selden's and Townsend's work identified them with the Maoist approach to mobilization. Activism is generated by struggle; party agitators whip up "hatred, resentment and a capacity for aggression" among activists in a process of emotional manipulation (Solomon 1969, 90, 86). Solomon also echoes Vogel's finding that ambition and the rivalry brought about by "the numbers of non-Party people willing to compete for Party membership" drive the emergence of activists (Solomon 1969, 98, italics omitted). Michel Oksenberg, too, associated activism with career opportunism in an essay published around the same time. Generally speaking, for the ambitious to get ahead they had to undercut their peers and had trouble getting along with them while so doing, as he put it (Oksenberg 1970).[6]

This theme is further developed in two later accounts, both of which focus on activists' role in the everyday politics of the school or work unit, and not merely on their role in political campaigns.[7] Susan L. Shirk and Andrew G. Walder made the idea that competition for career advancement and material rewards motivates activism central to their analyses of sociopolitical dynamics in high schools and state enterprises, respectively.[8] In *Competitive Comrades*, employing a rational-choice approach, Shirk asserts that "the systematic patterns of Chinese individual behavior are explicable as personal attempts to increase benefits and reduce costs in an environment where the rewards and penalties associated with various actions are established by regime policies" (1982, 5, italics omitted). Shirk's informants defined an activist as "a person who always takes the lead in political, labor and social activities and who is eager to carry out directives from teachers and school authorities." For high school students, adopting an activist stance was a "strategic decision"; she contrasts activists with those who tried to distinguish themselves by concentrating on their studies. Although students sought to maintain "moral integrity" and "peer respect" as well as to pursue "economic advancement," the latter goal was primary because the system rewarded political virtue in the high-stakes competition for a limited number of career opportunities. To prove themselves, activists had to do things like publicly criticize their classmates and hence were shunned by their peers (Shirk 1982, 86, 63, 7–10, 91).

Although Shirk sees several factors, including class background and student ability, playing into the decision of whether to become an activist, Walder's *Communist Neo-Traditionalism* makes a stronger claim, that the choice of an active or passive strategy is itself "easily the most politically salient social-structural cleavage" in the factory, superseding all other group affinities and defining the nature of workplace life: "No matter what their current income or skill level, worker political orientations are determined by their adoption of active-competitive or passive-defensive strategies. Every occupational group or stratum, no matter how defined, is divided by the social distinction between activist and nonactivist that pervades everyday life. . . . Information about group characteristics, boundaries, and their inferred interests, no matter how complete, cannot tell us anything about these networks and allegiances" (Walder 1986, 166, 244).

As in Shirk's book, the party's dominant role in doling out scarce rewards to its favorites is the root cause of divisions among the dependent rank and file. Workers depend on management for crucial benefits like housing and scarce opportunities like career advancement. In contrast to Shirk's view that payoffs go to those who display political rectitude, Walder finds a partially degenerated type of authority he calls principled particularism, in which "it is no longer the conformity to ideals of political virtue itself that is rewarded, but the concrete loyalty of workers to the party branch and shop management," as manifested in patron-client ties (1986, 131). Activists are those loyalists who "are positively oriented to the party and who actively do its bidding," for instance by snitching on their coworkers in "little reports" to the leaders (Walder 1986, 89). They reap the fruits of this betrayal but also suffer resentment and abuse: "The antagonism displayed toward activists is a reflection of a deeper social fact: that activists have sided politically with the party and management, that they have entered into a special relationship with representatives of the party and act routinely against the interests of the group as a whole, and that they will eventually become leaders themselves" (Walder 1986, 167).

These studies were based on the Mao era, and clearly China has undergone much political "decompression," in Linz's phrase, since then (2000, 113–114). Moreover, the neighborhood setting is, as Chapter 4 showed, at some remove from the arena of schools and workplaces, where one's future career could be at stake. Still, we lack an understanding of state-fostered voluntary participation in institutions that are more embedded in the governing apparatus than the kinds of organizations that Haddad studied in Japan, yet less politically pressurized than prereform China (2007).

Neighborhood Participation in Beijing and Taipei

Although it has always been a somewhat imprecise term, the word "activist" (*jiji fenzi*) is a concept familiar to RC staff and residents alike, commonly used in both official and popular language. Indeed, in the early decades of urban administration in the People's Republic of China (PRC) there was less of a distinction between members of the residents' committee and neighborhood activists; the staff themselves were by nature activists, working for a very small amount of pay or none at all. Activists today are not always called *jiji fenzi*, however. The term is still employed in some contexts and avoided in others, perhaps because of its dated, Maoist tone. (In some places "community volunteers" is now preferred; one Beijing community, by 2010, called its activists harmony promoters [*hexie cujinyuan*], an outlandish adaptation of a Hu-era buzzword.) It is thus necessary to turn to the nomenclature actually in use. Each neighborhood has a set of people who serve as the RC's liaisons to the households around their own homes. These liaisons go under varying appellations in different neighborhoods. For instance, where residents live in multistory apartment blocks, each building may have a building head (*louzhang*). In addition to, or instead of, a building head there are usually entryway heads (*loumenzhang*) where housing units are arranged vertically around common stairwells sharing an outside door, or floor heads (*cengzhang*) if units are arranged horizontally and open onto hallways. Older neighborhoods where homes are clustered around courtyards have designated courtyard heads (*yuanzhang* or *yuan fuzeren*). Thus, both terminology and the spatial distribution of activists vary in accordance with the layout of housing and the natural patterns of human interaction that arise from it.

In some instances, these household clusters are also considered residents' small groups (*jumin xiaozu*), whereas in other cases small groups may exist separately and have their own leaders (*xiaozuzhang*). In principle these volunteer post holders are known to all residents in their cluster, although the residents' awareness of or concern with these most local of representatives varies. The RC sometimes posts organizational charts specifying the names of those who hold these positions. Article 14 of the 1998 residents' committee organizational law stipulates that the small-group heads are to be chosen (*tuixuan*) by the residents' small groups.[9] In practice, the RC selects these contact people itself, replacing them when it wants to. It may or may not take residents' preferences into account, but its choices are generally activists or at least people who are willing to cooperate with it on most matters.

Taiwan's cities have less terminological profusion, and the term "activist" is not used. Straightforwardly, each neighborhood subsection (*lin*) has a leader known as a *linzhang*. In some cases, citizens reported that they took part in discussions about who would serve as their *linzhang*.[10] Officially speaking, though, there is no stipulation that the *lin*-leaders must be picked by their peers; the warden is free to choose his or her team of *linzhang* as one of the prerogatives of office. The national Local Government Act says nothing about the duties of the *linzhang* in either cities or villages, but city-level regulations spell out procedures for their appointment (*linpin*) and dismissal (*jiepin*). In Taipei, they are appointed by the district chief at the warden's recommendation, subject to certain restrictions: they must have reached the age of twenty; they must live in the *lin* that they serve; their household registry must reflect this; and individuals under certain kinds of legal sanction, such as a prison sentence, lose eligibility. A *linzhang*'s four-year term is indefinitely renewable (City of Taipei Civil Affairs Bureau 2003a).

In the PRC and the Republic of China alike, serving in such posts, generically translated as "block captains" here, is not the only avenue through which to volunteer at the neighborhood level. Residents may also, for instance, take part in security patrols (*zhian xunluo* in Beijing and *shouwang xiangzhu xunshoudui* in Taipei). These part-time citizen-sentinels can be seen strolling about the lanes in groups, proudly sporting their red sleeve bands or glowing vests. There are also teams engaged in neighborhood beautification and environmental protection.[11] Some Beijing neighborhoods have other RC spin-off organizations, such as a birth control association, composed of activists who have committed to lending a hand with a particular domain of RC work.[12] In Taipei, there are other forms of state-organized auxiliaries such as police volunteers (*yijing*), which are not directly related to *li* governance but constitute part of the pool of people who participate in these general ways at the ultra-local level.

Table 6.1 shows the frequency with which Beijing and Taipei residents participate in neighborhood activities. Three of the categories presented here overlap between the two cities, but four do not. Community development associations (CDAs; *shequ fazhan xiehui*) are unique to Taiwan, along with the kinds of local meetings and hearings indicated in the third row of

TABLE 6.1
Participation in neighborhood activities, by type of activity

Participation categories	Beijing: Respondents (%)	Taipei: Respondents (%)
Donates to neighborhood organization's charity drives	64.9	Not asked
Voted in most recent neighborhood election	15.6	50.4
Holds a neighborhood volunteer post	5.1	1.0
Has attended neighborhood meetings or hearings	Not asked	14.0
Participates in community development association	Not applicable	17.5
Participates in neighborhood patrols	13.1	Not asked
Participates in social events of the neighborhood organization	11.2	22.1
n	1,018	1,140

SOURCE: 2001 Beijing Law and Community Survey and 2006 Taipei Neighborhoods Survey.

NOTE: In the first, second, and fifth categories, respondents could indicate varying degrees of participation, rather than merely yes or no. Here the reported percentages combine those who participate "often" and "sometimes." The term *neighborhood volunteer post* refers to *linzhang* in Taipei and to several types of post in Beijing, including *jumin xiaozu zuzhang, louzhang, loumenzhang,* and *cengzhang.*

the tables (*limin dahui, shuominghui, gongtinghui*), at least as of the 2000s.[13] As many as 65 percent of respondents in the Beijing survey reported at least occasionally donating in response to the RC's requests for charitable contributions. Although this gives another indication of the very broad footprint of RC activity in society as a whole, such donations are usually small and, more important, are negligible in terms of time outlay. Table 6.1 also shows an immense gap between the cities in terms of rates of voting in neighborhood elections. The fact that far more Taipei residents vote is, of course, only to be expected, given the vast institutional differences detailed in Chapter 3.[14]

Holding a volunteer post represents a much more committed form of involvement compared to charitable giving or voting. Post holders constituted about one-twentieth of the population in the Beijing sample but only one-hundredth of the sample in Taipei. Although both cities recruit substantial numbers of citizens into these service roles, a larger proportion occupy such positions in Beijing. This is in spite of the fact that, as Table 2.2 showed, Beijing's residents' small groups and Taipei's *lin* are about equal in number relative to the total population of the city. In that data, Beijing had a small group for every 268 residents, and Taipei a *lin* for every 275.

It is instead because of the other categories of posts that overlap with and go beyond the scope of the small groups alone. As of the year 2000, my ten Beijing field sites had between 17 and 123 post holders each, numbers that do not include other forms of participation such as security patrolling. There was, in these neighborhoods, about one post holder for every twelve households on average, or one for every thirty-four members of the population. By 2010, the divergence between old and new neighborhoods had become quite striking: the much-expanded Chongxing claimed to have one courtyard head per eighteen residents, whereas a development of twenty-four-story buildings had just one building head or floor head per seventy-one residents. Although activists are not evenly scattered among neighborhoods, it is clear from these numbers, as well as aggregate official statistics, that their distribution is widespread. The Beijing city government put the total number of neighborhood activists at 108,000 in 1997 and at "approximately 140,000" in 1999.[15]

The last row of Table 6.1 shows that residents of Taipei take part in neighborhood social activities at about twice the rate of those in Beijing. In both cities, more than half of the population never participates in community-level gatherings, but the proportion of such abstainers is smaller in Taipei. Figure 6.1 further shows that a greater fraction of younger people take part

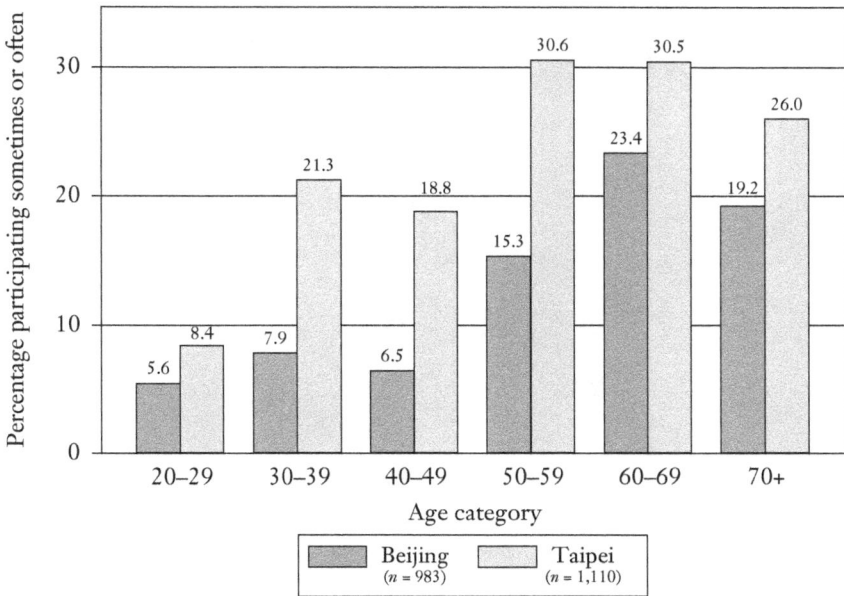

Figure 6.1.   Participation in neighborhood social activities, by age group.
Data are from the 2001 Beijing Law and Community Survey and the 2006 Taipei Neighborhoods Survey.

in neighborhood activities in Taipei. In both cities, the fifty-and-older age brackets contain the highest rates of participation, but in Taiwan's capital, more among those in their thirties and forties took part, too.

In the Venn diagrams of Figure 6.2, each circle shows the fraction of the city's sample that participates regularly in a given activity.[16] Not all categories are identical between the cities: the upper-right circle includes patrol duty in Beijing and meeting attendance in Taipei. The larger size of the circles illustrates the greater prevalence of all three of these activities in Taipei as compared to Beijing. In the latter, one-quarter of the sample had engaged in at least one of the three activities more than rarely; in the former, the corresponding figure is 60 percent. The graphs depict the previously documented contrast in reported voting rates. In both cities, we see considerable overlap among the circles, showing the mutually reinforcing nature of neighborhood participation. For example, in both cities, most of those who took part in the community's social activities also engaged in other forms of service or

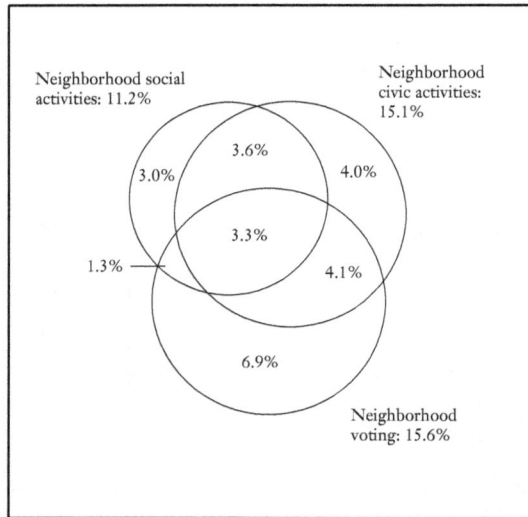

Beijing

Neighborhood social
activities: 11.2%

Neighborhood
civic activities:
15.1%

3.6%

3.0%

4.0%

3.3%

1.3%

4.1%

6.9%

Neighborhood
voting: 15.6%

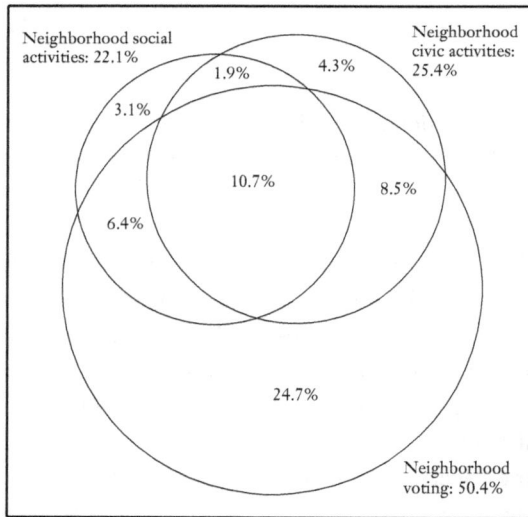

Taipei

Neighborhood social
activities: 22.1%

Neighborhood
civic activities:
25.4%

1.9%

4.3%

3.1%

10.7%

8.5%

6.4%

24.7%

Neighborhood
voting: 50.4%

Figure 6.2.   Neighborhood participation: Venn diagrams.
Areas of the squares represent the full survey samples from each city (Beijing *n* = 1,018,
Taipei *n* = 1,140). Areas of the circles are exactly proportional to the subsample percentages; areas of overlap among the circles only approximately so. In Beijing, 73.8 percent
of respondents belonged to none of the three categories, and in Taipei, 40.4 percent.
Neighborhood civic activities included service as a volunteer block captain in both cities,
as well as security patrols in Beijing and attendance at meetings of the neighborhood and
community development associations in Taipei. Data are from the 2001 Beijing Law and
Community Survey and the 2006 Taipei Neighborhoods Survey.

participation. At the same time, in neither case is voting confined to those who attend social functions or serve as volunteers. In Beijing, the RCs invite some locally prominent, cooperative residents to join in the election rituals, whereas Taipei's wardens and their teams of supporters mobilize many people who are otherwise uninvolved in neighborhood events (here, a full quarter of the sample) to turn out on Election Day.

Thus, each city has a core of particularly committed participants at the neighborhood level, and that kernel is larger in Beijing than in Taipei. As shown later in this chapter, community leaders in both capitals put considerable effort into building team spirit among this primary group of supporters. But Taipei has a larger penumbra of residents, beyond the core, that come into more casual and less administratively oriented forms of neighborhood participation. Indeed, had the survey been repeated after the 2010 three-in-one elections, in which turnout rose so dramatically, the circle of voters would bulge to even greater proportions.[17] How should what we might call Taipei's larger outer core of participation be explained? With regard to voting in particular, Taiwan's far more open and meaningful elections obviously encourage more residents to take part. Another possible explanation for broader participation in Taipei is the wardens' relatively deep entanglement in the thick and interwoven strands of local society, from clan networks to temple boards to parent-teacher associations. Another likely reason is that the *lizhang* have incentives to involve as many voters as possible in their festivals and other gatherings. That is part of the way in which they build name recognition and support in preparation for the next round of elections, when challengers might try to steal away their backers. In Beijing, in contrast, building broad-based support in the neighborhood is not an electoral imperative for RC incumbents. Instead, the committees are under greater pressure to reinforce the loyalty and selectively expand the ranks of their committed activists. Thus, their social events are more likely to be geared toward entertaining the relatively narrow clique of committed activists as opposed to pulling in a broader circle.

All these types and categories of participation point to ways in which people engage in supportive activity that is useful to neighborhood leaders and city government. Taipei's wardens aim to choose reliable supporters as their block captains, just as RCs in Beijing pick residents whom they can count on for help. But neighborhood-level voluntary participation is complex. A floor leader in an apartment building, for example, may indeed actively and enthusiastically provide assistance to the RC, or she might merely have allowed herself to be so designated in order to oblige the committee's need to fill out its roster. Status or connections may dictate the choice of block captains possessing special prestige. At the same time, many supporters of the neighborhood organization may not hold an official volunteer post.

Thus, there can be no perfect measures, but it is possible to create indices that capture the core idea of actively contributing to neighborhood governance on a volunteer basis. For this purpose, I divided each city's survey sample into participants and nonparticipants. In Beijing, the former were defined as those who had served as the RC's volunteer post holders, as well as those who regularly participated in neighborhood security patrols. In Taipei, this group comprised those who had served as *linzhang*, or who had attended neighborhood hearings or meetings, or who had taken part in community development associations. Factors predicting these forms of participation were explored using logit regression (Table 6.2).

Who are the people who take part in neighborhood service? In Beijing, those in their fifties and older are far more likely than others to participate. That volunteer patrol teams tend to draw from this demographic comes as no surprise to anyone who has spent time strolling through that city's streets and alleys. In Taipei, those in this category also make up a large proportion of local volunteers, but younger people are also fairly well represented, such that age does not statistically predict participation in the logit model. The average age of neighborhood participants was fifty-one in Taipei and fifty-six in Beijing.

Other pieces of information provided by the survey data illuminate important aspects of the neighborhood systems. In Beijing, the gender ratio of participants in certain RC-sponsored activities is strongly tilted toward women, whereas less of a gender divide is seen in Taipei. Fully 70 percent of those who held volunteer posts in Beijing were women. In Taipei, 52 percent of neighborhood participants were men.[18] What explains these contrasting sex ratios? To some extent, trends in employment and unemployment may lie behind the relative abundance of women among Beijing's activists. Women there were hit especially hard by layoffs, often being shunted into early retirement, thus making them more available for neighborhood activities. But economic trends alone do not explain these gaps. As previously noted, nearly four-fifths of RC staff members themselves in Beijing were women as of 2006, and indeed this pattern is found in cities around the country as well. Though sex does not statistically predict neighborhood activism overall, specific forms of participation clearly are gendered phenomena.

TABLE 6.2

Predicting voluntary neighborhood participation: Logit regressions

BEIJING			TAIPEI		
Variable	*Coef.*	*SE*	*Variable*	*Coef.*	*SE*
DEMOGRAPHIC			DEMOGRAPHIC		
Female	0.369	(0.225)	Female	−0.258	(0.197)
Age	0.040*	(0.016)	Age	0.007	(0.010)
Education, years	−0.074*	(0.036)	Education, years	−0.096**	(0.033)
Income, 2006 USD (1000s)	0.426	(0.784)	Income, 2006 USD (1000s)	−0.009	(0.059)
Retired	1.088***	(0.322)	Retired	0.585	(0.348)
Homeowner	0.168	(0.233)	Homeowner	0.491	(0.275)
Size of household	0.063	(0.126)	Subethnicity: Mainlander	−0.154	(0.380)
Life satisfaction	0.072	(0.126)	Subethnicity: Minnan	−0.137	(0.325)
Single rather than married	0.083	(0.400)			
POLITICAL AND ADMINISTRATIVE			POLITICAL AND ADMINISTRATIVE		
Approval: police and courts	0.072	(0.144)	Trust in city government	0.140	(0.151)
CCP or CYL member	0.111	(0.262)	Party ID: Pan-Blue	0.017	(0.239)
Correct household registry	0.216	(0.369)	Party ID: Pan-Green	−0.605	(0.310)

(continued)

TABLE 6.2 (*continued*)

	BEIJING			TAIPEI	
Variable	*Coef.*	*SE*	*Variable*	*Coef.*	*SE*
SOCIAL			SOCIAL		
Years in neighborhood (log)	−0.015	(0.170)	Years in neighborhood (log)	−0.193	(0.155)
Neighbors known (log)	0.443***	(0.113)	Neighbors known (log)	0.466***	(0.107)
Sociability: Associations	0.296**	(0.111)	Sociability: Associations	0.528***	(0.095)
			Generalized trust	0.111	(0.118)
NEIGHBORHOOD			NEIGHBORHOOD		
High-rise building	0.028	(0.427)	High-rise building	−0.300	(0.248)
1- or 2-story building	0.897***	(0.273)	1- or 2-story building	0.232	(0.340)
Neigh. avg. income, 1000s yuan	0.433	(0.295)	Low-income pop. in *li*	0.001	(0.001)
			Area of *li*, km^2	0.002	(0.002)
			Age of warden	0.010	(0.011)
Constant	−7.850***	(1.326)		−3.526***	(1.070)
Observations	861			719	
Pseudo-R^2	0.230			0.145	

NOTE: The outcome variable is a dichotomous measure of the respondent's participation in the neighborhood, as described in the text. Separate models were estimated for Beijing and Taipei, and not all predictor variables were the same for both cities. Robust standard errors were used in Beijing because of clustering by neighborhood.

*p < 0.05. **p < 0.01. ***p < 0.001.

In the ten Beijing field sites the preponderance of women among the most dedicated entryway heads and floor heads, those who regularly came in to visit and hobnob with the RC staff, was overwhelming. It was not uncommon for activist conclaves to be completely devoid of men. (Security patrols, however, were more evenly split between the sexes.) In Taipei, conversely, men were more likely to have held a *linzhang* post or to have attended a neighborhood meeting, although men and women voted in warden elections and participated in *li* social activities in roughly equal ratios.

One would expect political factors to predict neighborhood participation much more strongly than turns out to be the case. In Taipei, trust in the city government has no correlation with joining and volunteering in this way. As well, Blue-leaning residents are no more likely than nonpartisans to take part, despite the *li* system's long domination by the Kuomintang (KMT).[19] In Beijing, Communist Party members, and those more warmly disposed toward state institutions, are no more likely than others to be recruited into these service roles. All this suggests that in neither city should block captains be thought of primarily as foot soldiers in party machines.

The results instead spotlight the class dimension of neighborhood participation. In both cities, those with less education are more likely to take part in this form of volunteer service. This parallels the finding in Figure 3.1 that those with less schooling had a much greater tendency to vote in Taipei's warden elections. As with the gender differentials, this, too, seems to reflect the social makeup of the neighborhood leaders themselves. We also see that those with a tendency to join associations in general were more likely than others to take part in neighborhood service. This fact, too, points to the social nature of institutions like the RCs' many volunteer positions and their *linzhang* counterparts. Their appeals, as we will see, are of a piece with the attractions that draw people into other forms of organizational life.

As previously noted, my Beijing field research sites varied substantially in terms of the prevalence of neighborhood participation. In the case of Wutai, a newly built neighborhood, the RCs and their networks of affiliates remained in an early stage of development as of 2000, although in later years they matured and their ranks filled out. Here the ratio of post holders to ordinary citizens was markedly low. On the other end of the scale, three of the highest ratios were found in neighborhoods near the city center with single-story, courtyard housing: Chongxing, Shuangqiao, and Xiyingjie. It is in these older areas that the RCs' circles of activists are most densely established—indeed, Table 6.2

clearly reflects this—whereas in new developments the committees must work gradually to attract supporters. Anfeng, a small and particularly well-organized neighborhood occupied primarily by retired cadres from a national ministry, had numerous volunteers and stood out as a partial exception. In Taipei, with less growth, construction, and upheaval in the neighborhoods, the *lin* appeared to be more stable and evenly distributed.

To sum up this section: those who voluntarily lend a hand with the official neighborhood administrative structures in Beijing are not entirely the mirror image of their counterparts in Taipei. The gender contrast stands out, in particular. Yet they share a number of basic characteristics. They tend to be deeply rooted in their residential surroundings and closely familiar with the people who live around them. Indeed, in both cities, the local volunteers reported a personal acquaintance with, on average, slightly more than seventy of their neighbors, almost three times the average for nonparticipants.[20] In both cities, the pattern that emerges is one of a core of individuals—in neighborhood after neighborhood—contributing some spare time and energy to these organizations. Although they form only a modest percentage of the population, in the aggregate they constitute an immense number of people who provide assistance to the systems centered around the residents' committees and the *li-lin* apparatus. Given their wide dispersal, few urbanites live far from the home of a volunteer of some kind; they are well positioned to keep in touch with the residents around them. In addition to and overlapping with those who engage in volunteer service is a broader set of individuals who take part in neighborhood social activities—a stratum that is larger in Taipei than in Beijing.

These figures have provided a basic quantitative portrait, one that highlights the social nature of the RC and neighborhood warden systems. With this as a backdrop, we now employ a mostly qualitative approach to address the questions of what it is that the activists do, why they do it, and how they are perceived by their neighbors.

The Volunteers' Role in the Neighborhood

GATHERING INFORMATION AND OTHER ADMINISTRATIVE TASKS

In Beijing and other cities of mainland China, one of the state's primary motivations for having the residents' committees cultivate activists so systematically is the information that they help to collect—information about those who live around them and about what goes on in the neighborhood in general. The activists do many other things as well, but from the authorities' perspective what is most important is that, scattered as they are throughout the neighborhood, they are naturally well positioned to observe what is going on outside their windows, down the hallway, or across the courtyard. The information they provide can be crucial at moments of special exigency, such as cases of crime or threats to the state, but it also plays a cumulatively important role in everyday administration. Neighborhood activists are part of a patient investment by the state in people who contribute to its micro-level knowledge of society and therefore sharpen its capacity to intervene, both for broader social purposes and for maintaining the hegemony of the Communist Party.

Activists regularly stopped by the residents' committee offices in my field sites to apprise the staff of local happenings. The entryway heads and those in similar positions formed an integral part of the system through which RC staff routinely updated their files in programs like birth control, household registry, and the administration of migrants. In Xianningjie, the committee staff asked activists to sign birth-control responsibility letters (*jisheng zeren shu*), in which they formally accepted the duty of keeping an eye peeled for pregnancies in the homes around them, along with other tasks. Generally, however, no such documents were needed; activists took it upon themselves to tell the RC about all types of problems actual and potential, from fights among neighbors to strangers lurking in stairwells and a water pipe that had been hit by a truck and had burst open.[21]

Committee members also systematically queried the activists for information they needed. The Xianningjie staff were particularly adept at casually grasping opportunities for an update from their trusted volunteers. One March afternoon, a building head strolled in for a visit. In the midst of general banter, the genial but focused Liu Xiaomeng took the opportunity to inquire about birth control among some newly moved-in residents: did they have children? Director Cao jumped into the conversation as well, probing about whether she might expect a friendly or frosty reception from one of the newcomers were she to undertake a personal visit: "Is she tough [*lihai*]?" On another occasion Officer Dai, the beat cop, following up on a report about a local follower of the *falun gong* spiritual sect, first came to the RC office to get the name and phone number of the head of the entryway in which the follower lived and then called her for information before pursuing the matter himself.[22]

One Friday the following month, six or seven of the neighborhood volunteers, all women in their fifties or sixties, gathered in the back room for their weekly choral session, which featured patriotic songs led by Ge Yanhua, the RC's social coordinator. After honing their vocal skills, the women filtered back through the main office, where the other staff members engaged them in conversation, characteristically mixing casual chatter and soberer administrative matters. Liu talked sympathetically to one entryway head about her elderly father and his dementia. She then smoothly segued into reminding her of the necessity of staying on the qui vive for pregnancies among the younger residents, especially renters; a woman in a nearby neighborhood had recently flown to the Czech Republic to have a second child. Liu asked about the people in the activist's entryway and was assured that all was well. Another committee member, Yi Hanfeng, then joined the conversation from her desk, asking that the volunteer watch out for residents conducting home renovations so that the committee could ensure that they follow proper procedures for waste disposal. Liu rounded out the visit with an appeal for help in soliciting donations to support the establishment of a nearby public park.[23]

Acquiring information through the activist network helps the RC staff in a number of ways. It clues them in to events that they would not otherwise observe and may have no way of inquiring about. Even information that might be accessible to them through home visits and telephone inquiries with residents is much more efficiently gathered through third parties; this saves them the trouble of staying late and plodding up and down stairwells to find residents in their homes. As the scenes above indicate, having the activists make contact with new residents allows the committee staff to prepare for initiating their own contacts by providing them background information and a sense of how receptive the residents will be. Furthermore, it makes the gathering of information less obtrusive.

Taipei's *linzhang*, too, connect ordinary residents to the neighborhood organization and higher levels of administration. Wardens are required to hold quarterly meetings with them, which government officials and police attend as well. The government-mandated tasks of the *linzhang* include conveying announcements and rules from the city to their neighbors, passing on greetings and small gifts for the elderly, and (in some cases) serving on security patrols. They may report trouble if they see it, and occasionally assist the police or the *liganshi*; in some cases they are even asked for information about neighbors to update the household registry records. Yet they are not called on for surveillance purposes in anything like the way that the RCs' activists can be. Indeed, in terms of day-to-day governance responsibilities, the Taipei authorities seem to ask relatively little of the city's block captains. Significant administrative tasks are generally handled by the *li* office without drawing on or delegating to the *linzhang*, a point on which Taiwan's institutions differ from China's.

A BIT PART IN THE PERFORMANCE OF GOVERNANCE

Particularly in China, neighborhood volunteers have what might be called a performance role along with their other para-administrative duties. By turning out to patrol their locality singly or in teams, marked by their armbands, they provide a display of strength and numbers on behalf of the state. Of course, neighborhoods are not the only setting in which such displays are organized. Like other communist rulers, China's authorities are accomplished producers of mass pageants. As the nation's capital, Beijing is, of course, the site for many such spectacles, which have in recent years included ostentatious troop reviews on anniversaries of the PRC's founding in 1999 and 2009, the opening ceremony of the 2008 Olympics, and rallies celebrating events like reunification with Hong Kong and Macau. Though not as grand as these extravaganzas, RC-organized patrols are a way of showing the state's capacity to mobilize support not merely occasionally in public arenas like Tiananmen Square but also on a recurring or everyday basis in neighborhoods throughout major cities. On special occasions like holidays and major political meetings, Beijing's committees are instructed to mobilize increased numbers of patrollers to come out in force and make the rounds. During the March 2000 two-meetings period (*liang hui qijian*), the annual convening of the National People's Congress and the National People's Political Consultative Conference, the local police station told the Shimen team to have eight armband-sporting patrollers turned out for every hundred residents in the neighborhood. The previous year's National Day had brought a similarly tall order.[24]

The link between patrolling local streets and alleys and the lofty symbolic events of national politics is instructive. It suggests that one of the attractions of serving as an activist is precisely the sense of being a part of the broad project of maintaining order and governance. Although they occupy the humblest of stations in the administration of the city, the feeling of responsibility and affiliation with the state conferred by activist status provides affirmation to this category of people, many of whom have few other claims to social prestige. As one RC staff member put it: "They don't have much else to do. And it makes them feel satisfied. They feel: 'I'm retired or don't have work, but they still come to me for things.'"[25] Older activists are sometimes so keen on their posts that they try to continue on even after becoming physically incapable of carrying out their duties well; RC staff spoke of having to take the awkward step of dismissing such infirm enthusiasts. This loss of responsibility can be a harsh disappointment for some. As one Beijing resident slightly derisively described her aunt, who had been relieved of a volunteer position: "The old woman here was an entryway head; she only stopped recently. She's felt psychologically let down [*xinli shiluo*] ever since. . . . The old woman still has those bad habits—she still peeks out the window all the time, and if she sees anything going on, she wants to report it . . . give me a break [*lei bu lei*]."[26]

Taipei's neighborhood-level volunteers, too, evince a strong sense of pride in the service they render to the city. Unlike in Beijing, they are no longer called up in the kind of grand mobilizations that the authorities there stage to mark major events, although they once were. Still, they, too, see themselves as performing a part in a network of service that spans local government and the community. From their government-mandated charters to their newsletters and reports to the district authorities, community development associations stress their officially approved status, along with grants and awards bestowed on them by the city. The *linzhang*'s city-issued letter of appointment adds to his or her sense of official recognition and acknowledged importance. So, too, do the security patrollers' reflective vests and flashlights. A forty-eight-year-old woman in the Nangang district spoke glowingly of her *li*'s patrol team, organized into five subteams, each with a leader and assistant leader: "Having us out there on patrol can reduce social problems to some extent. In this neighborhood people are really enthusiastic about taking part. We have the most participants in the entire city of Taipei, as many as eighty people! And we're ranked number one or two in terms of our accomplishments, which isn't bad either. . . . In our lane alone there are nine people that go on patrol."[27]

HELPING NEIGHBORS, AND WATCHING THEM

The Nangang patroller's comment conveys pride not only in playing a part in maintaining order in the capital city and standing tall among other locales but also in doing something of benefit to the area. In neither Beijing nor Taipei do block captains and the like see their roles merely in terms of the governance-related responsibilities that the state formally or informally delegates to them. To fully understand these volunteers, one must also take into account their view of themselves as contributing in small ways to the well-being of their neighbors and the community in general. Although individuals of course vary in how well they live up to this, quite a few stand out by pitching in around the neighborhood, taking care of chores, and pursuing public-spirited tasks—and this in turn shapes the way others perceive them.

In both capitals, block captains take on tasks that help the neighborhood organization perform its duties, such as disseminating announcements of various types or picking up and dropping off minor documents like senior citizens' discount passes. In Taipei, block captains inform residents about upcoming festivals or about public meetings on issues of importance to the neighborhood, and they convey complaints and opinions to the warden. In Beijing, they sometimes look in on disabled residents or welfare recipients on behalf of the RC.[28] They often go door-to-door to collect fees for sanitation, gas, or electricity, although sometimes all residents and not just the activists take turns doing this. Naturally, these kinds of tasks are most significant in older neighborhoods without commercial property management. Other aspects of the block captains' service role are more ad hoc. One neighborhood boasted an elderly volunteer who fixed small household appliances for token fees.[29] In Xianningjie, a courtyard head stopped in to discuss job possibilities on behalf of a forty-one-year-old woman living nearby who had just been laid off from her work unit.[30] Others would clear trash away from a yard, sweep and mop the hallway in a large apartment building, or take in mail or newspapers.

Much of this, of course, is the kind of thing that neighbors anywhere might help one another with. What is notable is the way that much of this type of casual assistance is subsumed within the subculture of state-mobilized neighborhood participation. This means that, in Beijing, activists interact with those around them in benign and useful capacities, whereas any snooping or informing they might do is quiet and behind the scenes. Correspondingly, residents' views of the activists there seem to be quite varied. Some say that they are wary of the activists among their neighbors and avoid them as much as possible. This may particularly be the case for residents who have something to hide, such as illegally subletting a state-owned home; it may also reflect a taste for privacy and discomfort with the sense of being watched. In other cases, residents get along fine with the activists around them and appreciate their assistance and neighborliness.

Both those who are critical of the activists and those who are positively inclined toward them tend to describe them with terms like *ai guan shi* or *ai guan xianshi*. This term could be translated benignly as "liking to look after things," neutrally as "liking to take charge of things," or more sinisterly as "liking to get involved in [other people's] business." Beijingers themselves are ambivalent in how they use the phrase—it means "nosiness" to some, "helpfulness" to others. Sometimes a single informant used different meanings of the term in the same interview. One forty-two-year-old female barber had a generally negative perception of the activists in her housing complex, which belonged to a state work unit that was built in the 1950s. She felt that things like security patrols were not particularly useful: "What exactly do they do? They stop peddlers from coming into the compound without permission. They don't really stop thieves—I've lost eight bicycles!" She disparaged RC staff and activists alike as people who have nothing better to do than "*guan xianshi*." But later in the conversation she talked about her mother, who had served as an RC director for ten years up until the Cultural Revolution: "Back then they got no pay. It was truly selfless contribution to society. My mother really liked to *guan xianshi*. She liked to help people who had relatives who died, or who got sick; she liked helping the childless old people and resolving disputes."[31]

Just as respondents expressed mixed feelings about this form of concern for others, they were divided in their overall perceptions of activists as well. The more guarded type of reception can be seen in this comment from an intellectual in her late thirties, which also indicates her mother's more welcoming perspective:

> She [the activist] loves to stop by, drop off the mail, chat about things, and ask about your family's situation. She insists on coming into our apartment. Once she even came around at 7 o'clock in the morning on the weekend and I had to receive her in my bathrobe, and close the doors to the bedrooms so she

wouldn't peek in. She would know everything about who lived where in the neighborhood, how old they were, and so on. My mother really liked to chat with her; my mother is from a small town and is used to having a closer sense of community.[32]

In contrast, this middle-aged, laid-off worker in her fifties expressed the more benign view:

There is an old man in this courtyard who is in touch with the RC, named Guo. He's probably seventy-five years old. He is enthusiastic, and loves to *guan xianshi*. [Question: Was Guo selected or elected by the residents themselves in any way?] Of course he wasn't elected. He does things like picking up mail for people at the post office, and newspapers. Sometimes the RC will have him pass announcements on to the residents. . . . [He] sometimes cleans up the courtyard, and sometimes gets upset when people don't help him. His relationship with us is pretty good; we're happy with him. [Question: Are you worried about people like him informing on you?] We haven't done anything reactionary, so we're not worried about him.[33]

Interviews in Taipei asking residents about the *linzhang* found a similar range of responses. One woman spoke positively about hers, who lived across the hallway from her. "If there's an activity, she'll tell the people around here about it. She's a leader of the patrol team, and goes and asks people with free time to take part in it. If the health department comes by for an inspection, the warden will tell us about it, but the *linzhang* will also mention it."[34] Even though in Taiwan there is no possibility of the kind of quiet political surveillance that can take place in China, not all interviewees in Taipei spoke favorably of their block captains. One said: "I don't know him and so I don't have contact with him. . . . [The] purpose of the *linzhang* is not so obvious to people; they are not of much use."[35] Some with this type of attitude also felt it wasteful for the city to provide monetary compensation to these volunteers. Because block captains are chosen by the warden, Taipei residents have no more input than do Beijingers in the selection process, formally speaking. Yet they often may exercise control indirectly, as one woman related: "The man who was the old *linzhang* was a volunteer policeman, but he would drink at night. The worst was when he had a fight with his son and threw a gas canister outside. It was most likely because so many residents complained that the

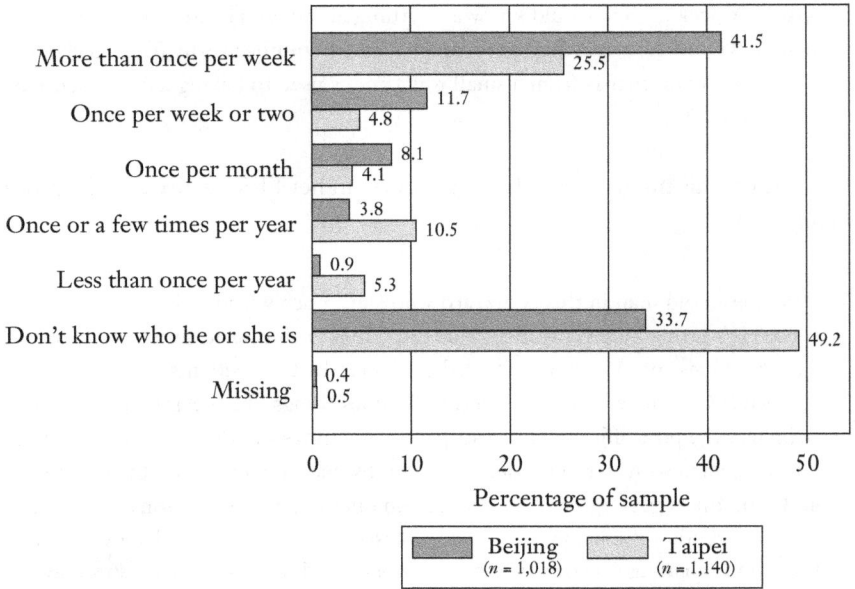

Figure 6.3.   Frequency of contact with block captain.
Data are from the 2001 Beijing Law and Community Survey and the 2006 Taipei Neighborhoods Survey.

block captain was switched. We all felt that the old woman was a good choice to replace him. We said that this lady is very active, so let's have her be our *linzhang.*"[36]

Data from the surveys give some perspective on how often residents of Beijing and Taipei come into contact with the neighborhood volunteers around them and what they think of them. As previously discussed, on a per capita basis as well as in absolute numbers, there are simply more such volunteers in China's capital than in Taiwan's. This fact is reflected in Figure 6.3, which shows that ordinary people in Beijing come into contact with block captains much more frequently than Taipei residents do. It also shows that although nearly half of all those surveyed in Taipei did not know who their *linzhang* is, the comparable proportion for those in Beijing was substantially smaller, only 34 percent.

Questions in both surveys assessed residents' openness toward or trust in the post holder responsible for their subsection of the neighborhood. These

TABLE 6.3

Openness with block captain

BEIJING		TAIPEI	
Answer category	Percentage	Answer category	Percentage
Can talk about anything	7.7	Very trusting	6.2
Can discuss most things	14.6	Fairly trusting	20.1
Can discuss a few things or fairly reserved	20.4	A bit reserved	26.8
Do not talk, or must be cautious	17.4	Quite cautious and reserved	21.8
Don't know	39.2	Don't know	24.9
Refused or missing	0.7	Refused	0.2
n	966		1,129

SOURCE: 2001 Beijing Law and Community Survey and 2006 Taipei Neighborhoods Survey.

NOTE: These two questions were not identically worded in the Beijing and Taipei surveys. Individuals who were themselves block captains were removed from the samples for this table. Because of rounding, columns may not sum precisely to 100 percent.

questions were not identically worded in the two cities, but they suffice to give us a starting point for comparison.[37] The results show, in both cities, a modest segment of the population that was entirely or largely at ease with the block captain: 22 percent in Beijing and 26 percent in Taipei (Table 6.3). Between two-fifths and a half in each city felt wholly or fairly distant from these volunteers, whereas significant numbers did not know the block captain or did not have an assessment of openness toward him or her. In Taipei, respondents had somewhat less trust in the *linzhang* than in the neighborhood warden, or even in people in general.[38] In the Beijing survey, a further question asked whether the block captain strived to be helpful to his or her neighbors. About half of the interviewees found their floor head or entryway head to be somewhat or very hardworking on behalf of neighbors. Fewer than 10 percent gave an answer of neutral or not hardworking; others did not know.

These mixed perceptions found in the survey data parallel the ambivalence expressed in the qualitative interviews. For many people, the neighborhood volunteers are seen as making efforts not merely to assist the RC or warden but also as being useful to others. For these respondents, the work that activists undertake on behalf of the state does not seem particularly intrusive. Clearly, the way in which neighborhood post holders provide casual assistance to those around them lightens public perceptions of them. Yet, for many others, there is something off-putting about these enthusiasts, whether that is nosiness or the suspicion that they might have ulterior motives. This is true even in Taipei, where the *linzhang* can hardly be viewed as eavesdroppers for the government. For still others, the world of the neighborhood volunteers is simply far removed from their own cares and concerns.

MATERIAL INCENTIVES

As we saw at the outset of this chapter, accounts of activism in China and other state-socialist systems have often explained such behavior as driven by material payoffs and clientelist relationships. Indeed, acts of supportive participation generally raise the question of what kinds of incentives might be involved. Do the block captains receive substantial instrumental rewards in return for the help they provide to neighborhood organizations?

Material compensation to activists varied somewhat from place to place among my Beijing sites. Neighborhood activists do receive minor gifts from the RCs, and in a few areas these gifts even take the form of small cash payments in exchange for certain types of service. But the material value of these rewards is in most cases trivial, even by local standards, and never amounts to more than a modest incentive. The holders of positions like small-group head and entryway head received cash for their efforts in only one of the neighborhoods I studied, where floor leaders were given several dozen yuan each at the lunar New Year party. Instead of cash, the activists commonly receive gifts several times a year: bars of soap; a few pounds of commodities like sugar, cooking oil, flour, and green peas; towels, sheets, or blankets; or snacks like candy or melon seeds. In the case of regular security patrollers, who usually put in a set number of hours per week, some received only periodic gifts such as the above, whereas others received small monthly payments. The best-paid security patrollers that I learned about were given 40 yuan per month for an hour and a half of patrolling each day. Though not entirely negligible, this was no overwhelming incentive—40 yuan could buy, for instance, about eight packs of cheap cigarettes or a dozen bottles of beer. More commonly, patrollers received no cash, and the RC staff took pride in that fact.

The RCs often had explicit budgets from the street offices that supervised them to provide for these gifts and payments, as well as the occasional group outing. One well-funded committee was allocated more than 5,000 yuan every six months for this purpose, which it spent on supplies for parties as well as gifts (not cash, in this case) for its more than fifty activists. This implied an average of 17 yuan in monthly expenditure per person. In short, to the extent that activists received material compensation at all, this was for the most part a token thank-you.

Given the prevalent notion that material rewards motivate state-supportive volunteering in Communist Party–led systems, it is somewhat ironic that Taipei features more tangible and standardized monetary payments to block captains. There, *linzhang* received a fixed subsidy from the city government of NT$2,000 (about US$60) per month.[39] Indeed, it was in part the proposal to cut this so-called transportation allowance (*chema fei*) in half that spurred the neighborhood leaders into action against the 2003 reform program. Clearly, they felt that to gut these allowances would tangibly diminish their block captains' enthusiasm, no doubt to the detriment of their service activities and their aid in reelection campaigns. Thus, these sums are modest but not a matter of indifference.

I discussed with many knowledgeable people in Beijing and Taipei the question of what backdoor benefits local volunteers might receive, such as special treatment by neighborhood staff, city authorities, or the police. One RC staff member, whom I came to trust because of her frank answers on many matters, pooh-poohed the idea that the activists were out for favoritism: "It's possible that a few have that in mind, but most don't. There wouldn't be many opportunities to favor them. For instance, there was a case where an activist had stacked coal bricks to dry in front of someone else's window, and that person complained to the RC. Now, could we just side with the activist?"[40]

A Taipei *liganshi* related the story of a block captain whose illegal rooftop home addition was reported by neighbors and who had to dismantle it just like anyone else would have to, at a cost of more than US$15,000.[41] Chapter 4 contained a discussion of the degree to which a neighborhood organization might give special treatment to its supporters. It would certainly be within the realm of possibility for an RC member or a higher-level contact to tip the scales in favor of an activist or an activist's friend or relative on certain matters: eligibility for welfare benefits, transfers of household registry, approval to run a shop or other business, and conceivably legal cases. Similarly, Taipei wardens can and do make choices that favor their supporters, as Chen Boyu did in discouraging food stalls that competed with local restaurants like the porridge shop. Or they might look the other way rather than reporting things like parking or housing-code violations. Still, in few cases in either city did the prospect of such favors seem to constitute a primary motivation for residents volunteering as a block captain or neighborhood patroller, or in other capacities. Given the relative infrequency of occasions when the neighborhoods are in a position to exercise discretion over matters of real pecuniary value, this seems an unlikely motivation for most supporters.

In Taipei, the block captains' stipends—though hardly putting them in a position of dependency with respect to the warden—clearly form one part of the mixture of incentives that bring them into this regularized service role. In Beijing, the relatively paltry nature of the gifts that the activists receive emphasizes that their purpose is mainly to convey a symbolic reward and to reinforce the real attractions of this role, which, in both cities, lie in the social and psychological realms. One interviewee said of her mother, a former neighborhood activist: "She didn't get anything for her efforts but a bar of soap. She would do patrol duty. She would clean up the neighborhood. She would also keep watch in the alley on holidays. She felt important. When she got the soap she would tell people: 'This was given to me by the street office! [*Zhe shi jiedao gei de!*]'"[42]

CONNECTING WITH PEERS

Rather than in material handouts, the key to neighborhood participation in both cities lies in its social dimension. As much as any other motivation, residents get involved in officially sponsored events and programs because it provides a chance to get out of the home and spend time socializing with like-minded peers.

Particularly in Beijing, this aspect of neighborhood volunteering is not coincidental or epiphenomenal but rather is painstakingly encouraged by the RCs themselves and systematically cultivated by the street offices. The committees sponsor a variety of regular recreational programs, including choral societies, dance clubs, and exercise groups. The latter practice both traditional tai chi (*taijiquan*) and things like the *jianshenqiu*, a rubber ball attached to a bungee cord used to whack oneself therapeutically on the back in a series of synchronized movements. Some neighborhoods provide tables and tiles for low-stakes or no-stakes sessions of mah-jongg (*majiang*). In some cases staff displayed real creativity in keeping these activities up to date. One RC director in a relatively affluent, newly built neighborhood organized her circle of middle-aged-and-older associates into a fashion-show team, which got together to show off their latest sartorial acquisitions; on another occasion, her colleagues arranged a youth soccer tournament.[43] One Tuesday my note taking in a different RC office was interrupted by loud noise coming from outside the building: the pulsing thump of electronic music that would not have seemed out of place in even the most au courant of Beijing's nightclubs. Poking my head out the door, I found the RC social coordinator leading about twenty middle-aged women and a few men in a series of dance moves.[44] Weng Lan, the staff member of the Dengdao RC formally responsible for such cultural and sports activities (*wenti huodong*), took time one day to show off the collection of equipment she had accumulated for her various groups. These included fans for the fan dance, a collapsible sword for the sword dance, and kerchiefs for the kerchief dance, not to mention equipment for tai chi and other exercise classes. Her sessions, held outside the office on a concrete patio, regularly attracted ten to twenty residents, most of them in their forties or fifties, and Weng expressed pride in the attendance rates. Later that morning, a street office staff member stopped by the office and demonstrated that these activities are not just fun and games but something the state takes very seriously. Weng's superior criticized her for having made little progress on the year-end report that was coming due. "You need a plan, a summary, and an activities log. What, you don't have a summary? It's already November!" She conveyed dissatisfaction with Weng's record keeping and was particularly concerned that no photographic record of the cultural and sports activities had been established for verification.[45] The reason that the institutions of urban governance care about fan-dance classes and the like is that these recreational and social activities play an important role in cementing the RC's relationship to its supporters.

In Taipei, assisting with neighborhood arts, culture, and sports activities also is among the wardens' assigned duties, and the city government promotes such things through community centers and the like. The authorities hardly need to crack the whip to make this happen—rather, many *lizhang* do so of their own initiative, as the electoral system gives them strong incentives for it. Not all leaders organize recreational events, but those who do not miss out on obvious opportunities to win the goodwill of constituents who are engaged with the community and thus likely to vote. Indeed, in some neighborhoods, elected leaders vie with other organizations for the opportunity to host such get-togethers.

In Beitou district in the northernmost part of the city, a nonpartisan warden, Ni Jinfeng, won election in a neighborhood with a long-standing,

KMT-leaning community development association. Envious of the high turnout at the activities this faction put together for residents, and correctly perceiving in it a hotbed for potential rivals, Ni began to horn in on events like the Mother's Day walk. "He wouldn't take part in our event, and he put on his own instead, so it was one group of people walking with the warden, and another group walking with the director of the association," one of the association stalwarts related. "Usually it's the *linzhang* who help the warden put on his activities, and with the CDA it's all of our directors, supervisors, and small-group members putting on our activities." Ni also took over sponsorship of the neighborhood's traditional Mid-Autumn Festival party, and its Winter Festival, although he nonetheless went down to defeat in the 2006 elections at the end of his first term.[46]

The Venn diagrams in Figure 6.2 showed the degree to which those who take part in neighborhood social functions also participate in other local activities. It illustrated the way in which the events that the RCs and neighborhood wardens sponsor are part of an ongoing effort to build and maintain a lively subculture of supportive participants, for whom volunteer service and socializing are two sides of the same coin. In fact, Figure 6.2 only begins to delineate the social dimensions of neighborhood service. Security-patrol duty is usually itself a group activity, with two to five participants strolling around the neighborhood together or keeping an eye on things from a stoop or a bench. As well, the meetings that the RC convenes for its post holders, though carefully structured, are not mere bureaucratic exercises but rather double as parties. Over the course of the year RC staff organize a number of such assemblies, around events like National Day, Lunar New Year, Women's Day, May Day, and so forth. Festive banners are displayed; candy, nuts, and tea are served; and participants compare notes on one another's families and catch up on gossip before and after sitting down to receive special instructions, exhortations, thanks, and encouragement from the RC staff and representatives of the street office.

Many RCs also organized bus trips to parks and tourist attractions outside of Beijing for activists, party members, retired RC staff, and other affiliates. These are not, generally speaking, intended as outings to which everyone in the neighborhood is invited; rather, they are intended as a way to thank the RC's supporters and to boost their esprit de corps. In Taipei, city-subsidized excursions, called self-strengthening activities (*ziqiang huodong*), often perform much the same function. Although these are intended to be open to all residents, in practice the block captains and other core backers tend to be first in line for the tours. For example, in 2006 one warden took his *linzhang* across the Taiwan Strait to Jinmen for a three-day excursion; the city defrayed NT$1,000 of each traveler's NT$5,500 cost. The subsidy thus constitutes a modest material benefit, but few would go along on such jaunts if they did not relish the companionship of others in the circle of community regulars.

In addition to taking part in such planned get-togethers, volunteers also spend quite a bit of time hanging around the neighborhood, often in the company of others like them. Some Taipei wardens arrange for their block captains to take shifts staffing the *li* office and receiving visitors. In Beijing, many activists dropped in at the RC office with great regularity, sometimes to convey a particular piece of news or discuss a problem and sometimes simply for chitchat. The RC staff occasionally even complained about having to entertain such guests at length and getting behind in all their other work as a result.[47] Quite often one encountered activists perched on chairs or standing together, with or without red sleeve bands, watching who comes and goes and sometimes asking them to explain who they are and what they are up to.

In short, service as a neighborhood volunteer provides a social focal point for this particular category of individual. In some cases such service and the camaraderie associated with it become quite central to their lives and a substitute for other types of human interaction in the world beyond the neighborhood. For others, it is merely one part of a more extensive set of leisure activities. Certainly, one cannot account for its appeal without understanding its social aspects.

Possibilities for Exercising Broader Influence

It is beyond dispute that the networks of neighborhood volunteers in both Beijing and Taipei were originally conceived as obedient components of the apparatus of government. By design, they were to facilitate projects and directives handed down from above. But does their state-cultivated nature doom them perpetually to such subservience? Is it possible for such structured associations to permit or encourage the expression of alternative societal voices and ideas at the ultra-local level?

In the case of Beijing, the ways in which neighborhood activists support the RC by supplying it with information and by contributing to symbolic displays are central to their role. But activists do not merely support the committee; they also have an impact on it in limited ways. As noted in Chapter 3, neighborhood volunteers could at certain times affect the selection of members of the RC staff, whether by voting (as residents' representatives) in the highly constrained elections or by influencing street office officials' choices for the candidate lists. These input functions must be kept in proper perspective. In elections, the activists were able to exercise sway over only one or two of the RC seats, and not over its leadership. One cannot find here robust veto power or democratic authority. Rather, the importance of the activists' modest influence on the RCs lies in what it tells us about their own conception of the role they play.

Activists sometimes take the lead in pointing out local problems to the committee, discussing, and addressing them. Although the agenda for an activist meeting is determined in advance and involves much more top-down assigning of tasks than bottom-up input, such meetings do include requests for suggestions and criticisms from those assembled. One committee, for instance, was told by its activists to pay more attention to security and sanitation, prone as the neighborhood was to petty thievery and sewage problems.[48] Because street office staff attend these meetings, it gives them a chance to hear feedback on the performance of the committee. As well, new RC staff are obliged to introduce themselves to the activists individually and listen to their opinions on how the neighborhood should be run. One newly appointed director described this process to me almost as though she had been campaigning to win their votes in a contested election, even though her installation as director had essentially been a foregone conclusion.[49] The examples show that the activists do at times have the power to act as a check on the committee staff. Even more important, they illustrate that activists see themselves not merely as ground-level lackeys of the party-state but also as contributing to neighborhood administration in ways that can be critical as well as supportive. Still, in its current formulation the residents' committee system does relatively little to empower its volunteers or otherwise encourage independent social action.

In Taipei, neighborhood volunteers have a more complex relationship to the skeins of local power. The *linzhang* are, to be sure, appointed by the warden and serve at his or her pleasure. But in a democratic era, the nature of that service does not just mean providing assistance when the warden or the city government ask for it. As one warden observed about the meetings that he holds twice a year with his block captains: "These meetings existed during the authoritarian period, but now they're different. In the past it was giving orders from above. Now it's the *linzhang* expressing residents' opinions on their behalf. Its function is completely different."[50] The block captains and others involved in local activities now often shape the micropolitics of the *li* in lively and influential ways.

An unusual transition took place in early 2007 in a neighborhood on the slopes of Yangming Mountain. Zhang Junhua, who had served as the neighborhood's district liaison officer (*liganshi*), retired from the civil service to run against Hong Guocheng, the incumbent he had worked with for eight and a half years. Hong, part of a well-established local family, had reputedly taken to excessive drinking and become sloppy in his work. Zhang soundly defeated his former colleague, winning 58 percent of the vote. Closely familiar with the area, Zhang had given serious thought to the *linzhang*. He planned to keep about half of Hong's block captains but build a new team of his own:

> I want younger ones, with vigor, who can serve people, and who have patience. Not ones that will have conflicts with people all the time. . . . You need various kinds of people to be *linzhang*. One kind are those that are part of the big clans around here; naturally you need to be in touch with them, along with all their relatives. Another kind is people who are good at service, and another kind is the young people, who can walk up and down the mountain. The most important is that this time I will have some people who are in their twenties. They want to give it a try. They never had a chance in the past. They have jobs. But they'll be OK. We only have two meetings a year. We can just use evenings to keep in contact. . . . They're mainly to be representatives, to express their views, and to bring people's opinions to me.[51]

Zhang's planning makes clear that he saw *linzhang* as conduits through which to keep in touch with, and receive input from, the multiple parts of his constituency. By carefully maintaining such lines of communication, he aimed to prevent the kind of embarrassing unseating that he had just dealt his predecessor.

Although they are themselves unelected, the block captains are thus an integral part of the city's electoral mechanisms. As Chapter 3 began to show, they are closely caught up in the contests that determine neighborhood leadership. Sitting *linzhang* form part of the team through which an incumbent mobilizes support in reelection campaigns. An aspiring warden often designates shadow *linzhang*, men and women who are promised these positions in the event of the candidate's victory. In both Beijing and Taipei, there is gradual turnover in the ranks of the block captains, but in Taipei, this is linked to the periodic, institutionalized scrimmages that determine leadership.

As Chapter 3 mentioned, Huang Maosen suffered an eighty-one-vote defeat in the 2006 elections after twelve years of service in Pingshan Li. Three weeks after this painful loss, I came upon Huang while he was packing up his office. He resignedly checked off items on a list of public property that he was responsible for turning over, including equipment used in the aftermath of major storms: one large gasoline-powered water pump, two chainsaws, a weed whacker, a tree trimmer, a generator, and a megaphone the size of a small tuba. Later, Huang and his friend Fan Yuqin sat down at a coffee shop to explain what had happened.

Part of Huang's problems related to the challenges posed by his geographically and socially complex *li*. Its territory encompassed several ordinary city blocks but also an expansive section of mountainside rising to elevations well above one thousand feet. Huang had strongly supported the construction of a pump station to connect those living in the upper reaches with running water from city pipes, but relatively few households lived on the hillside and stood to benefit from the water-pressure station. Fan laid out an election postmortem, a critique so unsparingly frank that it caused Huang visible distress. Huang underutilized his neighborhood volunteers, she explained. "For example, after the typhoon he went up the mountain to cut down fallen trees all by himself. It should be the community that does this together. He should have had his *linzhang* do this."[52] In this way, Huang's toil went unnoticed by the voters. He and his wife had also not wished to put his block captains and the members of his community development association to the trouble of knocking on doors for his reelection. He had neglected to mobilize the potential of his supporters.[53]

Wu Jiaqian, the retired bus company manager who distributed bold flyers attacking Huang in the closing days of his successful campaign, seemed unlikely to make that mistake himself. When I first visited Wu, he was in the midst of planning a nineteen-table victory banquet for his supporters and was on the phone discussing who would make a suitable master of ceremonies for the occasion. He presented his own perspective on the election. Wu's base of support lay in the more than four hundred voters living alongside him in a state housing complex (*guozhai*). Situated at the foot of the hillside, this subcommunity had little regard for those at higher elevations on whose behalf Huang had labored. Born in Nanjing in 1948, Wu shared a military background with many of his neighbors. He once served as a *linzhang* but got along poorly with Huang, seven years his junior, who relieved him of this position after the 2003 election. Wu became active in the security patrol, which split from Huang's neighborhood office and changed its name. Thus, the volunteer networks in which Wu was enmeshed helped to amplify opposition to the incumbent and propel him into office.[54]

Taiwan's CDAs were first established in 1991, during the administration of President Lee Teng-hui. Lee encouraged them in part as a potential alternative or counterweight to the existing *cun-li* structure, which came under criticism as overly bureaucratic (although not every observer embraced these alternative associations, either).[55] They have offered a vehicle for local groups to pursue common interests and projects from book clubs to traditional arts to eco-ponds (Sheng 1995; Wang 2008). The Society Bureau of the Taipei municipal government oversees all of the city's CDAs, which numbered 370 as of early 2007. An official there said that they view the associations' jostling with the wardens as "a positive form of competition," but she also wondered whether Taiwan had made a mistake in fostering a second major form of organization at the neighborhood level: "our system is kind of chaotic."[56] The groups are allowed to span more than one *li* but generally remain small in scope. As associations (*tuanti*), they do not have the administrative role of the *li*. Their leaders (*lishizhang*) are elected by the membership without the involvement of city government. But they are required to have at least one large meeting every year, and their boards of directors must submit reports to the Society Bureau. The organizations are eligible to apply for project grants from the city government, equivalent to several hundred or a few thousand U.S. dollars in value. The city also evaluates them; in 2006, twenty-six of Taipei's community associations were given awards and prize money for excellence, ranging from US$600 to US$2,000.

It is common in Taipei for CDAs and other neighborhood groups to serve as springboards for *lizhang* candidacies, and they can afford defeated wardens a government-supported locus of organization. Incumbent neighborhood leaders often cultivate loyal CDAs, but oppositional relationships are also common. The Songshan district official in charge of community development associations estimated that of the thirty-one such groups there, half stood in opposition to a neighborhood's warden.[57] In the mid-2000s, 77 percent of the city's CDAs were led by someone other than a warden (Chuang 2005, 103).

Puzhao Li, located in one of Taipei's central districts, provides an example of the complex and contentious interactions among the several kinds of organizations that operate at the *li* level and can potentially act as local power centers.[58] As the *liganshi* explained, three mountaintops (*shantou*), or factions, were jockeying for power. The neighborhood's CDA was founded in 1994, under a warden backed by the KMT. Although not all of its members belonged to the Nationalist Party, many of its board members did, and the organization generally had a Blue cast to it. For three years it received annual grants worth between US$600 and US$900 from the Ministry of the Interior for its newsletter, proudly edited by a retired reporter from the KMT-dominated Central News Agency. In the 2003 election, the neighborhood's three-term incumbent warden was ousted by Zeng Yalang, a shopkeeper and Democratic Progressive Party (DPP) member nursing ambitions of running for the city council, who headed a second faction. Puzhao's volunteer security patrol team, led by a retired police officer, constituted the third mountaintop.

By the time of the late-2006 elections, no love was lost among the three factions. As warden, Zeng had pursued and, with help from DPP members of the city council, pushed through an aggressive program of repaving local streets and preventing water backups by dredging drainage pipes. This solidified the support of some residents but alienated others who had been inconvenienced or whose businesses had been harmed by the construction. Zeng, a vituperative critic of all things Kuomintang and particularly of then-mayor Ma Ying-jeou, had also lodged a slew of complaints against the police, business proprietors, and even local dog owners. He accused his KMT- and CDA-backed rival, Xiao Zhuquan, of running an illegal gambling den (Xiao said this was just a friendly game of mah-jongg) and claimed that his opponent's supporters had physically attacked him. The neighborhood watch team, too, resented Zeng. In 2004 he had cut off support for the patrollers, apparently aiming to deny their leaders a platform from which to run against him.

With his opponents split, Zeng won reelection by a margin of 248 votes over Xiao, resolving one chapter in this struggle though no doubt laying the groundwork for more to come. Many in Taipei wince at the unseemly aspects of this kind of neighborhood bickering, but it is through such contention that new aspirants bring novel ideas and perspectives into neighborhood leadership. These dynamics are enhanced by the continual possibility of new issues and leadership candidates bubbling up from the ranks of *linzhang* and volunteers in other community-level groups—the most important of which are also, like the *li* system itself, backed by the city. In other words, substantial competition is found even in a collection of publicly funded organizations on the periphery of the official governance system.

Conclusion

Previous theories of state-supporting participation were built on studies of different settings and different points in time. The Chinese political system has changed considerably in the decades since the period from which those accounts were developed. To apply them to noncommunist settings would further defy plausibility. The kinds of supportive volunteer activity found in the neighborhoods of Beijing and Taipei is not well explained by careerism, material incentives, and other such factors highlighted by earlier generations of researchers.

Even under the dictatorship of the CCP, coercion is hardly what impels people to lend a hand in neighborhood governance, contrary to some accounts of how mass organizations work. As noted in the review at the outset of this chapter, the threat of punishments or sanctions may have been a motivation for some activists in the Mao era—for instance, the student from a bad class background who adopted an activist stance in an attempt to head off political trouble (Oksenberg 1970, 322). Research on urban neighborhoods in today's China provides no evidence that people become activists to avoid the consequences of past wrongdoing or other stigma, or indeed that threats of any kind motivate such participation. Residents are entirely at liberty to abstain from activism without suffering any mistreatment.

Solomon and others may well have been correct in identifying the activist as a key part of the Maoist approach to mobilization (1969). But the view from the contemporary neighborhood in China seems to show that active participation can exist without the resentment and aggression that he saw as central to that form of mobilization. Vogel and later writers highlighted the way in which the state deliberately created a schism between activists and their peers (1965, 1967). But neighborhood volunteers are not now intended to alienate themselves from those around them; in fact, the state's purposes are quite the opposite. Their behavior does not necessarily involve harming their neighbors. Rather, the degree to which one feels that the floor leader down the hall is a helpful or a discomforting presence depends heavily on individual circumstances and orientations. Accordingly, activists' relationships with their peers are highly variable; some of their neighbors shun or ignore them, yet others welcome them.

Competition theories of activism, like those of Shirk and Walder, stem at heart from the high stakes of the career game in schools and factories in the 1960s and 1970s (Shirk 1982; Walder 1986).[59] In contrast, neighborhood life and administration today is—for most people, most of the time—a low-stakes arena. It is cumulatively very important to the state to be able to draw on the assistance of a set of supporters dispersed throughout the neighborhood, and therefore well worth the funds and painstaking efforts it devotes to maintaining this network via the RCs. But most ordinary residents have relatively little to gain, and little to lose, from their interaction with the state's local deputies and their affiliates. Certainly nothing of the magnitude of careers and housing allotments is on the line, although RCs might occasionally be in position to dispense much more modest favors. To be sure, the small monthly payments that Taipei's block captains receive are part of what motivates their service. Still, the benefits that such volunteers receive for their efforts seem to be ones that lie in the background of these previous accounts, not the ones they emphasize most. Their relationship with those who organize them is not one of hierarchical dependency, although it is not one of equals either.

At the other end of the spectrum, the synergy perspective posits harmony rather than conflict between the residents of the neighborhood and those who administer it. To the extent that this picture holds true, service as a regular supporter of the RC or *li* office should create little or no tension with others. The volunteers themselves certainly see things in this light; they would hardly acknowledge any trade-off between helping the neighborhood organization and helping their neighbors. The evidence presented in this chapter shows a more complex picture, particularly in Beijing. On the one hand, we saw that, even in China, activists do perform functions that are widely perceived as useful by others, and they are seen by a substantial fraction of their nonactivist counterparts as benign and even trustworthy. We find no jagged social fault line separating them from their neighbors. On the other hand, to portray Beijing's activists as entirely in solidarity with all of their peers would also be an error. Residents are certainly aware that the activists' responsibilities include keeping an eye on their neighbors, and for most this leads to at least a degree of circumspection in their dealings with them, and sometimes to deep suspicion. Even in Taipei, some survey respondents and interviewees indicate wariness toward their *linzhang*.

The choice to serve as a neighborhood-level volunteer hardly amounts to a strategy. It is not independent of and prior to other aspects of an individual's sociopolitical life, but is clearly interrelated with demographic and other characteristics. In some Taipei neighborhoods, local groups take on the color of broader party allegiances, with Blue and Green partisans sometimes rubbing shoulders but often belonging to different camps. In both capitals, official volunteering venues draw those who are sociable by nature and provide a means to connect with others. Such service is one way in which individuals who largely fall within a particular demographic category—well into middle age or beyond, and outside the paid workforce—try to participate in the locality around them in a personally rewarding and meaningful way. At the same time, the earlier models are by no means entirely irrelevant to contemporary patterns. Neighborhood volunteer service indeed emerges from systems established to encourage and reward such patterns of behavior. It illustrates the state's powerful influence in shaping the associational patterns and channeling the participatory energies of some of its citizens. Through its cultivation of these supporters, both Beijing and Taipei create important social facts in the structure of neighborhood life.

State-mobilized service of this kind expresses and provides support for the existing order, yet it also embodies an impulse to become involved in local affairs and to contribute to neighborhood administration in a way that can mean speaking up, requesting changes, and expressing demands. Officially sponsored volunteering substitutes for self-initiated local organizations and citizen initiatives, thus providing participants with many of the same benefits and pleasures. One must appreciate the commonalities between neighborhood activists in these cases and participants in civic activities in other political systems without losing sight of the political apparatus in which they play an important part.

Chapter Seven

Thin Networks and the Appeals of Organic Statism

Chapter 6 trained a spotlight on a special subset of the neighborhood's constituents, those core supporters who choose to participate in its social and service programs. But it is not merely these individuals who look favorably on the residents' committees (RCs) and the neighborhood wardens. As Table 7.1 shows, even among survey respondents who never or only "very rarely" participate in its official activities, it is still the case that most are positively inclined toward the organization. In both Beijing and Taipei, clear majorities of nonparticipants indicated approval of their RC or warden. In Beijing, more than half of those who do not take part in the committee's activities nonetheless expressed willingness to provide assistance to it in a variety of circumstances.[1] In Taipei, two-thirds of nonparticipants said they would prefer to maintain the neighborhood warden system rather than to abolish it. Thus, although these institutions are in part rooted in the strong ties among those who deeply enmesh themselves in community sociability, that is only one part of their basis.

This chapter aims to account for the origins of this approval outside of and apart from the subculture of neighborhood volunteers. The argument advanced here is that the RCs and neighborhood wardens draw on several sources in winning goodwill for themselves among constituents. First, the personnel composing these ultra-local organizations are, in many cases, not strangers but rather community members who are familiar to the neighbor-

TABLE 7.1

Attitudes toward RC or NW, comparing participants and nonparticipants

Item	BEIJING		TAIPEI	
	Participants	*Nonparticipants*	*Participants*	*Nonparticipants*
Positive satisfaction with respondent's own RC or NW	84.2%	68.4%	82.1%	66.1%
Positive assessment of usefulness of RC or NW as an institution	89.8%	69.3%	64.6%	47.9%
Positive score on index of willingness to cooperate with RC (Beijing only)	77.2%	52.7%	N.A.	N.A.
Wants to maintain, not abolish, NW system (Taipei only)	N.A.	N.A.	75.4%	66.4%
n	169	849	290	850

SOURCE: 2001 Beijing Law and Community Survey and 2006 Taipei Neighborhoods Survey.

NOTE: In Beijing, participants were defined as those who held a volunteer post in the neighborhood or took part in security patrols "often" or "sometimes." In Taipei, the category included those who had served as block captains, attended formal meetings, or taken part in community development associations. Those who had taken part only in social activities are not counted as participants here.

hood and possessed of some measure of authority in it. This does not hold true equally for all parts of the cities in question, however, and not at all in the newest of Beijing's condominium towers. It applies best in places where staff and residents have lived in the same area for many years and are well acquainted with one another. Moreover, it holds most true in quarters where poor housing conditions and underdeveloped infrastructure increase the demand for the organizations' assistance. In newer neighborhoods where property management companies handle many aspects of maintenance and administration, the role of the RC and the neighborhood warden is at least somewhat diminished.

Second, the organizations provide a variety of forms of assistance and services. Beijing's residents' committees in particular offer a range of minor material goods, low-cost conveniences, and help with the handling of documents. Taipei's wardens do similar things, albeit on a somewhat smaller scale. All of these services are modest in scope, yet they cumulatively win considerable appreciation and shape part of the way that the organizations are popularly perceived.

The third factor is somewhat less tangible, yet perhaps most important of all. As the neighborhood's officially designated, all-purpose contact people, the RCs and the wardens provide a permanent presence that many constituents welcome. Actively and passively, they keep an eye on the neighborhood, giving a sense that someone takes responsibility for its well-being and can respond in the event of minor problems or large emergencies. They offer a place for residents to bring an immense variety of questions, problems, complaints, grievances, and suggestions. Although the neighborhood leaders may not be able or willing to act on all the concerns that are brought to their doorstep, to many they still convey the sense that someone is at least willing to listen.

In short, the kind of state-society fusion that these organizations represent possesses considerable appeal to many. As Chapter 5 emphasized, this appeal is far from universal. Some reject it entirely. Residents recognize that these parastatal organizations have strong obligations to the city authorities who hire and pay them. Yet their special link with the government has positive as well as negative aspects from the residents' point of view. It provides resources and performs functions that—for all their other possible merits—civil society organizations would be hard pressed to duplicate.

Providing Small Services

We have seen that the large majority of Beijing residents have at least a modest amount of contact with their residents' committee staff; in Taipei, there is also a great deal of such interaction, though not as much everyday brushing of shoulders as in Beijing. The surveys offer further perspective into the nature of this contact by measuring how common it is for individuals to approach the staff of grassroots institutions for specific purposes. One section of the questionnaire listed a series of reasons, gleaned from fieldwork, people might visit their local neighborhood office and asked respondents whether they had ever done so for that reason (Table 7.2). The most relevant of the items were replicated in the Taipei survey.[2] These data provide a backdrop for the remainder of the chapter, which employs interview and site-based information to explain the nature of this interaction and what it tells us about perceptions of these administrative grassroots systems as a whole.

TABLE 7.2
Contacting the neighborhood organization for specific reasons

Respondent has been to the RC or NW office . . .	Beijing: Respondents (%)	Taipei: Respondents (%)
To pay or discuss fees (e.g., fees for trash, water, gas, heating, electricity, cable television)	26.6	Not asked
To discuss welfare-related matters (e.g., relief cards, minimum guaranteed income, aid)	7.6	Not asked
To take care of documents and permits, or to get something stamped	30.6	17.5
To discuss or give input on neighborhood issues	24.3	22.7
For free or low-cost services or goods	50.6	Not asked
Because of a dispute with a neighbor	6.2	4.9
Because of a dispute in the family	2.6	Not asked
n	1,018	1,140

SOURCE: 2001 Beijing Law and Community Survey and 2006 Taipei Neighborhoods Survey.

NOTE: Some questions in this set were asked in Beijing but not Taipei because the telephone interview format in Taipei necessitated a shorter questionnaire.

Citizens interact with these organizations in a variety of modes, ranging from the purely bureaucratic to far more substantive and meaningful encounters. One of the residents' committees' functions in Beijing (something not found in Taipei) has been to collect fees for certain kinds of utilities and neighborhood services. In many areas of the city, as of the 2000s, residents came to the committee office every three or six months to pay cable television bills, for example. Typically, the RC also hired migrants or the unemployed to carry out basic cleaning duties like sweeping the yards and mopping indoor hallways, and for this the committee would collect a small fee. Though not necessarily perceived as a service provided by committees, such routine transactions bring residents into the office and into conversation with the committee staff—whether by design or by coincidence.

In a similar vein, the neighborhood organizations provide a place to handle certain kinds of bureaucratic chores. The reception counters in some of the new community offices make these functions especially plain, though at the risk of seeming coldly institutional, like a window at the post office. The RCs have long served such purposes, however. For instance, when it comes time to renew one's national identity card (*shenfen zheng*) or to update one's household registry booklet (*hukou ben*), Beijing residents can drop these documents off at the committee office rather than having to stand in line at the police station.

This service has a close parallel in Taipei, where *li* offices also accept identity cards to take to processing centers for renewal. One warden took this a step further, setting up a digital camera and printer to take the required passport-style photos for residents at his own expense. The RCs handled a steady trickle of things like government-issued senior citizens' discount cards (*laonian ren youdai zheng*), which entitle the bearer to low-cost entry to parks, museums, and movies; lower bus fares and priority seating; free use of pay toilets; and the like. This, too, found a very close analogue in Taipei, where wardens and *liganshi* could help the elderly renew their discounted subway and bus passes.

In Beijing, RCs commonly distributed or sold at a discount small material items, a practice less common in Taipei. The committees served as a conduit through which the municipal government gave out things like water-conserving spigots aimed to stem the city's serious water shortage. Sometimes they also doled out other products that are of public benefit, like poison to use against roaches and rats. The committees themselves purchase bulk goods like rice, cooking oil, and dish-washing detergent, then resell them to residents at prices slightly lower than retail rates. As Table 7.2 shows, almost half of the Beijing Law and Community Survey respondents had visited an RC for the purpose of obtaining such things. These offerings were somewhat less common in Taipei, although parallels could certainly be seen: in the summer of 2010, for instance, warden offices were doing a brisk business in tickets to the city's upcoming International Flora Exposition.

The organizations also offered special services that appealed to specific members of their constituencies. For example, in both Beijing and Taipei, many neighborhood offices had been equipped with simple blood-pressure meters, and staff were trained to take readings. It was quite common for middle-aged and older residents to stop by the office for a free hypertension check. Modest though it may seem, a blood-pressure test perfectly embodies the kind of small service provided in the neighborhood that can build personal rapport and contribute to the benevolent side of the organizations' popular image.

One sixty-year-old Taipei man living in the Daan district was skeptical of the neighborhood warden system in many respects, calling them "electoral tools" and associating them with a Kuomintang (KMT) machine that he strongly disliked. Yet even he had found things to appreciate about them: "Why do I not vote in the *lizhang* elections, yet I say the *lizhang* system should be kept? I know it's contradictory. It's because he [the warden] is doing things for society as a whole, even if I personally don't have any special feeling about it. When I went to take care of my daughter's identity card, I had my blood pressure taken, and my blood sugar tested. In the *lizhang*'s office there was a nurse there from the clinic."[3]

The neighborhood offices also serve as lively clearinghouses for useful information of many kinds. A dinner conversation with one Taipei warden was repeatedly interrupted by a parent calling the warden's cell phone with questions about getting her child into the local school.[4] In Beijing, unemployed residents come to the committees to ask whether they know of anyone in the neighborhood who might be interested in hiring them on an hourly basis to cook or do chores. For the more affluent, the committees may have suggestions as to where to find a nanny to take care of one's children. The Shuang-qiao committee was especially well informed about openings for low-level jobs, such as a part-time janitor position at a nearby hospital or a restaurant that was looking for a hostess.[5] The RCs' introductions were not merely in the economic realm; some RC staff members took special pleasure in trying to play matchmaker for single residents, especially middle-aged or elderly ones.[6]

Officials of the Ministry of Civil Affairs and of city governments are keenly aware that boosting the RCs' service-provision role is important for making them more appealing to constituents; indeed, this is at the heart of the concept of community services (*shequ fuwu*). Some cadres articulate this strategy quite straightforwardly. Jia Zheng, director of the community services office of the Civil Affairs Bureau of Beijing's Xicheng district, said, "In Xicheng, we want to get residents to approve of [*renke*] the residents' committee, and so we must get the committees to provide services in order to strengthen residents' sense of identification [*rentonggan*] with them."[7] A city-level official said: "The ordinary citizens think that the residents' committees are too oriented toward administration, and not enough toward service; that they are too repressive [*yazhi*]. People need services, but they don't care who provides them. They are not used to running things on their own."[8] One district cadre described the meaning of community services with an extended discussion of a metaphor: like a restaurant, the government should serve up whatever the residents order.[9] These comments illustrate both the government's eagerness to find more and more needs to satisfy via the neighborhood, as well as its assumption that it should indeed be the RCs through which these needs are met rather than through residents' self-organization, the market, or other mechanisms.

Taipei is less saturated with the rhetoric of community services, and its authorities less steeped in such paternalism. Still, it shows some of the same dynamics—public provision of highly visible bits of assistance, which enhances residents' rapport with the government's grassroots liaisons—albeit through somewhat different and more participatory mechanisms. The wardens have more control than do the RCs over what kinds of accoutrements and embellishments are airlifted into their localities. Many of Taipei's *li*, for example, receive compensation funds (*huikui jin*) from nearby facilities that generate pollution or noise, such as crematoria, the city's immense trash incinerators, and Songshan Airport. These funds are used for projects and equipment of the warden's choosing, under the supervision of the *liganshi*.

Always keeping an eye on reelection, the wardens are adept at making the most of such monies as well as their own resourcefulness. "I would like to boast a bit," Bai Zhengmin announced one Sunday afternoon, leaning back on his living-room couch, expounding proudly as an elder statesman of *li* politics. With a characteristic mix of pride and self-deprecation, he asked, "How do I go about running the neighborhood and tricking people into voting for me?" His first technique, he went on to explain, was to "snare the parents by coddling the kids," for instance through his annual neighborhood talent show. This was, he said, a worthwhile exercise for the children and a way to provide something to the community that had, at that point, elected him twice. "But my secret purpose is to butter up their parents, grandparents, aunts and uncles." Other techniques included personally sending reminders to seniors age sixty-five and older of their approximately US$30 annual respect-for-the-elderly gift from the government (*jinglao jintie*), arranging for nurses to come to the neighborhood to give free flu shots and tests to the elderly, and sponsoring a musical performance. He might have added the many classes and activities in the community center that he had wangled for his *li*.

Although, as we have seen, Taipei residents have varied perceptions of the usefulness of the warden system, these kinds of activities and services stand out in the minds of many. One interviewee felt that some of the everyday doings of the *lizhang* proved their worth, such as counseling thoughtless neighbors not to dump trash and helping plant trees on a nearby mountainside.[10] Another approvingly mentioned that his new neighborhood leader had installed fire extinguishers and repaired the children's slides in the playground.[11]

For Beijing residents like this retired teacher, the RCs' similar kinds of services were what came to mind when asked about the committees:

When I'm with the residents' committee people there's no feeling of authority [*quanwei gan*]. A few days ago when they were checking on sanitation, they went and did the cleanup work themselves, as well as going to find people at home in the evening. The residents' committee is something that can't be done without in life. When the TV breaks, you call the RC on the phone, and they find someone [to fix it] for you. They take responsibility for ordering coal; they have the activists leave notes for each family informing them which day it will be delivered, and on that day the RC brings it around. In the past they also took orders for cabbage, but now standards of living have risen, and people don't buy it anymore.[12] The RC gave us the phone number of the police emergency line. On May Day and October First [National Day] they stand at the intersection on guard duty, and they even stand at the intersection around Chinese New Year, in case people set off firecrackers.[13]

Some of these services—passing on the telephone number of the police—seem trivial, but this highlights the fact that even minor favors can convey the impression of benevolence. Other interviewees brought up similar kinds of help as reasons they are favorably disposed toward their committees, mentioning things like the RC informing residents of opportunities to change canisters of cooking gas and loaning out a shovel, as well as the kinds of common activities discussed above.[14]

Still another way in which Beijing's RCs come into occasional contact with residents is through their charity drives. As previously noted, about 65 percent of respondents there reported taking part in RC charity activities "often" or "sometimes," which indicates an immense amount of participation if we extrapolate from the sample to the population as a whole. Of course, self-reported data on socially approved behavior like charitable giving may be somewhat inflated. But this is corroborated by my field observations of well-established RCs, which indeed achieved high rates of giving, often bringing in at each effort thousands of yuan or impressive volumes of material goods like clothing and blankets. Most of these drives centered on causes that had received publicity in the news, such as an earthquake in Inner Mongolia or a child suffering from a terrible disease at a nearby hospital. The RC staff put up notices on chalkboards calling for donations, buttonholed everyone who walked through the door of their office, sent out requests through their volunteer network, and sometimes went door-to-door. Most donations were small and cost residents little. With China's nonprofit sector in its infancy and subject to political constraints, there were relatively few organizations competing with the RC network for contributions.

A Place to Be Heard

The retired teacher quoted earlier in this chapter mentioned specific problems that the RC helped resolve for her—obtaining coal, finding someone to fix her television, and so forth. But implied in what she said was an appreciation for having the staff on hand in a permanent way, potentially to help with any number of possible contingencies. This points to a second fundamental way in which such organizations appeal to constituents, apart from the provision of more tangible goods and services: by providing a presence in the neighborhood, being available for a great range of purposes on an ongoing basis.

Anyone who spends prolonged periods stationed in one of Beijing's residents' committees will be struck by the parade of people who drop in, one by one, to explain their problems and ask for advice or help: A woman who feared that her pet dog had been stolen. A man nearing retirement age trying to decide whether to take his pension as a onetime lump sum or as a series of monthly payments. A resident whose sleep was repeatedly interrupted by a car alarm.[15] In Taipei, a very similar procession of visitors and callers can be observed: demanding that something be done about feral cats, complaining that the streetlights go on too late at night, looking for help in paying for a costly hospital visit.[16]

Week after week, RC staff and wardens listen to a tremendously varied assortment of complaints, questions, and suggestions from their constituents. Densely distributed around the city and readily accessible, they can be the first place certain types of people turn to for help, whether on neighborhood matters, problems in the home, or dealings with government. Sometimes the personnel are willing and able to act on these requests or demands, and other times they are not. Regardless of their actual efficacy, many residents view the organizations as a potential source of solutions—or at least as a place to vent their frustrations and receive a sympathetic hearing.

One portion of the organizations' sounding board role is reflected in Table 7.2, which earlier in this chapter showed whether survey respondents had ever contacted the RC or neighborhood warden to discuss or give input on neighborhood issues.[17] In both cities, around 23 percent of those in the samples reported having done so. The striking similarity of these proportions suggests that this particular function is quite parallel in the two capitals. The most common problems prompting residents to make a trip to the neighborhood offices include noise, trash and waste disposal, and crime prevention. The Beijing committees I studied fielded a large number of reports of things like backed-up sewers and burned-out street lights. In one neighborhood located next to a street where taxi drivers would congregate to eat lunch and fraternize, a resident alleged that the men had developed a habit of relieving themselves on the sidewalk rather than taking the trouble to find a public bathroom. The same RC also received multiple complaints of kitchen smoke from a nearby restaurant wafting into residents' windows. In the case of the taxi drivers, Director Ouyang was reluctant to confront the offenders, explaining to the complainer: "I'm a female comrade; I can't watch out for them doing that." The smoke grievances, however, led her to contact the city management cadres at the street office, who promised to have environmental authorities send someone to inspect the restaurant's chimney.[18]

The quantitative data likely understate the frequency with which residents go to neighborhood organizations with questions, comments, and complaints. The survey could not possibly capture the endless variety of individual problems and conundrums, large and small, that lead people to contact these offices. In Beijing, visitors frequently stopped in at the RC office to get directions to specific buildings and people; representatives of work units, for instance, came to the committees to get in touch with retired employees.[19] Questions about the conversion from coal gas to natural gas that was under way in buildings throughout the city at the time, and the attendant need to install new meters and appliances, cropped up frequently. One woman sought special permission to park her three-wheeled flatbed pedal cart in the neighborhood bicycle shed.[20] Two interviewees noted that they relied on the RC to get help from the public housing authorities whenever pipes began to leak.[21] Residents sometimes brought reports of petty theft to the RC rather than going to the police, as in the case of one elderly woman who suspected that a bedsheet had been taken from her clothesline.[22] In one Taipei neighborhood, parents left house keys in a bowl at the warden's home for their children to pick up after school.[23] In another, residents enlisted the *lizhang* to help them try to negotiate lower fees from the cable television company.[24] Constituents in both cities

often came to the neighborhood office for coaching about the best way to approach branches of government on matters such as obtaining a duplicate copy
of one's marriage license or transferring one's household registry.

In private interviews, citizens often voiced appreciation for the ready availability of these institutions. The proprietor of a Taipei pharmacy employed a
geometry metaphor, describing the warden as a plane that intersects with the
single point of the city government and the lines of the district offices, thus
allowing for broad transmission of information that otherwise might not be
available to residents.[25] One thirty-six-year-old man had no interest in neighborhood activities but expressed confidence that he could take problems to the
warden and have a good chance of getting them resolved, a better chance than
if he went directly to police or city councilors.[26] In Beijing, a laid-off worker in
her forties said: "We have an RC director living in our courtyard. Whenever
there's a problem everybody goes looking for her, and when there's a problem
in other courtyards people come looking for her too."[27] A state cadre in his fifties noted, "If it's noisy outside, or if someone's selling things [in an unwanted
fashion], or if construction work nearby is going on at odd hours, you can go
to the RC."[28] One man pointed out that it can be convenient to obtain the
committee's help in finding someone's home in an unfamiliar neighborhood.[29]
The owner of a small photography shop said of the neighborhood across town
where he lived: "There are four or five people working in my RC. I know them
pretty well. They are neither a big nuisance, nor a big help, to people. They
are not very important for people's livelihood. But they are useful, for instance
for telling people where I am if someone is looking for me."[30]

To think of this merely as satisfying needs, answering questions, or fixing
problems would miss much of the point. Perhaps most essential is the human
dimension of these interactions: the respect and sympathy that the inquirers
can receive, as was the case with an old woman who stopped by the Pingshan
li office every three or four days to be shown to a chair and asked about her
grandchildren.[31] As one Taipei warden mused: "When people want something
they never just ask you for it straight out. They sit down and tell you the
whole story, from start to finish, including years ago when it all started, and
the conversation goes all over the place. We're like psychological analysts for
people."[32]

Not every neighborhood leader is equally cordial and patient, of course.
Nor are all visitors treated with equal solicitude. Chronic malcontents might
be turned away brusquely. Elderly and high-status guests tend to be received

with special warmth. It was common for men and women in their seventies or eighties who came to the RC office to be met with a polite display of welcome. The committee members would stop what they were doing, stand up from their desks to greet the visitor, insist that he or she sit down, and pour a cup of tea from their hot-water bottles. This type of hospitality was especially pronounced in the case of local notables, no matter what their age. Dr. Zhu, a practitioner of Chinese medicine whose husband served as director of a major city hospital, visited the Dengdao office after having donated three new blankets to its clothing drive for disaster relief. All four of the committee members stood up; Director Lin came over and held Zhu's hand; they thanked her profusely and asked about her health.[33]

It is readily understandable why Taipei wardens greet constituents warmly and receive guests enthusiastically. Like any democratically elected leader, they see each such encounter as an opportunity to build support for the next campaign. In the case of Beijing, there is essentially no such accountability at the ballot box, but RCs have less tangible motivations. In the case of a local influential like Dr. Zhu, the committee members might very well ask favors from her for themselves or for constituents. Yet committees often gave similar treatment to guests who appeared to have no special resources at their disposal. The Xianningjie staff stood listening indulgently as a retired professor of urban planning sat and held forth for more than half an hour on how the street office was wrong to have taken away what used to be the senior citizens' center and rented it out for business use, along with many other complaints, as well as reminiscences about his deceased wife.[34]

Late one afternoon as the Shimen staff were preparing to leave for the day, a man in his forties arrived at the office. The committee had asked to speak to him because neighbors were complaining about disturbances caused by his mother. As the man poured out the story of his family's troubles, Director Ding ended up staying with him long after the usual 5 P.M. closing time; far from an occasion to reprimand him, their talk became something close to a counseling session. His mother, it emerged, was half crazy, alcoholic, and incontinent; his father was gravely ill and living in a hospital. The man spent all his time washing his mother's clothes and cleaning the apartment. He and his brother and sister lacked money to take care of his parents; he had gone thousands of yuan into debt to friends from his days of military service to pay for their care. Director Ding listened patiently and expressed her understanding and support as he told this story, even as he digressed into lengthy and bitter complaints about the bribery necessary to get treatment at hospitals and the household registry fraud required to get his children into desirable out-of-district schools.[35]

Some of this hospitality and solicitude, particularly toward seniors, is culturally de rigueur in China and Taiwan. In other aspects it is simply a part of the "emotional work" that paid neighborhood service entails.[36] One might dismiss the warmth with which neighborhood leaders sometimes receive visitors as an empty show. Certainly, the mere fact of being treated graciously may not substitute for concrete action to address the visitor's concerns. It is also not easy to quantify; in the surveys I made no attempt to measure respondents' subjective perceptions of the tenor of most encounters with their neighborhood staff. Nonetheless, it is hard to deny that the availability of the RCs and wardens as an outlet for fielding residents' questions and complaints, together with the sympathetic hearing they may receive, add up to an important element of these institutions' public images. It is part of how they build and maintain a subtle network of thin ties linking themselves with their communities.

Mediating Disputes

"Mediating disputes among residents" was one of the five explicit duties written into the original 1954 residents' committee organizational law, and it was reaffirmed with nearly identical wording in the law's 1989 revision. As mentioned in Chapter 2, this single function alone has attracted a considerable amount of research and debate (Lubman 1967, 1997; Clark 1989; Wall and Blum 1991; Diamant 2000a; Guo and Klein 2005; Read and Michelson 2008). But of all the ways in which RCs are intended to help their constituents, mediation would, on the face of it, appear to be the most open to doubt. Government publications routinely make extravagant claims about the efficacy of mediation; this 1994 report from officials of Beijing's Xicheng district provides just one example: "Conscientiously carrying out the mediation of civil disputes, the 4,828 full-time and more than 23,000 voluntary mediators of the entire district did a large amount of work in resolving neighborhood disputes and preventing the escalation of contradictions. According to statistics, escalation was prevented in 132 civil disputes last year, averting the unnecessary injury or death of more than 180 people. The success rate of mediation was greater than 99.7 percent. This played a positive role in stabilizing society" (Pan and Cao 1994).

The near-perfect success rate and the supernatural knowledge of counterfactual casualty figures bring to mind the long and sometimes egregious history of official book cooking in China and other communist systems, and are the kind of thing that gave me a highly skeptical attitude toward mediation at the outset of my research. Fieldwork confirmed that official statistics on mediation cases should not be taken at anything like face value, as the RCs along with other levels of the public security and judicial bureaucracy have incentives to report impressive mediation achievements in their quarterly and annual work summaries. A number of mediation cases I observed were chronic disputes that had dragged on for years, casting doubt on the idea that any city district could bring such a high percentage of disputes to resolution.

Nonetheless, the kind of mediation that RCs do is far from meaningless. The disputes that mediation addresses are much like the other kinds of problems on which residents seek help from the committees, discussed previously. The committees' availability as a potential source of help in small-scale disputes is one more way in which they make themselves useful to their constituents, although it is not the most frequent. Because of the Beijing Law and Community Survey's special emphasis on residents' disputing behavior, this section of the chapter focuses on Beijing. Mediation is also a significant neighborhood- and district-level phenomenon in Taipei, as other evidence from that city makes clear, although it does not figure prominently among the wardens' officially assigned tasks.

Table 7.2 presents the percentages of survey respondents who said they had sought the RC or warden's help in a dispute with a neighbor. A slightly larger fraction of the Beijing than the Taipei interviewees answered that question in the affirmative: 6.2 percent in the former and 4.9 percent in the latter. In Beijing, the survey also asked about disputes within one's own family; only 2.6 percent of the sample reported having sought mediation from the RC for that reason. All told, in Beijing, 7.1 percent of respondents had requested assistance in either of these two circumstances. It must be borne in mind that these questions measure only whether the respondent him- or herself had taken the initiative to bring a dispute to the committee's attention. As individuals may become involved in mediation efforts initiated by other residents, or by the RC itself, mediation happens more often than these numbers suggest.

TABLE 7.3
Types of dispute by resolution channel pursued in Beijing

Type of dispute	Cases	RESPONSE TO DISPUTE			BREAKDOWN OF THOSE SEEKING THIRD-PARTY HELP			
		"Lumping it" (%)	Direct response (%)	Seeking third-party help (%)	Informal third party (%)	Residents' committee (%)	Work unit or gov't (%)	Police, lawyer, court, or other (%)
Neighbor	46	43.5	4.3	52.2	12.5	54.2	8.3	25.0
Consumer	32	68.8	18.8	12.5	50.0	25.0	0.0	25.0
Other	11	27.3	0.0	72.7	12.5	25.0	25.0	37.5
Property damage or loss	81	50.6	1.2	48.1	2.6	12.8	10.3	74.4
Home renovation	27	33.3	25.9	40.7	45.5	9.1	27.3	18.2
Property title or deed	51	47.1	0.0	52.9	7.4	7.4	22.2	63.0
Personal injury	22	36.4	0.0	63.6	14.3	7.1	28.6	50.0
Hiring discrimination	55	72.7	0.0	27.3	26.7	6.7	26.7	40.0
Collecting salary	68	77.9	1.5	20.6	35.7	0.0	57.1	7.1
Landlord or tenant	25	44.0	16.0	40.0	20.0	0.0	60.0	20.0
Will or inheritance	9	33.3	0.0	66.7	0.0	0.0	0.0	100.0
Divorce	5	60.0	40.0	0.0	0.0	0.0	0.0	0.0
Total	432	54.9	5.3	39.8	15.7	15.1	22.7	46.5

NOTE: Because of rounding, not all rows sum to 100 percent. Table is sorted by the percentage of those who sought third parties who went to the residents' committee.

The Beijing survey also probed the issue of neighborhood mediation in another way. Interviewees were asked whether they had ever experienced any of more than a dozen types of disputes, and if so, what they had done about the situation. This allowed us to gauge how the RCs compared with other potential sources of assistance, and it provided perspective on what types of problems are taken to it and what types are not. Based on these data, Table 7.3 shows the various ways in which Beijingers handled 432 disputes, sorted into twelve categories. The questions in this section of the survey were for the most part geared toward identifying major disputes that could potentially be legally actionable, and they omitted some important types of conflicts that lead residents to seek RC help, such as arguments within families. Because of this, Table 7.3 provides only a partial picture of the committees' role in managing local conflicts.

Table 7.3 shows clearly that RCs are sought out most frequently in disputes among neighbors, which certainly accords with the evidence from field research. It also tells us, though, that their help is sometimes requested in the event of several other kinds of conflict: disputes over property damage, property ownership, and home renovation, as well as disagreements between consumers and local businesses. In all categories but that of neighbor disputes, people were as likely or more likely to take problems to other venues, such as government offices, work units, lawyers, and the police. In other words, as of 2001, the RCs were most often sought for help in instances of low-level conflict that did not rise to the level of higher-stakes legal matters. This corroborates the argument presented so far in this study concerning the nature of the committees' power and jurisdiction: they do not themselves wield much authority over affairs of great material import but are an important resource on smaller, local matters. Even so, those who sought out the committees for help reported a higher rate of satisfaction with their experience than those who went to other potential sources of help, such as lawyers, a work unit, or police.[37]

Property or expenses that multiple families share provide one frequent source of disputes that are brought to the residents' committee. The use of common space in courtyards and hallways often causes friction, for instance when one neighbor attempts to enclose such areas for use as a kitchen or for storage. In older buildings there is great potential for conflicts over how to split the cost of utility bills. Even where living space is not shared, there are many ways for residents to impinge on one another's lives. In one alley, a new house had recently been built next to an older and shorter one, and rainwater from its roof drained into the neighbor's window. The complainant initially went to the housing office, but this agency refused to get involved, so he came to the RC. The committee's mediation officer talked to the person who lived in the new building, telling him, "If you lived in the other home, it'd be you who had water coming in your window." He eventually agreed to put up a gutter to catch the runoff.[38] In other cases, personal affronts can lead to the RC being summoned, as in a spat that arose when one resident maligned her neighbor as "not having real work," implying that she was a prostitute. The committee succeeded in getting these two individuals to agree not to talk to one another, at least for a time.[39]

The RCs are sometimes also alerted in cases of more ominous problems. One afternoon a woman in her forties arrived at the Shimen office, announcing, "I want to look someone up and find out if he's sick." Another resident of the neighborhood, a thirty-year-old bus driver, had been stalking her for no fewer than five years. She explained that he would hide behind trees or cars, then come out and ask her to talk to him, also accosting her when she was hanging out laundry on her balcony. She said that she was afraid for the safety of her fifteen-year-old daughter. Her mother had spoken to the mother of the stalker, but to no avail. Obviously concerned, the RC staff members spent forty-five minutes with her discussing details of the situation and the best way to handle it, eventually deciding that it should be brought up with the beat cop, Pan Yuan.[40] A crisis that arose elsewhere, in which an apparently deranged resident put glue in the locks of his neighbors' doors and attempted to stab one person with a knife, was directly referred to the police, as is the case with violence generally.[41] Even after passing such incidents on to other authorities, the RCs continue to follow up on them.

Requests for mediation in disputes within a single family are in some respects the most remarkable of all. Like other societies, Chinese culture contains elements that are resistant to washing one's dirty linen in public, as expressed in the phrase *jia chou bu ke wai yang*. Yet people with grievances against their own kin sometimes seek help from RCs nonetheless. One afternoon in Xiyingjie, a man in his early forties came in, hopping mad. The sixth son in a family of seven children, he had inherited from his father a home located close to the RC office. There had been a probate fight over the residence, and the court had recently ruled in his favor. But on that day his nephew (the loser of the probate case and the son of the third brother) had locked himself into the home and refused to come out. "Old Six," as the elder members of the RC staff called him out of familiarity, emphatically demanded that Director Dong come and talk his nephew into opening the door. While the RC was still going over the details of the case with him, his wife came in and announced that the nephew had relented and opened the door, whereupon Old Six politely took his leave.[42]

The RC staff often state that discord between mothers-in-law and daughters-in-law is a common impetus for residents to seek their services, and indeed several such cases cropped up during my fieldwork. In one instance, an elderly woman suspected her daughter-in-law of stealing money that she had placed on a pillow; she refused to leave the committee office until the staff intervened. The daughter-in-law denied the allegation and said that the woman was imagining things. The RC staff asked the woman to check other places where she might have put the money. She eventually came back, and admitted: "I did put it in the wrong place. I'm confused. I can't remember things anymore." The RC staff brought both sides together for the woman to say the same thing to her daughter-in-law, in hopes that this acknowledgment would cement a broader reconciliation. But later the old lady came back to complain that the daughter-in-law wasn't paying any attention to her. The staff went to the younger woman again to tell her to forgive the old lady; at least address her respectfully when you see her, they suggested.[43]

The exact degree of efficacy that the RC should be credited with in any given instance is not always easy to calculate. In the Shuangqiao neighborhood in September 2000, a man was carrying his child on his bicycle when he ran into an elderly woman and knocked her over. Although the hospital found no major physical injury, she was bruised and offended, and sought the residents' committee's assistance. A few days later no fewer than three committee members accompanied the cyclist's brother on a visit to the woman's home to make amends on his sibling's behalf with several bulging bags of fresh fruit. The incident was successfully smoothed over. However intangible its role, the committee had played a part in getting the two sides to reconcile with each other and, perhaps more important, had responded to its constituent's request and demonstrated usefulness.[44]

Often, however, mediation cases do not end in reconciliation. In one of the buildings belonging to Shimen, the residents of apartments 401 and 501—the latter located directly above the former—were locked in a dispute that had persisted for six years. The elderly man living in the lower unit accused the couple above of deliberately harassing him by stomping on the floor and even kicking his door on their way downstairs. He, in turn, would retaliate by pounding on the ceiling with a set of poles wrapped in cloth on one end, one stationed in each room, that he had fashioned specially for this purpose (initially telling his wife that they were for smashing mosquitoes). The residents' committee staff, led by mediation officer Tai Jin, repeatedly applied their standard technique of meeting separately with each party to confront them with their failure to compromise, then bringing the two sides together for a joint counseling session. After each of these efforts Tai optimistically pronounced the matter resolved. But in this chronic case, even the involvement of the police station, the street office's judicial bureau, and the courts, in addition to the RC's work, failed to bring an end to the ongoing feud. The committee, and the other state agencies as well, simply had no means to pressure the parties into a resolution. Nonetheless, by involving itself in even such intractable cases, committees at least affirm their role as a resource for constituents.

In private interviews, Beijing citizens sometimes drew attention to the usefulness of the committee's mediation function and helped to explain how it works. "It always helps to have a third party; any third party would be good," noted one man in his twenties.[45] This point granted, there is something distinctive about the RC stepping in to try to resolve a dispute, as opposed to just any would-be mediator. The committees have special advantages, in spite of the fact that they have little ability to enforce resolutions. Because they are often expected to play a coordinating role, they can sometimes bring about solutions that might not otherwise emerge, as this interviewee suggests:

> Conflicts are unavoidable in the big courtyards [da za yuan]. . . . Just a few days ago the director of the residents' committee convened a meeting of all seventeen of the courtyard's households about the problem with the electricity fees, with one representative from each household. There is only one overall meter for the whole courtyard, but because someone has been stealing electricity, the numbers on all the individual household meters always add up to a lot less than the number on the overall meter. The Electricity Bureau bills by the overall meter, so the rate each family pays for its electricity has gone higher and higher. The national guideline is 38 cents per kilowatt-hour, and we're now up to 50 or 60 cents; it's doubled. Everyone was very unhappy about this, and some publicly threatened to stop contributing to the electric bill. The outcome of the meeting was that the courtyard will be divided up into four sections, each with its own

meter. This way we'll be able to tell which section has the person stealing electricity in it, and it won't be so easy to steal anymore.[46]

The committees have a degree of authority by dint of their quasi-official status. "If my neighbor built something illegally, I wouldn't be able to tell him to take it down without the RC to intercede for me," said one interviewee.[47] This authority can derive from the seniority of the staff and from their legally defined position: "It sometimes gives people a way to back down from a confrontation without losing face [*gei yige taijie xia*]. . . . People respect RC members who come to mediate, especially if these same RC people watched them grow up."[48]

Limitations inherent in the telephone format of the Taipei survey made it impossible to collect fine-grained information about specific disputes that respondents had experienced. But the neighborhood leader's presence as a potential source of dispute resolution, and as a gateway to other venues where conflicts might be addressed, applies in Taipei in ways that are parallel to the Beijing case. Indeed, Taipei residents come to their wardens for many of the same reasons seen in Beijing, along with others. Disputes over noise, pipes leaking in apartment walls, kitchen and restaurant waste clogging drains—all were common fare. As in Beijing, residents were split in their assessments of the efficacy of the neighborhood leader in resolving such problems. Some were unimpressed, like the fifty-four-year-old owner of a rental property on Minzu East Road: "My tenant wanted to move out while still owing some management fees; he refused to pay them. The management committee there asked the warden to intervene and tell the tenant that he had to pay up before leaving. But then the warden came and wanted us to negotiate, telling my tenant: you don't have to pay the whole amount. He wanted to play the peacemaker [*heshilao*] and just get everyone to quiet down . . . but the tenant never paid. So a warden can only resolve these things if the other side is willing to give him face."[49]

Another, though, mentioned favorable experiences with the warden resolving conflicts over noise- and smoke-emitting machinery. "I feel that right now the *lizhang* is the closest to us common people. We don't need to try to use connections [*guanxi*]. If something comes up we can just go straight to the neighborhood office to find him and say something about it directly."[50] Others went to the warden in the course of acrimonious arguments concerning rainwater runoff or tensions between husband and wife.

Although the wardens themselves engage in quite a bit of mediation, they are not the only venue for such dispute resolution in Taipei. District offices also offer dedicated centers for this purpose. In Shilin, fifteen volunteer mediators, many of them with legal backgrounds, staffed this center. They met with disputants in private rooms in the district office building itself. According to the mediation chairperson, his district alone received six hundred or seven hundred cases per year, mostly civil cases concerning matters such as debts, tenancy, property rights, inheritance, and the like. Residents can be referred to the center by courts, officials, and neighborhood leaders, or they may apply directly for mediation.[51] The city recorded a total of 6,331 such mediation cases in 2010 (City of Taipei Department of Budget, Accounting, and Statistics 2011, 878). The availability of these facilities means that wardens need not always go to the trouble of resolving conflicts themselves. One interviewee felt that her warden was so eager to pass disputes on to the district-level institutions that "he was just like the nurse that screens you before you see the doctor."[52]

That so many disputes would be shunted to the more formal, semiprofessionalized forums of the mediation centers suggests one of the limitations of administrative grassroots engagement. Ultra-local leaders can, in some cases, use their local prestige and delegated authority to apply pressure to disputing parties, thus encouraging them to put aside their pride and accept compromises. But in practice, as Diamant noted, mediation can be a thankless task (2000b, 158). Many residents appreciate the warden's availability in case of conflict. Yet when a neighborhood leader actually intervenes, he or she risks offending the subject of the complaint while also failing to satisfy the person who lodged it, an outcome doubly detrimental to reelection prospects. Volunteer mediators in the district centers may not have the warden's extensive social networks, but in some cases an enhanced degree of legal authority can be more conducive than such ties to resolving conflict.

In an earlier era, state intervention in local disputes was interpreted as characteristic of totalitarian political systems, a way in which they amassed power. One scholar wrote that such regimes "achieve their nearly total control primarily by encouraging people to bring all their grievances, no matter how petty, to state officials," who would oblige by hauling off the offending party to "imprisonment, exile, or worse" (Black 1989, 78).[53] In today's authoritarian China and in democratic Taiwan, we perceive a distant and more benign reflection of this idea in the way that the state makes its neighborhood deputies available for addressing everyday quarrels. As we have seen, ordinary people in such settings are hardly able to wield mediation as a devastating weapon against their adversaries, and indeed the response can at times prove quite ineffectual. However imperfect, it constitutes a welcome resource that people turn to when coping with certain kinds of low-level conflicts that otherwise frustrate them.

Eyes on the Neighborhood

The previous two sections have explored important ways in which institutions like the RC and the neighborhood warden stand ready for constituents as an always-available source of advice, guidance, conflict management, and even comfort and companionship. The least tangible, but nonetheless highly salient, aspect of these institutions' permanent presence concerns observation, monitoring, and surveillance: the ongoing watch they keep over the locality. This is, once again, a general feature of administrative grassroots engagement. In some cases it is explicitly trumpeted: Cuba's Committees for the Defense of the Revolution, as we saw, make *vigilance* their watchword. More often it takes a quieter, even passive form. In the case of China's RCs, as previously explained, political surveillance of an ongoing and quiet kind is an essential part of the utility of the organizations to the state. But it would be a mistake to assume that monitoring and surveillance are relevant only in authoritarian contexts and of service only to government. Rather, many citizens in Beijing and Taipei alike welcome the general sense of having someone keeping an eye on things around the neighborhood and looking out for residents' interests.

As Chapter 1 pointed out, the juxtaposition of state-sponsored surveillance to the intimate setting of the residential neighborhood seems to be what Western observers have found both fascinating and unnerving about an institution like China's RCs. And certainly, as has been noted at points throughout this book, some residents of both cities prefer privacy and dislike any feeling of coming under quasi-official observation. Many others, though, express a near-complete lack of concern. As a middle-aged Taipei man said when asked about oversight by the *lizhang* and *linzhang*: "No one would feel that there's too much surveillance. In Taiwan, people emphasize friendship relations, and mutual concern for the community. This is a matter of national conditions and customs. It's because Taiwan and China both emerged from agricultural societies. They put value on neighborly relations, based on the care that people have for one another."[54]

Both perspectives are present, but the desire for privacy does not always predominate, nor do attitudes map neatly onto the divide between authoritarian China and democratic Taiwan. There is widespread concern among Beijingers about robbery, burglary, and other crime. Whether justified or not, this concern often focuses on rural migrants:

> In the past the floating population was smaller, and security was better; in the evenings we went to sleep without even closing the doors. Now the floating population is big and its moral character [*suzhi*] is poor. They come to the city looking for money, and the public security administration can't keep up with them. In the past when there was the *bao-jia* system, you needed a *luyin* to get into Beijing, which was like what we now call a letter of introduction. But now people can come and go as they please, so things like bicycle theft happen all the time. . . . My family has had things stolen twice: one year during the Spring Festival we had a television set stolen and a bicycle too.[55]

One interviewee singled out for praise the work the RCs do in keeping track of migrants: "China is too chaotic these days, and peasants don't stay on the land like they should. It's right to have someone taking charge of [*guan yi guan*] and controlling the floating population."[56] Thus, even though residents harbor considerable skepticism about the effectiveness of neighborhood-based anticrime measures such as the volunteer security patrols, many support the principle of monitoring and regulating these feared outsiders.

Taipei residents' security worries are not couched in the same terms, but concerns about crime or more casual wrongdoing similarly form a part of what shapes their expectations of neighborhood administration. The city's alleyway surveillance cameras, and popular attitudes toward them, highlight this fact. By the mid-2000s, many neighborhood leaders had used discretionary funds to install networks of cameras to monitor people and vehicles coming and going in the streets, lanes, and parks. In some areas, these fed into computer systems in the police station; in other cases, the lines went to the warden's office. Computer monitors displayed real-time images from the cameras, and large hard drives preserved a week's worth of jerky video. These archives were available for use by the warden, the police, or other authorities. Occasionally, residents asked to see the records, for example when a motor scooter had been stolen or a car sideswiped in a narrow alley. In principle, citizens could review the images only with police officers present.

The Taipei survey asked whether it was right to conduct such surveillance for reasons of security or whether it inappropriately violated individuals' privacy (*geren de yinsi*). The results were lopsided: more than 93 percent of the 1,140 respondents welcomed the cameras, and only 3 percent disapproved of them. In-depth interviews showed a similar pattern of overwhelming support. "I'm not worried about privacy; I'm concerned about burglars," one woman said. "Taiwan isn't all that safe; you can see how we put up metal bars outside the windows."[57] A forty-six-year-old man stated: "In terms of decreasing the crime rate, whenever something happens, the cameras can show an image from every single intersection and you can check it later. That way anyone who comes through here can't just slip away. If he came through he's under our surveillance [*jiankong*]."[58]

Only one Taipei resident stated opposition to the cameras in the interviews, as did one warden, Chen Boyu. "Today someone called me asking to see the video records because his foreign household worker [*wai lao*] ran away," he said with chagrin. Chen argued that the relatively low-resolution images produced by the cameras provided little help to detectives anyway and noted that the city had begun to discourage neighborhoods from spending further public funds on the systems because of their high maintenance costs. These scattered dissenting opinions notwithstanding, the citywide consensus favoring such cameras shows that the perceived public-safety benefits of surveillance trump privacy concerns.

Dispersing rather than collecting information, the broadcasting systems installed in many Taipei neighborhoods also shed light on issues of local public authority and its boundaries. By flipping a switch and speaking into a microphone, wardens can project their voices through a network of loudspeakers scattered throughout the *li*. Some reported using the system as often as several times per week. Reasons for broadcasts include suspected criminal activity in progress, such as a fraud artist going from home to home pretending to repair gas valves, notifying the owners of improperly parked vehicles, finding lost children or pets, and announcing special services like free flu shots.

A booming voice reverberating between apartment buildings, calling out instructions, may strike readers as having sinister overtones. No systematic data appear to exist on popular attitudes toward these broadcasts. One warden explained that, as a result of noise complaints, he used the system only from

10 A.M. until noon, and from 3 P.M. to 9 P.M. Chen Boyu explained that he had no loudspeakers, as his affluent, office-worker constituents wouldn't like it: "people want it quiet here." But interviewees referred to such announcements only in approving ways, citing them as evidence of a warden's conscientiousness and concern.

Both the cameras and the broadcasting systems tell us something about the intermingling of state and societal purposes through the *li-lin* system. Although opinion on them is hardly unanimous and not every neighborhood has such equipment, they show one way in which wardens are entrusted with a subtle form of authority and discretion over the locality, one that is broadly accepted even at the possible expense of forgoing some anonymity and tranquility. In short, many like the idea that a member of the community is keeping an eye on things.

This watchfulness, for many residents, means looking out not merely for their own interests but also for the interests of others, or on behalf of society as a whole. In other words, to borrow a term from theories of voting behavior, some citizens take a sociotropic, other-regarding perspective on the purpose and utility of these grassroots systems. To be sure, some interviewees expressed attitudes of condescension toward those who might need assistance from the neighborhood leader. One fifty-four-year-old Taipei woman, a graduate of a technical college, said: "I feel that it's only people whose level of knowledge is relatively low, people that don't know who to get help from, that would go to the warden. People like us who already know where to take a request, like where the tax bureau or the city government is, we don't need the warden. The ones who would are probably old women [*popo mama*] or working class, people who need help dealing with writing and documents, or are poorly informed."[59]

Much more commonly, however, a similar idea—that the *li-lin* system is worthwhile because of the assistance it provides to those in need of special help, such as elderly people living alone—was mentioned instead in a sympathetic light: "In fact the warden is really important. The low-income households go to the *lizhang* to get a document stamped, or children with disabilities, all kinds of disadvantaged people go to him. After all, they don't have other channels they can use. Sometimes a husband and wife will fight and she'll be injured and needs a witness, she might go to the police or she might go to the warden. There are some people who just go to work and have no contact with the *lizhang*, so they don't know how important he is to other people."[60]

In both Beijing and Taipei, some residents pointed to the neighborhood system's potential utility in the event of war, natural disaster, or other emergencies. This is hardly an abstract possibility for those who live in a region prone to earthquakes and, in Taipei's case, typhoons and landslides. One Taipei resident in her late sixties recalled World War II air raids, as well as more recent crises such as the deadly September 1999 quake, in supporting her view that wardens are especially needed in times of emergency. In such circumstances, she said, relief workers require cooperation and information from them to do their jobs well.[61]

The severe acute respiratory syndrome (SARS) epidemic of 2002–2003, which infected 5,327 people in mainland China and 346 in Taiwan, looms large in recent memory and provides an example of a crisis in which the ultra-local administrative apparatus was extensively mobilized in fighting a clear threat to the public.[62] In Beijing, Taipei, and elsewhere, neighborhood staff passed out disinfectant, along with other means of impeding the virus, and encouraged residents to use them. They also helped report potential infections to health officials and supported individuals under quarantine by maintaining contact with them and providing food. In so doing, they formed one component of a multidimensional state response. Not all residents consider the work done specifically by RCs or wardens to have been particularly significant or important, but for many, this kind of exigency is part of what makes such systems worth having around.

The sense that neighborhood leaders look out for the interests of the community extends to other kinds of circumstances as well. When faced with a choice between helping locals and helping strangers, Beijing's committees tend to choose the former. In two instances, RCs I was observing were approached by out-of-town visitors who sought help in collecting money they claimed to be owed by residents of the neighborhood. In both cases the RC politely refused to provide any assistance.[63] The committees emphasize their protective role by engaging in fire-prevention activities—in some neighborhoods including home inspections—and other public-safety announcements, such as reminding residents of the importance of proper ventilation in areas where coal is burned for cooking and heating.[64]

Another way in which the neighborhood organizations sometimes play a valued protective role is by shielding their constituents from demands of the state or by enforcing local rules in a lenient way. This should not be exaggerated; as previous chapters have indicated, China's RCs are under pressure from the street office not to slack in their duties, and the *liganshi* who work with Taiwan's wardens generally ensure that law and policy are followed. Still, residents often expect to receive exceptions or second chances. This can be as minor as refraining from reporting violations of the dog policy or letting a resident off without paying a deposit while doing home renovations. But, as in the cases of the *falun gong* adherents' family members discussed in Chapter 4, some residents also develop the sense that the committee will act on even more serious infractions in a way that takes their best interests into consideration, and often there is a real basis for this.

In the back alleys of both cities stand many homes or add-on structures that violate building codes (*weizhang jianzhu*). Gao Kunshan, the warden of Taipei's Yanping *li* before his defeat in the 2006 elections, said that as many as two hundred illegal houses littered the mountainside in the back of his neighborhood, occupied by elderly former military personnel. He had never asked them to move out, he said, because the residents had nowhere else to go: "If you ask them to leave, they will tell you that they're moving into *your* house." Gao and the city building authorities effectively gave them a permanent pass.[65] It was also common for *lizhang* to look the other way when residents did things like bending the parking rules or failing to register small temples. One man with long experience in local associations commented: "The more a warden helps residents do illegal things, the more they like him. If you were doing something legal, what would you need the warden for?"[66]

Late one December afternoon, Dai, the beat cop, announced to Director Ouyang, head of Beijing's Xianningjie RC, that he intended to levy fines on several dozen residents who were living in rented homes in the neighborhood. She replied: "Let's give them warnings instead of just fining them." Dai tried to push for immediate enforcement, saying that he had checked and that none of the renters had filed the appropriate forms; moreover, he said that such fines provided an important source of revenue to the district and would support the hiring of security guards. But in the end Ouyang insisted on posting warnings to the renters.[67] In another case, a staff member confided that the committee on which she served had refrained from turning in participants in the 1989 protest movement.[68] One proprietor of a small convenience store said that her committee helped her obtain business permits and interceded on her behalf with inspectors from the Industry and Commerce Bureau when they discovered that she had failed to put price labels on some of her inventory—even though the store was no longer an RC-sponsored business and the committee had nothing at stake financially.[69]

Conclusion

This chapter has elucidated the ways in which ordinary citizens—those outside the circle of supporters closest to the RCs and the wardens—look on and interact with these institutions. We must once again bear in mind that opinion toward these organizations is varied and idiosyncratic. Some citizens of Beijing and Taipei see nothing that is appealing in them and keep their distance, as detailed in Chapter 5. And yet a majority in both cities perceives them in at least a partially positive light. This chapter has aimed to explain that basic fact.

The dynamics of electoral competition in Taiwan factor into these perceptions. There, cities' quadrennial warden elections mean that incumbents and their would-be successors must climb stairs, as they put it, pounding their way up and down the walk-up apartment buildings to make personal contact with voters. More broadly, the choice process institutionalizes an accountability mechanism and empowers residents to choose neighborhood representatives for themselves—a power that their counterparts in mainland cities do not have at present. Boisterous, participatory elections are part of the culture of local governance in Taipei. Yet as we have seen, Beijing's RCs enjoy comparable levels of support, and indeed the official neighborhood system is perceived as valuable by a larger proportion of the populace in Beijing.

There is a fundamental similarity between the cities in what appeals to the majority of people about these institutions, what makes them feel like an acceptable or desirable presence, rather than alien impositions. Part of this has to do with interpersonal ties. Although some of the individuals who serve on Beijing's committees have no particular charisma or local rapport, others are well known in their neighborhoods and may have the benefit of constituents' respect because of seniority or the perception that they have served the neighborhood fairly. Still, relentless scaling up of neighborhood size and widespread demolition and relocation of communities continually disrupt these networks. Taipei is more stable in this regard; the occasional adjustments of *li* boundaries pale in comparison to Beijing's ongoing mergers and redevelopment churn. Many of Taipei's wardens are joined to clusters of supporters through kinship ties spanning multiple generations. In other cases, they draw on networks surrounding local temples, parent-teacher associations, and service activities of many stripes. In both cities, the day-to-day work of the neighborhood institutions, as this chapter and others have detailed, also generates and reinforces personal acquaintance and familiarity between leaders and certain segments of urban society.

Such networks are only part of the story, however. After all, some constituents have very little or no contact whatsoever with the men and women in the neighborhood offices, yet still approve of what they do. For such people and others, the organizations can still be a reassuring presence and a potential resource. Although generally of no help in addressing life's major imperatives like career and housing, it can provide small ame.nities, conveniences, favors, and support. Although it cannot solve every problem, it is at least a place to turn to. It offers a possible way of resolving conflicts with neighbors that might otherwise remain stuck at a galling impasse. Its oversight of the locality, whether through low-tech methods of watchfulness and word of mouth or through high-tech camera systems, is widely considered benign if not benevolent. For many, in other words, the organic statist vision of the neighborhood makes perfect sense.

As it turns out, the bases for affinity between communities and their official leaders are not unique to China and Taiwan but are also found in other cases of administrative grassroots institutions, to which we now turn.

Chapter Eight

The Landscape of Grassroots Administration
Comparative Cases

The preceding chapters have taken a close look at state-backed ultra-local administrative bodies in Beijing and Taipei. From the outset, though, this book has made the case for thinking of these two institutions as part of a broader family of governance arrangements found in many contexts. I argue that a comparative awareness of other cases is not just a thought-provoking coda to inquiry in China and Taiwan but in fact is essential for appreciating the two institutions on which this book focuses and for thinking clearly about the patterns of state-society interaction that they display.

Chapter 2 reviewed the historical threads tying together the East and Southeast Asian cases, and Chapter 3 glanced at leadership selection in several of them. Building on that foundation, this chapter fleshes out the argument for this common conceptual framework. It shows how examples of administrative grassroots engagement in other countries compare to the two primary cases, pointing out some basic commonalities as well as disparities. It draws on several particularly illuminating studies of the Japanese and Indonesian variants, my own modest field research on the South Korean case, and somewhat fragmentary evidence on Cuba's parallel organization. Each of the cases is unique in certain ways, and (like China and Taiwan) each contains important variation at the individual, neighborhood, and city level. Despite this, these institutions not only have significant similarities in terms of their organizational structure and the purposes to which states apply them but also exhibit common themes in ways that residents respond to and engage with these bodies.

Japan's Chōkai, Chōnaikai, and Jichikai

The neighborhood associations (*chōkai* or *chōnaikai*; also *jichikai*) of Japan are the most numerous and widespread of all the country's voluntary organizations; there are nearly three hundred thousand of these groups in existence, according to a recent study by Robert Pekkanen, Tsujinaka Yutaka, and Hidehiro Yamamoto.[1] Their origins and their development over time can be characterized as involving spontaneous, popular initiatives as well as state sponsorship by turns. The Edo period (1600–1868) supplied ancestors in the form of small household clusters similar to the Chinese *bao-jia* system, called *goningumi* and *tonarigumi*, although these were abolished in the later Meiji era and have no direct link to later phenomena. In the 1920s, the government looked approvingly upon locally formed associations and encouraged them to develop widely. The 1923 Kanto earthquake and the part that local groups took in relief efforts provided a further impetus for government to foster them. As the Japanese system turned more and more militarist and expansionist in the 1930s, the state wholly subsumed these neighborhood organizations, enlisting them in efforts to mobilize and regiment society. During World War II, city residents were compelled to participate in a hastily regenerated network of *tonarigumi* and *chōnaikai*, which undertook duties such as spreading propaganda, promoting civil defense, selling government bonds, and rationing food. Because they had been so closely interwoven with the war effort, the occupation authorities abolished them in 1947, but neighborhood groups quickly reemerged in the 1950s (Steiner 1965, 12, 55–60; Sullivan 1992, 136–140; Hastings 1995, 69–85; Mock 1999, 54–59; Pekkanen 2006, 102–108).

Those who study the contemporary *chōnaikai* report that officials of the Japanese government take pains to emphasize their distinctness from the discredited state appendages of the World War II period. And indeed they are distant. The leaders of today's neighborhood groups are chosen by locals in ways that are independent of government, as discussed in Chapter 3. Like parallel organizations elsewhere in East and Southeast Asia, the *chōnaikai* clearly do a great deal to foster neighborhood community ties and use those social networks extensively in their work. Although the size of these organizations varies, a typical group contains between fifty and five hundred households and, in urban areas, encompasses just a few city blocks.[2] Their scope is thus small enough that participants will be familiar with one another. The *chōnaikai* build interaction by sponsoring a range of social and voluntary activities. Pekkanen's research draws on several large-scale surveys by Japanese scholars to document the wide variety of community undertakings that neighborhood groups lead. Some of the most common include organizing local festivals, sports events, and clubs; supporting groups for children and the elderly; cleaning gutters and roads; and engaging in activities to prevent crime and fires (Pekkanen 2006, 92–95).

In his anthropological study, Bestor colorfully documents some of the volunteer activities that were organized in the Tokyo community he calls Miyamoto-chō. For instance, a group of grumbling but committed regulars undertook a monthly spraying of mosquito-control chemicals, receiving no pay for their toil but rewarded with a lunch provided by the *chōnaikai* and local restaurateurs (Bestor 1989, 122–124). He also describes the way in which local events like the annual festival centering around a Shinto shrine built solidarity and helped to "invest Miyamoto-chō with an aura of communal identity and autonomy" (Bestor 1989, 251). Subneighborhood bodies parallel the kind of elaborate structures found in other regional cases. Households were grouped into small clusters (*kumi*), which in turn were aggregated into geographical sections (*bu*).[3] Acting as a representative of one's *kumi* or *bu* in the broader *chōnaikai* organization was another way residents could serve in a voluntary capacity. All *chōnaikai* posts from the president down were unpaid (Bestor 1989, 170–176).

Unsurprisingly, participation in *chōnaikai* activities was not evenly distributed among the population. Bestor highlights the especially active role played by members of the "old middle class" of shopkeepers and other small-scale, self-employed entrepreneurs, and he observes that members of the "new middle class" like salaried professionals seemed to feel less welcome (Bestor 1989, 9–10, 263–264). Pekkanen notes that although an overwhelming majority of Japanese citizens are dues-paying members of their neighborhood association, only a portion of these are substantively involved in the organization. He nonetheless argues that the *chōnaikai* attract the active participation of "a majority of Japanese" and that "in comparative context, having half the adult population of Japan active in any organization seems to constitute a tremendously vital enterprise" (Pekkanen 2006, 90).[4]

Bestor gives attention as well to informal, person-to-person ties among neighbors that "maintain the social fabric of local life without which other, more organized activities and formally constituted groups simply could not exist" (1989, 193). These informal relationships were not an unmixed blessing, as they carried implicit obligations, possibly infringing on a household's desire for privacy. Nonetheless, they were valued by many residents and moreover allowed the neighborhood community to exert considerable social control over its members, as illustrated by the case of a local merchant who was pressured to remove a vending machine that sold pornographic magazines—even when the neighborhood organization declared itself powerless to intervene (Bestor 1989, 209–210). In his over-time study of a Sapporo neighborhood, Mock also emphasizes the ongoing relevance of the social functions of the neighborhood association, even as its overall power and prestige declined since the late 1940s (1999, 181–190).

Most intriguing for the purposes of this discussion are the ways in which both the formal organization of the *chōnaikai* and the informal neighborly bonds on which it rests are routinely tapped into by local government. Though self-constituting, Japanese neighborhood associations work closely with the state. They certainly do not have the same kinds of reporting and monitoring requirements that China's residents' committees (RCs) do, but they nonetheless carry out a range of activities on behalf of the authorities. These include communication functions like disseminating information through printed notices or through message boards that are circulated among households and conducting surveys on the government's behalf. They also are a channel through which the government endeavors to shape popular opinion on local matters, for instance in building support for public works projects. In many cases they also collect fees for the municipal government. The state often pays the neighborhood associations for services rendered, although such revenues are not the groups' main source of funds (Pekkanen 2006, 114–115; Pekkanen, Tsujinaka, and Yamamoto n.d., chap. 7).

Pekkanen and Bestor both emphasize that interaction between *chōnaikai* and government is a two-way street, with neighborhoods regularly lobbying officials on behalf of the locality's interests. Nonetheless, collaboration with the state is extensive, regular, and deeply rooted. Bestor writes that neighborhood leaders felt "inundated by almost constant, yet uncoordinated requests and demands for their cooperation in government projects." This stemmed in part from the fact that even in the postwar period, "the attitude endures at all levels of government that the lower, more local institutions do not exist as autonomous entities: lower levels are seen as existing to serve the needs and meet the demands of the higher strata of administration. Civil servants therefore see *chōkai*—the lowest institutions to which responsibilities are delegated (despite their legal standing as independent citizens' groups, not arms of the government)—as agents of the government's making and under its control, there to do the government's bidding." Consequently, "interaction with the government pervades [the *chōnaikai*'s] structure, its ethos, and its activities" (Bestor 1989, 105–106). Although Pekkanen analyzes the neighborhood groups as part of civil society, some scholars are thus reluctant to assign this form of association to the nonstate realm. One writes that it is "in an awkward position, because it has an intermediary nature which does not permit a clear separation between private and official matters" (Yoshihara 2000, 295).[5]

In short, the Japanese neighborhood groups constitute a powerful and pervasive example of state-society synergy, as presented in Chapter 1. They illustrate how the mechanisms of collaboration between government and community that Evans and others identified in the development context can be put to use in general administrative practices. The formal organization of the *chōnaikai* makes an irresistibly convenient focal point for government officials to employ as a conduit to the community; the dense interpersonal networks that sustain this organization provide a means through which announcements and requests can be widely communicated. As in other examples of such synergy, here communities are enlisted as partners to the state. Although this partnership can be burdensome to and at times even unwanted by *chōnaikai* leaders, it is conducted in a way that respects and even enhances the community's ability to organize itself and perpetuate its own solidarity.

Indonesia's Rukun Warga *and* Rukun Tetangga

As observed in previous chapters, municipal administration in Indonesia extends through several layers of city government all the way down to small clusters of households. At the very bottom level, the urban population is grouped into tiny associations known as *rukun tetangga* (RT), which also exist in villages. These had their origins in the *tonarigumi*, or "neighbor groups," introduced on Java in January 1944 by Japan's military occupation. Although the original Japanese-style institution was intended to contain just ten to fifteen households each, by the 1980s they ran to thirty to forty households (Sullivan 1992, 139–142; Niessen 1999). As of 2000, there were 260 residents per RT on average in Jakarta, according to official figures (Kurasawa 2009, 80n9). In turn, these subneighborhood groups are aggregated into community associations known as *rukun warga* (RW). Before the 1990s these took the form of somewhat larger units called *rukun kampung* (RK), *kampung* meaning village or lower-class neighborhood. The RT and RW work hand in hand with other networks of state-sponsored grassroots organizations, such as the women's association (Pemberdayaan Kesejahteraan Keluarga, or PKK), which, among other programs, has aimed to popularize birth control in cooperation with the national family-planning board (Shiffman 2002).

Ethnographic accounts of neighborhoods in Jakarta and Yogyakarta, each drawing on years of fieldwork during the Suharto era, emphasized the strongly community-centered nature of life in these urban localities, particularly the lower-class *kampung* districts (Logsdon 1974; Guinness 1986; Sullivan 1992). For example, members of local cells, or clusters of families, referred to one another using fictive kinship terms reflecting relative age and status—such as mother, uncle, elder brother, or sister—even when no actual kinship existed (Sullivan 1992, 47). Guinness wrote: "The RT ward community approximates that informal group of neighbors who provide immediate assistance to individual households in preparing slametan [communal feasts], erecting or repairing houses and providing support in times of emergency. Probably the imposition of RT administrative boundaries and the efforts of RT staff over the years to engender RT community co-operation have tended to fix the boundaries of intense social interaction, so that residents tend to think first of fellow RT members as their closest allies" (1986, 151). The RT were documented as organizing activities ranging from youth sports to rotating credit associations and joint ownership of a funeral trolley to defray burial expenses (Guinness 1986, 148–151).[6]

In the Suharto era, officers of the RT, RK, and RW served without pay and were drawn from the members of the locality in a process of selection that the state supervised closely. Whether through votes or through a consensus-building discussion, the RT leaders were chosen by the households they represented and served three-year terms. They, in turn, selected the staff of the RK apparatus, which could include a head, secretaries, treasurers, deputies for each of those positions, and committees responsible for matters such as social welfare, education, building, security, women, and youths. Guinness reported that RK staff in his field site served in their spare time and were expected to be on duty in the neighborhood office one afternoon per week, although some performed this obligation only spottily (1986, 24–25). Sullivan observed that the selection procedures for these officers were only quasi-democratic. The candidates themselves, as well as those who chose them, were limited to heads of households who were "free of Leftist taint" (Sullivan 1992, 143). Ritualized voting was sometimes expected to confirm a consensus outcome that had been reached in advance on the basis of argument, lobbying, and even threats. Yet Logsdon found that the process of discussion generally had real meaning and could influence the choice of RT head (1978, 101). Although government officials vetted leadership candidates carefully and had the power to appoint whomever they wished, in practice a kind of tacit balance obtained, as Sullivan described: "*kampungs* do not normally field candidates likely to dismay higher authorities and, realizing this and not wishing to create unnecessary ill feeling or resistance, higher authorities seldom intervene" (1992, 136, 143).

These accounts agree that the ultra-local administrative structure that emerged from this process was thoroughly embedded in dense local bonds. Like the Chinese RC, its duties included a number of functions aimed at maintaining order—often directly benefiting the local population but also facilitating Suharto-era repression. The RT and RW leaders frequently mediated disputes among neighbors, including marital squabbles within households (Guinness 1986, 37, 104, 142; Sullivan 1992, 144). They organized obligatory labor service, including night-watch duty. At the urging of city officials, they sponsored competitions among RT to "stimulate greater achievements of state-defined targets in tax contributions [and] acceptance of family-planning methods" (Sullivan 1992, 105–106, 147). They also assisted state officials in arresting Indonesian Communist Party members and sympathizers, and in monitoring paroled dissidents. Sullivan noted that the RW offices were required to "keep lists of returned political prisoners and similar suspects, monitor and constrain their movements, and help limit their employment opportunities" (1992, 168). Despite all this, residents generally had close relations with the RT head chosen from their midst, turning to him for information and assistance and seeing him as "the 'neighborhood's man'" rather than a tool of the authorities (Logsdon 1974, 67). She reported that in her 1969 sample of 548 Jakarta household heads, fully 90.2 percent of those from lower classes knew the name of their RT chair, whereas only 56.8 percent of upper-class respondents did (Logsdon 1974, 58).

In a follow-up study that tracked his original field site through the final years of the New Order regime, the democratic transition, and the first years under the emerging postauthoritarian system, Guinness continued to find formal and informal structures of authority closely woven together. The transition further accentuated the community-serving roles of the RT leaders. He found, for example, that in the 2000s residents felt all the more empowered to hold the RT and RW to account, and he cited their ability to take initiatives that helped the *kampung*, such as building a rudimentary bridge over a river (Guinness 2009, 83, 87–93). Aiko Kurasawa's participant observation in several locales, including a decade of occasional research in a Jakarta-area neighborhood from 1998 to 2008, also provides insight on the transition. She observed that although the post-*reformasi* ward office still seemed to exercise influence over the elections for the RT head, the procedures have become more open; after decades of leadership by Golkar supporters, candidates of the former opposition party, the Partai Demokrasi Indonesia Perjuangan (PDI-P), began to win this position after 2001. She found that the RT leader still acts as a liaison between the community and the local government but no longer tries to indoctrinate the residents or subject them to heavy-handed control. She also documents contextual changes that enhance accountability; even poorly educated residents have become more demanding of their RT heads and insist on transparency in decision making (Kurasawa 2009, 69–72, 74–76).

Having observed firsthand the important role these bodies played in monitoring and controlling society under Suharto, Kurasawa was struck by the fact that many longtime residents embraced the RT. Even after the transition, the RT continued to serve as a hub of neighborhood sociability and organization. It still hosted mutual-aid activities like rotating credit groups (*arisan*) and sponsored the local branch of the women's association, the youth association, and the Koran-chanting association, in addition to convening its own meetings. These various associations engaged the energies of roughly a third of the neighborhood, with longtime residents and homeowners particularly well represented. Clearly they were not a detested holdover from the authoritarian past but an integral part of the community, and evidence suggests that this finding applies in many similar areas. A World Bank study found the RT to figure prominently in the lives of the urban and rural poor, and indeed noted that such Indonesians widely consider it "a very important, effective, and trusted institution" (Mukherjee 1999, 94). Kurasawa also points out, however, that residents whose lives intersect less regularly with their residential surroundings (because of transience or the pressures of work) remain marginal to the RT structure and may not be well served by it. This underscores the fact that networks exclude as well as include, and systems of governance that rely on networks may have strong built-in biases (Kurasawa 2009).

The Indonesian system of urban governance thus emphatically underscores the fact that administrative grassroots engagement can coexist with robust local community, even under an authoritarian regime like the New Order. The above sources—convincing though they are—are limited to Java and surely cannot present every aspect of this state-society interface even there. Still, the broad consistency between the picture they paint and the synergy perspective is unmistakable. To paraphrase the title of Guinness's 1986 book, the image is one of overarching harmony within a structured hierarchy. Sullivan discussed how the local leaders' potentially conflicting obligations to community and state were kept in an apparently sustainable balance:

> The communities are realistic and by no means unreasonable taskmasters; they do not call for heroism from their leaders nor do they expect them to be any match for the state as they conceive it. Furthermore, they do not want their leaders to oppose state authorities to a degree or in a manner likely to antagonize those authorities and turn the machine against them. They are expected to cushion the community against state intervention as best they can, to connive and scheme on the kampung's behalf as far as practicable, but the kampung consensus is that the state is to be placated, not provoked. The state for its part adopts a placatory posture as far as it is able and only disrupts kampung life when it appears necessary. (1992, 170)

This image of realistic expectations and mutual accommodation within a broad structure of state domination bears a resemblance to Beijing and particularly its older neighborhoods, although as we have seen the widespread acceptance of the RC there does not extend to quite such an overwhelming consensus. Also, the accounts of Indonesia's *kampung* converge in stressing the centrality of the RT, the smallest unit of all, embedded in immediate day-to-day interactions and deep mutuality. In both Beijing and Taipei, the lowest-level units (small groups, floor heads, *lin*) lack this vitality; most of the energy and activity lies at the next higher tier. But in South Korea, the story is somewhat different.

South Korea's Tong *and* Ban

Chapter 2 observed that Korea's Joseon dynasty (1392–1910) employed local social control units similar to the *bao-jia*. Under Japan's rule, the population was organized into small groups called *ban*, and related structures persisted past the establishment of the Republic of Korea—flourishing particularly in the Park Chung-hee years with his launching of the new village movement in 1970 and the Yusin Constitution in 1972. They endured through the beginning of South Korea's democratization process in the mid-1980s and continue to exist today.

Very little academic research has been published on the official neighborhood governance apparatus, whether in Korean or in other languages.[7] The lack of detailed surveys or extended ethnographic studies made it challenging to incorporate them into the comparison in the same way as the other cases in this chapter, via secondary literature from country specialists. Instead, I visited Seoul myself for ten days in the summer of 2004. With the help of Hoi Ok Jeong, I conducted interviews with twenty-one residents, neighborhood leaders, city bureaucrats, academics, and officials of the Ministry of Government and Home Affairs. Brief and limited though this foray was, I present some observations from it to add to the discussion one more notable case of administrative grassroots engagement, one that otherwise could well go unnoticed.

The Republic of Korea, of course, has long been considered an archetypal example of a developmental state, although the elaborate manifestations of this state in the realm of urban administration are much less well known than its approach to economic governance.[8] Large cities are divided into districts (Seoul has twenty-five of them, called *gu*), which are further sectioned into wards (*dong*). In Seoul, each of the 522 wards contains a population of almost twenty thousand on average and has an office staffed by approximately a dozen full-time civil servants. They handle tasks that include civil defense, welfare programs, and the carefully maintained system of residential registration, along with things like notarizations and street cleaning.[9] Beneath each ward lie two levels of administrative grassroots engagement. First is the *tong*, headed by a part-time citizen *tongjang*. Seoul has 15,267 *tong*, or about twenty-nine on average in each ward.[10] Beneath them lie the *ban*, led by unpaid *banjang*, who resemble Indonesia's RT leaders, Taiwan's *linzhang*, and China's small-group heads. Policy details (e.g., minimum age) vary slightly among South Korea's scores of local governments, although the basic contours of the system are national in scope. In a country of some 49 million people, this stands as a huge organizational infrastructure: as of 2004, the country as a whole had 57,993 urban *tongjang*, assisted by 349,034 *banjang*.[11]

The *tongjang* whom I spoke with each handled an area containing between 100 and 450 households, significantly smaller than that overseen by a Taipei warden or a Beijing RC. They receive formal appointments from the district government for two-year terms. As noted in Chapter 3, some are selected by officials in the *dong* office, whereas others are recommended via written nominations from residents themselves; they are not chosen through formal balloting. In 2004 their stipends were fixed nationwide at 200,000 won per month (about US$175 at the time); they typically put in two to four hours of work every week on their official duties, although certain tasks or problems created elevated workloads. At the very lowest level, the position of *banjang* sometimes rotates periodically among families in a cluster of what is usually twenty to fifty households, whereas in other cases it is held for years by someone who happens to be willing to do it, and sometimes informal votes are held. The *ban* leaders receive no stipends, but at intervals district agencies give them gifts or cash in the range of US$20. Unlike their Taiwanese counterparts, the *tongjang* and *banjang* are forbidden to work for a politician's campaign in the ninety days before an election.

As a Seoul official in charge of local organizations put it, employing much the same language as is heard in China and Taiwan, *tongjang* and *banjang* form "a kind of bridge between the government and people."[12] Foremost among the *tongjang*'s administrative responsibilities are disaster preparedness and civil defense (something taken seriously in a capital lying within range of North Korean artillery), notifying civilian men of periodic military training, working with the *dong* office once or twice a year to update the residential registry, and helping the ward determine the eligibility of citizens applying for welfare support. They also distribute government magazines and announcements (e.g., informing citizens about changes in tax policy, encouraging them to refrain from driving their cars one day per week for traffic control), communicate with police about crime, and handle exigencies like flooding.

Comparatively, the duties of the *ban* leaders are light—they assist the *tongjang* with some of the above responsibilities, attend occasional meetings at the ward office, and help distribute government publications. In May 1976, the Park regime inaugurated a system of regular *ban* meetings (*bansanghoe*, or BSH). These were intended to bring together at least one member of

every household in the country on the twenty-fifth of every month, solidify-
ing national unity within grassroots gatherings.[13] The ban meetings continued as of 2004 and still constituted tangible links between community and
the national state. The Ministry of Government Administration and Home
Affairs compiled announcements monthly and circulated this material to local
governments, which then presented it at *tongjang* meetings and conveyed it
to *banjang*. Nonetheless, the system had relaxed substantially since Korea's
democratic transition. As the city-level official put it: "In the past, we used
the *bansanghoe* as a kind of method of controlling the people. Through them
we could gather information about the residents, and publicize our policies.
But today, things have democratized, so the BSH system became very voluntary. In the old days, the civil servants themselves attended the meetings, and
insisted that they be held. Now we have a more self-initiated system."[14]

As of the mid-2000s, most neighborhoods held BSH only every two or
three months, or even as little as two or three times per year, and local leaders
came under less pressure from government to drum up attendance compared
to the years of military dictatorship. For example, in Seoul's Dongjak district
only 883 out of 4,052 *ban* (22 percent) held the monthly meeting in June
2004. Indeed, some neighborhoods seem to have quietly dropped the meetings entirely.

Who takes part in these systems, and what is the nature of this participation? Some *tongjang* are homemakers, and many others run local businesses;
one of those with whom I had long interviews ran a small clothing store,
another a real estate office. In such cases, the part-time government work had
obvious synergies with their jobs, both of which involved close interaction
with the community. At the *ban* level, either the *banjang* hosts or households
take turns hosting the *bansanghoe*, which still feature readings of announcements from the government, followed by general discussion, the serving of
snacks, and such. In some neighborhoods, nominal fines (US$1 or $2 in value)
were levied on those who missed the meeting, although often there is only
social pressure to show up—or no pressure at all.

Just as neighborhood activities in Beijing and Taipei are attended much
more by some demographics than others, the same is true for the *ban*. In
Seoul, women clearly make up the majority of *banjang* and BSH attenders,
although no precise figures were available.[15] A common pattern was one of
more frequent meetings and avid participation in apartment blocks, where
middle-class homemakers had more time for such gatherings and more com-

mon concerns to discuss, as opposed to in areas of detached homes. Sometimes the BSH became a forum for urgent problems requiring group resolution, such as (in one instance) water leaks that required large maintenance expenditures in an apartment building. As in other cases of grassroots administration, community leaders serve as channels through which residents can contact city offices and inform them of troubles with things like streetlights and trash.

One thirty-nine-year-old Seoul woman with a master's degree in social work said that despite its authoritarian origins, the BSH "has a positive aspect": "Things totally changed in Kim Dae-jung's administration, which promoted civil society. Then people realized that the government cannot control us, we can express ourselves. In that sense, *bansanghoe* became a good chance to debate and reach agreement. The meetings had been mandatory in the past— everyone attended but it had no meaning for us. Today, BSH indicates that civil society has developed well."

She cited the way these meetings provide an opportunity to gather items to sell for charity and a forum for neighborhood decision making, arguing also that the state-backed framework of the BSH remained necessary and appropriate: "We don't want the government meddling, but we need a certain minimum of support. We don't want government control, but we need someone to encourage us to meet."[16]

In South Korea's *ban* and *tong*, then, we see a striking example of an institution that, much like the Indonesian and Taiwanese cases, once fit easily into the category of authoritarian mass organization, yet has persisted and evolved long after a national-level democratic transition. The government remains committed to it; to give a conservative estimate, the city of Seoul alone spends the equivalent of at least US$50 million on stipends and gifts for *tongjang* and *banjang* annually. The authorities still draw on it for a variety of purposes, motivated not least by South Korea's special need for civil defense, but also corresponding to a system in which societal cooperation in administrative tasks is largely considered normal. Since the Park and Chun Doo-hwan years it has become more flexible and adapted to community purposes while maintaining its highly state-structured character. In contrast to the wardens of Taiwan, *tongjang* work in their official capacity only a few hours a week and cover a relatively small population. They do not campaign for their positions the way *lizhang* do, and any role they have representing the neighborhood upward to the city seems to be a muted one. Just as in other countries, though, neighborhood institutions like the *ban* and its meetings have resonance among certain parts of the population. They are not everyone's cup of tea, but those with particularly strong ties to the immediate locality and time to spend in such gatherings find them valuable. These gatherings possess a gendered quality as well, much like RC work.

Cuba's Committees for the Defense of the Revolution

On September 28, 1960, just more than a year and a half after seizing power from Fulgencio Batista, revolutionary leader Fidel Castro announced the formation of what were to be called Committees for the Defense of the Revolution (CDRs). These ultra-local organizations were given the primary task of keeping a lookout for individuals or activities that threatened the new regime. Castro explained:

> We're going to set up a system of revolutionary collective vigilance. And then we shall see how the lackeys of imperialism manage to operate in our midst. Because one thing is sure, we have people in all parts of the city; there's not an apartment building in the city, not a corner, not a block, not a neighborhood, that is not amply represented here [in the audience]. In answer to the imperialist campaigns of aggression, we're going to set up a system of revolutionary collective vigilance so that everybody will know everybody else on his block, what they do, what relationship they had with the tyranny [the Batista government], what they believe in, what people they meet, what activities they participate in. (Fagen 1969, 69)[17]

Although this book has focused on East and Southeast Asian cases, which share a set of historical linkages, administrative grassroots engagement is not unique to that region. To ignore non-Asian cases altogether would overstate the geographic specificity of this phenomenon, examples of which appear in multiple settings where relatively strong states with weak or absent liberal norms confront security threats. Thus, it is worth taking a glance at Cuba's CDRs, the creation of a young revolutionary regime that perceived itself as menaced by forces of reaction both domestic and foreign, much like China at the time it established the RCs. Forming a natural pair for comparison given their Communist Party–led political contexts, the Cuban and Chinese cases remain similar overall, yet diverge in certain respects.

Instead of serving merely as a neighborhood-level auxiliary to the city government and police, the CDRs stand as an independent apparatus, with a national directorate of their own as well as provincial and municipal coordinating bodies. The RCs have always been a network of small local committees that attempt to build links to constituents but not to enroll the population into their ranks. The Cuban committees, in contrast, possess a huge mass membership and over the years have aimed continually to increase the percentage of the citizenry that belongs to the organizations. In this respect, they conform more closely to Kasza's model of the administered mass organization than their Chinese counterparts. The failed Bay of Pigs invasion by U.S.-backed Cuban exiles in April 1961 heightened the perception of external threat and led to a rapid expansion of CDR membership from seventy thousand people to more than a million in September of that year (Fagen 1969, 77). As of 1996, the authorities claimed that 7.6 million people belonged, or approximately 88 percent of adult Cubans (Colomer 2000, 135). In 2005, Juan Jose Rabilero Fonseca, national coordinator of the CDRs, stated that the organizations had more than 133,000 local units and more than 8,300,000 members (Kruger 2007, 107).

The ambition of subsuming the population en masse ensures a considerable gap between those who participate actively and those who are members in a nominal way only. Thus, within individual blocks the CDRs revolve around local leaders who are monitored by higher levels of the hierarchy. In this regard they have become more similar to the RCs, and although the extent to which local CDR leaders are paid regular stipends like their RC counterparts is uncertain, they clearly receive forms of material compensation (Colomer 2000, 126). Initially the CDRs were intended to have a presence in factories and other workplaces, but they were scaled back to encompass only residential settings like the RCs, although they are found in both urban and rural communities (Dominguez 1978, 262–263).

Functionally speaking, the CDRs grew to have quite a bit in common with their counterparts in the Asian cases. The Cuban state recognized early on that—apart from their role as monitors of the populace and as promoters of revolutionary values—the CDRs could be useful as local implementers of many different types of government programs. As Fagen writes: "Because of its capillary organization throughout the nation, the CDR system appeared almost from its inception to be an administrative arm of the state. Indeed, by the end of 1961 the leadership's most effective way of reaching quickly into every corner of the island for administrative purposes was through the CDR" (1969, 91). These tasks have included rationing, disaster relief, and efforts to stem undesired behavior from domestic violence to illegal migration to Havana (Halebsky, Kirk, and Hernández 1990, 178; Roman 2003, 217). In the 1960s and 1970s, the CDRs also encouraged participation in unpaid labor, first in agriculture, then in construction tasks (Dominguez 1978, 265). The sociologist Benigno Aguirre identifies the committees as a primary component of Cuba's system of social control, which has successfully "pushed dissent and civil society into less-organized and less-institutionalized forms," although he sees this system as weakening (2002, 87).

There can be no doubt that, as with China's RCs and communities, having the CDR provide benevolent social services has allowed it to present itself to constituents as something other than an oppressive watchdog. Their duties, for instance, have included things like ensuring that young people receive polio vaccinations, promoting literacy, enrolling children in school, and sponsoring sports events and local festivals (Fagen 1969, 80–103; Dominguez 1978, 265). Since 1985, CDRs have worked with local family physicians and nurses to provide basic health care to neighborhoods of five hundred to one thousand people. The CDRs' side of this medical mission includes helping promote campaigns against disease and unsanitary practices, helping organize health education sessions, and facilitating support for families with special needs (Santana 1990, 253–255). They are among the institutions that Cubans may turn to for local dispute resolution (Evenson 2003, 45). This highlights the fact that states that maintain this type of institution find it expedient to blend welfare, assistance, or recreational programs into the grassroots organizations' mix of functions.

But just how successful has Castro's regime been in promoting cooperative links between the CDRs and their communities through such service-oriented activities? Precise information is not available, and sources tend to take polarized positions depending on their overall stance toward the Cuban revolution. On the basis of visits to neighborhoods and interviews with CDR members, during which he observed residents working together, voluntarily, on projects like mosquito control, Kruger finds that the groups "provide the glue that attaches individual community members to the larger community." More generally he emphasizes the efficacy of these institutions for controlling crime and intervening with delinquent youth in ways that are finely tailored to the locale and the individuals involved (Kruger 2007, 107–112). There is, however, substantial evidence concerning factors that alienate some of the people who live under the eyes of this organization. Even more than their Chinese counterparts, the CDRs have taken "vigilance" against foes of the revolution not merely as one important task but as their most imperative duty and defining theme. The Cuban regime has periodically reemphasized the centrality of vigilance in the committees' work (Dominguez 1978, 263). Colomer cites the broad range of activities that CDR members have been expected to report to the authorities, including "receiving visitors from outside the neighborhood, purchasing unrationed goods, attending church, having family quarrels, listening to Radio Martí, wearing blue jeans, or making inconvenient political comments" (2000, 126). While China underwent economic reforms in the 1980s that in many ways embraced market forces, the CDRs retained the thankless task of reporting on widespread black-market activity that the command economy breeds, as well as other breaches of revolutionary values that have long since become commonplace or even condoned in China.

Moreover, the CDRs continue regular efforts to mobilize the population into formulaic displays of loyalty to the regime, whereas the RCs have retreated to a much less aggressive role in which they encourage only the willing to participate. Where the RCs set up undemanding security patrols for volunteers (often retirees) to join a few times a month during daytime hours, the CDRs have struggled to press even working people into service in the night watch, which at least in the 1960s and 1970s held shifts in the hours between midnight and dawn (Colomer 2000, 124). Apart from volunteer service, the CDRs have orchestrated a wide range of collective displays that include "the celebration of death and martyrs, the mass political gathering, the testimonial of solidarity, and the ceremonial of reception," according to Aguirre. Although the elderly and infirm may be excused from taking part, others "face unmitigated pressure to conform" (Aguirre 1984, 548–549). He argues that this type of participation is encouraged through highly instrumental incentives, with residents attending events in order to obtain favorable treatment. The CDRs' support is required for individuals to accomplish things like transferring a food-rationing card, obtaining scarce building materials, and gaining entry into university programs, which suggests a much higher degree of arbitrary authority than in today's RCs (Aguirre 1984, 546–547). In a similar vein, others have judged participation in and compliance with the CDRs to have declined over time, arguing that the committees' enforcement duties put them in a bleak position of ongoing conflict with their communities and that the state has lost the ability to reward loyalists enough to make them sustain this struggle (Golden 1994; Colomer 2000).[18]

Needless to say, it is not feasible to conclude here by adjudicating these conflicting perspectives on the CDRs and estimating the real level of support and neighborhood cohesion that they generate. But it is possible to note ways in which they parallel and diverge from the Chinese case. Both constitute massive networks that have, as a primary purpose, identifying and reporting threats to the hegemony of the ruling party. Both also undertake a slew of activities that involve helping people rather than reporting on them. There is evidence that, compared to the RCs, the CDRs make more onerous demands and impositions on their constituents, insisting that the great majority of citizens join and monitoring their actions more oppressively. Clearly, though, residents' perspectives on these organizations vary in relation with their general attitudes toward the Cuban state, which echoes the other cases discussed in this book.

Thematic Comparison

Considering the history and development of the RCs and *li-lin* together with their counterparts elsewhere, we have seen that in some cases institutional origins can be traced far back in time, as Chapter 2 showed. In others, such as Cuba (as well as Singapore), specific state imperatives rather than any local historical model seem to account for their creation. These local bodies exhibit other differences as well: the numbers of households within each unit; the exact relationship to local government; the amount of authority, latitude, and compensation accruing to individual leaders; and whether residents are formally considered members. They also show remarkable likeness: in their multiple levels of informal governance and in the essentially voluntary nature of participation by those at the bottom rung. In each case we see evolution over time, punctuated at points by ruptures such as the American occupation of Japan, but tending toward gradual change. Democratizations—those of Japan in the postwar period, of Taiwan and South Korea starting in the late 1980s, and of Indonesia starting in the late 1990s—have led administrative grassroots institutions to shed their more repressive practices and to come under greater community influence or control, but they have preserved substantial continuity as well. Even in China and Cuba, cases that have not democratized, the general trend in these grassroots organizations has been toward diminishing intrusiveness and moderation of political demands placed on constituents.

In the systems that descended from the dynastic *bao-jia* and wartime *tonarigumi*, modern governments have hardly wished to advertise a debt to prior systems of political control. And the local institutions embodied substantial departures from their antecedents, far from merely aping them. For example, the RCs of the 1950s, in keeping with the Chinese Communist Party's style of mass mobilization and guided participation, took on a great variety of educational and other service tasks, such as literacy classes and newspaper-reading groups. Nonetheless, the core functional echo of the past—recruitment and cooptation of local deputies to facilitate policing and governance through their ties with neighbors—can hardly be mistaken. As noted in Chapter 2, it is uncontroversial for people in Taiwan to refer to the dynastic and colonial organizations as precursors of today's institutions, and the same parallels are sometimes drawn in China, too.

Whether in nakedly oppressive contexts, as under the Qing, or in relatively liberalized settings, the purpose of these organizations has always been to draw on networks and local knowledge. This can be done in baldly coercive ways, such as requiring the *bao* heads to report criminals hiding in the neighborhood upon pain of collective punishment, or in far subtler ones. The accounts of Japan, Indonesia, and South Korea in particular make clear that organizational forms mandated or strongly encouraged by the government can take on purposes that serve the locality and become meaningful for some of its members, sometimes deeply so. The state's imposition of regimented patterns, its *jia* and its *bao*, its squads and platoons, may start in a cookie-cutter artificiality but can become an accepted, even taken-for-granted, part of community life. In other places or in the eyes of other subjects, they can remain unwanted, oppressive, or simply irrelevant.

This chapter began with the claim that a comparative awareness of cases like the four discussed above is crucial for understanding the primary subjects of this book. In part, this is because to look only at China and Taiwan would risk leaving an impression that overemphasized the partially interlinked past and culture of just those two specific systems. As well, appreciating other cases where ultra-local institutions developed under authoritarian regimes have retained relevance after democratic transitions helps to show why comparisons across regime types are not unreasonable. Pointing out parallels and commonalities does not mean asserting that the countries discussed here and in the rest of the book are all fundamentally alike, sharing some essential-ist "Asian" quality. The Cuban case, of course, provides one corrective for any such misimpression. Rather, responding to security threats, and in some cases invoking or building on historical templates, the states considered here have—each in its own ways—created and sustained governance institutions premised on a particularly intimate vision of the state-society relationship. For reasons that have broad similarities to those found in the Beijing and Taipei cases, these maintain resonance and acceptance in certain parts of their populations.

Chapter Nine

Conclusion

Whether in physics or architecture or politics, changes in scale between the macro and the micro, the colossal and the intimate, bring about far-reaching transformations. A meeting of five people is not the same as a meeting of two hundred people. Mass democracy is not the same creature as its historical predecessors in towns or small cities. The same is true of ultra-local organizations that are fostered or drawn on by government. Like water, which behaves one way in individual drops, yet differently in a tank containing many gallons, state authority can operate and be perceived in strikingly divergent ways when it works through interpersonal ties rather than in distant, faceless institutions.

This study took on three basic questions. It started with the fundamental issue of how individuals in Beijing and Taipei, and in different parts of society, perceive administrative grassroots engagement (AGE), and how they understand and respond to the kinds of authority and obligations that the state channels through it. Building on the answers to that, the book has also explored two other primary questions. It has asked what this phenomenon tells us about the intermingling of vertical and horizontal networks, and the sociopolitical effects of putting community ties toward state-mandated purposes. And it has sought to understand the extent to which state-fostered grassroots organizations can serve as focal points for democratic participation and channels for popular influence.

The nature of the subject matter confronts any researcher with the challenge of comprehending enormous variation at multiple levels. It must be emphasized again that the city cases of Beijing and Taipei cannot speak for all the cities of China and Taiwan collectively. Although the residents' committees (RCs) and *li-lin* are fundamentally national institutions, comparative glances—at points throughout the book, and discussed further in Appendix 2—have uncovered important ways in which other cities differ from the capitals in certain specific conditions and practices. Even when we narrow the focus to look at single neighborhood leaders, as we have done at times in examining individuals like Ding Xiaoli and Bai Zhengmin, we face the facts that each one plays multiple roles and that, even within a single locality, constituents' attitudes toward the same director or warden range widely. Still, the capital cities are by no means unrelated to their less politically central cousins, and evidence indicates that their neighborhood structures provide at least a starting place for understanding those of other large cities.

As Chapter 1 noted, part of what makes organizations like the RCs and the *li-lin* intriguing is their liminal stateness, their position on the boundary between government authority and community-level associational life. States are instruments of force and domination; coercive power is their hallmark. This is true of the government of Taiwan or anywhere else, although it is particularly obvious in the case of the Chinese state, which wields repressive power in many situations, sometimes mercilessly and without institutional checks and restraints. Yet even in Beijing, coercion is not the day-to-day currency in which the neighborhood organizations deal. To the extent that Ding succeeds in her tasks as intermediary and wins support and cooperation from her constituents, it is not through an iron fist. The committees have close links to police and other parts of the state apparatus that possess the ability to employ force. But on most matters the RCs cannot impose their will on constituents. With Taipei's wardens, this is all the more true.

Although there is much overlap among them, we have observed some important differences in the tasks that the organizations in Beijing and Taipei are given by their higher-ups in the street offices and districts, respectively. China's committees have the unenviable responsibilities of monitoring birth-control compliance and migrants, and they engage in more intrusive kinds of surveillance and information gathering, in the service of the Communist Party's expansive conception of public security. In Beijing, the blunter of the neighborhood staff will occasionally point out that some of their work involves *mo di*—feeling out the residents, trying to ascertain basic information about them. In contrast, acting as the government's agents in checking up on ordinary citizens is generally not what Taiwan's wardens do, especially since the democratic transition. In Taiwan, the wardens keep watch for criminal activity and other trouble, just like their mainland counterparts do, and they may provide information to the police and household registry offices, but they respect the civil liberties enjoyed in a free society. They often allow the *ligan-shi* to take the lead on duties of an administrative nature, such as distributing draft notices. Moreover, Taipei's institutions truly offer citizens a choice of neighborhood leader rather than merely pretending to. Thus, the *lizhang* have considerable independent standing (and little sense of threat from above, save in cases of wrongdoing), yet they face the possibility of election challenges (threats from below), a concept that remains foreign to the RC director. Indeed, the wardens have a distinctive role as actors in their own right in the world of city politics and decision making.

Despite these far-reaching differences, there is much that is similar in the worlds of the RC and the *lizhang*. Both act as primary points of contact between government and the population, and as such, they face a daily barrage of visits, calls, and queries from demanding constituents. Both have reasons to try to oblige or at least mollify those inquirers. Leaders in both cases build a set of core supporters with whom they develop close relationships. As Chapter 6 discussed, these supporters often become part of a subculture of social events and volunteer service that the neighborhood groups cultivate. At the same time, as Chapter 7 laid out in detail, staff also try to reach out beyond the ranks of their committed volunteers and win support among the residents in general by trying to demonstrate usefulness and benevolence. One might say that a common logic of ultra-local politics and everyday life underlies the similarities between neighborhood institutions in the two capitals.[1]

Perceptions

Neighborhood leaders in both systems seek to achieve at least benign familiarity with as many constituents as possible, even if this is only a thin form of acquaintance. Chapter 5 presented aggregate survey numbers that show the contours of residents' attitudes toward and interactions with these institutions. In Beijing, the RC's relationships with those outside its core of active supporters vary widely, with some constituents warmly disposed toward the committee, others bitterly detesting it, and most falling somewhere in between. The opinions of Taipei residents toward their wardens showed a generally similar distribution. The RCs and *lizhang* have plenty of detractors but also enjoy even more widespread approval, although that approval is generally muted rather than enthusiastic. A strong majority of Beijingers found the RCs to be useful, in comparison with about half of those surveyed in Taipei—yet even there, respondents preferred to keep rather than abolish the *li-lin* system, by an overwhelming margin.

Ideology and political culture undoubtedly play their part in explaining the degree of support that exists for these institutions. As noted at the outset, Whyte and Parish observed that strongly state-managed neighborhood organizations simply would not fly in a country like the United States, with its liberal traditions (1984). Grassroots engagement by states may be impossible in political cultures that contain strong and widely held elements of antistatism. In countries like Japan and Indonesia, by contrast, state-society collaboration is tightly swathed in prevailing belief systems, as the anthropological accounts reviewed in Chapter 8 indicated. For instance, the very names of the institutions known as *rukun tetangga* (RT) and *rukun warga* (RW) begin with a word meaning "social harmony" (Guinness 1986, 131).[2] The evidence from China and Taiwan provides considerable support for the possibility that political culture helps explain the prevalence of administrative grassroots engagement institutions and also gives reasons to refrain from overemphasizing this factor. The interviews have presented ample evidence that many residents of the two capitals embrace such conceptions as the primacy of the political order or organic statism, as discussed in Chapter 1 (Stepan 1978; Schwartz 1996). Although the presence of such legitimating ideas may be a necessary condition for the practice of grassroots engagement in these forms, individuals in a given national culture vary widely in their attitudes. Constituents weigh all requests and impositions in the context of an evolving set of expectations about the boundaries of privacy, and by no means do they welcome just any form of government oversight and intermediation. To win whatever public acceptance they might enjoy, institutions like the RCs and the *li* must continually prove their worth by providing services, leisure activities, neighborhood improvements, and general responsiveness. This indicates that they cannot rely on any timeless cultural values for legitimation. Rather, the vision of organic state-society fusion competes with other perspectives that would place tighter limits on the appropriate role of the state.

States can choose more or less onerous duties to impose on grassroots institutions, and these can be expected to have a strong influence on the way people perceive them. In the case of Cuba's Committees for the Defense of the Revolution, evidence indicates that zealous reporting of political and economic infractions earned these organizations considerable enmity in some quarters. The Chinese RCs, as we have seen, have undergone a quiet but highly consequential change over the decades. During the Mao era, these organizations helped create the environment of constant surveillance that many urbanites today look back on with distaste, if not dread. Even many ordinary residents experienced this in the form of late-night household registry checks and imperious treatment by RC leaders; those branded as class enemies suffered humiliation, expropriation, or far worse during political campaigns in which RCs directly figured. The integral role played by the committees in the ferreting out of *falun gong* practitioners starting in 1999 brought to the surface their normally half-submerged role as part of the Chinese Communist Party's repressive apparatus—although as we saw, Beijingers varied in their attitudes toward even this dramatic campaign.

Conducting political surveillance on behalf of an authoritarian regime distinguishes the RCs from organizations like the *li-lin* or the *chōnaikai*. It alienates some of those they watch over and leads to a certain wariness in many people's dealings with the committee. Sullivan wrote that in Suharto's Indonesia, communities simply accepted that the RT and RW leaders were obliged to assist the state when it demanded help, even if doing so meant acting against the interests of individual members of the neighborhood (1992). Evidence from China's RCs partly resonates with this, but it also suggests a more complex picture; the work they do for the state is alienating to some residents and endearing to others. To the extent that the RC's vigilance is viewed as largely directed against burglars and other menacing outsiders, it is often welcomed. Even when surveillance is aimed at one's neighbors, it may still win approval if it helps stop thoughtless or reckless residents from discarding refuse improperly, disturbing others with noise or commotion, or undertaking home improvement projects that detract from the safety or comfort of the homes around them. The legitimacy of the RC's requests for personal information regarding birth control, eligibility for welfare programs, and the like depends on individual attitudes toward those public policies. In short, as Chapters 4 and 5 showed, some residents dislike the RC's oversight, whereas others see it as appropriate, but relatively few have much to fear from their neighborhood leaders. Overall, the committees' monitoring functions, though still important, are not perceived as a significant threat by most Beijing residents.

In Taipei as well as in Beijing, residents are quite aware of the close relationship between the neighborhood organizations and the government. For some individuals, this linkage to the state is grounds for criticism. Yet this also has advantages in constituents' eyes. They often see the neighborhood leaders as well-informed sources of information about, for instance, which door of the bureaucracy they should knock on to solve their problems. The focal point of authority provides a basis on which to coordinate the handling of neighborhood troubles, whether of a routine or an emergency nature. Grassroots administrators become generalized go-to people who can at least listen to many kinds of laments and complaints. Indeed, as we have seen, many Beijingers (though somewhat fewer residents of Taipei) find it slightly outlandish to contemplate not having such organizations.

Kasza wrote that administered mass organizations "engender a habit of dependence in their members" (1995, 186). If so, then it is unsurprising that Beijing's RCs, which lie closer to the mass organization model, generate a more widespread feeling that their existence is needed.[3] There, a greater proportion of urbanites are accustomed to living and working within paternalistic structures in which oversight by the government and party is a given. The neighborhood organizations there simply have larger numbers of staff than in Taipei, and people come into contact with them more frequently. Less wealthy in the aggregate even as incomes rise, Beijing's population has, on average, more occasions to seek out their help and fewer alternative resources. Still, as we have seen, the notion of dependency can take us only so far; few urbanites depend on their RC or warden in any real way. Rather, many have an openness to or preference for the model of the state-society relationship that these organizations embody, a perspective that stems from broader historical, ideational, and social sources.

Networks and Clientelism

The great majority of adults in these cities have an opinion on their neighborhood organization, even if, for some, it is only weakly held. A smaller but still sizable fraction of the population actually knows the men and women who constitute these organizations. The essence of institutions of grassroots engagement is their suffusion throughout society, serving as conduits of information via myriad interpersonal ties. To carry out their duties efficiently and smoothly, the wardens, *liganshi*, and RC staff rely heavily on personal contact and familiarity with their constituents.

These connections start with the primary staff members, who choose an inner core of associates (e.g., *linzhang*, small-group heads). In theory though not always in reality, Beijing RC directors and members have close familiarity with constituents at the time that they join the community staff, by dint of longtime residency in the area. Sometimes those recruited for service already have the respect of many neighbors, whether because of mere seniority, a genial and helpful personality, leadership skills acquired in the workplace, having someone of high status in the family, or other characteristics. There can be no question that an RC leader like Ding Xiaoli was encouraged by the city government to join the RC after her retirement precisely because of her personal charm and local prestige, in addition to her work experience, party membership, and political reliability. As we have seen, committee staff are not always so closely rooted in their communities. In newly built neighborhoods, no one the street offices could find would have Ding's kind of cachet with residents, primarily because no one has lived there long enough to build such ties with neighbors. As the city government strives to rejuvenate the committees in the *shequ* structure, it is often obliged to pass over those with seniority and long-standing residential tenure in favor of younger staff with qualities that are seen as desirable for other reasons, like secondary or tertiary education. It has become increasingly common for members to live in places other than the neighborhoods in which they work.[4] And of course, not every RC staffer possesses winning personal qualities; some are dour clock watchers with little or no neighborhood rapport.

In Taipei, the electoral mechanism virtually ensures that incumbent wardens have extensive personal ties in their locality. As we have seen, these have historically taken the form of familial networks, but given the city's expanding population and the diminishing salience of old clans and their property holdings, many other kinds of relationships can also propel a hopeful to these leadership positions. They can instead be a well-established business proprietor's links to his customers, the networks surrounding temples or parent-teacher organizations, or in some cases ties that have formed in the process of micro-level movements and struggles. Sometimes *lizhang* have deep connections to only one area or social segment of their neighborhoods, as with Wu Jiaqian's backers in the state housing units. Regardless, it is essentially impossible to win a warden position in the absence of face-to-face familiarity with at least part of the *li*.

As discussed in Chapter 7, whether in Beijing or in Taipei, the very nature of grassroots institutions systematically builds further opportunities for neighborhood staff to interact with constituents, thereby deepening their pre-existing ties. By offering small conveniences and services, providing a place to ask questions or voice complaints, intervening in low-level disputes among neighbors, and working with police to address crime, the committees and wardens bring themselves into at least occasional contact with people who might otherwise never meet them. For the *lizhang*, these are not merely the obligations of office but also valuable opportunities to build rapport with the next election cycle in mind. All this helps to establish at least a degree of familiarity between leaders and a wide range of residents. In Beijing, the networks of various types of neighborhood volunteers were particularly extensive, and residents more frequently came into contact with the RCs for routine reasons, whereas Taipei featured a broader band of occasional participants in the social and festive activities of the *li*.

These kinds of connections to ordinary constituents are a form of weak ties. Like the tenuous bonds that Granovetter touted, they serve to link the neighborhood leaders to those outside the relatively small clique of their closest friends and supporters; they extend the institution's reach (1973). To a limited degree, such ties can also constitute a form of the kind of reciprocity identified by scholars of *guanxi*, or "relationships," in China (Yang 1994; Gold, Guthrie, and Wank 2002b). In common usage, *guanxi* means having an in or receiving special treatment from someone who owes you favors. As this book has shown, sometimes relations between neighborhood leaders and constituents can have this quality, but such a notion captures only a small segment of the ways that such networks matter.

In both cities, the thickest of the networks around these institutions are formed by the interpersonal bonds among the inner circle of neighborhood volunteers, those who participate in the various neighborhood service activities discussed in Chapter 6. These ties are in some ways indistinguishable from the networks found in nonstate voluntary organizations, a web of horizontal links among core enthusiasts that encourages them to contribute time and energy. In the first instance, block captains and the like draw on the potential for solidarity that comes about merely by dint of living near and encountering one another over the years. Residential proximity also means that they share an interest in the area's well-being. Many of their day-to-day pursuits pertain to matters that are of concern to urban residents anywhere, such as local security, sanitation, and maintenance. In all these respects, the entryway heads and courtyard heads of Beijing and the *linzhang* of Taipei are similar to the *kumi* representatives of Tokyo and the RT officers of Yogyakarta.

Just as in other voluntary associations, neighborhood participation— for instance, taking part in patrol duty together or attending meetings— strengthens these neighborly bonds. Ties among the active supporters are also promoted by the purely recreational get-togethers that the RCs and *li* offices sponsor, whether these are field trips to nearby tourist attractions or singing and exercise groups. Just as in any voluntary group, members join in largely for the simple rewards of companionship. But also as with other service-oriented associations, people take part because it gives them the sense that they are doing something useful with their time, that they are contributing something to the community or even to the broader governing system of which the community is a part.

The nature of the interpersonal ties that link the primary staff members, their associates, and the residents at large vary greatly from person to person, as we have seen, but it is possible to step back and point out general implications. The relationship between, say, Ding Xiaoli and one of her constituents in Beijing's Shimen neighborhood is partially but not strongly vertical. The investing of a certain amount of official authority in figures like the RC director and the *lizhang* hardly destroys their ties with neighbors, and indeed can strengthen them. As Chapter 4 showed, in most circumstances the practical authority that she wields is small. At the same time, the relationship is not fully horizontal; in many respects she speaks for, and acts on behalf of, the state. Her role differs in hue from that of a leader who emerges spontaneously from the grass roots, although in Ding's case it is possible to imagine her doing so in a different political setting. All the same, to say that there can be a hierarchical element in her ties to the neighborhood does not necessarily mean that those ties are those of patron to client. To assess the limited degree of clientelism in these relationships requires carefully parsing the circumstances of different individuals and evaluating shades of gray.

Clientelist ties take their most destructive form when used to fragment a subordinate group and turn its members against one another. Such a situation, with clientelist links to Communist Party cadres shattering any possibility of shop-floor solidarity among workers, is depicted in Walder's account of Chinese state enterprises in the late Mao era (1986). Clients were radically alienated from those around them; indeed, this alienation was in some senses deliberately induced by the system as a test of the activists' loyalty and to serve as a lightning rod for nonactivists' anger and grievances. Naturally, we would not expect to find such extreme polarization in the alleys of today's Beijing, let alone in nonauthoritarian settings. Still, a question remains as to whether visible support for the state-backed neighborhood organization might preclude or weaken one's links to neighbors. Glances at Indonesia's neighborhood groups indicated that, in researchers' judgment, it is entirely possible for people to do what the state requires of them while maintaining their membership in the community intact.

In Beijing we find mixed evidence. The activists have highly varied relationships with the nonactivists around them. Some residents welcome a neighbor taking the lead in addressing matters of common concern. Others are wary of or hostile to the activists, mindful that their floor head or courtyard head may someday be called on to report information about them to the RC or police. Activists rarely are entirely estranged from those around them, but at the same time their relations with neighbors can contain an element of tension that may be less present in cases like the *kumi* representatives of Japan. In Taipei we found less tension, but even there, certain residents stay distant from their *linzhang*.

Clientelistic dependency may also come about when power holders wield arbitrary authority over valuable material goods, opportunities, certification, or the enforcement of rules. A form of this kind of power can be seen in Kurasawa's description of New Order Jakarta, where one had to stay in the good graces of the RT head to receive letters of support that were necessary to obtain various official documents (2009, 65). In Indonesia, much of the RT head's arbitrary control seems to have vaporized with Indonesia's *reformasi*, however. Similarly, RCs may have possessed such power in the Cultural Revolution, when they were known to steer Red Guard raids toward the homes of the politically suspect or otherwise disfavored. These days, that kind of tyrannical power is essentially gone in the neighborhoods of Beijing; still less is it to be found in Taipei. Nonetheless, as Chapter 4 discussed, the residents' committees do have extensive dealings with rural migrants whose status and rights in the city are precarious. Both RCs and *lizhang* play an advisory role to the government on decisions over welfare benefits. The wardens, in particular, can weigh in on (though rarely decide single-handedly) choices that have real consequences for local businesses or developers, as seen in the issues concerning the selling of food in public spaces or even the building of temples, public works, and such. Thus, they potentially hold a degree of power over subpopulations with special needs or special interests. This is mitigated by institutional structures in both cities that sharply limit the discretionary power of neighborhood leaders. Actual decisions on things like welfare support are made at a higher level, and evidence indicates that needy households are not particularly vulnerable to having funds cut off arbitrarily. All told, true dependency is fairly rare in these settings, although elements of clientelism can be seen in relations with certain segments of urban society.

The *linzhang* of Taipei receive monthly payments equal to about US$60 for their service. In Beijing, RCs frequently offer token gifts to their activists. As we saw in Chapter 6, in the case of the security patrollers, these gifts occasionally take the form of small amounts of money, although that is unusual. In both cities, these select supporters of the neighborhood organization typically get first place in line to attend special parties and state-funded outings. Unlike classic situations of patronage, these are not relationships based on the exchange of loyalty by subordinates for substantial material rewards, career opportunities, or the like. The volunteers are hardly in a condition of dependency. Still, relatively modest though they may be, these are undeniably incentives that foster supportive behavior, thus enhancing the appeal of government-encouraged channels of service.

Electoral competition in Taiwan has many salutary effects, but it also brings into the *li* what Crenson's Baltimore study playfully called "foreign entanglements"—political forces from outside the neighborhood (1983, chap. 6). Indeed, a common theme throughout East and Southeast Asia is one of politicians drawing on local state-linked organizations for the purpose of drumming up votes. The threat here is that neighborhoods might be obliged to provide support for politicians in order to obtain material goods or city services, thus substituting short-term payoffs for deeper forms of representation and undermining democratic accountability. In the case of Japan, Pekkanen has aimed to debunk the idea that Japan's neighborhood associations are clientelist political vehicles. In his account, the groups are just one forum among many, providing gatherings where politicians have a chance to speak and appeal to voters but not to ensnare them in relationships of mutual dependency (Pekkanen 2006,

95–99). As we might expect, in Thailand, a less affluent and institutionalized country, Mahakanjana finds that the ties that politicians form with poorer neighborhoods through cooperative community groups can indeed be clientelistic (2009, 111). Chapter 3 noted that in Chiayi, Taiwan, outright vote buying at the neighborhood level remains alive and well. In Taipei, by contrast, the buying of votes has become very rare. There, the wardens commonly form enduring, mutually beneficial alliances with city council members. Some encourage their constituents to vote for favored politicians, but they do not act as brokers delivering votes en bloc.

As we have seen, the language of community saturates the official discourse about these organizations. But can such statist entities truly build community—in a human rather than an institutional sense? Vertical power need not actively smash horizontal solidarity; it can displace or preempt it in more subtle ways. It can cultivate bonds that center on political loyalists and are reinforced through activities geared toward serving the state rather than making demands on it. It can disrupt oppositional forms of solidarity by substituting for them. To the extent that residents interact with neighborhood leaders on a one-to-one basis, they reinforce social links that radiate out like the spokes of a wheel, from the center of the structure, through core participants, to the neighborhood population as a whole. Though not the most malignant kind of clientelism, this certainly may undermine spontaneous, nonhierarchical forms of association.

Particularly in the case of mainland China, many of the duties undertaken by activists consist of tasks that are assigned by the committee members, tasks that often originate in police stations and the functional bureaus of the street office. This is less true in Taiwan, but there, too, *linzhang* duty is conceived of and formalized as a kind of government service. This limits the pool of possible participants, giving it a lopsided quality; those individuals who are disinclined to work on behalf of the state are unlikely to join. The RC cannot, and the *lizhang* typically do not, galvanize commitment through the specific means of overt and contentious efforts to lobby local officials in the name of neighborhood interests. These stand as contrasts between the officially sanctioned networks of supporters and the type of voluntary or community associations with which Westerners are familiar.

The RCs generate community only very selectively, and in some important respects they suppress it. The committees sometimes act on constituents' behalf, but they forgo the potentially unifying effect of rallying the neighborhood to make demands on government. They do not employ in their repertoire of activities some practices that would seem to be obvious ways of developing solidarity: for instance, they almost never hold open public meetings in which all residents freely discuss neighborhood matters. Even when the RCs do seek citizen input, they dislike independent critical dialogue on local matters. Rather, they prefer to interact with nonactivist residents in a quiet and above all individualistic fashion. This works against the building of broad community networks outside of the committee's leadership.

In China, residents typically have few, if any, alternative neighborhood-level venues in which to participate, but in Taiwan, more such options are available. The exclusiveness of vertically organized associational channels is substantially mitigated in settings in which local groups face competitive pressures. Candidates from different parties (and in many cases, no party at all) vie for neighborhood leadership in Taipei. At a minimum, this puts pressure on wardens to diversify their support beyond a small coterie of partisans. As Chapter 6 showed, in Taipei a greater proportion of the citizens take part in neighborhood social activities than in Beijing, which may well be an indirect result of electoral competition—the vote-seeking *lizhang* apparently work harder than the RCs do to pull casual participants into their festivals and the like. Moreover, residents may form, at their own initiative, community development associations that can apply independently for city support. This helps prevent vertical linkages being used exclusively for the benefit of any one political clique.

In some circumstances, government backing for grassroots organizations seems actually to promote horizontal connections. The anthropological accounts from Indonesia cited in Chapter 2 testify to the flourishing of vibrant communities around the structure of some RT. Mahakanjana argues that Thai neighborhoods often lack preexisting associational foci, and thus state-fostered community groups create rather than supplant social capital (2009, 101–103). Moreover, she writes, government backing can give credibility to programs like cooperative burial insurance, which otherwise might be defeated by mutual distrust. And as Pekkanen insists, Japan's neighborhood groups could hardly have the astonishing extensiveness that they do without state assistance (2006, 85, 108).

Echoes of this can be seen in both the RCs and the *li-lin*. These government-supported systems work precisely by appropriating, incorporating, and encouraging types of networks that are typically thought of as belonging to the realm of communities or nonstate voluntary groups. The structures are deeply enmeshed in horizontal, neighborly ties, such as between the *linzhang* and those who live in their immediate vicinity. Indeed, the state-mobilized nature of these institutions stimulates a kind of arranged cohesion in the associational life surrounding them. The social capital that is embodied in such ties can potentially be drawn on by autonomous neighborhood groups and social movements that constrain and influence government. Indeed, in Taiwan and to a lesser extent in mainland cities, independent groups like homeowner associations and nongovernmental organizations (NGOs) do take root in urban communities. The system works in some ways to reinforce wholly horizontal ties, as with its sponsorship of local festivals and exercise groups. But in administrative grassroots engagement, these ties are selectively put to work in ways that center on the *lizhang* and RC staff.

These systems remind us that interpersonal relationships at the neighborhood level are potentially double edged and can be mobilized toward a diverse variety of ends. To be sure, not every specific link in such networks is immediately fungible—for instance, some residents would be willing to serve as a block captain under a Democratic Progressive Party warden but not under one affiliated with the Nationalist Party, or would attend a meeting of environmentalists but not a gathering of entryway heads. Yet in the aggregate and over time, networks that otherwise might serve different purposes can develop in state-sanctioned patterns. For better or for worse, they can provide broad forms of support for government and its endeavors, whether in limited ways, as with the *chōnaikai*, or in far-reaching ones, as with the *li-lin* system and the RCs. Although attention in research on associations and social capital has mostly been focused on relatively independent organizations like NGOs or self-governing local groups, it is not only in such entities that networks play a central role. In many ways, horizontal ties and mild forms of vertical authority can be highly compatible and mutually reinforcing.

Theorists of the concept of synergy have embraced precisely this insight, but what we see here constitutes a form of that phenomenon that puts existing theory into new light. The heart of the synergy idea is that states and communities each can possess valuable assets that the other requires: resources, reach, expertise, and authority on the one hand, and micro-level networks, interpersonal trust, and credibility on the other hand. The RCs and even the *lizhang* are not instances of synergy in the way that Evans and his collaborators posit this idea (1996a, 1997). Rather, they show that the basic logic and processes that those scholars identified have a much broader relevance than originally envisioned. The exemplary developmental projects that are showcased in the synergy literature are special cases, perhaps rare ones.[5] The outcomes are wholly felicitous, and the developmental projects are essentially unobjectionable to all involved. These are partnerships between communities and restrained branches of the state that respect their counterparts' right to organize themselves. If state actors intervene in the locality, it is mainly to help empower the citizens.[6]

Systems of grassroots administrative engagement are also mechanisms through which states build forms of embeddedness that promote development. But these institutions go well beyond the phenomenon of synergy in terms of functional scope, thus representing a more comprehensive form of state-society integration. They differ in two respects. First, although some of the outcomes they contribute to are developmental, such as birth control and public health, they facilitate general administrative and political programs as well, such as policing, welfare, and migration control. These can involve containing and even repressing society, not just giving it a helping hand. Second, the nature of the links they forge between state and citizen are more comprehensive and enduring. These are not just ways in which bureaucracies form partnerships with communities to accomplish jointly an agreed-on project. Here, states engage with societies in a sustained and pervasive fashion, forming dense networks reaching to a large proportion of the population at an individual level and involving some measure of personal familiarity.

Association, Democracy, and Representation

Conceptually, organizations like the *li-lin* and RC systems are a fundamentally different type of animal from those in the phylum of citizen-organized associations. In practice, they blur the boundaries between these categories, starting with the attractions they have to those who take part in them as volunteers. Analysts have largely viewed participation in state-fostered organizations, particularly in authoritarian settings, as brought about by compulsion or the self-interested pursuit of material rewards. But as we have seen, even in authoritarian China, let alone democratic Taiwan, residents are not threatened with state punishment for failing to join or participate. Material conditions do shape people's relations with the grassroots administrative apparatus.

Evidence from China and Taiwan reinforces accounts of Thailand and Indonesia in showing that participation is most concentrated in poorer neighborhoods. Kurasawa found, for example, that in these areas residents are more interested in taking part in things like the rotating credit groups (Kurasawa 2009). Relatively wealthy households, living in more modern forms of housing, tend to rely less on their communities and have less need for coordination with them.

Although people's practical needs and instrumental considerations are part of the story, in cases around East and Southeast Asia, the pleasures of sociability and the psychological rewards to be gleaned from serving alongside others in an official auxiliary of the state seem to be the most important parts of the appeal of these groups. This appears to hold under democracies and authoritarian regimes alike. Neighborhood groups in Beijing and Taipei lie at opposite ends of the spectrum of formal accountability, yet they both pull in teams of voluntary participants for things like block captain service and security patrols. Whether in China, Singapore, or Indonesia, most citizens are proud of their country, and administrative grassroots groups provide a way to serve the nation, even if only at the humblest of levels.

Thus, both these kinds of organizations and civil society offer residents opportunities to interact together and join in collective undertakings. From the perspective of individuals seeking ways to take part in group activities that are enjoyable and convey a sense of meaning, what such venues provide overlaps considerably with what autonomous organizations might offer. Indeed, as we have seen, the state-managed nature of the *li-lin* system and the RCs, though limiting them in certain respects, also bolsters their appeal as a locus for popular participation. The scale of government investment in these groups means that they are readily accessible in virtually every neighborhood. Their official status increases (rather than decreases) their appeal to certain types of volunteers, for whom participation provides a sense of taking part in an important civic project and a national mission. Thus the groups may, in effect, compete with civil society, soaking up citizens' participatory energies like so many widely dispersed sponges. Why form your own local association or Neighborhood Watch group when there is already one waiting for you right outside your apartment building? This effect is magnified in a setting like China, where civil society is embryonic and frail. This siphoning of civic energy should be thought of as a tangible cost of such institutions.

To point out ways in which certain functions of state-fostered organizations overlap with those of independent groups is to not elide this distinction or to deny the fundamental importance of civil society to good governance. We know how crucial civil society is in part by considering cases in which it is absent or cowed into quiescence. Countries that deny their citizens the right to organize wholly autonomous associations through which to address public issues and make political demands are markedly different in important ways from those that respect this right. We also know this from cases around the world in which citizen groups have led the way in bringing about sorely needed political change, whether at the regime level or in expanding rights and addressing injustices.

It is also demonstrably not the case that civil society in its contemporary meaning is unsuitable for Asian societies. Some have argued that this concept is too beholden to the individualistic bent of the liberal tradition, and thus unable to do justice to associations in non-Western societies (Wakeman 1993; Hann 1996). Yet any such argument goes too far. Although the term finds its intellectual origins in British and Continental philosophy, it has evolved a considerable distance from those roots and can be applied as an analytic category without reference to region. As Frank Schwartz and Muthiah Alagappa point out, the existence of civil society in Asia is an undeniable fact, though it is much more highly developed in some countries than in others (Schwartz 2003; Alagappa 2004b).

The problem with civil society studies is that in seeking to establish a discrete concept, they have set rigid definitional lines that obscure important boundary phenomena. The idea of a white-and-black, binary distinction between groups inside and outside of civil society has impeded knowledge in many ways rather than advancing it, thus hindering our understanding of whole galaxies of actual organizations. We must develop much finer-grained categories with which to comprehend the associational universe. This is, in fact, what some outstanding scholarship of recent years strives to do, whether we think of Mark E. Warren's categorizations; Verba, Schlozman, and Brady's analysis of the role of specific types of organizations (unions and churches) in building civic skills; or Lily Tsai's careful research on solidary groups in Chinese villages (Verba, Schlozman, and Brady 1995; M. E. Warren 2001; L. Tsai 2007). This has also been an aim of projects that pursue a functional rather than organizational definition of civil society, such as the Civicus Civil Society Index (Heinrich 2005). As we pursue this, we will likely find even more evidence that organizations that are independent of government have no monopoly on civic qualities, and that sometimes the state can—perhaps surprisingly—do more good than harm as it engages with associational life.

As we know from studies of mass organizations and state corporatism, crude top-down control of grassroots organizations unquestionably can render them lifeless as channels for meaningful political participation. Certainly this has been largely true with China's RCs. Yet apart from such extreme cases, empirical research on the nexus of state and association is still in its infancy. Links to the state have both benefits and drawbacks with respect to the capacity of grassroots organizations to stimulate civic engagement. Neighborhood structures in places like Taiwan and Indonesia suggest that even if state penetration of associations has negative effects, these can also be balanced with institutional features that reinforce popular accountability rather than undermine it. The key ingredients seem to be the inclusion of strong mechanisms to ensure democratic accountability, and the opening up rather than closing off of avenues by which ordinary people can meaningfully affect decision making in the state itself.

Is it possible for state-sponsored local organizations to be run democratically, to choose their own leaders and be held accountable to constituents? The answer is a strong yes. Indeed, the Taiwanese *lizhang* seem to represent the high-water mark in this regard in Asia and perhaps the world, as Chapter 3 shows. Their elections are overseen by the same commissions that handle races for offices like mayoralties, legislatures, and the national presidency. Just about anyone can run for these positions, and in most Taipei neighborhoods the races are competitive. Candidates issue formal statements of their campaign platforms, which are circulated to each household in detailed brochures from the election commission. The counting of ballots in each polling place is conducted as rigorously as in contests for higher offices, under police guard with the scrutiny of election officials and the public alike.

Beijing's RCs, of course, are a very different story; elections there were found to feature little competition, sharply limited participation by carefully picked voters, and a government-dominated process of candidate nomination. Although sometimes an element of genuine choice is offered at the margins, they essentially apply a veneer of faux democracy to the street office's staffing decisions. The different nature of these two institutions and the governments of which they are a part has clear effects on the type of participation that they encourage. The RCs mobilize larger teams of committed volunteers to assist with administrative tasks. But Taiwan's democratic warden elections brought a third or more of Taipei's citizens to the polls—even before their combination with the mayor and council balloting led to the jump in turnout of 2010—far more than those who vote in Beijing's heavily constrained elections.

We might further observe that the process of leadership selection in Taipei's *li* is considerably more democratic than in many civil society organizations. There is no guarantee that nonstate citizen groups automatically adopt democratic modes of operation. In fact, doing so can be difficult and inconvenient. Associations' leaders or most active members, having invested a great deal of personal time and effort, may neglect to hold the kind of open meetings or internal votes that give rank-and-file members veto authority. Sometimes, factional strife in an organization can paralyze all participation and decision making (Read 2008a). But well-functioning democratic states have the knowledge, infrastructure, and authority to run fair elections, and they can extend that competency to associations outside the government proper. In this way, Taiwan's culture of rigorous election procedures infuses its grassroots administrative structures.

An organization's internal democracy is analytically distinct from the external influence it wields. It is possible to have fair and rigorous elections for local leaders who nonetheless have little power to press demands on higher levels. So to what extent are grassroots administrative institutions able to represent their constituencies, to speak to the powerful on their behalf? When the state embraces local associations, does it in fact open itself to influence or transformation in the process?

In many instances, such upward representation is limited. China's RCs, for example, are strongly geared toward carrying out duties and facilitating programs defined by the state and the Communist Party. They have very little standing to talk back to the branches of municipal government that oversee them. After all, committee members were essentially chosen for their positions by the state in the first place and can be summarily dismissed for insubordination— thus illustrating an obvious connection between a lack of democratic accountability and a lack of representative voice. In cases like China, upward influence is generally confined to politely bending the ear of higher officials. They can call attention to individuals who need state assistance but are not receiving it. They can point out infrastructure that needs fixing or explain that a particular policy is not well received by residents and should be rethought. To be sure, some residents appreciate neighborhood staff acting on their behalf even in these low-key ways.

Even in democracies, grassroots representatives of this kind often confine themselves to a relatively subdued form of representation. Pekkanen argues that Japanese neighborhood associations do not evince much of an advocacy role (Pekkanen 2004, 2006). Several reasons seem to underlie this, in Japan and elsewhere. Association leaders may need government support, whether to keep their positions or to obtain resources. There are formal guidelines and informal norms that govern their behavior and that stipulate duties they owe to administrative higher-ups. They may also fall victim to "status seduction," as Jeffrey Broadbent posited in explaining neighborhood leaders who turn against their communities' wishes, swayed by the prestige that comes with playing a part in the great pageant of governance (Broadbent 1998, 190).

When Taiwan's wardens flex their political muscles, it is not necessarily for the benefit of their constituents; in resisting the 2002–2003 reforms, they aimed, with considerable success, to defend their own privileges. They tend to avoid noisy, contentious forms of claims making. Despite this, many of the *lizhang* do indeed pressure city authorities on matters of concern for their neighborhoods. They lobby for improvements to parks, sidewalks, and roads in their jurisdictions. They negotiate with state agencies, city officials, public utilities, and private companies. They weigh in on issues of development and redevelopment, from temples to apartment buildings to projects like the memorial tower. Their status as elected representatives, state liaisons, and (in some cases) savvy party operatives gives them solid standing from which to demand things from powerful actors at all levels of the city.

We noted in Chapter 3 that, despite the night-and-day contrast between the elections in Beijing and Taipei on democratic criteria, residents of the former city do not necessarily judge their neighborhood leaders to be less effective in representing them to higher levels of authority. Data presented in Chapter 5 indicated that, at least by one measure, residents of China's capital are more likely to view the essentially government-appointed RCs as important to the community's well-being, whereas residents of Taiwan's capital are more divided on the same question with regard to their elected wardens. On the face of it, one might interpret these results to mean that democracy does not matter much in grassroots administrative institutions. But that would be incorrect. As we have seen, democratization at the national and local levels had cumulatively powerful effects on the warden system, making it more open and responsive. And the survey data show that Taiwan's citizens strongly favor continuing to elect their *lizhang*. It is also true, however, that democracy is not a necessary condition for such institutions to win substantial support. In the end, representation per se is not the main function that most people associate with them. Those who are favorably disposed toward the RCs and *lizhang* like them primarily for their presence and immediate availability, not out of an expectation that they can move heaven and earth.

Administrative Grassroots Institutions and Their Implications for Asian Politics

Understanding the neighborhood organizations of Beijing and Taipei is important not merely for grasping the nature of urban governance in these two cities, but because it offers a window on a particular vision of the state-society relationship, as embodied in a type of institution that exists on an immense scale in many countries. As we have seen, many aspects of this vision cut across the usual lines of regime type used in political analysis. Situated in the larger context of East and Southeast Asia, the cases of administrative grassroots engagement listed in Table 1.1 remind us of how much more distance our theories have left to cover before they do justice to the actual global terrain of associational life and its links to the state. Most institutions in this category fall between the poles of the oppressive Leninist mass organization on the one hand, and the wholly self-initiated and independent citizens' group acting in civil society on the other hand. Many have, in fact, moved during the course of their existence from one position on this spectrum to another. This calls attention to the possibilities for change and evolution inherent in these institutions. Even more significant, it speaks to the fundamental malleability of intermediary bodies with regard to their multiple connections to the state. Once established, these links contain the potential for either governors or governed to renegotiate and convert them to new purposes.

East Asia has been known for its abundance of corporatist modes of organization. Broadly speaking, the neighborhood cells discussed in these pages could be said to constitute kinds of corporatist arrangements in that states use them in efforts to direct popular participation toward sanctioned channels. Yet the ultra-local scale and broad functional scope of these organizations distinguish them from the forms of corporatism that are most commonly known in the economic sphere. The more authoritarian forms of AGE seem reminiscent of the kind of corporatist fetters that were imposed on, for instance, Peruvian slum dwellers by military regimes. Yet in such instances, state corporatism served little purpose other than to suppress and supplant residents' voices. Even in a politically closed setting like Beijing, state-controlled grassroots organizations evince a much more complex set of dynamics, to say nothing of other cases like Indonesia or Taiwan. The difficulty that existing theories have in encompassing such variation attests to the fact that state-initiated corporatism remains both static and unrefined as a concept.

Although the degree of embeddedness of an RC or a *lizhang* depends heavily on the specific neighborhood and the qualities of the leaders, these organizations can be deeply entrenched indeed. This has a distinctive effect on the very nature of state-society interactions. It encourages ordinary citizens at least to try the neighborhood bodies as a channel through which to express voice, making a state liaison available for residents to contact for everything from replacing a hallway light bulb to personal crises. To the extent that RC members and *lizhang* or *liganshi* are well known to their constituents—which varies, it must be emphasized again—they can possess a degree of credibility that an outsider would not have. Things the staff do on behalf of government take on a human dimension, and this brings about a willingness at least to open the door for them, at least to listen to the rationale they have to offer. It facilitates an effort to legitimate state action, not through mass media but through a micro-level process of ongoing interpersonal dialogue.

Thus enrooted, these institutions play an important role in governance and policy implementation; indeed, from the state's perspective they must be described as a highly valuable asset. They significantly enhance its power, for better and for worse. To be sure, these local liaisons are costly to maintain and require constant supervision to try to ensure that they carry out their assigned duties. Even under the eyes of the street offices and districts, they sometimes pursue unauthorized sources of revenue, abuse their positions, or deviate in other ways. Nonetheless, the utility of the RCs and the *li* to their governments in facilitating the implementation of policy, in handling local problems, and in gathering information can hardly be overstated. The outcomes that these contribute to can be unequivocally benign or considerably oppressive (especially in the Chinese case), and they are commonly somewhere in between. Although they are by no means all-knowing, particularly in newer neighborhoods, they are generally quite effective in bringing local information to light, whether this means alerting authorities to the plight of an unemployed resident for possible remedy through welfare assistance or uncovering the same person's ineligibility for benefits. The role that neighborhood informants play in assisting the police in Beijing provides one means of addressing the problem of urban crime while also making it easier for the state to repress political and religious dissidents. Administrative grassroots engagement can help keep authoritarian regimes in power just as it helps bolster public health and social welfare. Yet as we have seen, for all their statism they are not incorrigibly authoritarian.

During the course of the reform era, China's ruling party has allowed some of the institutions that it established in its early years in power to go by the board. In the countryside, communes and collective agriculture were jettisoned. In the cities, the work unit, though still important in certain ways and in certain sectors, no longer has the kind of all-encompassing and enduring economic and administrative relationship with employees that it often had. Small groups, considered a crucial instrument of indoctrination and social control during the Mao era, have faded into a much looser and more passive existence—as is the case with neighborhood small groups—or else have disappeared entirely. Yet the residents' committees have not merely been spared a similar demise; the state has in fact redoubled its commitment to them, attempting to maintain and even enhance their administrative effectiveness in the new *shequ* framework. The ROC, too, has undergone far-reaching institutional overhauls, such as the reorganization of national and provincial government, the abolition of the National Assembly, and sweeping reform of the Legislative Yuan. Through all of this, it has kept the *li-lin* system intact.

The RCs today show a remarkably robust side of the administrative system of the PRC. This fits in with other studies that have found this system to have resilience and remarkably broad popular support (Nathan 2003; J. Chen 2004; Tang 2005; Walder 2009; Whyte 2010; Wright 2010). It is tempting to speculate that trends in urban China are undermining some of this strength. The committees' effectiveness depends on establishing channels through which information can be obtained. As we saw, city dwellers are increasingly acquiring both the desire for privacy and the means to secure it. The old neighborhoods in which committees have the closest links to constituents are being torn down and redeveloped at a brisk pace. It remains uncertain to what extent such ties can be regenerated in new housing complexes. The fact that maintenance and other functions in which RCs once played a part are now provided by management firms in such neighborhoods raises one question in this regard; the emergence of homeowners' associations as direct representatives of residents' interests also calls into question the RCs' privileged, state-mandated position (Read 2003, 2008a). Alternative routes through which citizens can achieve solutions to their problems, whether pursued through the market or through collective self-empowerment, may diminish the salience of the RCs. The long-term trend toward making committee work more like a paid job and less like a form of volunteer service has in some cases also jeopardized one of the human aspects of the institution that constituents find appealing.

The Taiwan case suggests limits to such a line of speculation, though. In Taipei, too, high-rise condo residents have less contact with their formal neighborhood leaders than others do. But even those living in such towering buildings, far above the lanes and alleys, still support the *lizhang* system by large margins. Their condominium management committees, moreover, seem to have few significant conflicts with the official *li* system, as noted in Chapter 4. Most people seem to accept that each of these two organizations has its own distinct set of legitimate functions. In short, although housing modernization is reshaping residential space in many ways, it would be facile to assume that the official governance institutions will fade from relevance.

Cases in which states sharply constrain the possible forms of citizen expression through local organizations and indeed use them to help identify and silence nonconforming voices, like China's RCs, can hardly be recommended as a template for other countries to apply. Even the most democratic of these organizations have much to learn from institutions designed specifically for empowering constituents to take the budgetary reins of local government, to participate in managing local schools, or to monitor the performance of the state (Abers 2000; Fung 2004; Cornwall and Coelho 2007; Fox 2007). Most of the Asian cases do too little to bring citizens together across the boundaries of small communities, and they may in fact perpetuate a form of social fragmentation. And whatever the merits or drawbacks of the organizations considered here, it is clear that much associational and political activity at the grassroots level should remain free from government links. Quite obviously, there are important forms of political action—such as transformative social movements, contentious calls for justice, noisy demands for redress of official malfeasance—that are unlikely to emerge from state-society hybrids.

Yet organizations sponsored by and plugged into local government contribute much to their societies and should not be rejected out of hand. They may mitigate some of the common problems found in neighborhood associations elsewhere, as discussed in the introduction. Whether we think of South

Korea's *tong* or Indonesia's RT, permanent governance structures overseen and supported by cities mean that neighborhood organization is not left to happenstance and the fickle energies of residents. Given their universal nature, covering (at least in theory) every city block, they need not inherently disadvantage less cohesive or affluent areas. Through its procedures for appropriating funds, government might ensure that resources are equitably distributed or even disproportionately allocated to areas in need, thus helping to mitigate inequality. Where immense networks of grassroots administrative institutions exist, even as legacies from unsavory periods of authoritarianism, a strong argument can be made for reforming rather than discarding them. There can be no single answer to the question of the appropriate configuration of authority and autonomy, cultivation and spontaneity, at the grass roots.

This study has focused on explaining these institutions as they currently exist, with glances toward their past. Looking to the future, one cannot rule out the possibility that Taiwan could do away with the *li-lin*; some voices have advocated such a step. But for now this seems quite unlikely, given the degree of popular support they enjoy, and their deeply entrenched position in urban politics and society. It is even harder to imagine, in the foreseeable future, the abolition of China's RCs and new community structures. Given what we have seen in these two cases, as well as patterns in other Asian states, one can predict gradual rather than radical change. The cases of Japan, South Korea, Taiwan, and Indonesia remind us that even national systemic transformation from authoritarianism to democracy need not spell the end of administrative grassroots engagement, although such change may greatly alter the ethos of its work and the purposes it serves. The *lizhang*, in particular, point to a way in which such institutions can evolve from authoritarian origins into highly democratic practices, all the while fitting snugly into a system of close state-society ties. All in all, the impetus toward this type of close and multifaceted intertwining of government and society remains remarkably enduring.

Reference Matter

Appendix One

Research Methods

A serious effort to answer the questions posed in this project required accurate information about a nuanced and in some ways delicate topic: the relationships and interactions between state-fostered neighborhood organizations and their constituents. The process of acquiring this information requires explanation.

Several factors make Taiwan's neighborhood wardens fairly tractable as subjects of up-close study. The Republic of China is, of course, a free and open system, one that places few if any special restrictions on political research. In this context, as Chapter 4 explains, the wardens operate as part of the city government's organizational structure, but the elections that bring them to their positions also give them independent standing and, in many cases, a critical distance from that structure. Individual *lizhang* in Taipei varied in the stance they took toward the historically KMT-dominated bureaucracy, some railing against it and others feeling entirely at home with it. In any case, they do not by and large see themselves as spokespeople for the city or for the state as a whole. As well, the civil servants (*liganshi* and other district officials) who work with the wardens do not act as gatekeepers—indeed, they themselves provide well-informed perspectives on neighborhood politics and the foibles of the governance system. To be sure, as with research subjects anywhere, trust building and over-time study were required to obtain a well-rounded sense of the actors and forces in play in Taipei's *li*. But Taiwan's institutions generally facilitate inquiry rather than impede it.

The residents' committees (RCs), in contrast, are more challenging as subjects of research than the wardens or independent neighborhood groups in liberal political systems. Accordingly, I took a particularly long-term approach to my research in China, and this process deserves special explanation here. As with many institutions in China, there is no presumption on the part of the authorities that the RCs should be open for study, whether by local or foreign scholars. Although these low-ranking organizations are not as forbidding as some parts of government, they are nonetheless inherently somewhat sensitive as extensions of the state. Many of their functions, for instance those related to security, birth control, and local Communist Party organization, are touchy by nature. Both the committee staff themselves and their higher-ups in the street offices, police stations, and other state units can be reluctant to cooperate with researchers. In a neighborhood office, the party leadership, if not the entire staff, generally maintains a disciplined and careful approach to dealing with guests.

Fortunately, these challenges are mitigated by a number of other factors that made serious study of the RCs quite possible. First, the beginning of my fieldwork coincided with increasing emphasis at all levels of government on reform of grassroots organizations, including both the RCs and their rural cousins, the villagers' committees. The fact that community building had become a buzzword on the lips of leaders from General Secretary Jiang Zemin on down had salutary effects. It provided a politically acceptable rationale for wanting to study local organizations, and it motivated officials and RC staff alike to try to impress outsiders with what they portrayed as the advances made under reforms. Partly as a result of the official priority given to the community-building drive, Chinese social scientists had already begun to give new attention to the RCs at the time I began my research, which provided opportunities for collaboration and consultation.

The sheer size of the network of residents' committees makes it an easy target in some respects. Even medium-size cities have hundreds of RCs. If one committee is not inclined to entertain questions and visits, the next one down the street might be. Even if the RCs themselves were entirely closed to researchers, which turns out certainly not to be the case, it would remain true that the very nature of the institution brings it into contact at one time or another with a large proportion of the urban population. This means that many ordinary citizens can serve as research informants—particularly if it is precisely the RC-constituent relationship that is under study, as in this book.

Indeed, Whyte and Parish exploited this fact by studying the RCs via émigrés even when China itself was inaccessible (1984).

Chapter 1 provided a short overview of the research that I undertook in Beijing; Taipei; and to a much more limited extent, other cities in China and Taiwan as well as Seoul, South Korea. As noted there, my work in the two primary cities comprised a mixture of neighborhood site visits; survey research; interviews; and exploration of government documents, election records, and other published sources. Here I discuss just the site visits and the surveys.

Neighborhood Site Visits

The approach I took to developing neighborhood field sites in Beijing was driven by two considerations. First, I wanted sites that were not Potemkin-village model neighborhoods. As anyone who has conducted journalistic or academic research in China knows, there is a strong tendency for officially arranged visits to be shunted toward local showcases. (One neighborhood I was shown by government hosts in Qingdao boasted that it had received no fewer than 1,133 official visitors in the previous year alone.) Although such exercises can be useful for certain purposes—for instance, they may be harbingers of what will become general trends, or they may at least provide a glimpse of goals that the state is striving toward—there are obvious dangers in generalizing from model neighborhoods to more ordinary ones. Second, I wanted to sample a variety of neighborhoods so as to understand how the same institution functions in different social contexts.

With these goals in mind, I contacted RCs in Beijing through three different methods: cold visits, private introductions by acquaintances, and formal requests through government channels. In the five committees contacted through cold visits, I identified neighborhoods of interest, then knocked on the doors of RC offices, introducing myself as a visiting student doing research on community organizations and presenting a letter of introduction from my host unit, the Chinese Academy of Social Sciences. If the RC was willing to tolerate my first visit, I returned later for ongoing follow-up visits. In three other cases, three separate acquaintances provided entrée to an RC by introducing me to a committee member.

Two committees were contacted through formal requests. In fact, the two committees belonged to a single street office that a fourth acquaintance had introduced me to. At the insistence of local officials there, I obtained formal permission for my research by means of a short proposal submitted to the district government on my behalf by the Chinese Academy of Social Sciences. The street office arranged for me to visit two of its RCs; after one of them turned out to have model-neighborhood characteristics, the street office obliged my request to visit a different one (Chongxing) instead. Although my first visit to each of these two neighborhoods was monitored by a street office cadre, subsequent trips were unaccompanied, as were all of my visits to the eight other sites. (In one neighborhood, Duzhuang, I did my research not through office visits but through a series of private interviews with one particularly obliging and candid RC staff member. In three other neighborhoods I had private, one-on-one interviews with committee members in addition to my site visits.)

To what extent did this strategy of case selection introduce bias? My fourteen attempts at cold visits in Beijing were evenly split between successes and failures (I opted to discontinue study of two of the successful cases, even though they raised no objection to my presence.) Were the committees that tolerated my visits systematically distinct from those that were unwilling to be studied? This possibility cannot be completely dismissed. It may be that committees that turned me away were generally less hospitable or more bureaucratic. But in fact I believe this to be only a minor, if not negligible, problem. In several of the failure cases, the RCs themselves did not object to me; rather it was police or street office staff that caused my disinvitation. Even in cases in which the RC itself said no to me, this cannot necessarily be taken as representative of the orientation of the committee as a whole, as it usually appeared to be one particularly suspicious member who vetoed my inquiry. Moreover, the committees receive different visitors in very different ways. An RC has every reason to turn away an inquiring Western researcher, but it has an interest in giving its constituents a more helpful reception. Finally, I gathered corroborating information from the other prongs of my research strategy, which were not subject to the same kind of potential selection bias at the neighborhood level.

Once having established a relationship with a committee, I returned repeatedly without advance notice. Part of what I did during these visits was to ask questions. This was useful for gathering basic information about the neighborhood and the functions of the committee, for obtaining the RC members' perspectives on things, and for clarifying specific issues. Even more fruitful than asking questions, though, was having the chance to spend hours at a time listening in on the committee's internal discussions and observing its interaction with residents and others who came to the office. I took notes off and on during these sessions and typed them up within a few days.

Needless to say, there are limitations to this research strategy. After all, I was no fly on the wall, but a green-eyed, big-nosed foreigner, and my presence at times affected the way the committee behaved. On occasion, when my visits coincided with sensitive items of RC business, it created palpable tension, and I wore out my welcome entirely in two of the committees to which I had been introduced through acquaintances. Nonetheless, there were considerable benefits to this strategy of repeated visits. After the first few encounters, the committees—some more than others—became less concerned to feed me a happy, sanitized story about their jobs and their neighborhood. More important, the nature of the committees' work meant that they were constantly responding to new problems and developments, from constituents arriving to ask questions or deliver tirades to street office staff calling to give instructions or impose discipline. The RC had little control over what contingencies might crop up during my visits.

Even so, it was important to build as much trust as possible with each of the residents' committees I visited, and the degree to which I succeeded in doing so varied. In the two RCs that eventually asked me not to return, there was a frequent sense of wariness and awkwardness during my visits. In others, the staff became quite welcoming and even generous; two committees held dumpling parties for me at the end of my initial fieldwork. The more trusting of the RCs seemed to enjoy confiding in me about the endless trials and tribulations that their work entailed. One even enlisted my help in tasks like filling in stacks of multiple-choice answer sheets for a Macao knowledge quiz to feign completion of its assignment of administering the test to residents on the eve of the former colony's return to mainland control. To borrow James Scott's terms, the site visits provided moments in which it was possible to glimpse certain kinds of hidden transcripts at odds with the public transcript that official institutions strive to present to outsiders (1990, 1–16). But the nature of performances on the stage (as it were) of the committee office fluctuated constantly depending on which RC members were in the room, their level of comfort with me, whether police or street office personnel were present, what was being discussed, and so forth. The raw material of my encounters with the neighborhood organizations, and their encounters with constituents, required continual between-the-lines parsing and interpretation.

To introduce an element of reciprocity in my relationships with the committees, I did things like donate readily, though not extravagantly, to their charity drives. Occasionally, I took RC members out to lunch or dinner. For a period of time I held four hours per week of English classes in my apartment for several children of the staff of two RCs. For the most part, however, my access to the neighborhood committees was based merely on their understanding and acceptance of the fact that I was a researcher carrying out a scholarly project.

In Taipei, as described in Chapter 1, I also carried out a set of site visits to neighborhood offices. I met some of the wardens through personal contacts, others through introductions by academic colleagues or other *lizhang*, and others at my own initiation. I went to seven neighborhoods only once or twice, but I made three or more visits to six other locales over a period spanning multiple years. In three of these cases I made a particularly intensive effort to get to know the warden and others in the area, and I made as many as sixteen trips to one *li*. Although some neighborhood leaders in Taipei gave remarkably open and revealing interviews even in the first encounter, the in-depth cases were still important. They provided a fuller sense of the nature of and limitations on the warden's power, his or her relationship to political parties and the government, the range of economic and political interests at play in the neighborhoods, and the kinds of help that constituents seek from their local leaders.

The method of inquiry I pursued in the Beijing and Taipei sites that I visited multiple times bears some resemblance to the ethnographic techniques of cultural anthropologists, but in fact it was far more modest in that I did not attempt to acquire a comprehensive understanding of each neighborhood and all its residents. There was inevitably a trade-off between the desire for deep knowledge of each locality and the goal of developing multiple field sites as well as other sources of information—trade-offs that I have explored elsewhere (Read 2010). The basic aim of the neighborhood visits was to gain a qualitative grasp of the subject matter on key points of interest, to be supplemented and verified by other types of data.

Surveys

The Beijing Law and Community (BLC) Survey was part of a legal sociology project led by Ethan Michelson, then of the University of Chicago, and

Professor Li Lulu of People's University, funded primarily by the Ford Foundation. Most of the survey aimed to acquire information about how citizens dealt with various types of disputes or problems they had experienced, as well as their beliefs and attitudes regarding legal institutions such as the police and the courts system. The principal investigators generously allowed me to add to the questionnaire a battery of questions concerning respondents' residents' committees, and the Mumford Center for Comparative Urban and Regional Research at State University of New York–Albany provided support for my participation in this project.

The BLC survey was administered through in-home visits to residents of Beijing in the summer of 2001 by the Beijing Social Psychology Research Institute (BSPRI), which developed the sampling frame and hired interviewers. Despite strenuous efforts to ensure quality of execution, the administration of the survey was not trouble-free. A total of 1,394 questionnaires were completed. After receiving these questionnaires from the BSPRI, we subjected them to a verification process that combined follow-up interviews by student research assistants, handwriting analysis, checks on missing value patterns, and tests for logical consistency. There were indications that eight out of thirty-one interviewers may have filled out one or more questionnaires falsely or improperly, and consequently, the questionnaires submitted by these interviewers were rejected. For purposes of this book, a handful of respondents currently working as residents' committee staff were also dropped, leaving 1,018 respondents in the sample.

Another problem was the failure of the BSPRI to collect information on would-be respondents who declined to be interviewed; the interviewee response rate is unknown. If there were a large number of nonrespondents, this would raise the question of the degree to which there were systematic differences between individuals who chose to participate in the survey and those who did not. Because of this potential problem, as well as general principles, we paid special attention to the question of the survey's representativeness.

The target population of the survey was not the entire population of the city but adults between the ages of twenty-five and seventy; this was because it was believed that very young adults (between the ages of eighteen and twenty-five) or very old ones would be less likely to have had recent experiences with disputes. Available demographic information on Beijing tends to cover the entire population, however. To determine the representativeness of the sample, Ethan Michelson conducted an analysis that took advantage of the fact that the questionnaire collected information not merely on the respondent but also on each of the respondent's family members. He constructed an expanded data set containing basic information on all 3,501 members of the households in the survey and compared this with published information on the overall population of Beijing. He then compared the survey respondents with other members of their households.

The results of this analysis are generally encouraging. In terms of household size, age distribution, and gender distribution, our household sample falls very close to figures in the 2001 Beijing Statistical Yearbook (BSY), which reports data from 2000. The proportions of retirees match almost exactly, with 24.9 percent in the BSY and 24.7 percent in the household sample.[1] In our household sample, 77.1 percent of those who are employed work in state-owned units, whereas the BSY sample of one thousand households reports 81.2 percent.[2] The annual per capita household income in our sample is slightly lower than that found in the BSY: 8,993 yuan as opposed to 10,350 yuan. Our data is roughly on target in terms of the highest education level achieved by respondents, although relative to the BSY data our sample has fewer middle-school graduates, more high school graduates, and slightly fewer recipients of postsecondary education. Finally, there appears to be little or no difference between survey respondents and other adult members of their own households in terms of age, education, marital status, Communist Party membership, employment status, occupation, job rank, and work unit ownership. In summary, despite concerns raised by the aforementioned flaws in survey execution, there is good reason to believe that the BLC sample is highly representative of its target population.

The Taipei Neighborhoods Survey was simpler and more straightforward than its Beijing counterpart in certain respects. It took the form of a telephone survey conducted in the evenings of March 28–30 and April 3, 2006, by trained interviewers working in the call center at Focus Survey Research (Shanshui Minyi Yanjiu) using a computer system. I developed the thirty-nine-question instrument in consultation with academic colleagues in Taiwan and the Focus staff. It replicated key questions from the Beijing survey but was thoroughly adapted to the Taipei context, using local terminology and expressions (some interviews were conducted in Taiwanese rather than Mandarin). Given the understandably limited patience of telephone interviewees, only some parts of the Beijing survey could be duplicated. In contrast with the Beijing survey, in which respondents were clustered in neighborhoods, here the random-digit-dialing sampling technique generated 1,140 interviews that were dispersed throughout the city. Of 2,703 answered phone calls, 42 percent resulted in completed interviews with Taipei residents age twenty and older. The company's supervisors and I monitored the forty-eight interviewers carefully throughout the calling. About twelve minutes in duration on average, the interviews were digitally recorded and remain on file with the author.

Women are slightly overrepresented, constituting 57 percent of the sample, as opposed to 52 percent of a 2004 reference data set based on government records of the city's entire adult population (ROC Ministry of the Interior 2005). Young adults are somewhat underrepresented in the sample, with 40 percent of the phone interviewees age fifty or older, compared to 37 percent of the reference data set. Those with a four-year college degree formed 34 percent of the phone sample, compared to 28 percent of the general adult population. As noted in Chapter 3, about 52 percent of respondents who were eligible to vote in the 2003 warden elections reported doing so, but the actual turnout was 38 percent of those eligible to vote—no doubt reflecting a mixture of selection bias toward voters along with interviewees saying they had voted when in fact they had not. All in all, the Taipei telephone survey appears to have achieved a sample reasonably well matched to the underlying population.

Appendix Two

Beyond the Two Capitals

This study focused on Beijing and Taipei. Here I explain this emphasis on just one city in the People's Republic of China and one in the Republic of China, and also supplement it with perspectives obtained from short visits to other cities. Creating a full empirical portrait of neighborhood organizations throughout all of China and Taiwan was not my goal; rather, it was to explore the theoretical questions laid out in Chapter 1. Even if these capitals turned out to be very different from other places in terms of the political, economic, and social environment in which neighborhoods are governed, they would still be important cases with much to teach us about administrative grassroots engagement. Nonetheless, intercity comparison is by no means irrelevant. No doubt this would not be the exact same book if it compared, say, Guangzhou and Kaohsiung. The question is how different it would be.

Some research has already made progress in comparing neighborhood institutions among more than one of China's cities (Derleth and Koldyk 2004; Heberer and Göbel 2011). But in the absence of data that could provide a rigorous comparison between random samples, making generalizations about intercity differences is challenging. It is difficult to know whether locally observed phenomena reflect factors at the individual or neighborhood level, for instance, or whether they represent systematic contrasts between cities. Nonetheless, the purpose of my short (three- to ten-day) visits to cities outside of Beijing and Taipei was to try to understand, in rough terms, how RCs

TABLE A2.1

Research sites outside of Beijing and Taipei

City	Population at time of visit	Neighborhoods visited	Description
Benxi, Liaoning	960,000	3	Located in China's northeastern Rust Belt; once a center of coal production and still a producer of steel and cement; high unemployment
Chiayi City, Taiwan	275,000	5	Small inland city located in the southern half of Taiwan between Taichung and Tainan
Guangzhou	7,010,000	6	Flourishing metropolis on the Pearl River near Hong Kong, long a leader in reform
Hengyang, Hunan	700,000	3	Economically troubled city located on major lines of rail, highway, and water transportation
Qingdao, Shandong	2,900,000	4	Former German and Japanese colony on the ocean; home to Hai'er and other relatively successful industrial enterprises
Shanghai	9,900,000	5	Megacity near the mouth of the Yangzi River; was under colonial administration in late 19th and early 20th centuries; launching pad for the careers of Jiang Zemin and other top leaders; major industrial, commercial, and financial center
Shijiazhuang, Hebei	2,100,000	2	Midsize provincial capital in North China

NOTE: In Qingdao, I also participated in a group discussion with representatives of nine residents' committees.

and wardens varied among different municipalities. Table A2.1 lists these cities. I considered developing one or more of the other locales into full-blown cases in which I would pursue long-term, intensive neighborhood studies and surveys of the population. Eventually, I concluded that my particular project would best be served by exploring variation within the neighborhoods of the capitals alone.

In part, I made this decision on practical grounds: I did not have the time or the money to replicate in two other cities the kind of prolonged research I did in Beijing and Taipei. But resource constraints were not the only reason for this choice. I also found, in my forays to China's provinces, that residents' committees (RCs) in the different parts of the country that I looked at displayed considerable consistency in terms of basic institutional characteristics and day-to-day operations. (Although these secondary cities spanned a range of latitudes and sizes, none was in the western reaches of the PRC or minority autonomous regions.)¹ Specific details of RC and *shequ* organization and practices vary somewhat, but these institutions are governed by the same law, have similar core duties, and are in many respects minor variations on the same theme. Much the same is true of *li*-level organization in Taiwan.

The most obvious contrast among the seven cities I investigated in China lay in the amount of resources available for RC work. Economically and fiscally well-endowed areas were better able to fund the neighborhood system and thus provide it extra vitality, and presumably effectiveness. As noted in Chapter 2, at the time I began my research, cities across the country were experimenting with RC reforms. Thus, for instance, one district in Qingdao, Shinan district, hired an extra staff member for most committees, known as a community work assistant (*shequ gongzuo zhuli*), who was better paid and typically younger and more educated than other staff; this program paralleled a similar initiative in Beijing. In experimental neighborhoods in Benxi, RCs were being supplemented with community advisory committees (*shequ canyi weiyuanhui*), which were given the duty of monitoring and providing counsel to the committees and which also had counterparts in the capital. As with other reforms, it did not appear that these bodies represented a step toward greater democratic representation, as candidates were carefully vetted, and most were party members. Although it is possible that they allowed for increased popular input into RC work, it was clearer that they were designed to give voice to state institutions in and around the neighborhood; most seats were occupied by leaders of state enterprises, police officers, and the like.

These efforts to tweak the organizational structure of the RCs were not the only, or necessarily the most important, source of cross-city variation. Neighborhood committees in every city encouraged residents to participate in voluntary service as building heads, small-group heads, and the like—and as Chapter 6 argues, this is an important part of how the RCs strive to carry out their administrative duties. Still, the specific forms of voluntary service varied somewhat; in Guangzhou, for instance, few neighborhoods still mobilized volunteer security patrols, having switched instead to a system of paid guards (Beijing neighborhoods were just beginning to hire the like). Committee members in Shijiazhuang claimed that they still attempted to perform mediation in efforts to reconcile married couples who sought a divorce; their Beijing brethren had given up this particularly challenging form of intervention. Shanghai's RCs were, relatively early on, given important new duties as implementers of that city's effort to move social welfare functions away from enterprises and into new municipal institutions. Thus, in the spring of 2000, RCs there were already in the process of handling application forms (including photographs and fingerprints) for social guarantee cards (*shehui baozhang ka*), which were to be linked to accounts through which pensions, health care, and other programs would be channeled. Similar cards came to Beijing several years later. As I have noted elsewhere, Shanghai took a distinctive approach to the new homeowner organizations as well, encouraging rather than discouraging their formation but making strong efforts to shape and guide them (Read 2008a, 1248).

Most significant seemed to be the contrast between wealthy, politically prominent cities and more economically troubled, peripheral ones. In Hengyang in the year 2000, for example, some neighborhoods had only one or two RC staff members. In many cases, at least one committee member was assigned and paid by a local work unit rather than by the city government. A city's financial circumstances appeared to influence the degree to which RCs were allowed or encouraged to engage in economic activity. Although this was officially limited (but often winked at) in major cities, in smaller and poorer ones like Hengyang and Shijiazhuang, the trickle of income that sponsorship of local businesses could bring to the RCs was deemed indispensable by local officials. In Hengyang, some staff members' salaries were in arrears, and others said that their personal earnings depended entirely on what revenue their committees could generate through business activity. In poorer locales, committees sometimes lacked telephone lines or even offices. It seemed likely that low levels of staffing and inadequate compensation affected the committees' ability and willingness to provide the kinds of everyday services that, as Chapter 7 argues, are important for building positive relationships with constituents.

Although organizational reforms and other types of local variation were noteworthy and call for more study, they must be viewed in conjunction with the broad similarities that were evident among RCs in all the cities I visited. In all cases, the committees were closely managed by street offices and other parts of the city government. Their set of top-priority responsibilities pertained to the same programs, including birth control, security, welfare, the administration of migrants, and the maintenance of the household registry. In all six cities as well as Beijing, local officials were consolidating the RC system by merging smaller neighborhoods into larger ones and by hiring staff with stronger formal credentials. Committee members everywhere spoke of similar types of daily challenges and rewards.

In Taiwan, time constraints allowed me to explore just one city-level case outside the capital, so I chose one that contrasted with Taipei in a number of respects. With a population of 275,000, Chiayi is a small city (*shi*), lower in rank than the larger municipalities (*zhixiashi*), which lies in the southern half of the island of Taiwan, fifteen miles inland from the western coast. It had been governed since the early 1980s by a series of female mayors. Its politics were marked by competition between powerful clan networks as well as the divide between the two major national parties. When I visited in the spring of 2006, it had a total of 108 *li* (and 1,797 *lin*) in two districts; these neighborhoods are thus smaller than Taipei's, with just 2,500 people per *li* on average. Turnout in the most recent warden elections had been an impressive 49 percent of eligible voters. As in Taipei, though, a majority of Chiayi's wardens (56 percent) ran as Kuomintang (KMT) candidates, whereas 41 percent ran without party affiliation, and many in the latter category leaned toward the Democratic Progressive Party.[2]

Interviews with five wardens, three city officials, and a prominent local KMT leader revealed a few ways in which neighborhood governance in Chiayi was distinctive. For example, wardens received no fixed budgets for small local projects and had to apply to the districts or the mayor for such funds. The *liganshi* were not required to report daily to the neighborhood offices but worked out of a set of local centers. Block captains received no cash from the city, just a newspaper subscription and an annual group excursion. Most notably, as discussed in Chapter 3, wardens in many cases still served as conduits through which city council candidates bought votes, a practice that had faded in the capital. Many particulars, though, were largely or wholly identical to what I found in Taipei. Much of their get-out-the-vote work on behalf of candidates for city council, mayors, and national offices was entirely legal and took familiar forms like distributing campaign literature. Wardens received the same monthly NT$45,000 stipend; sponsored similar kinds of local activities, including night patrols in many areas; and reported the same sorts of requests from residents. Like their counterparts in the capital, they generally preferred not to bother with the annual residents' meeting they are supposed to hold. And in meetings I attended with city and district officials, wardens did not defer to those authorities but persisted in voicing their own opinions, the same kind of dynamic that is found in Taipei.

In short, brief research trips to other municipalities allowed me to place the capitals' neighborhood organizations in national context, if only in a preliminary way. It was not feasible for me to conduct either long-term qualitative study or survey research on the seven other cities. As noted, other scholars have begun to pursue intracity comparisons, and in-depth research will no doubt reveal new patterns and complexity. This book has attempted to explain differences in individual responses to administrative grassroots institutions through factors such as beliefs about the state's role vis-à-vis society, residents' everyday pursuits and needs, community-level activities and relationships, and the kinds of low-level assistance that neighborhood institutions provide. It is my strong hunch that much of the variation to be found among different cities can be explained largely in these terms. I look forward to having this hunch confirmed or corrected.

Notes

1. The honors include loving the motherland, serving the people, working hard, and obeying the law; the shames are their opposites.

2. Site visit, Chongxing, Beijing, August 26, 2010.

3. Site visit, Wenchang, Taipei, August 12, 2010.

4. As we will see, in some cases there are multiple forms of neighborhood organization, official and unofficial. In Japan, *chōnaikai* and *jichikai* are no longer mandated but have a near-universal presence nonetheless.

5. For instance, Dutton's study of policing deals, in part, with neighborhood institutions (1992). Also see Yao's study of the *bao-jia* in Taiwan (2002).

6. Multiple accounts discuss the Peruvian case (e.g., Stepan 1978, chap. 5; Castells 1983, chap. 19).

7. See the following pages of the Anchor Books edition of *Wild Swans* (Chang 1991): 69, 77, 114, 137, 173, 216, 265, and 306. Pagination is not the same in other editions.

8. There are certainly exceptions: sensitive and compelling accounts that do not conform to the typical pattern described here (e.g., Frolic 1980, 224–241; Dutton, Lo, and Wu 2008, chap. 3).

9. Sheryl WuDunn, "In China's cities, the busybodies are organized," *New York Times*, March 13, 1991, 4; Lisa Movius, "Mrs. Li is watching me: In China, SARS isn't just threatening public health—it's bringing back the Orwellian neighborhood committees of the Cultural Revolution," June 19, 2003, http://www.salon.com/2003/06/19/sars_2/.

10. The well-known 1990 comedy sketch "Excess-Birth Guerrillas" (*chaosheng youjidui*), for instance, features a rural couple with three young children on the run from the small-footed tracking squads and birth control enforcement in the city. In the past, some of the women serving in RCs indeed had been subject to the practice of foot binding in childhood, although that generation has long since disappeared from neighborhood service.

11. See, for instance, "Lien Chan lizhang toupiao changtan si nian linzhang xinde" [Lien Chan votes in warden election and talks about what he learned in four years as a block captain], TVBS, January 4, 2003, http://www.tvbs.com.tw/news /news_list.asp?no=alisa20030104114439, accessed March 4, 2011.

12. The language of bridges is, of course, applied to other structures as well, such as officially sanctioned business associations (Unger 1996).

13. I thank Neil Diamant for bringing this essay to my attention.

14. Yet Crenson resisted the notion that neighborhood polities should be relegated "to the twilight zone of 'parapolitical systems,' along with private groups like churches, trade associations, or universities" (1983, 13).

15. Diamond defines civil society as "the realm of organized social life that is open, voluntary, self-generating, at least partially self-supporting, autonomous from the state, and bound by a legal order or set of shared rules" (1999, 221).

16. A number of scholars have advanced general claims about the democratic benefits of associations (Cohen and Rogers 1992; Walzer 1995; Diamond 1999, 239–250; M. E. Warren 2001, 60–93; Anheier 2004; Heinrich 2005). Although these enjoy wide acceptance, other studies have found that civil society helps create or improve democratic governance only under certain conditions (Berman 1997; Bermeo and Nord 2000; Kaufman 2002; Alagappa 2004a; Sampson, McAdam, MacIndoe, and Weffer-Elizondo 2005).

17. Information on these commissions is available at the Web site of the Advisory Neighborhood Commissions, http://anc.dc.gov, accessed October 7, 2011.

18. Philippe C. Schmitter's oft-cited definition, referring to interest groups that accept constraints on the leadership they choose and the demands they make in exchange for receiving a representational monopoly in their category of activity, seems too narrow for a general statement of this concept (1979, 13). State constraints and shaping can take many forms, and corporatist groups need not have monopolies. David Collier and Paul S. Adams provide reviews of the concept (Collier 1995; Adams 2002).

19. For instance, state controls on labor in the authoritarian period of South Korea and Taiwan, the organization of Indonesian society under Suharto, and business groups in today's China (Deyo 1989; Liddle 1996; Unger 2008).

20. Not all images of mass organizations are quite so bleak. Some studies have cast the organizations in a more benign or at least neutral light (Townsend 1967, 145–173; Fagen 1969; Friedgut 1979).

21. Kasza wrote that "[a]ll functioning AMOs concentrate power in the hands of nondemocratic regimes" (1995, 190). This, and the definition of the concept itself, seems to leave open the possibility that such organizations could exist in democratic states. In other respects, though, Kasza's concept seems tailored to authoritarian regimes, and specifically those of the "single-party and military-bureaucratic" type (8). In discussing the legacy of AMOs, the book suggests, for instance, that mass

organizations might evolve into interest groups but does not explore the possibility of state-structured hybrids lying between these two types (Kasza 1995, 183–188).

22. There is debate over the degree to which interpersonal networks per se are a necessary part of the civil society argument. Some point out that citizens' organizations can be effective in pressing for their political goals even when they do not involve face-to-face interaction among members but instead rely on the activities of a professional staff paid by donations and dues from supporters (Berry 1999; Skocpol and Fiorina 1999).

23. In his comparison of associational life in China and Taiwan, Robert Weller observes that such bonds persist in both democratic and authoritarian systems and in both formal and informal groups (Weller 1998; 1999, 41–44, 56–59). Putnam and Goss acknowledge that horizontal networks can be ambiguous in their social and political effects (2002, 9).

24. Jonathan Fox's research on Mexico provides other examples of clashing vertical and horizontal pressures (1994, 2007). In a similar vein, some studies of grassroots groups and NGOs have found that the acceptance of government funding or mandates by such organizations can damage their internal unity or their accountability to members and stakeholders (Arnstein 1969; Smith and Lipsky 1993). It can lead to toothless, co-opted groups that avoid playing the roles of advocate for constituents' interests or critic of government policy (Hulme and Edwards 1997).

25. The several articles on synergy in the June 1996 issue of *World Development* were republished in book form the following year (Evans 1997).

26. For example, Ostrom describes a Brazilian program that actively involves local citizens in the planning and maintenance of sanitation systems in their own neighborhoods (1996). Wai Fung Lam analyzes the complicated ways in which the water resources bureaucracy in rural Taiwan interacts with local farmers through irrigation groups and particularly "water guards," who draw on their local knowledge and community seniority to help allocate water and resolve disputes (1996).

27. Eisenstadt and Roninger give a far-ranging discussion of variation in patron-client relations, for example (1984, 220–268). Scott's and Landé's treatments leave considerable room for the affective component of such "instrumental friendships" (Scott 1972, 1976; Landé 1977).

28. In addition to the other essays in Gold, Guthrie, and Wank's 2002 volume and work discussed below, key readings in the literature on *guanxi* and similar connections include studies by several other sociologists and anthropologists (Bosco 1992; Yang 1994; Yan 1996; Kipnis 1997; Wank 1999).

29. Stokes defines clientelism as "the proffering of material goods in return for electoral support, where the criterion of distribution that the patron uses is simply: did you (will you) support me?" (2007, 605). Kitschelt and Wilkinson define clientelist accountability as "a transaction, the direct exchange of a citizen's vote in return for direct payments or continuing access to employment, goods, and services" (2007, 2).

30. As Evans acknowledges, "Communities need capable public institutions desperately, but, unfortunately, they need states quite different from the ones that currently confront them" (2002b, 236).

31. On the definition of Leninism, see Jowitt 1992. On technocratic leadership, see Li 2001 and Andreas 2009.

32. Jay Taylor's biography of Chiang Kai-shek emphasizes Chiang's admiration for the CCP organization and his efforts to rebuild the KMT along Leninist lines in its early years on Taiwan (2009, 411, 442).

33. In addition to material cited elsewhere in these pages, at least two edited volumes have presented statements of this perspective (Migdal, Kohli, and Shue 1994; Migdal 2001).

34. Even just within the discipline of political science alone, a number of researchers have applied techniques of ethnography and participant observation (Fenno 1978; Scott 1985; Wedeen 1999; Wood 2003; L. Tsai 2007; Morris MacLean 2010). Edward Schatz's compilation collects essays about and examples of work of this type (2009).

CHAPTER TWO

1. To be clear, sometimes the term "grass roots" (including its Chinese translation, *caogen*) is used to refer exclusively to autonomous, self-initiated action or organization. I employ it in connection with ultra-local administrative institutions to highlight the fact that states till and contest the grass roots.

2. I have not attempted to create a systematic index of these two variables; the coding illustrated here is rough and schematic but adequate for present conceptual purposes.

3. The Web site of the People's Association, http://www.pa.gov.sg, accessed October 7, 2011, contains further information.

4. One urban-rural comparison is Benewick, Tong, and Howell (2004). Chan, Madsen, and Unger's updated discussion of Chen Village, which became urbanized but retained the self-governing capacity it had as a village, highlights this contrast (2009, 342–346). Chang and Keng discuss two cases of urbanized villages (2008). Village institutions have an even more central role in dispute resolution than urban neighborhoods (Read and Michelson 2008).

5. Taiwan's community development associations are discussed in the chapters that follow.

6. The *bao-jia* system also had precursors in several previous dynasties.

7. For example, Yao notes that the system "appealed directly to the private and intimate spheres of the people: the affections, relations and solidarities both within and between families. In other words, by using the 'natural unity' of the local community to organise the hoko, and by persuading the landlord and gentry to be the

hosei, the colonial state was actually taking advantage of people's familial feelings and loyalties, and, more important, of the long-standing patriarchal system in Taiwan" (2002, 246).

8. Joseon dynasty (1392–1910) systems organized households into units of five and required subjects to carry identification tags (Lee 1984, 184).

9. The following discussion of the residents' committees up to the reform era draws on a number of sources in addition to those specifically cited in the text (Barnett 1964; Schurmann 1966; Townsend 1967; Salaff 1967, 1971; Sidel 1974; Frolic 1980; Whyte and Parish 1984).

10. Wang Zheng argues that women's participation in the residents' committees of the 1950s, along with other organizations, complicates any simple notion of a patriarchal socialist state (2005).

11. On this, see in particular Diamant's study (2000b).

12. Phillips discusses the KMT's establishment of what was at first highly limited local self-government on Taiwan (2003, 102–114).

13. Aspects of the development of such neighborhoods, and the lifestyles of those who purchase homes there, have been explored in several studies (e.g., Davis and Lu 2003; Fleischer 2010; Hsing 2010; Zhang 2010).

14. As of the end of 2010, 104 urban renewal (*dushi gengxin*) projects were under way, totaling thirty-three hectares in area. See the Web site of the Taipei City Urban Redevelopment Office, http://www.uro.taipei.gov.tw, accessed October 7, 2011.

15. In the 2006 Taipei telephone survey, 23 percent of respondents reported living in large apartment buildings.

16. Relevant laws are available at the Web site of the ROC Ministry of the Interior, http://www.moi.gov.tw, and in published compilations (ROC Ministry of the Interior 2002).

17. For example, "Danwei people become citizens," *Economist*, September 6, 2003. In fairness, such assertions are sometimes made in passing as part of well-informed surveys of China's development (Gilboy and Heginbotham 2001, 30).

18. Lisa Movius, "Mrs. Li is watching me: In China, SARS isn't just threatening public health—it's bringing back the Orwellian neighborhood committees of the Cultural Revolution," June 19, 2003, http://www.salon.com/2003/06/19/sars_2/.

19. The many studies of village governance reforms run from early articles (O'Brien 1994; Kelliher 1997) to more recent contributions (L. Tsai 2007; Manion 2009; O'Brien and Han 2009; Schubert 2009; Kennedy 2010).

20. Examples of model communities in Beijing included Liuyin Jie and Baiyun Lu.

21. They were given a label roughly translating to "community institutional cadres" (*shequ shiye ganbu*), signaling their belonging to a more formalized part of the street offices' staff rosters.

22. In Beijing, as of 2006, 84 percent of RC directors were party members, and in 67 percent of neighborhoods, the director also served as party secretary. These

figures were calculated from an unpublished Beijing city government report, on file with the author.

23. In 1999, for example, there were 114,815 RCs nationwide (Ministry of Civil Affairs 2000, 164).

24. The earlier figures come from Hsi and Fan's study (2003, 83–84).

25. The population figure for 2000 is from the city's statistical yearbook (Beijing Municipal Bureau of Statistics 2001). The number of RCs for that year comes from an unpublished Beijing city government report, on file with the author.

26. New residents' committees and communities are established in stages after the building of new housing developments. In the most high-end, exclusive neighborhoods, the presence of the RC can be difficult to discern, especially at first; it may conduct much of its business through the property management company. Conflicts sometimes arise between property developers and city agencies over the provision of office space for the committees.

27. More specifically, the figure was 6.2 members per community residents' committee in 2006; unpublished Beijing city government report, on file with the author.

28. Unpublished Beijing city government report, on file with the author.

29. Site visit, Xianningjie, Beijing, August 24, 2010.

30. The trio of party committee, residents' committee, and service-stand facilitators is referred to as three horse carts rolling side by side (*san jia mache bingxing*).

31. After the 2010 elections, women made up 18 percent of Taipei's wardens, according to results posted on the Web site of the Taipei Election Commission, http://www.mect.gov.tw, accessed February 15, 2011.

32. Chen Qiao, "Minzhengbu ni quanguo fanwei nei chexiao jiedao ban, qianghua jumin zizhi" [Ministry of Civil Affairs plans to abolish street offices on a nationwide scale, strengthening residents' autonomy], *Jinghua Shibao*, September 5, 2011, http://news.qq.com/a/20110905/000061.htm, accessed October 12, 2011.

CHAPTER THREE

1. In this paragraph I draw on ten days of interviews I conducted in Seoul in July 2004.

2. Figures on the total number of *dong* in Seoul were given to me by officials of the Ministry of Government Administration and Home Affairs in a photocopied table, dated December 31, 2003. This number had not changed as of April 1, 2011, according to information accessed on that date on the city's Web site, http://english.seoul.go.kr.

3. Interview, Dongjak District Office, Seoul, July 9, 2004.

4. See also Pekkanen's earlier study (2006, 100).

5. On arrangements in the New Order period, see Guinness (1986, 24) and Sullivan (1992), in addition to Kurasawa's study. Guinness's recent treatment of his Yogyakarta research site also touches on elections (2009, 41, 53).

6. For example, only some of Thailand's cooperative community groups hold elections, whereas the leaders of others are chosen by city officials (Mahakanjana 2009).

7. John Pomfret, "Chinese tiptoe toward the vote; some residents, in some cities, may choose from among limited candidates," *Washington Post*, February 20, 2000; Erik Eckholm, "China's neighborly snoops reinvent themselves," *New York Times*, April 11, 2000; Mure Dickie, "China's democratic model may be toothless tiger," *Financial Times*, October 13, 2003.

8. Site visit, Shimen, Beijing, June 23, 2000.

9. On *jiaweihui*, see Chapter 4.

10. The numbers in this section come from unpublished Beijing city government reports, prepared after the elections of 2000, 2003, and 2006, respectively, on file with the author.

11. Interview, Duzhuang RC member, Beijing, July 1, 2000.

12. These do not exhaust the ways in which elections are controlled. In each round, authorities arbitrarily choose not to hold elections in certain neighborhoods. Also, second elections are held in a small number of neighborhoods, presumably where something in the first election did not go as planned.

13. Middle-aged and older party members sometimes are unable to join party activities at their *danwei* because of the dissolution or reorganization of those work units or because they no longer live nearby.

14. I was not able to obtain details of the most recent round of elections in Beijing, but interviews and site visits in 2010 indicated that nothing substantial had changed.

15. Li Fan has tirelessly called attention to such examples and possibilities; for instance, see his report "Zhongguo jiceng minzhu de fazhan he zhengzhi gaige [The development of base-level democracy and political reform in China]," http://www.chinaelections.org/newsinfo.asp?newsid=58899, accessed October 20, 2011. See also Trott 2006 (cited with permission); Chen and Lu 2007, 425; and Chen, Lu, and Yang 2007, 509.

16. Candidates in 2003, for example, were repaid NT$30 (a little less than US$1) for each vote they received, if they obtained at least one-third of the winning number of votes (City of Taipei Election Commission 2003, 210).

17. A press release from the City of Taipei Election Commission, dated July 25, 2006, explained that the practice of discouraging frivolous candidacies in *lizhang* elections had been modeled on other cities such as Kaohsiung and Yilan, and that Taipei's wardens had been polled to determine an appropriate amount for the deposit.

18. This figure includes incumbents who chose not to defend their seats as well as those defeated by challengers at the ballot box.

19. Forty-eight percent identified with parties in the pan-Blue camp, and 31 percent said there was no particular party they leaned toward.

20. In November 2010, Su won a respectable 44 percent of the Taipei vote, though not enough to beat KMT incumbent Hau Lung-Bin.

21. Warden candidates who have obtained a political party's recommendation (*tuijian*) are identified accordingly on the election announcements circulated by the government, although party affiliation is not printed on ballots.

22. Data on the four major cities outside of Taipei came from the database section of the Central Election Commission's Web site, http://db.cec.gov.tw/cec /cechead.asp (February 16, 2011).

23. The following account is based on sixteen visits to Wenchang between 2003 and 2010, with vote counts and other facts supplied or verified by the Taipei Election Commission reports for the relevant years.

24. Chuang found that the most common items in the published campaign platforms for the 2003 elections called for improving neighborhood security systems, adding amenities such as activity centers and reading rooms, and bolstering volunteer activities (2005, 60).

25. This proportion is more than ten percentage points higher than the actual turnout figures, a gap no doubt attributable in part to respondents misremembering or misreporting their participation, as well as to a modest bias in the sample toward people who spend more time at home (thus answering the phone) and who are more connected to neighborhood affairs.

26. I am grateful to the Ministry of the Interior and to Professor Chen for making the questionnaire, data, and report from their 2004 survey available to me (C.-M. Chen 2004).

27. The deliberately broad question wording surely captured groundless impressions as well as actual cases of vote buying. As the accounts presented here show, it is not uncommon for warden candidates to level wild accusations at opponents.

28. Following the 2010 elections, prosecutors moved to annul the election of one Taipei City neighborhood warden (and two in New Taipei) as a result of allegations of vote buying. A total of fifteen such cases were reported in warden campaigns in the five special municipalities, which reflects the fact that other localities have more of this abuse than Taipei City does. Lin Changshun, "Shi Jian ti 3 lizhang dangxuan wuxiao" [Shilin District Prosecutors Office moves to annul three warden elections], *Central News Agency*, January 4, 2011, http://news.cts.com.tw/cna /society/201101/201101040644855.html, accessed October 12, 2011.

29. Interview, Chiayi, April 1, 2006.

30. Unlike most figures in this book, Figure 3-3 omits the missing values. Of respondents, 158 in Beijing and 418 in Taipei said that they did not know how effective their neighborhood organization was at representing them. This reflects differences in the amount of everyday contact that residents of the two cities have with these organizations, which are explained in Chapter 5.

CHAPTER FOUR

1. These figures are derived from tables 1-1 and 3-3 of the Beijing Statistical Yearbook 2010 (2009 data), http://www.bjstats.gov.cn/nj/main/2010-tjnj/index.htm, accessed March 30, 2011.

2. In addition to the neighborhood-level perspective provided by my ten primary RC field sites, this section also draws on interviews at the Bajiao Street office in Shijingshan district, Beijing, October 20, 1999, and with officials at two other street offices elsewhere in the city.

3. "Merger of four Beijing districts is approved, Xuanwu and Chongwen districts to become history," Xinhua, July 1, 2010.

4. The former are formally dubbed *shoudu gongneng hexin qu* and the latter *chengshi gongneng tuozhan qu*, carrying the awkward English translations of "core districts of capital function" and "urban-function extended districts." See Beijing Municipal Bureau of Statistics 2007, table 3-3.

5. By 2006 they were no longer called *jiaweihui* but were designated as transitional communities (*jiaweihui duli zhuan zhi shequ*). The original term is short for *jiashu weiyuanhui* or "family members' committee," which reflects the idea that these organizations would administer the dependents of work unit employees. In 2000, 41 percent of Beijing's RCs were *jiaweihui*; by 2006, only 12 percent were considered former *jiaweihui*.

6. Site visit, Shimen, Beijing, April 27, 2000.

7. This occurred in Wutai and Xianningjie RCs.

8. Interview, *liganshi*, Taipei, December 22, 2003.

9. Interview, *liganshi*, Taipei, January 24, 2007.

10. Site visit, Wenchang, Taipei, January 9, 2007.

11. Interview, district chief, Taipei, March 20, 2006.

12. Site visit, Wenchang, Taipei, January 9, 2007.

13. According to city records and newspaper reports, seven others had died in office, and one went missing.

14. "Just convicted, a warden stabs and injures a peddler, and is arrested," *Liberty Times*, March 18, 2006, http://www.libertytimes.com.tw/2006/new/mar/18/today-so3.htm, accessed October 30, 2009.

15. "Chen Chin-chi's mother cries at the injustice of a reduced sentence for the hirer of a murderer," *Liberty Times*, July 22, 2005, http://www.libertytimes.com.tw/2005/new/jul/22/today-so12.htm, accessed October 30, 2009.

16. Site visit, Wenchang, Taipei, January 9, 2007.

17. The six geographically defined electoral districts did not include two seats reserved for aboriginals.

18. Site visit, Shengfeng, Taipei, January 3, 2007.

19. Site visit, Shengfeng, Taipei, January 3, 2007.

20. Site visit, Shengfeng, Taipei, January 27, 2007.

21. The street names in this passage are pseudonyms.

22. Mayor Ma's administration defended the election postponement as a necessary step given the adjustment of neighborhood boundaries. DPP critics charged that the purpose was to keep many longtime KMT vote mobilizers (*zhuangjiao*) in place until after the December 2002 mayor and city council elections; this arrangement, it was argued, would give them extra motivation to help their party's candidates in the earlier election in return for assistance in their own races immediately thereafter.

23. Interview with warden, Taipei, January 17, 2007. Yang stated that the main reason for his protest was the election postponement.

24. Yang kept his position and its perquisites, however; he won reelection to a second term in 2006 before losing to a challenger in 2010.

25. These events received extensive coverage in newspapers: Yun-ping Chang, "Mayor Ma admits errors as borough wardens protest," *Taipei Times*, January 17, 2003, 3; *China Post*, "Ward chiefs protest against Taipei City government," January 17, 2003; Qin Fuzhen, "Beishi lizhang hong Lin Zhengxiu xia tai" [Taipei wardens shout Lin Cheng-hsiou off the stage], *Lianhe Wanbao*, January 16, 2003, 2. See also City of Taipei 2003. In August 2003, Lin was moved to the directorship of the city's Research, Development, and Evaluation Commission. He maintains that the postponement of the election was the primary cause of the protests. Interview, December 18, 2003, and personal communication.

26. Site visit, Wenchang, Taipei, December 16, 2003.

27. Site visit, Chongxing, Beijing, March 31, 2000.

28. Site visit, Shimen, Beijing, February 25, 2000.

29. Site visit, Wutai, Beijing, October 20, 1999.

30. Site visit, Shimen, Beijing, February 17, 2000.

31. A kilowatt-hour of electricity cost 0.39 yuan at the time.

32. Site visit, Shimen, Beijing, February 17, 2000.

33. Site visit, Chongxing, Beijing, March 31, 2000.

34. Site visit, Dengdao, Beijing, May 10, 2000.

35. Site visit, Wutai, Beijing, March 28, 2000.

36. One committee member had recommended a more aggressive course of action, including charging the vegetable seller a full 400 yuan and going on to set up an entire morning market full of vendors, but the others feared that the Street Office would take the revenue away from them. Site visit, Xianningjie, Beijing, October 18, 1999.

37. The RC members grumbled that the informant was probably an unemployed local resident who had sought their permission to open his own vegetable stand but had been turned down on the grounds that one was enough and the Daxing farmer's prices were lower. Site visits, Xianningjie, Beijing, June 8 and 23, 2000.

38. In one case, the staff member had been accused of appropriating relief aid intended for a welfare recipient and was summarily dismissed, although her trouble was apparently aggravated by conflicts with other members and the fact that her husband had been discovered to be a former felon. In the other, the committee member in charge of migrants had been accused of accepting free clothes and haircuts from them. She was not dismissed but resigned rather than face an election in which her being voted out by the thirty-eight representatives was the prearranged conclusion. Site visit, Chongxing, Beijing, April 28, 2000, and interview, Duzhuang RC member, Beijing, July 1, 2000.

39. Site visits, Xianningjie, Beijing, October 25, 1999, and Shuangqiao, Beijing, October 19, 1999.

40. Interview, Duzhuang RC member, Beijing, July 1, 2000.

41. Site visit, Shimen, Beijing, May 18, 2000.

42. Site visit, Chongxing, Beijing, April 28, 2000.

43. Site visit, Shimen, Beijing, November 20, 2000.

44. Site visit, Xianningjie, Beijing, March 21, 2000.

45. Site visit, Xianningjie, Beijing, September 4, 2000. It should be noted that enforcement in other parts of the city was at times draconian, including the confiscation and killing of noncompliant animals.

46. Site visit, Chongxing, Beijing, March 31, 2000.

47. Site visit, Anfeng, Beijing, November 3, 2000.

48. Spiegel provides one attempt to assess the extent and violence of the government's campaign (2002). Books on *falun gong* by Chang and Ownby contain chapter-length treatments of the suppression (Chang 2004; Ownby 2008).

49. Interview, Duzhuang RC member, Beijing, November 13, 1999.

50. Site visit, Shawan, Beijing, February 21, 2000.

51. Site visits, Shimen, Beijing, September 16 and December 17, 1999.

52. The RC turned away such an application in at least one case I learned about. An elderly man named Guo approached them to try to obtain a temporary residence permit on behalf of a young woman who had found lodging in the neighborhood while ostensibly making a living by offering private dance lessons. The RC believed her to be a prostitute, however, and even titteringly quoted her fee scale to me. They had told her to leave the neighborhood once before. Site visit, Shuangqiao, Beijing, February 23, 2000.

53. Not all those who ran neighborhood businesses under the sponsorship of the residents' committee were migrants. Permanent residents, especially those who had been laid off from state-sector jobs, would open small convenience stores and the like, sometimes by converting part of their home into a storefront. Such individuals were relatively few in number, as a single neighborhood would generally have only two to six RC-sponsored proprietorships. Like migrants, they, too, might well depend on the committee's good will, although their irrevocable urban household registry made their overall citizenship status much higher than that of migrants.

54. Site visit, Shuangqiao, Beijing, March 22, 2000.

55. Site visits, Shawan, Beijing, April 24, 2000, and Shimen, Beijing, September 16, 1999.

56. Site visits, Shimen, Beijing, May 18 and April 17, 2000.

57. Site visit, Shuangqiao, Beijing, April 17, 2000.

58. Site visit, Wenchang, Taipei, January 9, 2007.

59. The mother claimed that the individual in question was her brother, and the committee member did not challenge this assertion. Site visit, Chongxing, Beijing, December 12, 2000.

60. Ding stated to me privately that she believed that Shao's rental income would disqualify her from receiving the benefits she sought. Site visit, Shimen, Beijing, March 23, 2000.

61. "If even someone as awful as Mao could be given a three-seven split [the official evaluation of the deceased leader's deeds as having been 30 percent erroneous but 70 percent meritorious], then we ought to be even more forgiving of people who have only committed trifling faults."

62. A member of one family whose home was in the Shimen neighborhood had spent the last eight years in a mental health hospital. Director Ding of the RC realized that he could be eligible to be designated a "disabled person," thus giving the family access to some 200 yuan per month in state support as well as favorable tax status should they choose to open a business. Although committee members accompanied them on numerous trips to hospitals and other institutions to get the appropriate certification, the family still criticized Ding for not doing enough to help them, and the RC staff complained bitterly about their ingratitude. Site visits, Shimen, Beijing, February 17 and February 25, 2000.

63. Site visit, Chongxing, Beijing, November 30, 2000.

64. Jia was at that time the party secretary of Beijing and a member of the Politburo.

65. Site visit, Chongxing, Beijing, March 31, 2000.

66. In the second of the two cases described above, the Street Office eventually did instruct the committee to produce a statement—in support of the other party.

67. Site visits, Xiyingjie, Beijing, September 13, November 7, and November 30, 2000.

68. Site visit, Puzhao, Taipei, April 6, 2006.

69. Site visit, Shengfeng, Taipei, January 3, 2007.

70. Interview No. T1, Taipei, December 21, 2003.

71. Interview No. T23, Taipei, April 2, 2006.

72. Contributors to Schwartz and Shieh's book on NGOs and state organizations grapple with these and related questions (2009).

73. These struggles, in major cities around the country, have garnered substantial scholarly attention (e.g., Read 2003, 2007, 2008a, 2008b; Zhu 2004; Cai 2005; Tomba 2005; Yip and Jiang 2011).

74. Interview, city housing official, Beijing, November 8, 2000; interview, home-owner activist, August 17, 2010. It is common for YWH to be formed through non-democratic processes under the control of property developers or street offices.

75. Interview at NGO office, Taipei, January 18, 2007.

76. Site visit, Shengfeng, Taipei, January 22, 2007. By "Urban-Rural Institute" (Chengxiangsuo), he meant the National Taiwan University unit whose English name is the Graduate Institute of Building and Planning, a hotbed of initiatives in urban planning and reform.

77. Interview, January 27, 2007; real name used by permission.

78. Interview, warden, Taipei, January 17, 2007.

79. Interview, warden, Taipei, January 17, 2007.

80. The Maokong Gondola project, http://gondola.trtc.com.tw, has received extensive media coverage.

CHAPTER FIVE

1. Ninety-four of the 133 informants were from Guangdong Province. As émi-grés, they may have differed from the general population; for instance, they might have been particularly disaffected (Whyte and Parish 1984, 377–389).

2. The Taipei interviewers pushed harder than those in Beijing to obtain either a positive or a negative answer, although they accepted neutral responses from 3.5 percent of interviewees.

3. A comparable question was not asked in the 2001 Beijing survey out of what may have been an exaggerated fear that such a question would be too politically sensitive.

4. The full question wording was as follows: "Question D25: Please tell me whether in the following circumstances you would be certainly willing, perhaps willing, perhaps unwilling, or certainly unwilling to cooperate with the work of the residents' committee: (1) Helping the residents' committee publicize the relevant content of new policies, for instance policies concerning the vaccination of infants; (2) Informing the residents' committee about the situation when a dispute breaks out among neighbors; (3) Helping the residents' committee learn about things like your neighbors' identity or household registry status; (4) If your neighbor were receiving state welfare funds, helping the residents' committee learn about other sources of income he/she had."

5. All other variables were set at their means for this purpose.

6. In Taipei, though not in Beijing, it was possible to include in these analyses publicly available information on the wardens themselves, which showed the age of the warden also to have a modest effect on perceptions. Superannuated *lizhang*, for example, elicited less satisfaction than younger ones did.

7. In Taipei, identifying as a *waishengren*—coming from a family that arrived from the mainland around the time of the Kuomintang influx of the late 1940s—is

not significant, which suggests that this much-debated subethnic cleavage was not very relevant to this institution by the time the survey was conducted. More generally, it supports the notion that the *li-lin* system, from the early years of KMT rule in Taiwan, was used as one way to mitigate polarization along these lines.

8. This is true in three of the four models reported here.

9. In both cities, these relationships are found only in attitudes toward respondents' specific RC or NW, not in perceptions of the system's overall usefulness.

10. In Beijing, residents who had lived in the same neighborhood for many years tended to have less favorable assessments of the usefulness of the RC than did others. This may reflect a form of what Mary Gallagher has termed, in a separate but related context, *informed disenchantment* (Gallagher 2006). In other words, although Beijingers for the most part have a positive opinion of the usefulness of these neighborhood bodies, those with long years of exposure to a particular RC may develop a heightened awareness of its limitations.

11. This format was adopted in the Beijing survey with the intention of reducing social or political bias toward positive answers; it was retained for the Taipei survey.

12. Site visit, Shuangqiao, Beijing, February 23, 2000.

13. Interview, Duzhuang RC member, Beijing, November 13, 1999.

14. Interview No. DT14, Beijing, November 27, 2004.

15. Some aspects of social change in postwar Taipei are addressed in Marsh (1996).

16. "Taibeishi di 5 jie shizhang, di 11 jie yiyuan ji di 11 jie lizhang xuanju houxuanren ge qu, ge li depiao ji dangxuan qingxing," retrieved from the Taipei election commission's Web site, http://www.mect.gov.tw/, on February 15, 2011.

17. In the Taipei survey, "high-rise" (*da xia*, as pronounced there) was one of the categories in which respondents reported their type of housing. In Beijing, respondents reported the total number of floors in their building; those with fourteen or more floors were coded as high-rise buildings.

18. Site visit, Wutai, Beijing, May 10, 2000.

19. Interview No. T16, Taipei, March 25, 2006.

20. Interview No. T13, Taipei, March 25, 2006.

21. Interview No. C14, Beijing, July 9, 1998.

22. Interview No. D2, July 13, 2000. In one interview, a Taipei man indicated a related form of skepticism that his neighborhood leader could be responsive to the community: "The people with power in the locality put forward one of their own people; that's who the warden really is. . . . He's about forty years old, and the people in his family are big landowners around here." Interview No. T14, Taipei, March 25, 2006.

23. Interview, city housing official, Beijing, November 8, 2000.

24. Interview No. D30, Beijing, August 27, 2000.

25. Interview No. C31, Shanghai, July 25, 1998.

26. Interview No. C10, Beijing, September 27, 1999.

27. Interview No. C34, Shanghai, July 29, 1998.

28. Interview No. C40, Beijing, August 3, 1998.

29. Interview No. T6, Taipei, March 19, 2006.

30. Interview No. T12, Taipei, March 25, 2006.

31. Interview No. T20, Taipei, March 29, 2006.

32. The committee was trying to tidy up the neighborhood in preparation for the fiftieth anniversary of the founding of the People's Republic. Interview No. C64, Beijing, September 3, 1999.

33. Interview No. T6, Taipei, March 19, 2006.

34. Interview No. C19, Beijing, July 11, 1998.

35. Interview No. T2, Taipei, March 14, 2006.

36. Interview No. T26, Taipei, December 29, 2006.

37. Interview No. T10, Taipei, March 23, 2006.

38. Interview No. C28, Beijing, July 21, 1998.

39. Interview No. D4, Beijing, July 14, 2000.

40. Interview No. T16, Taipei, March 25, 2006.

CHAPTER SIX

1. The work of Qingwen Xu represents an effort to place RC-mobilized action into a broader context of community participation (2007).

2. Elizabeth J. Perry's study of worker militias examines the history of one widespread form of citizen auxiliary force in the People's Republic of China and in earlier periods (2006).

3. See also Townsend's discussion of neighborhood organizations (1967, 158–165).

4. In this passage, Townsend goes on to identify activists as "those who fill official or unofficial positions of more or less regularized responsibility during the course of the movement," people who invest "a disproportionately high degree of time, energy, and commitment in political activity" (1967, 132–133).

5. See also Gold's post–Cultural Revolution critique (1985). Vogel has dealt with activism in other work, as has Victor Falkenheim (Vogel 1967; Falkenheim 1978).

6. Oksenberg, it should be noted, gave consideration to several other motivations as well.

7. Activists' special role in political campaigns has received continued attention in other accounts, however, including the well-known *Chen Village* (Chan, Madsen, and Unger 1984, 50–51).

8. Both Shirk and Walder report facts about activists' motivations that add nuance to, but also stand in tension with, the essence of their theoretically streamlined accounts. Shirk points out that "students distinguished between two categories

of activists: those who were sincerely committed to the revolution and those who were hypocrites" (1982, 114). Walder's informants report a variety of activist types corresponding to motivations including raw opportunism but also a sense of duty, ideological belief, commitment to serving the people, and work ethic (1986, 148).

9. The law only mentions small-group heads, not the other terms.

10. For example, Interview No. T3, Taipei, March 15, 2006, and Interview No. T11, Taipei, March 24, 2006.

11. Drawing on city records, Chuang found a total of 786 volunteer teams across Taipei (2005, 71).

12. Outi Luova describes the closely related community volunteers' associations of Tianjin, dubbing them "multipurpose partners of the party-state" (2011).

13. Conversely, questions on charity and security-patrol participation were omitted from the Taipei survey to keep the questionnaire short enough for the telephone format.

14. As pointed out in Chapter 3, the actual voting rate in Taipei's 2003 *lizhang* elections was 37.7 percent. It is likely that, in both cities, some respondents erroneously reported having voted and that both surveys contain a sampling bias toward individuals who were more likely to have voted.

15. The 1997 figures are from an interview on August 26, 1998, with officials of the Beijing city government; the 1999 figures are from page four of *Shequ jianshe zhong de juweihui gongzuo shouce*, edited by the city's Civil Affairs Bureau and published internally in 2000. The 1997 figures were said not to include security patrollers; the scope of the 1999 figures is unclear.

16. "Regularly" meaning an answer of "often" or "sometimes" in the survey.

17. As it stands, the 2006 participation data show the proportion of Taipei residents who cared enough about warden elections to show up at the polls even without the extra draw of the mayoral and city council races.

18. Looked at from a different perspective, in Beijing, 19 percent of women had participated in RC activities but only 13 percent of men. In Taipei, 28 percent of men were neighborhood participants but only 23 percent of women.

19. Supporters of the DPP appear slightly less inclined to participate, but the relationship falls just shy of statistical significance at the .05 level.

20. Naturally, this leaves unanswered the question of whether the participants knew so many neighbors before or as a result of their voluntary service; the answer is likely a mixture of both.

21. Site visits, Shimen, Beijing, October 31, 2000; Shuangqiao, Beijing, November 10, 2000; and Xianningjie, Beijing, May 19, 2000.

22. Site visits, Xianningjie, Beijing, March 14 and April 24, 2000.

23. Site visit, Xianningjie, Beijing, April 14, 2000.

24. Ding explained that it had been unrealistic to expect her to produce such a turnout and that she had countered with a proposal that they "come up with a

local method [*zamen lai ge tufa ba*]," in other words, cut corners and make do with a smaller number of patrollers. Site visit, Shimen, Beijing, November 2, 1999.

25. Interview, Duzhuang RC member, Beijing, October 10, 1999.

26. Interview No. C69, Beijing, December 5, 2000.

27. Interview No. T24, Taipei, April 2, 2006.

28. Site visit, Xianningjie, Beijing, February 21, 2000.

29. Site visit, Xiyingjie, Beijing, March 16, 2000.

30. Site visit, Xianningjie, Beijing, February 15, 2000.

31. Interview No. C42, Beijing, September 3, 1999.

32. Interview No. C70, Beijing, December 16, 2000.

33. Interview No. C66, Beijing, September 26, 1999.

34. Interview No. T4, Taipei, March 16, 2006.

35. Interview No. T3, Taipei, March 15, 2006.

36. Interview No. T11, Taipei, March 24, 2006.

37. The wording of this question, in Beijing, paralleled that of the question presented in Chapter 5 concerning residents' openness toward their RC staff or warden. In Taipei, it paralleled the standard trust question that was also asked concerning the respondent's warden.

38. About 41 percent of Taipei respondents said they were very or somewhat trusting toward their wardens, and about 37 percent were very or somewhat trusting toward people in general.

39. Taipei block captains also received NT$300 to NT$450 for newspaper subscriptions.

40. Interview, Duzhuang RC member, Beijing, July 1, 2000.

41. Site visit, Puzhao, Taipei, January 24, 2007.

42. Interview No. C66b, Beijing, December 9, 2000.

43. Site visits, Wutai, Beijing, March 28, 2000, and July 11, 2003.

44. Fittingly, these were not improvised moves but a structured sixteen-step (*shiliu bu*) routine that meshed perfectly with the four-four beat. Site visit, Xianningjie, Beijing, March 14, 2000.

45. Site visit, Dengdao, Beijing, November 6, 2000.

46. Interview No. T18, March 26, 2006.

47. Site visit, Shimen, Beijing, March 3, 2000.

48. Site visit, Chongxing, Beijing, March 7, 2000.

49. Site visit, Xianningjie, Beijing, January 26, 2000.

50. Site visit, Wenchang, Taipei, December 16, 2003.

51. Site visit, Luzhou, Taipei, January 21, 2007.

52. She referred to Typhoon Nari, which hit Taiwan with deadly impact in September 2001.

53. Site visits, Pingshan, Taipei, January 17 and 25, 2007.

54. Site visit, Pingshan, Taipei, January 25, 2007.

55. Essays by the sociologist Hei-Yuan Chiu, for instance, give a sense of the debates. See, for instance, "The crisis and hope of civil communities," and "A confused and authoritarian community development policy," available at his Web site, http://140.109.196.10/hyc/.

56. Interview, Society Bureau official, Taipei, January 11, 2007.

57. Interview, district official, Taipei, January 24, 2007.

58. The following account is based on election records for 2003 and 2006, along with site visits in 2006 and 2007, including two interviews with the warden, a group interview with leaders of the CDA, and an interview with the *liganshi*.

59. Anecdotal evidence suggests that such career-oriented activism persists in schools and work units, although it is surely diminished in many cases by the much greater availability in the reform era of alternative career paths to those controlled by the CCP.

CHAPTER SEVEN

1. For more information on the set of questions concerning cooperation, see Figure 5.3. Even on the most demanding measure of willingness to cooperate with the RC that was included in the Beijing survey instrument—the question asking whether the respondent would turn in a neighbor for welfare cheating—more than 30 percent of all nonparticipating respondents answered affirmatively.

2. The limitations of the telephone survey format made it impractical to replicate all of the items on the Beijing survey.

3. Interview No. T1, Taipei, March 11, 2006.

4. Site visit, Yanping, Taipei, August 13, 2010.

5. Site visits, Shuangqiao, Beijing, September 21, 1999; October 19, 1999; and November 15, 1999.

6. Site visit, Xianningjie, Beijing, March 2, 2000.

7. Interview, Beijing, September 6, 2000.

8. Interview, Civil Affairs Bureau, Beijing, September 6, 1999.

9. Interview, district Civil Affairs official, Beijing, December 10, 1999.

10. Interview No. T4, Taipei, March 16, 2006.

11. Interview No. T5, Taipei, March 19, 2006.

12. Beijing residents' once-prevalent practice of laying in a large stock of Chinese cabbage (*da baicai*) to last through the winter months has waned as the supply of vegetables has become more reliable.

13. Interview No. D15, Beijing, September 23, 2000.

14. Interview No. C33, Shanghai, July 27, 1998; interview No. D10, Beijing, August 26, 2000.

15. Site visits, Shuangqiao, Beijing, November 2, 1999; Chongxing, Beijing, November 15, 2000; and Shawan, Beijing, July 10, 1998.

16. Site visits, Puzhao, Taipei, January 4, 2007, and Wenchang, Taipei, January 9, 2007, and December 22, 2003.

17. In the Beijing survey, this was asked as two separate questions, which inquired whether the respondent had gone to the RC "to discuss or give input on neighborhood security issues" and "to discuss or give input on other neighborhood issues (such as construction noise, sanitary conditions, the condition of hallways, etc.)." Table 7-2 reports positive responses to either of these questions.

18. Site visits, Xianningjie, Beijing, April 24 and September 4, 2000.

19. Site visits, Xiyingjie, Beijing, March 24, 2000; Shimen, Beijing, April 27, 2000; Chongxing, Beijing, December 2, 1999.

20. Site visit, Shawan, Beijing, April 24, 2000.

21. Interviews No. C29, Shanghai, July 25, 1998, and No. C51, Beijing, August 10, 1998.

22. In this case, the committee members were inclined to believe that she had merely misplaced it. Site visit, Xianningjie, Beijing, November 1, 1999.

23. Site visit, Wenchang, Taipei, December 22, 2003.

24. Site visit, Pingshan, Taipei, March 9, 2006.

25. Interview No. T21, Taipei, March 30, 2006.

26. Interview No. T25, Taipei, April 1, 2006.

27. Interview No. D8, Beijing, July 20, 2000.

28. Interview No. C19, Beijing, July 11, 1998.

29. Interview No. C44, Beijing, August 5, 1998.

30. Interview No. C65, Beijing, September 21, 1999.

31. Site visit, Pingshan, Taipei, March 21, 2006.

32. Interview with Fushou warden, Taipei, January 17, 2007.

33. Later, one of the committee members specially wrote out a letter of commendation to the street office on behalf of the donor, keeping a carbon copy for their own files. Site visit, Dengdao, Beijing, October 23, 2000.

34. Two of the younger staff members expressed agreement with his criticisms and told him to complain to the street office; they could not complain themselves, they said, or they would lose their jobs. Site visit, Xianningjie, Beijing, December 13, 1999.

35. Site visit, Shimen, Beijing, January 24, 2000.

36. Research on emotional work includes studies by Hochschild (1983), Pierce (1996), and Whitelegg (2002).

37. Out of 126 disputes in Beijing where respondents sought third-party help, 47.8 percent of those who went to residents' committees reported that it met or exceeded their expectations. The corresponding figures for other sources of help were as follows: informal third parties such as friends, 45.0 percent; lawyers or courts, 40.0 percent; government offices of various kinds, 35.7 percent; work units, 30.8 percent; and police, 25.8 percent.

38. Site visit, Xiyingjie, Beijing, March 31, 2000.

39. Site visit, Shimen, Beijing, May 18, 2000.

40. Although they took the position that it would be somewhat more reasonable if the two parties were not both married, the committee members considered the man's behavior unacceptable. Site visit, Shimen, Beijing, January 24, 2000.

41. Site visit, Xianningjie, Beijing, February 21, 2000.

42. Site visit, Xiyingjie, Beijing, March 31, 2000.

43. Interview, Duzhuang RC member, Beijing, July 1, 2000.

44. Site visit, Shuangqiao, Beijing, September 5, 2000.

45. Interview No. C15, Beijing, July 9, 1998.

46. Interview No. D11, Beijing, August 26, 2000.

47. Interview No. C65, Beijing, September 21, 1999.

48. Interview No. C8, Beijing, June 25, 1998.

49. Interview No. T17, Taipei, March 26, 2006.

50. Interview No. T22, Taipei, March 30, 2006.

51. Interview, district mediation director, Taipei, January 18, 2007.

52. Interview No. T10, Taipei, March 23, 2006.

53. Black cited Jan Gross, who wrote: "The real power of a totalitarian state results . . . from its being at the disposal, available for hire at a moment's notice, to every inhabitant" (1984, 69). I thank Ethan Michelson for bringing these passages to my attention.

54. Interview No. T3, Taipei, March 15, 2006.

55. Interview No. D11, Beijing, August 26, 2000.

56. Interview No. C1, Beijing, June 20, 1998.

57. Interview No. T10, Taipei, March 23, 2006.

58. Interview No. T22, Taipei, March 30, 2006.

59. Interview No. T17, Taipei, March 26, 2006.

60. Interview No. T15, Taipei, March 25, 2006.

61. Interview No. T4, Taipei, March 16, 2006.

62. World Health Organization, "Summary of probable SARS cases with onset of illness from 1 November 2002 to 31 July 2003," http://www.who.int/csr/sars /country/table2004_04_21/en/index.html, accessed October 4, 2009. Schwartz highlights the role of RCs in the state response to the crisis (2009). See also the collection of local perspectives on the epidemic edited by Deborah Davis and Helen Siu (2007).

63. Site visits, Xiyingjie, Beijing, November 7, 2000, and Xianningjie, Beijing, May 8, 2000.

64. Site visit, Chongxing, Beijing, November 15, 1999.

65. Site visit, Yanping, Taipei, March 16, 2006.

66. Interview No. T23, Taipei, April 2, 2006.

67. Site visit, Xianningjie, Beijing, December 14, 2000.

68. Interview, Duzhuang RC member, Beijing, November 13, 1999.

69. Interview No. D31, Beijing, August 27, 2000.

CHAPTER EIGHT

1. This English-language manuscript (n.d.) is translated from the published Japanese book (Tsujinaka, Pekkanen, and Yamamoto 2009). All told, 18,404 out of the sample of 33,438 associations responded to the survey on which this book draws.

2. The data of Pekkanen, Tsujinaka, and Yamamoto show 69 percent of the associations responding to their survey lying within that size range (n.d., chap. 3).

3. Pekkanen discusses *kumi* as well (2006, 103).

4. Three-quarters of the associations participating in the 2006–2007 survey reported membership rates of at least 90 percent (Pekkanen, Tsujinaka, and Yamamoto n.d., chap. 4). See also Haddad on community volunteering in Japan (2004, 2007).

5. The quoted passage comes from the English-language synopsis of Yoshihara's 2000 book.

6. Guinness and Sullivan differ in that the former emphasizes the self-generated nature of *kampung* community within the overlay of the RT, RK, and RW, and the latter calls special attention to the state's role in creating and reinforcing such community through its ultra-local organizations and ideology. Guinness thus takes issue with Sullivan's book in places (Guinness 2009, e.g., 11–15). Yet the accounts can largely be read as two sides of the same coin.

7. One exception is Im (2004).

8. On South Korea as a developmental state, see, for example, Evans (1995), Woo-Cumings (1999), Kohli (2004), and Vu (2010).

9. The *dong* offices, with staff waiting behind counters, bear a resemblance to the reception areas of some of Beijing's new *shequ*.

10. These figures on Seoul's districts, wards, and *tong* come from the city government's Web site, http://english.seoul.go.kr, accessed April 1, 2011.

11. These figures were provided by officials of the South Korean Ministry of Government Administration and Home Affairs in an interview with the author, July 12, 2004. Seoul had 98,234 *ban* in 2004.

12. Interview, city official, Seoul, July 13, 2004.

13. Jungmin Seo's paper discusses their symbolic dimensions (2002).

14. Interview, city official, Seoul, July 13, 2004.

15. Surprisingly, both national and Seoul officials lacked basic information such as demographic figures on the people who serve in these capacities.

16. Interview, Seoul, July 7, 2004.

17. The bracketed phrases are Fagen's.

18. The account of Freedom House's Arch Puddington also emphasizes the oppressive nature of the CDRs (1995).

CHAPTER NINE

1. I thank an anonymous reviewer for suggesting a point along these lines.

2. Chapter 6 of Guinness's book discusses at length the meanings of *rukun* (1986). Sullivan, too, emphasizes the widespread embracing of this concept, although he highlights the state's promotion of this ideology of harmony and notes that the word could also be translated merely as group or association (1992, 106–109, 139, 148–149).

3. Here we take members to mean "constituents," setting aside the fact that the official neighborhood organizations of China and Taiwan do not have a mass membership per se.

4. In 2006, 66 percent of RC members in Beijing's eight core districts either lived in the neighborhood they served or were registered as living there. Beijing city government report, on file with the author.

5. One analysis drawing on a comparison of neighborhoods in South Korea and Thailand points out that synergy may be quite difficult to obtain in many settings (Douglass, Ard-am, and Kim 2002).

6. This generalization does not apply to every scholar working in the synergy framework; some explore both empowerment and demobilization (Fox 1996).

APPENDIX ONE

1. The Beijing Statistical Bureau data include a "retired, reemployed" category as well as "retired"; the 24.9 percent figure includes both these categories.

2. Our data also contain an "other" category, and most of those in this category seem to work in military or government units; adding in these to the original figure of 73.8 percent brings the apparent total proportion of employees in the state sector to 77.1 percent.

APPENDIX TWO

1. Filmmaker Duan Jinchuan's documentary *No. 16, Barkhor South Street* provides a vivid glimpse of one RC in Lhasa.

2. Figures on the neighborhoods and elections in Chiayi come from interviews with city officials and the official records of the 2002 elections (City of Chiayi Election Commission 2002).

References

Abers, Rebecca Neaera. 2000. *Inventing local democracy: Grassroots politics in Brazil.* Boulder, Colo.: Lynne Rienner Publishers.

Adams, Paul S. 2002. Corporatism and comparative politics: Is there a new century of corporatism? In *New directions in comparative politics*, edited by H. J. Wiarda and P. S. Adams, 17–44. Boulder, Colo.: Westview Press.

Aguirre, Benigno E. 1984. The conventionalization of collective behavior in Cuba. *American Journal of Sociology* 90 (2): 541–566.

———. 2002. Social control in Cuba. *Latin American Politics and Society* 44 (2): 67–98.

Alagappa, Muthiah, ed. 2004a. *Civil society and political change in Asia: Expanding and contracting democratic space.* Stanford: Stanford University Press.

———. 2004b. Introduction. In *Civil society and political change in Asia: Expanding and contracting democratic space*, edited by M. Alagappa, 1–21. Stanford: Stanford University Press.

Alpermann, Björn. 2009. Institutionalizing village governance in China. *Journal of Contemporary China* 18 (60): 397–409.

Amsden, Alice H. 1989. *Asia's next giant: South Korea and late industrialization.* New York: Oxford University Press.

Andreas, Joel. 2009. *Rise of the red engineers: The Cultural Revolution and the origins of China's new class.* Stanford: Stanford University Press.

Anheier, Helmut K. 2004. *Civil society: Measurement, evaluation, policy.* London: Civicus.

Arnstein, Sherry. 1969. A ladder of citizen participation. *Journal of the American Institute of Planners* 8 (3): 216–224.

Baker, Andy, Barry Ames, and Lucio R. Renno. 2006. Social context and campaign volatility in new democracies: Networks and neighborhoods in Brazil's 2002 elections. *American Journal of Political Science* 50 (2): 382–399.

Barnett, A. Doak. 1964. *Communist China: The early years, 1949–1955.* New York: F. A. Praeger.

Beijing Municipal Bureau of Statistics. 2001. *Beijing tongji nianjian 2001* [Beijing statistical yearbook 2001]. Beijing: China Statistics Press.

———. 2007. *Beijing tongji nianjian 2007* [Beijing statistical yearbook 2007]. Beijing: China Statistics Press.

———. 2010. *Beijing tongji nianjian 2010* [Beijing statistical yearbook 2010]. Beijing: China Statistics Press.

Bendix, Reinhard. 1974. *Work and authority in industry: Ideologies of management in the course of industrialization.* Berkeley: University of California Press.

Benewick, Robert. 1991. Political institutionalisation in government. In *The Chinese state in the era of economic reform: The road to crisis,* edited by G. White, 243–264. Armonk, N.Y.: M. E. Sharpe.

Benewick, Robert, Irene Tong, and Jude Howell. 2004. Self-governance and community: A preliminary comparison between villagers' committees and urban community councils. *China Information* 18 (1): 11–28.

Berman, Sheri. 1997. Civil society and the collapse of the Weimar republic. *World Politics* 49 (3): 401–429.

Bermeo, Nancy, and Philip Nord, eds. 2000. *Civil society before democracy: Lessons from nineteenth-century Europe.* Lanham, Md.: Rowman and Littlefield.

Berry, Jeffrey M. 1999. *The new liberalism and the rising power of citizen groups.* Washington, D.C.: Brookings Institution.

Berry, Jeffrey M., Kent E. Portney, and Ken Thomson. 1993. *The rebirth of urban democracy.* Washington, D.C.: Brookings Institution.

Bestor, Theodore C. 1989. *Neighborhood Tokyo.* Stanford: Stanford University Press.

Black, Donald. 1989. *Sociological justice.* Oxford: Oxford University Press.

Bosco, Joseph. 1992. Taiwan factions: Guanxi, patronage, and the state in local politics. *Ethnology* 31 (2): 157–184.

Bray, David. 2006. Building "community": New strategies of governance in urban China. *Economy and Society* 35 (4): 530–549.

———. 2008. Designing to govern: Space and power in two Wuhan communities. *Built Environment* 34 (3): 392–407.

Broadbent, Jeffrey. 1998. *Environmental politics in Japan: Networks of power and protest.* Cambridge: Cambridge University Press.

Brown, Archie. 2009. *The rise and fall of communism.* New York: Ecco.

Brown, L. David. 1998. Creating social capital: Nongovernmental development organizations and intersectoral problem solving. In *Private action and the public good,* edited by W. W. Powell and E. S. Clemens, 228–241. New Haven, Conn.: Yale University Press.

Brown, Melissa J. 2004. *Is Taiwan Chinese? The impact of culture, power, and migration on changing identities.* Berkeley: University of California Press.

Burke, Edmund. 2007. *Reflections on the revolution in France.* New York: Cosimo Classics. Original edition published in 1790.

Cai, Yongshun. 2005. China's moderate middle class: The case of homeowners' resistance. *Asian Survey* 45 (5): 777–799.

———. 2007. Civil resistance and rule of law in China: The defense of homeowners' rights. In *Grassroots political reform in contemporary China*, edited by E. J. Perry and M. Goldman, 174–195. Cambridge, Mass.: Harvard University Press.

Caldeira, Teresa Pires do Rio. 2000. *City of walls: Crime, segregation, and citizenship in São Paulo.* Berkeley: University of California Press.

Castells, Manuel. 1983. *The city and the grassroots: A cross-cultural theory of urban social movements.* Berkeley: University of California Press.

Chan, Anita, Richard Madsen, and Jonathan Unger. 1984. *Chen village: The recent history of a peasant community in Mao's China.* Berkeley: University of California Press.

———. 2009. *Chen village: Revolution to globalization.* 3rd ed. Berkeley: University of California Press.

Chang, Jung. 1991. *Wild swans: Three daughters of China.* New York: Anchor Books.

Chang, Maria Hsia. 2004. *Falun Gong: The end of days.* New Haven, Conn.: Yale University Press.

Chang, Ya-Wen, and Shu Keng. 2008. Zhongguo dalu jiceng xuanju zhong de wuzhi youyin yu toupiao dongyuan: Yi Shanghai "Xianjin," "Fada" liang shequ "cungaiju" wei li [Electoral mobilization and monetary inducements in China: Case studies of Xianjin and Fada communities]. *Dongwu zhengzhi xuebao* 26 (4): 145–195.

Chen, Ching-Chih. 1975. The Japanese adaptation of the *pao-chia* system in Taiwan, 1895–1945. *Journal of Asian Studies* 34 (2): 391–416.

———. 1984. Police and community control systems in the empire. In *The Japanese colonial empire, 1895–1945*, edited by R. H. Myers and M. R. Peattie, 213–239. Princeton, N.J.: Princeton University Press.

Chen, Chun-Ming. 2004. *Cun-lizhang zhi gongneng ji dingwei wenjuan diaocha* [A questionnaire survey concerning the functions and position of village and neighborhood wardens]. Taipei: Ministry of the Interior.

Chen, Jie. 2004. *Popular political support in urban China.* Stanford: Stanford University Press.

Chen, Jie, and Chunlong Lu. 2006. Does China's middle class think and act democratically? Attitudinal and behavioral orientations toward urban self-government. *Journal of Chinese Political Science* 11 (2): 1–20.

———. 2007. Social capital in urban China: Attitudinal and behavioral effects on grassroots self-government. *Social Science Quarterly* 88 (2): 422–442.

Chen, Jie, Chunlong Lu, and Yiyin Yang. 2007. Popular support for grassroots self-government in urban China: Findings from a Beijing survey. *Modern China* 33 (4): 505–528.

Chen, Yung-fa. 1986. *Making revolution: The communist movement in eastern and central China, 1937–1945.* Berkeley: University of California Press.

Choate, Allen C. 1998. *Local governance in China, part II: An assessment of urban residents committees and municipal community development*. San Francisco: Asia Foundation.

Ch'ü, T'ung-tsu. 1962. *Local government in China under the Ch'ing*. Cambridge, Mass.: Harvard University Council on East Asian Studies.

Chu, Yun-han. 2008. The evolution of political values. In *Political change in China: Comparison with Taiwan*, edited by B. Gilley and L. Diamond, 27–48. Boulder, Colo.: Lynn Rienner Publishers.

Chuang, Heiw Yuan. 2005. *Taibeishi li-lin zuzhi yunzuo zhi yanjiu* [Organization and operation of Taipei City's boroughs and neighborhoods]. M.A. thesis, Ming Chuan University.

City of Chiayi Election Commission. 2002. *Taiwansheng Jiayishi di liu jie lizhang xuanju zong baogao* [General report on the sixth round of neighborhood warden elections in Chiayi City, Taiwan Province]. Chiayi, Taiwan: City of Chiayi Election Commission.

City of Taipei. 2003. *Lizheng gaige goutong bu zu Ma shizhang zhiqian* [Mayor Ma apologizes for inadequate communication about the neighborhood administration reforms]. News release, March 24.

City of Taipei City Council. 2003. *Taibei shizhengfu "lizheng gaige" zhuan'an baogao* [Special report on the City of Taipei government's "neighborhood administration reforms"]. *City of Taipei City Council Bulletin* 67 (9): 1813–1819.

City of Taipei Civil Affairs Bureau. 2003a. *Taibeishi linzhang linpin jiepin shishi yaodian* [Key implementation points on the appointment and dismissal of block captains, City of Taipei]. In *Taibeishi lizhang fuwu shouce* [City of Taipei neighborhood warden service handbook], edited by City of Taipei Civil Affairs Bureau. Taipei: City of Taipei Civil Affairs Bureau.

———. 2003b. *Taibeishi lizhang fuwu shouce* [City of Taipei neighborhood warden service handbook]. Taipei: City of Taipei Civil Affairs Bureau.

City of Taipei Department of Budget, Accounting, and Statistics. 2011. *Zhonghua minguo 99nian Taibeishi tongji nianbao* [Taipei city statistical yearbook 2010]. Taipei: City of Taipei Department of Budget, Accounting, and Statistics.

City of Taipei Election Commission. 1985. *Taibeishi di wu jie lizhang xuanju shilu* [Factual record of the fifth round of neighborhood warden elections in Taipei City]. Taipei: City of Taipei Election Commission.

———. 1990. *Taibeishi di liu jie lizhang xuanju shilu* [Factual record of the sixth round of neighborhood warden elections in Taipei City]. Taipei: City of Taipei Election Commission.

———. 1994. *Taibeishi di qi jie lizhang xuanju shilu* [Factual record of the seventh round of neighborhood warden elections in Taipei City]. Taipei: City of Taipei Election Commission.

———. 1998. *Taibeishi di ba jie lizhang xuanju shilu* [Factual record of the eighth round of neighborhood warden elections in Taipei City]. Taipei: City of Taipei Election Commission.

———. 2003. *Taibeishi di jiu jie lizhang xuanju shilu* [Factual record of the ninth round of neighborhood warden elections in Taipei City]. Taipei: City of Taipei Election Commission.

———. 2006. *Taibeishi di shi jie lizhang xuanju shenqing dengji wei houxuanren ji she jingxuan banshichu, zhi zhuxuan yuan zhuyi shixiang* [Notice of matters concerning applications for candidacy, establishing campaign offices, and designating campaign assistants for the tenth round of neighborhood warden elections in Taipei City].

Clark, John P. 1989. Conflict management outside the courtrooms of China. In *Social control in the People's Republic of China*, edited by R. J. Troyer, J. P. Clark, and D. G. Rojek, 57–69. New York: Praeger.

Cohen, Joshua, and Joel Rogers. 1992. Secondary associations and democratic governance. *Politics and Society* 20 (4): 393–472.

Collier, David. 1995. Trajectory of a concept: "Corporatism" in the study of Latin American politics. In *Latin America in comparative perspective: New approaches to methods and analysis*, edited by P. H. Smith, 135–162. Boulder, Colo.: Westview Press.

Colomer, Josep M. 2000. Watching neighbors: The Cuban model of social control. *Cuban Studies* 31: 118–138.

Cornwall, Andrea, and Vera Schattan Coelho, eds. 2007. *Spaces for change? The politics of citizen participation in new democratic arenas*. London: Zed Books.

Crenson, Matthew A. 1983. *Neighborhood politics*. Cambridge, Mass.: Harvard University Press.

Das Gupta, Monica, Helene Grandvoinnet, and Mattia Romani. 2000. State-community synergies in development: Laying the basis for collective action. World Bank Policy Research Working Paper No. 2439, World Bank, Washington, D.C.

Davis, Deborah S., and Hanlong Lu. 2003. Property in transition: Conflicts over ownership in post-socialist Shanghai. *European Journal of Sociology* 44 (1): 77–99.

Davis, Deborah, and Helen Siu, eds. 2007. *SARS: Reception and interpretations in three Chinese cities*. New York: Routledge.

Derleth, James, and Daniel Koldyk. 2004. The Shequ experiment: Grassroots political reform in urban China. *Journal of Contemporary China* 13 (41): 747–777.

Deyo, Frederic C. 1989. *Beneath the miracle: Labor subordination in the new Asian industrialism*. Berkeley: University of California Press.

Diamant, Neil J. 2000a. Conflict and conflict resolution in China: Beyond mediation-centered approaches. *Journal of Conflict Resolution* 44 (4): 523–546.

———. 2000b. *Revolutionizing the family: Politics, love, and divorce in urban and rural China, 1949–1968*. Berkeley: University of California Press.

Diamond, Larry. 1999. *Developing democracy: Toward consolidation*. Baltimore: Johns Hopkins University Press.

Dickson, Bruce J. 1997. *Democratization in China and Taiwan: The adaptability of Leninist parties*. New York: Oxford University Press.

Dominguez, Jorge I. 1978. *Cuba: Order and revolution*. Cambridge, Mass.: Harvard University Press.

Douglass, Mike, Orathai Ard-am, and Ik Ki Kim. 2002. Urban poverty and the environment: Social capital and state-community synergy in Seoul and Bangkok. In *Livable cities? Urban struggles for livelihood and sustainability*, edited by P. Evans, 31–66. Berkeley: University of California Press.

Duara, Prasenjit. 1988. *Culture, power, and the state: Rural North China, 1900–1942*. Stanford: Stanford University Press.

Dutton, Michael Robert. 1992. *Policing and punishment in China: From patriarchy to "the people."* Cambridge: Cambridge University Press.

Dutton, Michael Robert, Hsiu-ju Stacy Lo, and Dong Dong Wu. 2008. *Beijing time*. Cambridge, Mass.: Harvard University Press.

Eckert, Carter J. 1990. *Korea, old and new: A history*. Seoul: Ilchokak Publishers.

Eisenstadt, S. N., and Louis Roniger. 1984. *Patrons, clients, and friends: Interpersonal relations and the structure of trust in society*. New York: Cambridge University Press.

Evans, Peter. 1995. *Embedded autonomy: States and industrial transformation*. Princeton, N.J.: Princeton University Press.

———. 1996a. Government action, social capital and development: Reviewing the evidence on synergy. *World Development* 24 (6): 1119–1132.

———. 1996b. Introduction: Development strategies across the public-private divide. *World Development* 24 (6): 1033–1037.

———, ed. 1997. *State-society synergy: Government and social capital in development*. Berkeley: University of California Press.

———. 2002a. Introduction: Looking for agents of urban livability in a globalized political economy. In *Livable cities? Urban struggles for livelihood and sustainability*, edited by P. Evans, 1–30. Berkeley: University of California Press.

———, ed. 2002b. *Livable cities? Urban struggles for livelihood and sustainability*. Berkeley: University of California Press.

Evenson, Debra. 2003. *Law and society in contemporary Cuba*. 2nd ed. The Hague: Kluwer Law International.

Fagen, Richard R. 1969. *The transformation of political culture in Cuba*. Stanford: Stanford University Press.

Fainstein, Norman I., and Susan S. Fainstein. 1974. *Urban political movements: The search for power by minority groups in American cities*. Englewood Cliffs, N.J.: Prentice-Hall.

Falkenheim, Victor C. 1978. Political participation in China. *Problems of Communism* 27 (3): 18–32.

Fenno, Richard F., Jr. 1978. *Home style: House members in their districts.* Boston: Little, Brown.

Fischer, Claude S. 1982. *To dwell among friends: Personal networks in town and city.* Chicago: University of Chicago Press.

Fleischer, Friederike. 2010. *Suburban Beijing: Housing and consumption in contemporary China.* Minneapolis: University of Minnesota Press.

Forrest, Ray, and Ade Kearns. 2001. Social cohesion, social capital and the neighbourhood. *Urban Studies* 38 (12): 2125–2143.

Fox, Jonathan. 1994. The difficult transition from clientelism to citizenship: Lessons from Mexico. *World Politics* 46 (2): 151–184.

———. 1996. How does civil society thicken? The political construction of social capital in rural Mexico. *World Development* 24 (6): 1089–1103.

———. 2007. *Accountability politics: Power and voice in rural Mexico.* Oxford: Oxford University Press.

Freedman, Maurice. 1966. *Chinese lineage and society: Fukien and Kwangtung.* London: Athlone Press.

Friedgut, Theodore H. 1979. *Political participation in the USSR.* Princeton, N.J.: Princeton University Press.

Friedman, Edward, and Joseph Wong. 2008. *Political transitions in dominant party systems: Learning to lose.* Abingdon, U.K.: Routledge.

Frolic, B. Michael. 1980. *Mao's people: Sixteen portraits of life in revolutionary China.* Cambridge, Mass.: Harvard University Press.

Fung, Archon. 2004. *Empowered participation: Reinventing urban democracy.* Princeton, N.J.: Princeton University Press.

Gallagher, Mary E. 2006. Mobilizing the law in China: "Informed disenchantment" and the development of legal consciousness. *Law and Society Review* 40 (4): 783–816.

Gilboy, George J., and Eric Heginbotham. 2001. China's coming transformation. *Foreign Affairs* 80 (4): 26–39.

Gilley, Bruce. 2008. Comparing and rethinking political change in China and Taiwan. In *Political change in China: Comparison with Taiwan,* edited by B. Gilley and L. Diamond, 1–23. Boulder, Colo.: Lynn Rienner Publishers.

Glasze, Georg, Chris Webster, and Klaus Frantz, eds. 2006. *Private cities: Global and local perspectives.* New York: Routledge.

Gold, Thomas B. 1985. After comradeship: Personal relations in China since the Cultural Revolution. *China Quarterly* (104): 657–675.

Gold, Thomas, Doug Guthrie, and David L. Wank. 2002a. An introduction to the study of *guanxi.* In *Social connections in China: Institutions, culture, and the changing nature of Guanxi*, edited by T. Gold, D. Guthrie and D. L. Wank, 3–20. Cambridge: Cambridge University Press.

———. 2002b. *Social connections in China: Institutions, culture, and the changing nature of Guanxi*. Cambridge: Cambridge University Press.

Golden, Tim. 1994. Guardians of Castro's Cuba have fallen on hard times. *New York Times*, November 7.

Granovetter, Mark. 1973. The strength of weak ties. *American Journal of Sociology* 78: 1360–1380.

Grootaert, Christian, and Thierry van Bastelaer, eds. 2002. *The role of social capital in development: An empirical assessment*. Cambridge, Mass.: Harvard University Press.

Gross, Jan T. 1984. Social control under totalitarianism. In *Toward a general theory of social control: Volume 2, selected problems*, edited by D. Black, 59–77. Orlando, Fla.: Academic Press.

Gui, Yong, Joseph Y. S. Cheng, and Weihong Ma. 2006. Cultivation of grass-roots democracy: A study of direct elections of residents committees in Shanghai. *China Information* 20 (1): 7–31.

Guinness, Patrick. 1986. *Harmony and hierarchy in a Javanese kampung*. Singapore: Oxford University Press.

———. 2009. *Kampung, Islam and state in urban Java*. Honolulu: University of Hawaii Press.

Guo, Haini, and Bradley Klein. 2005. Bargaining in the shadow of the community: Neighborly dispute resolution in Beijing hutongs. *Ohio State Journal on Dispute Resolution* 20 (3): 825–909.

Haddad, Mary Alice. 2004. Community determinants of volunteer participation and the promotion of civic health: The case of Japan. *Nonprofit and Voluntary Sector Quarterly* 33 (3): 8S–31S.

———. 2007. *Politics and volunteering in Japan: A global perspective*. Cambridge: Cambridge University Press.

Halebsky, Sandor, John M. Kirk, and Rafael Hernández. 1990. *Transformation and struggle: Cuba faces the 1990s*. New York: Praeger.

Hann, Chris. 1996. Introduction: Political society and civil anthropology. In *Civil society: Challenging Western models*, edited by C. Hann and E. Dunn, 1–26. London: Routledge.

Hao, Zhidong, and Kunrong Liao, eds. 2008. *Liang'an xiangcun zhili bijiao* [A cross-strait comparison of township and village administration]. Beijing: Social Sciences Academic Press.

Hastings, Sally Ann. 1995. *Neighborhood and nation in Tokyo, 1905–1937*. Pittsburgh: University of Pittsburgh Press.

He, Yanling. 2007. *Dushi jiequ zhong de guojia yu shehui: Le Jie diaocha* [State and society in the lanes of the metropolis: A study of Le Street]. Beijing: Shehui Kexue Wenxian Chubanshe.

Heberer, Thomas. 2009. Institutional change and legitimacy via urban elections? People's awareness of elections and participation in urban neighborhoods. In *Regime legitimacy in contemporary China: Institutional change and stability*, edited by T. Heberer and G. Schubert, 79–106. Abingdon, U.K.: Routledge.

Heberer, Thomas, and Christian Göbel. 2011. *The politics of community building in urban China*. Abingdon, U.K.: Routledge.

Heinrich, Volkhart F. 2005. Studying civil society across the world: Exploring the thorny issues of conceptualization and measurement. *Journal of Civil Society* 1 (3): 211–228.

Hinton, William. 1966. *Fanshen: A documentary of revolution in a Chinese village*. New York: Vintage Books.

Hochschild, Arlie Russell. 1983. *The managed heart: Commercialization of human feeling*. Berkeley: University of California Press.

Howard, Marc Morjé. 2002. The weakness of postcommunist civil society. *Journal of Democracy* 13 (1): 157–169.

———. 2003. *The weakness of civil society in post-communist Europe*. Cambridge: Cambridge University Press.

Hsi, Dai Lin, and Zhong Yuan Fan. 2003. *Taibei shizhengfu jiceng zuzhi gongneng zhi yanjiu* [A study of the functions of the Taipei city government's local-level organizations]. Taipei: City of Taipei Research, Development, and Evaluation Commission.

Hsiao, Kung-ch'üan. 1960. *Rural China: Imperial control in the nineteenth century*. Seattle: University of Washington Press.

Hsing, You-tien. 2010. *The great urban transformation: Politics of land and property in China*. New York: Oxford University Press.

Hulme, David, and Michael Edwards. 1997. *NGOs, states and donors: Too close for comfort?* New York: St. Martin's Press, in association with Save the Children.

Huntington, Samuel P. 1991. *The third wave: Democratization in the late twentieth century*. Norman: University of Oklahoma Press.

Hurst, William. 2010. Urban China: Change and contention. In *Politics in China: An introduction*, edited by W. A. Joseph, 250–268. New York: Oxford University Press.

Im, Dobin. 2004. *Hanguk jibang jojik ron: Haengwija, jeonryak, geim* [publisher's translation: Action theory of local organizations; author's translation: A theory of local organizations in Korea: Actors, strategy, games]. Seoul: Pakyoungsa.

Jowitt, Ken. 1992. *New world disorder: The Leninist extinction*. Berkeley: University of California Press.

Kasza, Gregory J. 1995. *The conscription society: Administered mass organizations*. New Haven, Conn.: Yale University Press.

Kaufman, Jason. 2002. *For the common good? American civic life and the golden age of fraternity*. Oxford: Oxford University Press.

Kelliher, Daniel. 1997. The Chinese debate over village self-government. *China Journal* 37: 63–86.

Keng, Shu, and Yi-ling Chen. 2007. Zhongguo dalu de shequ zhili yu zhuanxing qianjing: Fazhan cuzhuan huo zhengquan weiwen [Community self-governance and prospects for democracy in China: Modernization theory or regime stability?]. *Yuanjing jijinhui jikan* 8 (1): 87–122.

Kennedy, John James. 2007. The implementation of village elections and tax-for-fee reform in rural Northwest China. In *Grassroots political reform in contemporary China*, edited by E. J. Perry and M. Goldman, 48–74. Cambridge, Mass.: Harvard University Press.

———. 2010. Supply and support for grassroots political reform in rural China. *Journal of Chinese Political Science* 15 (2): 169–190.

Kennedy, Scott. 2005. *The business of lobbying in China*. Cambridge, Mass.: Harvard University Press.

Kipnis, Andrew B. 1997. *Producing Guanxi: Sentiment, self, and subculture in a North China village*. Durham, N.C.: Duke University Press.

Kitschelt, Herbert, and Steven I. Wilkinson. 2007. Citizen-politician linkages: An introduction. In *Patrons, clients and policies: Patterns of democratic accountability and political competition*, edited by H. Kitschelt and S. I. Wilkinson, 1–49. Cambridge: Cambridge University Press.

Klinenberg, Eric. 2002. *Heat wave: A social autopsy of disaster in Chicago*. Chicago: University of Chicago Press.

Koh, David Wee Hock. 2006. *Wards of Hanoi*. Singapore: Institute of Southeast Asian Studies.

Kohli, Atul. 1994. Where do high growth political economies come from? The Japanese lineage of Korea's "developmental state." *World Development* 22 (9): 1269–1293.

———. 2004. *State-directed development: Political power and industrialization on the global periphery*. Cambridge: Cambridge University Press.

Kokubun, Ryosei, and Kazuko Kojima. 2002. The "Shequ Construction" programme and the Chinese Communist Party. *Copenhagen Journal of Asian Studies* 16: 86–105.

Kruger, Mark H. 2007. Community-based crime control in Cuba. *Contemporary Justice Review* 10 (1): 101–114.

Kuhn, Philip A. 1970. *Rebellion and its enemies in late imperial China: Militarization and social structure, 1796–1864*. Cambridge, Mass.: Harvard University Press.

———. 1975. Local self-government under the Republic: Problems of control, autonomy, and mobilization. In *Conflict and control in late Imperial China*, edited by F. E. Wakeman and C. Grant, 257–298. Berkeley: University of California Press.

———. 1979. Local taxation and finance in Republican China. Select Papers from the Center for Far Eastern Studies No. 3, University of Chicago.

Kurasawa, Aiko. 2009. Swaying between state and community: The role of RT/RW in post-Suharto Indonesia. In *Local organizations and urban governance in East and Southeast Asia: Straddling state and society*, edited by B. L. Read with R. Pekkanen, 58–83. Abingdon, U.K.: Routledge.

Lam, Wai Fung. 1996. Institutional design of public agencies and coproduction: A study of irrigation associations in Taiwan. *World Development* 24 (6): 1039–1054.

Landé, Carl H. 1977. The dyadic basis of clientelism. In *Friends, followers, and factions: A reader in political clientelism*, edited by S. W. Schmidt, L. Guasti, C. H. Landé, and J. C. Scott, xiii–xxxvii. Berkeley: University of California Press.

Landry, Pierre F., Deborah Davis, and Shiru Wang. 2010. Elections in rural China: Competition without parties. *Comparative Political Studies* 43 (6): 763–790.

LaPalombara, Joseph. 1975. Monoliths or plural systems: Through conceptual lenses darkly. *Studies in Comparative Communism* 8 (3): 305–332.

———. 1978. Political participation as an analytical concept in comparative politics. In *The citizen and politics: A comparative perspective*, edited by S. Verba and L. W. Pye, 167–194. Stamford, Conn.: Greylock Publishers.

LaRamée, Pierre M., and Erica G. Polakoff. 1997. The evolution of the popular organizations in Nicaragua. In *The undermining of the Sandinista Revolution*, edited by G. Prevost and H. E. Vanden, 141–206. New York: St. Martin's Press.

Lau, Siu-kai. 1983. *Society and politics in Hong Kong*. Hong Kong: Chinese University Press.

Lee, Ki-baik. 1984. *A new history of Korea*. Cambridge, Mass.: Harvard University Press.

Lei, Jieqiong. 2001. *Zhuanxing zhong de chengshi jiceng shequ zuzhi: Beijingshi jiceng shequ zuzhi yu shequ fazhan yanjiu* [Urban local community organizations in transition: A study of local community organizations and community development in the city of Beijing]. Beijing: Beijing Daxue Chubanshe.

Li, Cheng. 2001. *China's leaders: The new generation*. Lanham, Md.: Rowman and Littlefield.

Li, Clara. 2002. City gets first taste of grassroots polls. *South China Morning Post*, January 15.

Li, Lianjiang, and Kevin J. O'Brien. 1999. The struggle over village elections. In *The paradox of China's post-Mao reforms*, edited by M. Goldman and R. MacFarquhar, 129–144. Cambridge, Mass.: Harvard University Press.

Liddle, R. William. 1996. *Leadership and culture in Indonesian politics*. Sydney: Allen and Unwin.

Lin, Ruisui. 1996. *Shequ fazhan yu cunli zuzhi gongneng wenti zhi tantao* [An exploration of issues in community development and the self-governance functions of villages and neighborhoods]. Taipei: Xingzhengyuan Yanjiu Fazhan Kaohe Weiyuanhui.

Linz, Juan J. 1975. Totalitarian and authoritarian regimes. In *Handbook of political science*, edited by F. I. Greenstein and N. W. Polsby, 175–411. Reading, Mass.: Addison-Wesley Publishing.

———. 2000. *Totalitarian and authoritarian regimes*. Boulder, Colo.: Lynne Rienner Publishers.

Linz, Juan J., and Alfred Stepan. 1996. *Problems of democratic transition and consolidation: Southern Europe, South America, and post-communist Europe*. Baltimore: Johns Hopkins University Press.

Little, D. Richard. 1976. Mass political participation in the U.S. and the U.S.S.R. *Comparative Political Studies* 8 (4): 437–460.

Liu, Rong. 2008. Maokong gai lingguta? Shangjia kangzheng [Will a memorial tower be built in Maokong? Businesses contest the issue]. *Ziyou Shibao*, September 6.

Logan, John R. 2002. *The new Chinese city: Globalization and market reform*. Oxford, U.K.: Blackwell Publishing.

———. 2007. *Urban China in transition*. Oxford, U.K.: Blackwell Publishing.

Logsdon, Martha Gay. 1974. Neighborhood organization in Jakarta. *Indonesia* 18: 53–70.

———. 1978. Traditional decision making in urban neighborhoods. *Indonesia* 26: 95–110.

Lubman, Stanley B. 1967. Mao and mediation: Politics and dispute resolution in communist China. *California Law Review* 55 (5): 1284–1359.

———. 1997. Dispute resolution in China after Deng Xiaoping: "Mao and Mediation" revisited. *Columbia Journal of Asian Law* 11 (2): 229–391.

Luova, Outi. 2011. Community Volunteers' Associations in contemporary Tianjin: Multipurpose partners of the party–state. *Journal of Contemporary China* 20 (72): 773–794.

Madsen, Richard. 2007. *Democracy's dharma: Religious renaissance and political development in Taiwan*. Berkeley: University of California Press.

———. 2008. Religion and the emergence of civil society. In *Political change in China: Comparison with Taiwan*, edited by B. Gilley and L. Diamond, 79–94. Boulder, Colo.: Lynn Rienner Publishers.

Mahakanjana, Chandra. 2009. Municipal governments and the role of cooperative community groups in Thailand. In *Local organizations and urban governance in East and Southeast Asia: Straddling state and society*, edited by B. L. Read with R. Pekkanen, 101–120. Abingdon, U.K.: Routledge.

Manion, Melanie. 2009. How to assess village elections in China. *Journal of Contemporary China* 18 (60): 379–383.

Marsh, Robert Mortimer. 1996. *The great transformation: Social change in Taipei, Taiwan since the 1960s*. Armonk, N.Y.: M. E. Sharpe.

McKenzie, Evan. 1994. *Privatopia: Homeowner associations and the rise of residential private government*. New Haven, Conn.: Yale University Press.

Meyer, Alfred G. 1965. *The Soviet political system: An interpretation.* New York: Random House.

Meyer, Megan, and Cheryl Hyde. 2004. Too much of a "good" thing? Insular neighborhood associations, nonreciprocal civility, and the promotion of civic health. *Nonprofit and Voluntary Sector Quarterly* 33 (3): 77S–96S.

Migdal, Joel S. 1988. *Strong societies and weak states: State-society relations and state capabilities in the Third World.* Princeton, N.J.: Princeton University Press.

———, ed. 2001. *State in society: Studying how states and societies transform and constitute one another.* Cambridge: Cambridge University Press.

Migdal, Joel S., Atul Kohli, and Vivienne Shue, ed. 1994. *State power and social forces: Domination and transformation in the Third World.* Cambridge: Cambridge University Press.

Miller, Warren E., and J. Merrill Shanks. 1996. *The new American voter.* Cambridge, Mass.: Harvard University Press.

Ministry of Civil Affairs. 2000. *Zhongguo minzheng tongji nianjian 2000* [China civil affairs statistical yearbook 2000]. Beijing: China Statistics Press.

———. 2009. *Zhongguo minzheng tongji nianjian 2009* [China civil affairs statistical yearbook 2009]. Beijing: China Statistics Press.

Mock, John Allan. 1999. *Culture, community and change in a Sapporo neighborhood, 1925–1988: Hanayama.* Lewiston, N.Y.: Edwin Mellen Press.

Molina, Oscar, and Martin Rhodes. 2002. Corporatism: The past, present, and future of a concept. *Annual Review of Political Science* 5: 305–331.

Moore, Barrington, Jr. 1966. *Social origins of dictatorship and democracy: Lord and peasant in the making of the modern world.* Boston: Beacon Press.

Morris MacLean, Lauren. 2010. *Informal institutions and citizenship in rural Africa: Risk and reciprocity in Ghana and Cote d'Ivoire.* Cambridge: Cambridge University Press.

Mukherjee, Nilanjana. 1999. *Consultations with the poor in Indonesia.* Washington, D.C.: Poverty Reduction and Economic Management Network, World Bank.

Nathan, Andrew J. 2003. Authoritarian resilience. *Journal of Democracy* 14 (1): 6–17.

Naughton, Barry. 2007. *The Chinese economy: Transitions and growth.* Cambridge: Massachusetts Institute of Technology Press.

Nelson, Robert H. 2005. *Private neighborhoods and the transformation of local government.* Washington, D.C.: Urban Institute Press.

Niessen, Nicole. 1999. *Municipal government in Indonesia: Policy, law, and practice of decentralization and urban spatial planning.* Leiden: Research School CNWS, School of Asian, African, and Amerindian Studies, Universiteit Leiden.

O'Brien, Kevin J. 1994. Implementing political reform in China's villages. *Australian Journal of Chinese Affairs* (32): 33–59.

O'Brien, Kevin J., and Rongbin Han. 2009. Path to democracy? Assessing village elections in China. *Journal of Contemporary China* 18 (60): 359–378.

Offe, Claus, and Susanne Fuchs. 2002. A decline of social capital? The German case. In *Democracies in flux: The evolution of social capital in contemporary society*, edited by R. D. Putnam, 189–243. Oxford: Oxford University Press.

Oksenberg, Michel. 1970. Getting ahead and along in communist China: The ladder of success on the eve of the Cultural Revolution. In *Party leadership and revolutionary power in China*, edited by J. W. Lewis, 304–347. Cambridge: Cambridge University Press.

Öniş, Ziya. 1991. The logic of the developmental state. *Comparative Politics* 24 (1): 109–126.

Ooi, Giok Ling. 2009. State shaping of community-level politics: Residents' committees in Singapore. In *Local organizations and urban governance in East and Southeast Asia: Straddling state and society*, edited by B. L. Read with R. Pekkanen, 174–190. Abingdon, U.K.: Routledge.

Ostrom, Elinor. 1996. Crossing the great divide: Coproduction, synergy, and development. *World Development* 24 (6): 1073–1087.

Ownby, David. 2008. *Falun Gong and the future of China.* Oxford: Oxford University Press.

Pan, Yi, and Changsheng Cao. 1994. *Beijing shi Xicheng qu juweihui gongzuo shang shuiping* [Residents' committee work in the Xicheng district of Beijing reaches a higher level]. *Chengshi Jieju Tongxun*, June 24–25.

Peerenboom, Randall. 2007. *China modernizes: Threat to the West or model for the rest?* Oxford: Oxford University Press.

Pekkanen, Robert. 2004. Japan: Social capital without advocacy. In *Civil society and political change in Asia: Expanding and contracting democratic space*, edited by M. Alagappa, 223–256. Stanford: Stanford University Press.

———. 2006. *Japan's dual civil society: Members without advocates.* Stanford: Stanford University Press.

Pekkanen, Robert, Yutaka Tsujinaka, and Hidehiro Yamamoto. N.d. Local governance and neighborhood associations in Japan. Unpublished manuscript.

Peng, Zhen. 1991. *Peng Zhen wenxuan (1941–1990)* [Selected works of Peng Zhen (1941–1990)]. Beijing: Renmin Chuban She.

Perry, Elizabeth J. 2006. *Patrolling the revolution: Worker militias, citizenship, and the modern Chinese state.* Lanham, Md.: Rowman and Littlefield.

Phillips, Steven E. 2003. *Between assimilation and independence: The Taiwanese encounter nationalist China, 1945–1950.* Stanford: Stanford University Press.

Pierce, Jennifer. 1996. Rambo litigators: Emotional labor in a male-dominated occupation. In *Masculinities in organizations*, edited by C. Cheng, 1–28. London: Sage.

Po, Ching-Chiu. 1971. Taiwansheng cun-li zhidu zhi yanjiu [A study of the village and neighborhood system of Taiwan Province]. *Si Yu Yan* 9 (4): 13–45.

Puddington, Arch. 1995. Revolutionary defense committees. In *Cuban communism, 1959–1995*, edited by I. L. Horowitz, 489–498. New Brunswick, N.J.: Transaction Publishers.

Putnam, Robert D. 1993. *Making democracy work: Civic traditions in modern Italy.* Princeton, N.J.: Princeton University Press.

———. 2000. *Bowling alone: The collapse and revival of American community.* New York: Simon and Schuster.

Putnam, Robert D., and Kristin A. Goss. 2002. Introduction. In *Democracies in flux: The evolution of social capital in contemporary society,* edited by R. D. Putnam, 3–19. Oxford: Oxford University Press.

Read, Benjamin L. 2000. Revitalizing the state's urban "nerve tips." *China Quarterly* (163): 806–820.

———. 2003. Democratizing the neighbourhood? New private housing and home-owner self-organization in urban China. *China Journal* (49): 31–59.

———. 2006. Site-intensive methods: Fenno and Scott in search of a coalition. *Qualitative Methods* 4 (2): 9–13.

———. 2007. Inadvertent political reform via private associations: Assessing home-owners' groups in new neighborhoods. In *Grassroots political reform in contemporary China,* edited by E. J. Perry and M. Goldman, 149–173. Cambridge, Mass.: Harvard University Press.

———. 2008a. Assessing variation in civil society organizations: China's home-owner associations in comparative perspective. *Comparative Political Studies* 41 (9): 1240–1265.

———. 2008b. Property rights and homeowner activism in new neighborhoods. In *Privatizing China: Socialism from afar,* edited by L. Zhang and A. Ong, 41–56. Ithaca, N.Y.: Cornell University Press.

———. 2010. More than an interview, less than Sedaka: Studying subtle and hidden politics with site-intensive methods. In *Chinese politics: New sources, methods, and field strategies,* edited by A. Carlson, M. Gallagher, K. Lieberthal, and M. Manion, 145–161. Cambridge: Cambridge University Press.

Read, Benjamin L., and Ethan Michelson. 2008. Mediating the mediation debate: Conflict resolution and the local state in China. *Journal of Conflict Resolution* 52 (5): 737–764.

Rigger, Shelley. 1999. *Politics in Taiwan: Voting for democracy.* London: Routledge.

———. 2011. *Why Taiwan matters: Small island, global powerhouse.* Lanham, Md.: Rowman and Littlefield.

ROC Ministry of the Interior. 2002. *Cun-li faling huibian* [Compilation of laws and orders on villages and neighborhoods]. Taipei: ROC Ministry of the Interior.

———. 2005. *Zhonghua Minguo Tai-Min diqu renkou tongji* [Population statistics of the Taiwan-Fujian region of the Republic of China]. Taipei: Ministry of the Interior.

Roeder, Philip G. 1989. Modernization and participation in the Leninist developmental strategy. *American Political Science Review* 83 (3): 859–884.

Roman, Peter. 2003. *People's power: Cuba's experience with representative government.* Rev. ed. Lanham, Md.: Rowman and Littlefield.

Rose, Richard, William Mishler, and Christian Haerpfer. 1997. Social capital in civic and stressful societies. *Studies in Comparative International Development* 32 (3): 85–111.

Rosenstone, Steven J., and John M. Hansen. 1993. *Mobilization, participation, and democracy in America.* New York: Macmillan.

Rossi, Peter H., and Eleanor Weber. 1996. The social benefits of homeownership: Empirical evidence from national surveys. *Housing Policy Debate* 7 (1): 1–35.

Rothstein, Bo. 2002. Social capital in the social democratic state. In *Democracies in flux: The evolution of social capital in contemporary society,* edited by R. D. Putnam, 289–331. Oxford: Oxford University Press.

Rowe, William T. 1984. *Hankow: Commerce and society in a Chinese city, 1796–1889.* Stanford: Stanford University Press.

Salaff, Janet Weitzner. 1967. The urban communes and anti-city experience in communist China. *China Quarterly* (29): 82–109.

———. 1971. Urban residential committees in the wake of the Cultural Revolution. In *The city in communist China,* edited by J. W. Lewis. Stanford: Stanford University Press.

Salamon, Lester M. 1995. *Partners in public service: Government-nonprofit relations in the modern welfare state.* Baltimore, Md.: Johns Hopkins University Press.

Sampson, Robert J. 2004. Networks and neighbourhoods: The implications of connectivity for thinking about crime in the modern city. In *Network logic: Who governs in an interconnected world?,* edited by H. McCarthy, P. Miller, and P. Skidmore, 157–166. London: Demos.

Sampson, Robert J., Doug McAdam, Heather MacIndoe, and Simón Weffer-Elizondo. 2005. Civil society reconsidered: The durable nature and community structure of collective civic action. *American Journal of Sociology* 111 (3): 673–714.

Santana, Sarah M. 1990. Whither Cuban medicine? Challenges for the next generation. In *Transformation and struggle: Cuba faces the 1990s,* edited by S. Halebsky and J. M. Kirk, 251–270. New York: Praeger.

Schafferer, Christian. 2003. *The power of the ballot box: Political development and election campaigning in Taiwan.* Lanham, Md.: Lexington Books.

Schatz, Edward, ed. 2009. *Political ethnography: What immersion contributes to the study of power.* Chicago: University of Chicago Press.

Schmid, Hillel. 2001. *Neighborhood self-management: Experiments in civil society.* New York: Kluwer Academic and Plenum Publishers.

Schmitter, Philippe C. 1979. Still the century of corporatism? In *Trends toward corporatist intermediation,* edited by P. C. Schmitter and G. Lehmbruch, 7–52. Beverly Hills, Calif.: Sage Publications.

Schubert, Gunter. 2009. Village elections, citizenship and regime legitimacy in contemporary rural China. In *Regime legitimacy in contemporary China: Institu-*

tional change and stability, edited by T. Heberer and G. Schubert, 55–78. Abingdon, U.K.: Routledge.

Schurmann, Franz. 1966. *Ideology and organization in Communist China.* Berkeley: University of California Press.

Schwartz, Benjamin I. 1996. The primacy of the political order in East Asian societies. In *China and other matters*, edited by B. I. Schwartz, 114–124. Cambridge, Mass.: Harvard University Press.

Schwartz, Frank J. 2003. Introduction: Recognizing civil society in Japan. In *The state of civil society in Japan*, edited by S. J. Pharr and F. J. Schwartz, 1–19. New York: Cambridge University Press.

Schwartz, Jonathan. 2009. The impact of crises on social service provision in China: The state and society respond to SARS. In *State and society responses to social welfare needs in China: Serving the people*, edited by J. Schwartz and S. Shieh. New York: Routledge.

Schwartz, Jonathan, and Shawn Shieh, eds. 2009. *State and society responses to social welfare needs in China: Serving the people.* New York: Routledge.

Scott, James C. 1972. Patron-client politics and political change in Southeast Asia. *American Political Science Review* 66 (1): 91–113.

———. 1976. *The moral economy of the peasant: Rebellion and subsistence in Southeast Asia.* New Haven, Conn.: Yale University Press.

———. 1985. *Weapons of the weak: Everyday forms of peasant resistance.* New Haven, Conn.: Yale University Press.

———. 1990. *Domination and the arts of resistance: Hidden transcripts.* New Haven, Conn.: Yale University Press.

———. 1998. *Seeing like a state: How certain schemes to improve the human condition have failed.* New Haven, Conn.: Yale University Press.

Seah, Chee Meow. 1987. Parapolitical institutions. In *Government and politics of Singapore*, edited by J. S. T. Quah, C. H. Chee, and C. M. Seah, 173–194. Singapore: Oxford University Press.

Selden, Mark. 1971. *The Yenan Way in revolutionary China.* Cambridge, Mass.: Harvard University Press.

Seo, Jungmin. 2002. *Bansanghoe* (1976–present) and the politics of symbolism in Korea. Paper presented at the annual meeting of the American Political Science Association, Boston, August 28.

Sheng, Virginia. 1995. Here comes the neighborhood! *Free China Review* 45 (5): 4–13.

Shi, Tianjian. 1997. *Political participation in Beijing.* Cambridge, Mass.: Harvard University Press.

Shiffman, Jeremy. 2002. The construction of community participation: Village family planning groups and the Indonesian state. *Social Science and Medicine* 54 (8): 1199–1214.

Shirk, Susan L. 1982. *Competitive comrades: Career incentives and student strategies in China*. Berkeley: University of California Press.

Shue, Vivienne. 1988. *The reach of the state: Sketches of the Chinese body politic*. Stanford: Stanford University Press.

Sidel, Ruth. 1974. *Families of Fengsheng: Urban life in China*. Baltimore: Penguin.

Sitrin, Marina. 2006. *Horizontalism: Voices of popular power in Argentina*. Edinburgh: AK Press.

Skocpol, Theda, and Morris P. Fiorina. 1999. Making sense of the civic engagement debate. In *Civic engagement in American democracy*, edited by T. Skocpol and M. P. Fiorina, 1–23. Washington, D.C.: Brookings Institution and Russell Sage Foundation.

Smith, David Horton. 2000. *Grassroots associations*. Thousand Oaks, Calif.: Sage Publications.

Smith, Stephen Rathgeb, and Michael Lipsky. 1993. *Nonprofits for hire: The welfare state in the age of contracting*. Cambridge, Mass.: Harvard University Press.

Solinger, Dorothy J. 1999. *Contesting citizenship in urban China: Peasant migrants, the state, and the logic of the market*. Berkeley: University of California Press.

———. 2008. Business groups: For or against the regime? In *Political change in China: Comparison with Taiwan*, edited by B. Gilley and L. Diamond, 95–114. Boulder, Colo.: Lynne Rienner Publishers.

Solomon, Richard H. 1969. On activism and activists: Maoist conceptions of motivation and political role linking state to society. *China Quarterly* (39): 76–114.

Spiegel, Mickey. 2002. *Dangerous meditation: China's campaign against Falungong*. New York: Human Rights Watch.

Steiner, Kurt. 1965. *Local government in Japan*. Stanford: Stanford University Press.

Stepan, Alfred. 1978. *The state and society: Peru in comparative perspective*. Princeton, N.J.: Princeton University Press.

Stokes, Susan C. 2007. Political clientelism. In *The Oxford handbook of comparative politics*, edited by C. Boix and S. C. Stokes, 604–627. Oxford: Oxford University Press.

Sullivan, John. 1992. *Local government and community in Java: An urban case-study*. Singapore: Oxford University Press.

Swindell, David. 2000. Issue representation in neighborhood organizations: Questing for democracy at the grassroots. *Journal of Urban Affairs* 22 (2): 123–137.

Tang, Wenfang. 2005. *Public opinion and political change in China*. Stanford: Stanford University Press.

Taylor, Jay. 2009. *The generalissimo: Chiang Kai-shek and the struggle for modern China*. Cambridge, Mass.: Harvard University Press.

Taylor-Robinson, Michelle M. 2009. Clientelism. *APSA-CP Newsletter* 20 (2): 15.

Thomson, Ken. 2001. *From neighborhood to nation: The democratic foundations of civil society*. Hanover, N.H.: University Press of New England.

Tomba, Luigi. 2005. Residential space and collective interest formation in Beijing's housing disputes. *China Quarterly* (184): 934–951.

Tong, James W. 2009. *Revenge of the forbidden city: The suppression of the Falungong in China, 1999–2005.* Oxford: Oxford University Press.

Townsend, James R. 1967. *Political participation in communist China.* Berkeley: University of California Press.

Trott, Stephen. 2006. Political reform in China's cities: Introducing community elections. Paper presented at the annual meeting of the Canadian Political Science Association, Toronto, June 1–3.

Ts'ai, Hui-Yu Caroline. 1990. One kind of control: The "hoko" system in Taiwan under Japanese rule, 1895–1945. Ph.D. diss., Columbia University.

Tsai, Kellee S. 2007. *Capitalism without democracy: The private sector in contemporary China.* Ithaca, N.Y.: Cornell University Press.

Tsai, Lily L. 2007. *Accountability without democracy: How solidary groups provide public goods in rural China.* Cambridge: Cambridge University Press.

Tseng, I-jen. 2004. *Cun-lizhang shifou gai wei youjizhi zhi yanjiu* [A study of whether village and neighborhood wardens should be changed to salaried positions]. Taipei: Ministry of the Interior.

Tsujinaka, Yutaka, Robert Pekkanen, and Hidehiro Yamamoto. 2009. *Gendai nihon no jichikai/chonaikai* [Local governance and neighborhood associations in Japan]. Tokyo: Bokutakusha.

Unger, Jonathan. 1996. "Bridges": Private business, the Chinese government and the rise of new associations. *China Quarterly* (147): 795–819.

———, ed. 2008. *Associations and the Chinese state: Contested spaces.* Armonk, N.Y.: M. E. Sharpe.

Verba, Sidney, Kay Lehman Schlozman, and Henry E. Brady. 1995. *Voice and equality: Civic voluntarism in American politics.* Cambridge, Mass.: Harvard University Press.

Vogel, Ezra F. 1965. From friendship to comradeship: The change in personal relations in communist China. *China Quarterly* 21: 46–60.

———. 1967. Voluntarism and social control. In *Soviet and Chinese communism: Similarities and differences,* edited by D. W. Treadgold, 168–184. Seattle: University of Washington Press.

———. 1991. *The four little dragons: The spread of industrialization in East Asia.* Cambridge, Mass.: Harvard University Press.

Vu, Tuong. 2010. *Paths to development in Asia: South Korea, Vietnam, China, and Indonesia.* New York: Cambridge University Press.

Wade, Robert. 1992. *Governing the market: Economic theory and the role of government in East Asian industrialization.* Princeton, N.J.: Princeton University Press.

Wakeman, Frederic, Jr. 1993. The civil society and public sphere debate: Western reflections on Chinese political culture. *Modern China* 19 (2): 108–138.

Walder, Andrew G. 1986. *Communist neo-traditionalism: Work and authority in Chinese industry.* Berkeley: University of California Press.

———. 2009. Unruly stability: Why China's regime has staying power. *Current History* 108 (719): 257–263.

Wall, James A., Jr., and Michael Blum. 1991. Community mediation in the People's Republic of China. *Journal of Conflict Resolution* 35 (1): 3–20.

Walzer, Michael. 1995. The civil society argument. In *Theorizing citizenship*, edited by R. Beiner, 153–174. Albany: State University of New York Press.

Wang, Audrey. 2008. Reclaiming a sense of community. *Taiwan Review* 58 (4): 56–61.

Wang, Chin-Shou. 2004. Democratization and the breakdown of clientelism in Taiwan, 1987–2001. Ph.D. diss., University of North Carolina at Chapel Hill.

Wang, Chin-Shou, and Charles Kurzman. 2007. Logistics: How to buy votes. In *Elections for sale: The causes and consequences of vote buying*, edited by F. C. Schaffer, 61–78. Boulder, Colo.: Lynne Rienner Publishers.

Wang, Zheng. 2005. "State feminism"? Gender and socialist state formation in Maoist China. *Feminist Studies* 31 (3): 519–551.

Wank, David L. 1999. *Commodifying communism: Business, trust, and politics in a Chinese city.* Cambridge: Cambridge University Press.

Warner, Mildred. 1999. Social capital construction and the role of the local state. *Rural Sociology* 64 (3): 373–393.

Warren, Mark E. 2001. *Democracy and association.* Princeton, N.J.: Princeton University Press.

Warren, Mark R. 2001. *Dry bones rattling: Community building to revitalize American democracy.* Princeton, N.J.: Princeton University Press.

Wedeen, Lisa. 1999. *Ambiguities of domination: Politics, rhetoric, and symbols in contemporary Syria.* Chicago: University of Chicago Press.

Weller, Robert P. 1998. Horizontal ties and civil institutions in Chinese societies. In *Democratic civility: The history and cross-cultural possibility of a modern political ideal*, edited by R. W. Hefner, 229–247. New Brunswick, N.J.: Transaction Publishers.

———. 1999. *Alternate civilities: Democracy and culture in China and Taiwan.* Boulder, Colo.: Westview Press.

———. 2008. Responsive authoritarianism. In *Political change in China: Comparison with Taiwan*, edited by B. Gilley and L. Diamond, 117–134. Boulder, Colo.: Lynne Rienner Publishers.

Wellman, Barry. 1988. The community question re-evaluated. In *Power, community and the city*, edited by M. P. Smith, 81–107. New Brunswick, N.J.: Transaction Books.

White, Gordon. 1991. Basic-level local government and economic reform in urban China. In *The Chinese state in the era of economic reform: The road to crisis*, edited by G. White, 215–242. Armonk, N.Y.: M. E. Sharpe.

————. 1993. *Riding the tiger: The politics of economic reform in post-Mao China.* Stanford: Stanford University Press.

White, Gordon, and Xiaoyuan Shang. 2003. State entrepreneurship and community welfare services in urban China. In *Asian politics in development: Essays in honour of Gordon White*, edited by G. White, R. Benewick, M. J. Blecher, and S. Cook, 173–194. London: Frank Cass.

White, Tyrene. 2006. *China's longest campaign: Birth planning in the People's Republic, 1949–2005.* Ithaca, N.Y.: Cornell University Press.

Whitelegg, Drew. 2002. Cabin pressure: The dialectics of emotional labour in the airline industry. *Journal of Transport History* 23 (1): 73–86.

Whyte, Martin King. 2010. *Myth of the social volcano: Perceptions of inequality and distributive injustice in contemporary China.* Stanford: Stanford University Press.

Whyte, Martin King, and William L. Parish. 1984. *Urban life in contemporary China.* Chicago: University of Chicago Press.

Wirth, Louis. 1938. Urbanism as a way of life. *American Journal of Sociology* 44 (1): 1–24.

Wong, Aline K. 1972. *The Kaifong associations and the society of Hong Kong.* Taipei: Orient Cultural Service.

Wong, Linda, and Bernard Poon. 2005. From serving neighbors to recontrolling urban society: The transformation of China's community policy. *China Information* 19 (3): 413–442.

Woo-Cumings, Meredith, ed. 1999. *The developmental state.* Ithaca, N.Y.: Cornell University Press.

Wood, Elisabeth Jean. 2003. *Insurgent collective action and civil war in El Salvador.* New York: Cambridge University Press.

Woolcock, Michael. 1998. Social capital and economic development: Toward a theoretical synthesis and policy framework. *Theory and Society* 27 (208): 151–208.

Woolcock, Michael, and Deepa Narayan. 2006. Social capital: Implications for development theory, research, and policy revisited. In *The search for empowerment: Social capital as idea and practice at the World Bank*, edited by A. Bebbington, M. Woolcock, S. Guggenheim, and E. A. Olson, 31–62. Bloomfield, Conn.: Kumarian Press.

World Bank. 1993. *The East Asian miracle: Economic growth and public policy.* Washington, D.C.: Oxford University Press.

————. 2004. State-society synergy for accountability: Lessons for the World Bank. World Bank Working Paper No. 30, World Bank, Washington, D.C.

Wright, Teresa. 2001. *The perils of protest: State repression and student activism in China and Taiwan.* Honolulu: University of Hawaii Press.

————. 2010. *Accepting authoritarianism: State-society relations in China's reform era.* Stanford: Stanford University Press.

Wu, Fulong. 2007. *China's emerging cities: The making of new urbanism.* Abingdon, U.K.: Routledge.

Xu, Qingwen. 2007. Community participation in urban China: Identifying mobilization factors. *Nonprofit and Voluntary Sector Quarterly* 36 (4): 622–642.

Yan, Yunxiang. 1996. *The flow of gifts: Reciprocity and social networks in a Chinese village*. Stanford: Stanford University Press.

Yang, Mayfair Mei-hui. 1994. *Gifts, favors and banquets: The art of social relationships in China*. Ithaca, N.Y.: Cornell University Press.

Yao, Jen-to. 2002. Governing the colonised: Governmentality in the Japanese colonisation of Taiwan, 1895–1945. Ph.D. diss., Department of Sociology, University of Essex.

Yip, Ngai-ming, and Yihong Jiang. 2011. Homeowners united: The attempt to create lateral networks of homeowners' associations in urban China. *Journal of Contemporary China* 20 (72): 735–750.

Yoshihara, Naoki. 2000. *Ajia no chiiki jyumin soshiki: Chonaikai Kaibokai RT/RW* [Asia's self-governing residential organizations: Chonaikai, kaifong, RT/RW]. Tokyo: Ochanomizu Shobo.

Yu, Yanyan. 2006. *Shequ zizhi yu zhengfu zhineng yanbian* [Community self-governance and the evolution of the functions of government]. Beijing: Zhongguo Shehui Chubanshe.

Zhang, Li. 2001. *Strangers in the city: Reconfigurations of space, power and social networks within China's floating population*. Stanford: Stanford University Press.

———. 2010. *In search of paradise: Middle-class living in a Chinese metropolis*. Ithaca, N.Y.: Cornell University Press.

Zhu, Jiangang. 2004. Not against the state, just protecting the residents' interests: A residents' movement in a Shanghai neighborhood. *Perspectives* 5 (3): 25–40.

Index

Italic page numbers indicate material in tables or figures.

The authorized representative in the EU for product safety and compliance is:
Mare Nostrum Group
B.V Doelen 72
4831 GR Breda
The Netherlands

www.ingramcontent.com/pod-product-compliance
Lightning Source LLC
Chambersburg PA
CBHW020333270326
41926CB00007B/164